Politics of National Identity in Italy

This book focuses on the politics of national identity in Italy. Only a unified country for just over 150 years, Italian national identity is perhaps more contingent than longer-established nations such as France or the UK.

The book investigates when, how and why the discussions about national identity and about immigration became entwined in public discourse within Italy. In particular it looks at the most influential voices in the debate on immigration and identity, namely Italian intellectuals, the Catholic Church, the Northern League and the Left. The methodological approach is based on a systematic discourse analysis of official documents, interviews, statements and speeches by representatives of the political actors involved. In the process, the author demonstrates that a 'normalisation' of intolerance towards foreigners has become institutionalised at the heart of the Italian state.

This work will be of particular interest to students of Italian politics, nationalism and comparative politics.

Eva Garau is a Research Fellow in Contemporary History at the University of Cagliari, Italy.

Routledge Studies in Extremism and Democracy

Series Editors: Roger Eatwell, *University of Bath*, and Matthew Goodwin, *University of Nottingham*

Founding Series Editors: Roger Eatwell, *University of Bath*, and Cas Mudde, *University of Antwerp-UFSIA*

This new series encompasses academic studies within the broad fields of 'extremism' and 'democracy'. These topics have traditionally been considered largely in isolation by academics. A key focus of the series, therefore, is the (inter-)*relation* between extremism and democracy. Works will seek to answer questions such as to what extent 'extremist' groups pose a major threat to democratic parties, or how democracy can respond to extremism without undermining its own democratic credentials.

The books encompass two strands:

Routledge Studies in Extremism and Democracy includes books with an introductory and broad focus which are aimed at students and teachers. These books will be available in hardback and paperback.

Titles include:

Understanding Terrorism in America
From the Klan to al Qaeda
Christopher Hewitt

Fascism and the Extreme Right
Roger Eatwell

Racist Extremism in Central and Eastern Europe
Edited by Cas Mudde

Political Parties and Terrorist Groups (2nd edition)
Leonard Weinberg, Ami Pedahzur and Arie Perliger

The New Extremism in 21st Century Britain
Edited by Roger Eatwell and Matthew Goodwin

New British Fascism
Rise of the British National Party
Matthew Goodwin

Routledge Research in Extremism and Democracy offers a forum for innovative new research intended for a more specialist readership. These books will be in hardback only. Titles include:

1. Uncivil Society?
Contentious politics in
post-communist Europe
*Edited by Petr Kopecky and
Cas Mudde*

**2. Political Parties and
Terrorist Groups**
*Leonard Weinberg and
Ami Pedahzur*

**3. Western Democracies and the
New Extreme Right Challenge**
*Edited by Roger Eatwell and
Cas Mudde*

**4. Confronting Right Wing
Extremism and Terrorism
in the USA**
George Michael

**5. Anti-political Establishment
Parties**
A comparative analysis
Amir Abedi

6. American Extremism
History, politics and the militia
D.J. Mulloy

7. The Scope of Tolerance
Studies on the costs of free
expression and freedom of the press
Raphael Cohen-Almagor

8. Extreme Right Activists in Europe
Through the magnifying glass
Bert Klandermans and Nonna Mayer

**9. Ecological Politics and
Democratic Theory**
Mathew Humphrey

10. Reinventing the Italian Right
Territorial politics, populism and
'post-fascism'
Carlo Ruzza and Stefano Fella

11. Political Extremes
An investigation into the history of
terms and concepts from antiquity
to the present
Uwe Backes

**12. The Populist Radical Right
in Poland**
The patriots
Rafal Pankowski

**13. Social and Political Thought of
Julius Evola**
Paul Furlong

14. Radical Left Parties in Europe
Luke March

15. Counterterrorism in Turkey
Policy choices and policy effects
toward the Kurdistan Workers'
Party (PKK)
Mustafa Coşar Ünal

**16. Class Politics and the
Radical Right**
Edited by Jens Rydgren

**17. Rethinking the French
New Right**
Alternatives to modernity
Tamir Bar-On

18. Ending Terrorism in Italy
Anna Bull and Philip Cooke

19. Politics of Eugenics
Productionism, population and
national welfare
Alberto Spektorowski

**20. Politics of National Identity
in Italy**
Immigration and 'Italianità'
Eva Garau

Politics of National Identity in Italy

Immigration and 'Italianità'

Eva Garau

 Routledge
Taylor & Francis Group

LONDON AND NEW YORK

First published 2015
by Routledge
2 Park Square, Milton Park, Abingdon, Oxon OX14 4RN

and by Routledge
711 Third Avenue, New York, NY 10017

Routledge is an imprint of the Taylor & Francis Group, an informa business

British Library Cataloguing in Publication Data
A catalogue record for this book is available from the British Library

Library of Congress Cataloging in Publication Data
Garau, Eva.
Politics of national identity in Italy : immigration and 'Italianità' / Eva
Garau.
  pages cm
Includes bibliographical references and index.
  1. Nationalism–Italy. 2. National characteristics, Italian. 3. Italy–Politics
and government–20th century. 4. Italy–Politics and government–21st
century. I. Title.
  DG451.G36 2015
  320.540945–dc23
              2014028111

ISBN: 978-0-415-62779-5 (hbk)
ISBN: 978-1-315-73333-3 (ebk)

Typeset in Times New Roman
by Taylor & Francis Books

Printed and bound by CPI Group (UK) Ltd, Croydon, CR0 4YY

To Giovanni, Marisella and Laura

Contents

Preface   x
Acknowledgements   xiii

Politics of national identity in Italy: introduction   1

1   Italian intellectuals and the 'death of the homeland': antagonistic
    identities in Italy since 1945   18

2   The Catholic Church and the debate on identity and immigration   53

3   The Northern League and the debate on identity and immigration   102

4   The Italian legislation on immigration   145

5   Recent debates on identity and otherness: everything needs to
    change, so that everything stays the same?   181

6   Conclusion   207

Bibliography   215
Index   240

Preface

Anna Cento Bull

In a recent collected volume focusing on the relationship between the incorporation of migrants in their host societies and public representations of the past, the editors put forward an important question: 'Does the multicultural makeup of many societies today [...] mean that national foundation myths and conceptions of the nation may have to be reworked to take into account countries' heterogeneous realities?'[1] While the question is rhetorical, the reality, regrettably, points to a situation in which national identities in most countries continue to be constructed in exclusionary ways, so much so that 'they now appear to exacerbate social tensions'.

Eva Garau's book addresses these issues in relation to Italy, a country which has become *de facto* multicultural but which has failed to acknowledge this diversity other than in negative terms. Her work provides a fascinating, insightful and timely account of how this has come to pass, which goes beyond any facile explanation revolving around the rise and success of the party known as Lega Nord (Northern League). Rather, she demonstrates that this party's blatantly xenophobic discourse and increasingly influential role in policy-making related to migrant incorporation was made possible by the ways in which a variety of actors positioned themselves in the public sphere in relation to the migrant presence. Among these actors the book explores in depth prominent intellectuals, including many directly concerned with historical legacies and with the need to revisit and reconstruct national myths and narratives, who nevertheless were seemingly unable to address the issue of migrants' invisibility and silence in collective images and narratives. Carefully examining those aspects of the past which Italian intellectuals prioritised in their public debates and representations in the 1990s and at the beginning of the new century, Garau highlights violent conflicts and civil wars, especially the fascist dictatorship, the Second World War and the Resistance (recently redefined as a civil war between fascist and anti-fascist Italians). In so doing, intellectuals privileged domestic, ideologically inspired conflicts over colonial or international conflicts. While this is to some extent understandable, especially in the light of persisting political divisions in Italy during the period dominated by Berlusconi and his (post)fascist allies, the debate on national identity among intellectuals represented a wasted opportunity in terms of revisiting the country's established memories and counter-memories as well as overcoming selective forgetting in relation to its colonial history and emigrant past.

While Italian intellectuals bear a collective responsibility for failing to incorporate representations of past immigrant and/or colonial experiences in their debates on national myths and narratives, the Catholic Church carries a heavier responsibility for developing a 'model' of citizenship with various points of contact with the openly exclusionary one constructed by the Lega Nord. The vision of society put forward by the Catholic Church following mass migration has been seriously under-researched in scholarly work, therefore this part of the book fills an obvious gap and provides an important analysis of great interest beyond the Italian case. While acknowledging the positive role of social support and services provided to migrants by Catholic associations, the book defines the model of citizenship developed in authoritative Church documents as a case of 'selective solidarity', whereby only Catholic immigrants are openly welcomed and fully incorporated into society, whereas non-Catholics and especially Muslims are relegated to liminal spaces and destined never to become incorporated into the national community (given that the latter is redefined as Catholic).

Obviously there is a huge difference between this model and the fully exclusionary model developed by the Lega Nord, which Garau analyses in highly novel ways and which is applicable to the vision of society advocated by comparable radical right movements across Europe. And yet at the core we find a similar use of Catholicism in order to reconstruct national identities as homogeneous rather than diverse. Furthermore, this approach has proven attractive also to mainstream political parties, so much so that, as Garau argues, many issues and themes popularised by radical right movements have been successfully 'mainstreamed', starting with the securitisation of migration and migrants.

An important chapter deals with public policy and shows how the most vociferous actors in the public sphere – the Catholic Church and above all the Lega Nord – are also those which were able to influence policy-making the most. Yet it was only in 2008 that new legislation passed by the Berlusconi government seemingly attempted to apply, at least on a symbolic level, the radically exclusionary model of citizenship advocated by the Lega Nord. In this scenario, in which mainstream politicians resort to developing and implementing policies inspired by extreme 'niche' parties, the only hope lies with a possible change of direction within the Catholic Church, following the election of Bergoglio as Pope Francis on 13 March 2013, and with the migrants themselves, provided they are able to make their voices heard.

Going back to the question posed at the outset, this book confirms in an original and novel manner the tension between the need to revisit 'national foundation myths' in ways that construct the nation as heterogeneous and current trends directed at reaffirming narratives of homogeneity and of migrants' invisibility. It also demonstrates the crucial importance of the symbolic and rhetorical level in such constructions and the very real and demonstrable impact the latter have upon the sphere of policy-making and legislation.

Note

1 See *History, memory and migration: Perceptions of the past and the politics of incorporation*. Edited by Irial Glynn and J. Olaf Kleist, Basingstoke and New York: Palgrave Macmillan, 2012. The quotations are from the introductory chapter by the editors, entitled 'The Memory and Migration Nexus: An Overview', pp. 3–32 (p. 6 and p. 8).

Acknowledgements

Work for this book began during my years at the University of Bath. I am grateful to many people who helped in different ways at different stages while it was being conceptualised and researched.

I am extremely grateful to Roger Eatwell, who supported the project from the start, providing invaluable advice, always being available to discuss it, and encouraging me to publish the findings.

I owe my deepest gratitude to Anna Cento Bull. This book is the result of a constant dialogue with her. I must thank Anna for posing new questions and challenges as the writing progressed, allowing me constantly to rethink this book through, and for the time she devoted to reading the manuscript several times in the last year.

I am grateful to Karoline von Oppen, for her friendship, her generosity, patience and support, and for the hours she spent sitting in a pub discussing this book with me, asking questions and finding problems I would not have thought of.

I must thank Gino Bedani for his advice and Jacqueline Andall for her inspiring work and for her support.

I would like to thank my mentors, friends and colleagues at the University of Cagliari, where I completed the writing. In particular, I am grateful to Annamaria Loche for bringing me back to where it all started and giving me the chance to continue my research at the Department of Philosophy, and to Professor Francesco Atzeni for giving me the opportunity to work with him in the Department of History.

I must thank Marina Falbo, who after our graduation convinced me I needed to leave Italy to understand it better. I can now see how right she was.

I would like to thank my family and in particular my parents, who supported me over the years I spent researching and writing this book and my sister Laura for sharing my joys and worries and making me feel close to home during my years in Bath. I will never thank them all enough for accepting my emigration, for encouraging me and believing in me.

Finally, I would like to thank the editorial and production team at Routledge for their assistance and support throughout all stages of this project.

Politics of national identity in Italy
Introduction

1 Introduction

'We made Italy. Now we need to make Italians.' Massimo d'Azeglio's words in the aftermath of Italian Unification (1861–70) have become symbolic of the difficult process of construction of a unitary national identity. Long after the creation of the new nation-state, indeed, Italy was judged to be a mere 'geographical expression', where the village, the province or the region were still the point of reference for a population who did not share the same language and did not feel any sense of loyalty towards a nation that many felt had been imposed upon them.

The 150th anniversary of Unification (1861–2011) has been presented by opinion makers and politicians as an occasion to (re)open a dialogue on the meaning of *Italianness*, on whether such a shared common belonging has ever been successfully achieved, and on its core values. Paradoxically, the organisation of the celebrations for the anniversary exposed the still problematic/ fragile state of the feeling of national belonging. Doubts about the meaning of Italianness also emerge when looking at the titles of a series of books published to mark the anniversary: *It is Not the Country I Dreamt of – A Conversation with Carlo Azeglio Ciampi* (former president of the Republic), and *Excuse Me, Do You Feel Italian?* a collection of contributions on the meaning and the weakness of national identity.

A series of opinion polls launched at the time by several national newspapers show that many interviewees identify with the divided memories of Fascism and the Resistance – one of the reasons that explain the acknowledged weak national identity. Among the negative features of Italianness, mafia and corruption seem to be their first concerns, whereas the polls show that among the perceived threats to national identity is that of immigration. As the 2009 international survey 'Transatlantic Trends on Immigration' showed, Italy is the country where the perception of immigration is most distorted, as Italians believed there to be four times as many immigrants than is actually the case: 6.5 per cent according to Istat (the National Institute for Statistics), and 23 per cent according to the interviewees. With the current unrest and the explosion of civil wars in countries such as Libya and Egypt and the daily arrivals on Italian Southern shores of thousands of refugees, the popular image of immigration as 'an invasion' and a threat is not destined to fade.

In European countries with a longer tradition of immigration such as, for instance, Britain and France, the arrival of foreigners seeking better living conditions has contributed to opening a debate on models of integration as well as a discussion on different ideas of the nation-state and its role in granting political and civil rights. In these countries the construction of coherent responses to immigration also triggered a public discussion on national identity and its transformation and evolution in coming to terms with the presence of citizens of different origins. While the British debate on multiculturalism was recently reopened by Prime Minister David Cameron, in France the discussion on immigration in 2007 led to the creation of a Ministry of National Identity and Immigration.

The aim of this volume is to examine public discourses on national identity and immigration in contemporary Italy. In the past two decades, a broad literature on each of these themes has been produced, both in English and in Italian, by scholars of different disciplines. The contributions on the construction of Italianness and those on the transformation of Italy from a starting point to the final destination of the migratory process are pivotal in the analysis presented here and can be regarded as its pillars. This volume, however, has the ambitious aim of combining these two strands of scholarly interest, starting from the first appearance of these originally distinct debates in the public sphere in the early 1990s and following their intersecting development up to the present day. The following are the main questions that this book asks and aims to answer: What model, if any, is Italy following in responding to immigration? How and to what extent does this response to the growing number of arrivals include opening and promoting a debate on the need to renegotiate the feeling of national belonging in order to make it more inclusive of alternative/minority identities? What actors are taking part in the debates on identity and otherness, and what impact does their rhetoric have on public opinion and state policy?

I believe that the provisional answers to these questions could be of interest to scholars and students of Italian history, politics and culture, as well as for those studying the issues of national identity and immigration at a more theoretical level or from a comparative perspective.

The book sets out to fill the gap in the literature on the relation between public debates on identity and immigration by following a chronological and thematic approach. It will start with an overview of the concepts of identity and otherness as presented in classical literature and the dominant models of integration developed by individual countries according to their political and historical traditions, which will be presented in this Introduction. The first four chapters will then explore the Italian debates on national identity and immigration, analysing the positions of, and the dialogue between, those Italian political and social actors which, for their role in the public sphere, can be expected to have an important voice in such a discussion. More precisely, the first chapter will focus on the role of Italian intellectuals and opinion makers in the debate on national identity and immigration, while the second and third chapters will take into account the position of, and model of integration proposed by, the Catholic Church and the Northern League, respectively, on the same matters. The fourth chapter will analyse the Italian legislation on citizenship and immigration in order to establish whether it has been informed by any specific model and whether any of the actors mentioned above has influenced or shaped the state's response to immigration. The fifth chapter will bring together the changes and shifts in the rhetoric of the three main political actors taken into account, while contextualising the employment of a discourse on Italianness and immigration in the last three years. This last part of the book will assess the impact of a series of factors, from the 150th anniversary of the Unification of Italy to the resignation of Pope Benedict XVI and the advent of the Francis era, to the scandals and the change of leadership within the Northern League, to the abrogation of the crime of illegal entry.

2 Methodology

Given the scope of this volume, the methodological approach chosen is one that brings to light and explains the different interpretations of the phenomenon and the models of integration and citizenship put forward by single actors as well as by the state. The research method applied here is that of discourse analysis, and more precisely discourse theory as it has been conceptualised by Ernesto Laclau and Chantal Mouffe: 'Issues of identity formation, the production of novel ideologies, the logic of social movements and the structuring of societies by a plurality of social imaginaries are central objects of investigation for discourse theory' (Howarth and Stavrakakis, 2000: 2). Laclau and Mouffe argue that the only scientific method to define social groups/classes is that of not attributing to them characteristics that they do not exhibit in society, in concrete situations. The critique of social, economic and historical determinism is conducted starting from the general assumption that meanings are not fixed (Laclau and Mouffe, 1985). 'Discourse theory sees all social phenomena as discursive constructions, and assumes that all social phenomena can be studied by discourse analysis. It is in this sense that discourse theory turns social phenomena into language, and language into an object for discourse analysis' (Pedersen, 2009: 5). Laclau and Mouffe's interpretation of discourse analysis results from deconstructing other theories: from structuralist linguistics they take the principle that the smallest unit in language is the sign and that discourse is a system of signs where every sign is different from the others. Following post-structuralism, they establish that the content of signs (signified) is always contingent and never fixed. Finally, neo-Marxism inspires their belief that the 'articulation', which infuses a meaning into the signs, is embedded in a political process. If the discourse is a system of signs whose meaning comes from the articulation, this latter has to be intended as a conflict between subjects aiming to achieve a political status by imposing a specific idea of the world, taken for granted and presented as a-problematic (Laclau and Mouffe, 1985: 140–42). According to them, discourse analysis can therefore be used to map this conflictual process as a political process, which involves finding the nodal points that give the signs their meaning as well as bringing to light the process of allocation of meanings. A nodal point is a central concept, for instance that of democracy, around which conflict takes place. Discourse theory assumes that all discourses are ideological precisely because they are presented as objective and therefore contribute to creating alternative realities, and that meaning is created through politics and by politics. In this sense, institutions do not exist independently of discourse: on the contrary, they are purely discursive constructions without any extra-discursive status (Laclau and Mouffe, 1985: 130; Pedersen, 2009: 5–6):

> The fact that every object is constituted as an object of discourse has nothing to do with whether there is a world external to thought, or with the realism/idealism opposition. An earthquake or the falling of a brick is an event that certainly exists, in the sense that it occurs here and now, independently of my will. But whether their specificity as objects is constructed in terms of 'natural phenomena' or 'expression of the wrath of God' depends upon the structuring of a discursive field. What is denied is not that such objects exist externally to thought, but the rather different assertion that they could constitute themselves as objects outside any discursive condition of emergence.
>
> (Laclau and Mouffe, 1985: 108)

To summarise, it can be said that discourse theory interprets as discourse any organised system of meanings. The elements of such a system do not exist on their own, outside the system, as they do not have fixed and pre-existent meanings. Therefore institutions or social/political groups do not have an a priori identity but as single elements of the system they acquire meaning only in relation to one another, when they form a regular configuration that turns them into 'signs'. As a result, meaning is relational and human actions acquire it through a regularly performed series of actions. If the meaning of each element is determined by its relation and interaction with the other elements in the system, then when a new signifier is added to the picture, it can only acquire meaning by establishing a relation with the other signs. In acquiring its meaning, the new signifier creates disruption in the order it finds when it first appears and therefore determines a change in the general meaning of the system as well as in that of each sign: this process is described by discourse theory as 'conflict' or antagonism (Laclau and Mouffe, 1985: 159–71).

Such a methodological approach becomes particularly helpful when applied to the research presented here, as it provides a theoretical framework to explain how the relations between single actors articulate and evolve. Applying discourse theory to the Italian discussion on national identity and immigration contributes to explaining how the different actors involved in the debate, be they intellectuals, the Church or the Northern League, articulate their own specific rhetoric in order to provide a coherent definition of the situation and alternative interpretations presented as 'true', 'objective' and a-problematic. Moreover, it allows us to expose the relations between these various systems of signs carrying antagonistic meanings, as well as the processes according to which they influence each other and renegotiate through conflicts their own positioning and the general meaning of the system of meanings they contribute to form. In this sense, it allows us to deconstruct the tensions within each group of actors, for instance by bringing to light the internal contradictions and antagonistic positions of the Catholic hierarchy. Moreover, while putting the claimed objectivity of alternative realities into perspective (in their being relative precisely because they all claim to be objective), it also allows us to understand how reality is performative – that is to say, how discourse reproduces reality while informing it.

Applying this concept to the Italian case and the debate on immigration also contributes to explain how the interpretations of the immigration phenomenon presented by intellectuals, political parties and the Church as objective have contributed to influence public perception of the issue. Hence the adopted methodological approach helps to explain how the discourse on immigration, seemingly resulting from an analysis of a 'real' situation (number of arrivals, issues linked to law and order, etc.), contributes to shape such reality, not least by turning public fears of immigration and perceptions of migrants as a threat into something more 'real' than any statistics. By focusing on the influence of discourse on social reality and vice versa, discourse analysis brings to light the mutual dependence of rhetoric and legislation, where the former shapes the latter, while the latter stimulates the creation of a new rhetoric inclusive of revised meanings.

The public sphere, according to the definition given by Habermas (1989a), is not encompassed by the state and therefore does not coincide with it: rather, it is a theatre where mediation and dialogue between the private sphere and the authoritative state take place. The public sphere is 'a realm of social life in which public opinion can be formed' (Habermas, 1989a: 30), 'a kind of social intercourse', which allows and encourages relations between heterogeneous, multiple, overlapping and opposing views (ibid.: 36). The expression 'public opinion' refers to 'the task of criticism and control which a public body of citizens informally – and, in periodic elections, formally as well – practices vis-à-vis the ruling structure organized in the form of a state' (ibid.: 146).

This interpretation justifies the choice to base this research on the debate as it emerged in the public sphere, taking the latter as the focus, rather than the media through which the debate developed. When a systematic analysis of the media has been carried out, as in the case of the qualitative analysis of articles and editorials published in the Northern League's newspaper, *La Padania*, this was due to the relevance that the views expressed there had acquired in the public debate on immigration. This also explains why the position of specific individuals who are part of the collective actors taken into account will not be further investigated, for instance through interviews, since the aim of this work is not that of establishing whether their attitudes towards immigration are genuine or where they originated. Rather, the aim of this book is to assess the ideas that until now have been presented in the public sphere, and to analyse their impact and their consequences. In other words, what matters here is reconstructing the (contrasting) narratives on immigration and national identity in order to provide a better understanding of the state of the debate in Italy as well as to expose the conflicts, alliances and interests underpinning the public and political debate and assess their impact on Italian legislation on immigration and citizenship.

3 From a country of emigration to a country of immigration: an historical overview

Since the end of World War II, the phenomenon of immigration and the presence of refugees and asylum seekers have begun to acquire relevance in the political and social life of Western European countries. The unprecedented waves of migration were characterised by a South–North movement, which originated mainly from Northern Mediterranean countries and were directed towards Northern Europe, particularly Belgium, Britain, France, Germany and Sweden. The colonial legacy of some of these Northern European countries represented a further pull factor, which attracted a considerable number of non-European nationals from the British, French and Dutch ex-colonies, who were granted special rights and preferential access to employment and citizenship. In times of reconstruction and economic development, the receiving countries often not only encouraged immigration but actively recruited a labour force through national companies and industries and through bilateral agreements with the sending countries (Triandafyllidou and Gropas, 2007: 1).

Scholars and historians of migration movements tend to agree on indicating 1973 and the oil crisis as the watershed that marks the era in which Southern European nations, such as Spain, Greece and Italy, turned from countries of emigration into countries of immigration, final destinations for those seeking better living and working conditions. This was due to international events as well as to the reaction of Northern European countries to the economic stagnation and rising unemployment that affected the whole of Western Europe, when they stopped recruiting workers abroad and in fact decided to close their doors and aim at a 'zero immigration policy' (Schain, 2008; Hollifield, 1992; Sciortino, 2000). Moreover, since 1989, the end of the Cold War, the Albanian crises and the war in former Yugoslavia contributed to opening new migration routes from the East to the West of Europe, making immigration increasingly visible in neighbouring countries such as Italy.

By that time the first countries of immigration had developed long-term strategies aimed at integrating a foreign presence that had become permanent or semi-permanent. Such models of integration resulted from both theoretical approaches to integration of difference and from more practical ideas of the state and its role in granting its citizens civil and political rights. The different strategies adopted by different countries were also based on specific definitions of the nation-state resulting from their individual history and traditions. Each of these first-wave immigration countries witnessed a debate on the nature of the state, on whether it had to be considered an empty box, neutral towards different ideas of the good life, in which all should be granted freedom of expression, or rather had to be interpreted as carrying a certain set of values and moral standards traditionally derived from a shared culture and seen as indispensable for the reaffirmation of a shared national identity. In the receiving countries, the construction of coherent responses to immigration also triggered a public discussion on national identity and its transformation or evolution in coming to terms with new internal characteristics, as will be shown later in the analysis of the dominant models of integration.

Italy is among those countries that in the early 1970s started to receive more people than they were sending abroad and therefore became countries of immigration. Traditionally considered as the starting point of many diasporas, between the end of the 19th century and the early 1920s, almost 15 million Italians left their country for Northern Europe, the United States, Latin America, Canada and Australia (Biggeri, 2005: 1). Italian culture has always been pervaded with a shared memory of the experiences of the 'emigranti', which is reflected in popular culture, cinema and music, and which contributed to create the myth of 'Italians abroad' as part of the national identity (Fortier, 2000; Gabaccia, 2000). The theme of the homeland as 'mother' and that of the journey by boat, the images of Italians disembarking on Ellis Island and of little Italys around the world, have become part of a narrative that has contributed to creating or reinforcing a common feeling of national belonging (Krase, 1996; Patriarca, 2001). The transition that brought Italy to the status of a receiving country went unnoticed for decades, neglected by the political world and irrelevant for public opinion, at least until the early 1990s, when it exploded, unexpectedly and suddenly.

Italy, today the fourth country of immigration in Europe, after Britain, France and Germany, is characterised by a 'polycentric migration population', by which is meant a population consisting of many nationalities from different parts of the world, with no one nationality or group of nationalities emerging as dominant. Indeed, in 2000 the three top nationalities (Moroccans, Albanians and Filipinos) represented only a quarter of the total immigrant population, whereas, for instance, in Germany the three main foreign nationalities (Turks, Yugoslavs and Italians) made up 40 per cent of the immigrant population (King, 2002: 4; Caritas-Migrantes, 2000). Until recently, immigrants in Italy (2,670,514 in 2005) accounted for 2.5 per cent of the total population, a proportion that remained below the average of most European countries. Since 2008, however, foreign citizens residing in the country have risen to almost 4.5 million (6.7 per cent), which is slightly higher than the European average, albeit still far from the numbers registered in Germany (8.2 per cent). In terms of arrivals concentrated in single years, 2008 and 2009 were the first two years in which Italy overtook countries such as Britain, whose immigrants account for 6.3 per cent. In terms of nationalities most represented, today the first group is that of Romanians, who represent 20.5 per cent of the total immigrant population, followed by Albanians (11.3 per cent) and Moroccans (10.4 per cent) (Caritas Migrantes, 2010: 5). Half of the foreign population (50.8 per cent) is composed of women not only migrating to accompany male migrants but mainly as independent labour migrants employed in the domestic sector. The number of migrants is evenly distributed across the peninsula with areas of concentration in big cities, particularly Rome and Milan, as well as the most populated provinces of the centre-North. This population is characterised by a low average age, with two thirds of immigrants aged 19 to 40; while older people remain significantly under-represented, it is difficult to get a picture of the number of children, which is clearly increasing but becomes noticeable only when looking at school enrolment data, as they do not appear in the statistics since they do not have individual permits (ibid.).

Given its new position as a country of immigration, Italy is today facing the same challenges that traditional receiving countries encountered decades earlier. However, the fact that it joined other countries of immigration late and that the level of its foreign population remained below the European average for decades, has heavily influenced the debate on immigration as well as the nature of migration policies put forward by different governments. In addition, the sudden and unexpected transformation of Italy into a final destination for migrants has determined a difficulty on the part of public opinion in evaluating impartially the phenomenon and its consequences. This has induced a radicalisation of perceptions and assessments of the immigrant presence which has not contributed to a full understanding of the complex and dynamic reality of the phenomenon and its various effects. On the political side, there was, and to a certain extent there still is today, a tendency to polarise the discussion between those generally in favour and those against immigration, which has prevented a coherent discussion on more pragmatic but also long-term solutions to deal with this new trend (Biggeri, 2005: 8–9).

As stated above, one of the aims of this book is that of investigating whether, in reacting to the growing number of arrivals, Italy has followed any of the models adopted by other European countries. Four hypotheses are formulated here. The first hypothesis is that the legislation to deal with immigration increasingly reflects the model of integration put forward by the Northern League. The second hypothesis is that it fits into the model suggested by the Church. The third possibility is that Italy is using a combination of the two models or, rather, developing an original model in order to deal with immigration, according to its own cultural, historical and constitutional traditions. Finally, a fourth hypothesis is that Italy is not constructing any coherent long-term strategy, nor is it opening an intellectual and political debate on the subject, but is rather coping with the phenomenon by relying on ad hoc measures aimed at dealing with individual 'unforeseen' emergency situations.

Before moving to the analysis of the Italian case, it is necessary to look briefly at the theoretical and ethical debate on identity, rights and justice, and how it has informed the responses to immigration in countries such as France and Britain. The following section will provide an overview of the main issues related to the representation of minority groups as they have been addressed in the complex and articulated dialogue between liberals and communitarians. It will address the main positions of, as well as criticism directed at these two strands of thought, and the models they inform: assimilation and multiculturalism. Defining these models is of central importance, as they will be used as a paradigm to assess the Italian position(s) on the issue. Thus the wider debate on individual and collective identity and the role of the state in promoting justice and equal opportunities is relevant as it will represent a term of comparison and will contribute to highlight, as we shall see in the course of this volume, both the absence of a similar debate in Italy and its occasional appearance, generally in highly critical and dismissive terms, in the discourse of some actors, notably the Church and the Northern League.

4 The debate on identity and justice: liberalism v. communitarianism

The second half of the 20th century has been characterised by an increasing presence, in the political scene of Western democracies, of organisations and movements representing the claims of disadvantaged groups, such as African-Americans, Native Indians and other ethnic, cultural and religious minorities, as well as social groups such as women, gays and lesbians. The demands and the ideologies of these social movements and minority groups have triggered a systematic debate on the concept of identity, its origin, nature and meaning, as well as the different issues linked to and derived from it, such as the current and future status of the particular identities being claimed and defended by these groups.

The politics of identity put forward by contemporary democracies is strictly connected to the ideas of oppression and discrimination, which presuppose the vulnerability of the minority group in the face of cultural imperialism as well as its experience of stereotyping, 'violence, exploitation, marginalization and powerlessness' (Young, 1990: 39). In demanding access to civil rights and acquiring visibility in the public sphere, members of minority groups went through a process of consolidation of group identities, increasing identification with social and cultural categories and thus reinforcing self-sameness. Claims for protection and representation indeed required a strong sense of belonging to an organised group sharing ethnic or cultural traits, which could act in a unitary manner in the struggle to achieve public recognition.

This resulted in the representation of identities alternative to the mainstream ones and also 'fixed', exhibiting predictable and unchangeable common characteristics. In this sense, being gay, lesbian, black or female became a stereotyped and monolithic identity, characterised by immutable traits (Calhoun, 1995: 193–99). To a certain extent, identification with a close community was the price minority groups had to pay in order to be recognised as such and granted access to rights and resources, and in this sense the simplification of representation was accepted by marginalised communities as transitory and functional to the achievement of immediate goals (Moller Okin, 1989; Young 1990). This contributes to explaining how, for decades, the constitution of identities has been presented as a harmonious process resulting in 'stable and minimally changing identity' (Calhoun, 1995: 218). As a result, the struggle and the tensions involved in the forging of identities and the fact that identities are fragmented were underestimated until relatively recently. However, more recent approaches have converged towards a systematic deconstruction of essentialist interpretations of social, ethical and religious groups, stressing the importance of multiple, conflicting or complementary identities and their respective and often contradictory demands (ibid.).

Since the 1970s, the debate on identity and participation has been polarised between two main interpretations aimed at finding a solution to issues of recognition, integration and participation in the public sphere. On the one hand, the liberal perspective, traditionally linked to the ideas of philosophers such as John Stuart Mill (1806–73) and Jeremy Bentham (1748–1832), and further developed by John Rawls in his *A Theory of Justice* (1971), interprets identity as individual and universal. On the other hand, the communitarian interpretation of identity, articulated as a critique of the liberal approach, and formulated by philosophers such as Michael Sandel, Charles Taylor, Michael Walzer and Alasdair McIntyre, views belonging as local, relative and collective. These two approaches reflect and inform different models of citizenship and integration put forward by Western democracies to foster inclusion and participation in the public sphere, to grant rights and access to resources, and to create a shared feeling of belonging. Before addressing the models resulting from liberal and communitarian interpretations of belonging, and particularly assimilation in France and multiculturalism in Britain, it is worth looking at the specific contents of these two perspectives.

In trying to identify the process according to which rights can be claimed by different individuals, Rawls developed a theory of justice based on the idea of 'the original position', according to which citizens have to imagine themselves as being in the position of equal and free persons who agree on general principles of social and political justice. The main characteristic of the original position is that 'a veil of ignorance' prevents participants from being allocated specific social and historical circumstances, which they ignore when making choices on fairness and desirable forms of participation. The role of the veil of ignorance is that of allowing impartiality of judgement when the subjects in the original position are demanded to choose between different ideas of justice that best represent and serve their interests. According to Rawls, the most effective and rational choices are achievable when taking into account two principles of justice. The first guarantees citizens equal basic rights and liberties necessary to pursue their different conception of the good life. The second provides equality of educational and employment opportunities while granting all of them minimum income and wealth to pursue their interests and to maintain their self-respect. When 'blind' citizens, unaware of their specific cultural, ethnic and religious circumstances, make choices on the allocation of resources and the type of participation they judge best, they will tend to include as many groups of people as possible among those who will be given access to rights, since they do not know in which situation they will have to live.

Rawls argues that the principles of fair justice can be identified through rational individual choices. In this respect, his theory of justice is somewhat close to the utilitarian approach to justice and representation, based on the idea of granting the highest level of happiness to the highest number of people (Bentham, 1996 [1781]). This liberal theory of justice originates from the concept of an ideal autonomous subject who 'successfully and rationally extricates himself from the entanglements of history and the characteristics and values that come with the entanglement' (Bell, 1993: 29). The idea of a subject or citizen as a self-sufficient agent who chooses a life plan and employs his/her will to pursue it, rests on the assumption that life is a result of individual rational decisions. In this sense, liberal theory does not take into account collective identities: rights are given to individuals on the basis of their choices, their demand for participation and the acknowledgement of their presence in the public sphere as individuals.

An inherent aspect of liberalism is that the state is presented as indifferent to any set of values or specific backgrounds that characterise the single citizens, neutral towards different interpretations of the good life, which liberalism defines as a life that is worth living. Criticism of this interpretation of the role of the state as purely procedural comes from within liberalism itself, as perfectionist liberals admit that the state should not be an empty box but should rather provide a minimum common denominator in terms of values, which allows citizens to develop a sense of belonging and loyalty. However, both strands of liberalism still consider the individual as the only beneficiary of rights (Galeotti, 1994; Kymlicka, 1995). Liberal utilitarianism has been criticised for not being applicable, as the idea of achieving the highest happiness for the majority of people has proven to be lacking rationality. Indeed, it can justify intolerant and cruel practices, as in the example of a community of 12 people wherein ten members link their happiness to torturing the other two. In this case, torture would be the utilitarian response to the popular will (Bell, 1993: 78).

Neutralist liberalism and Rawls's theory of justice have been criticised by communitarians for their atomistic and abstract conception of the individual as a rational agent. First, communitarians have argued that the idea of an abstract good life lacks substance, which explains why liberals do not provide examples of what they mean by it; second, making choices implies a judgement of different alternatives, which can only be made according to some sort of moral orientation. The possibility of choosing is only given when the subject has already learned a specific idea of the good, a framework which defines the type of life s/he aims to live. It is then the social worlds in which human beings are immersed that offer the moral horizon that determines what is worth achieving or being (Taylor, 1989: pt 2). This is the reason why 'we cannot make sense of our moral experience unless we situate ourselves within this given moral space' (Bell, 1993: 37).

Communitarians' critique of liberalism is based on the idea that human beings are ultimately social creatures, political animals, as they define them using Aristotle's definition (Barnes, 1984). Moreover, they reject the idea that human beings use rationality in order to decide what values matter most and consequently plan their lives. According to them, the highest attachment of individuals goes to their community, which can range from the family to a religious group, and does not require a rational choice, but rather assumes a 'pre-conscious' modus operandi, which is further influenced by the specific social and historical characteristics of the particular time and environment in which the subject lives. Rational choice intervenes only when the unreflective routine of everyday life is interrupted by an unusual event that creates a conflict between different pre-conscious values (Heidegger, 1927: 213; Bell, 1993: 33).

Communitarians believe that different groups based on ethnic, religious or sub-national shared identities should be given recognition as such in the public sphere and therefore the state should not be neutral towards their demands. Moreover, according to them, the state can never be really neutral as, in demanding citizens to leave all differences (such as religion, sexual orientation, ethnic background) out of the public sphere so that they do not interfere with the process of decision making, it proves to privilege main-stream groups, namely, in Western democracies, the so-called WASP (white Anglo-Saxon Protestant and mainly male citizens). These inner characteristics do not need to be left out of the public sphere as they are shared by the majority of the population and therefore are not perceived as different, whereas black, Muslim or gay citizens would be allowed to enter the public sphere not in the name of their identities, but despite them (Galeotti, 1994).

Communitarians have been accused of essentialism by feminists and post-structuralists, who argue that in identifying human beings mainly as members of specific groups, they do not take into account that oppression often comes from within the community, when members are marginalised or not allowed to leave when they come to a rejection of the communities' values (for instance in a patriarchal family or in ethnic groups where dissent is considered betrayal) (Young, 1990; Moller Okin, 1989; Kymlicka, 1995). In responding to this charge, communitarians argue that participation in one group does not exclude simultaneously belonging to other groups since loyalty stretches to more than one community and attachment to the family does not conflict with attachment to a religious group, a region or a nation (Sandel, 1982: 150; Anzaldùa, 1999). However, at the same time they define the breaking of ties with the community as a 'self-defeating' experience (Bell, 1993: 100–103), diagnosing those who lose this identification and commitment to the group as going through 'a painful and frightening experience' (Taylor, 1989: 26–27).

Finally, communitarians have been criticised for their inability to give a positive definition of the concept of community. This gap was filled by a central work for communitarian thought, Martin Bell's *Communitarianism and its Critics* (1993), in which the author identifies three types of communities: communities of memory, communities of place and psychological communities. Communities of memory, such as the nation, are based on their history, their common past, but also the future: 'beside tying us to the past, such communities turn us towards the future as communities of hope' (Bell, 1993: 125). Members aim to realise the ideals and the projects embedded in the past of such communities as a contribution to the common good (Bellah *et al.* 1985: 153). Communities of place are characterised by proximity and locality and usually by a common language, whereas psychological communities do not require geographical boundaries or shared memories but are rather based on personal interactions in small groups such as the family, church groups, civic associations and work units (Bell, 1993: 172).

Once again, however, the idea of constitutive communities has been criticised by gay/lesbian groups as it represents a limit in the definition of groups that should be recognised in the public sphere, by presenting other belongings of affiliation as 'interest groups', groups based on a single aim or interest and whose members do not share a deep common identity (Young, 1990). Finally, the communitarian interpretation of collective identity has been dismissed as relativistic in its attribution of equal value to a broad range of groups. If liberals argue that rational choice is good per se, communitarians believe that difference in itself is a value: both positions have been perceived as dogmatic (Kymlicka, 1995).

To conclude, communitarians think that rather than taking the 'original position' as the only condition to make rational and therefore fair decisions on representation and participation, we should instead judge what identity is by using the 'final position'. The citizen in the final position, which is the deathbed, can look back at his/her life and only then, after s/he has lived that specific life in a particular place and historical time, can decide what really mattered, what s/he was really attached to or, in other words, what constituted his/her identity as a social being (Bell, 1993: 187).

5 Assimilation and multiculturalism

'Tolerance' of religious, ethnic and inter-personal behavioural differences is the leitmotif of Western societies and their attempt to accommodate difference. Yet 'despite this reputation for liberalism there can be little doubt that, in the past decade or so within Western countries, there has been an increasing awareness of, and a hardening of attitudes towards people who are "different" and, in particular, towards immigrants' (Borooah and Mangan, 2009: 34).

Since the aftermath of World War II, traditional European receiving countries have adopted different long-term strategies to react to the growing number of arrivals resulting from their colonial legacy and their active recruitment of labour force (Fernando, 2009: 379). The presence of foreign nationals triggered a debate on integration and coexistence as well as on the role of the state and whether it should demand immigrants to adapt to the culture of the country of arrival or whether it should encourage them to retain their specific characteristics and grant them recognition as members of minority groups (Entzinger and Biexeveld, 2003). This section will provide a brief overview of the two main Western European models of integration, assimilation in France and multiculturalism in Britain, while highlighting how the liberal and communitarian perspectives on citizenship described above inform them.

Assimilation requires the absorption of minority cultures into the main-stream culture and is aimed at maintaining an ideally mono-cultural and mono-faith society, an approach that implies the loss of the main character-istics of the absorbed group. Legally all citizens are recognised as French citizens as opposed, for instance, to French Arabs (Borooah and Mangan, 2009: 34–36). When addressing the concept of assimilation, scholars tend to agree on the need to distinguish between structural assimilation and cultural assimilation. Structural assimilation measures the level of participation of individuals or groups in national institutions, assessing, for instance, their voting behaviour, whereas cultural assimilation looks at values and cultural orientation and the acquisition of a sense of belonging on the part of immi-grants. Structural assimilation and cultural assimilation do not necessarily go hand in hand, as foreign nationals can take part in the institutional life of the country while maintaining a separate moral and cultural attachment to a specific minority group or to the country of origin (Gordon, 1964). The French conception of citizenship stems from an historical and constitutional tradition based on the myth of the Republic, which implies the possession of a rich legacy of memories and values that presupposes 'a past and present-day consent and desire to live together' (Renan, 1990: 19). The nation is characterised by its ambition to transcend particular minority identities, such as affiliation to historical, ethnic, religious, economic and social groups. Such an abstrac-tion is pursued through citizenship intended as individual and universal at the same time. This does not mean that rational modern citizenship does not have to confront pre-existing national features linked to a specific history and cul-ture. The French idea of citizenship is both contractual and cultural, a dual nature that is not only abstract (Schnapper, 1994: 49).

Historically, assimilation originates from the pre-revolutionary *ancien régime*, when the Kingdom of France was unified and the inhabitants of the various regions and counties were integrated into the French state (Sahlins, 1989). French national identity is also based on the values of equality, free-dom and fraternity, as well as on laïcité, the separation between the state and the Church, implemented in the Third Republic (1870–1940), when a rigid distinction between individual culture and religion, confined to the private sphere, and the secular state was introduced (Weil and Crowley, 1994: 112). The same values have inspired the French Empire, its colonial expansion during the Third Republic and its civilisation mission, which predicated the intrinsic superiority of French culture and justified its imposition onto 'less civilised' cultures (Conklin, 1997). As Haddad and Balz explain, 'while *mission civilisatrice* [sic] no longer explicitly figures in French political discourse, the idea that French culture is inherently superior to the culture of immigrants remains a key element of French policy' (Haddad and Balz, 2006: 25). Immigrants, the majority of whom come from the ex-colonies, are expected to assimilate fully into French society as quickly as possible by actively giving up their former identities and voluntarily embracing a 'single, exclusively French identity' (ibid.). Indeed, the Republican model of integration does not contemplate the possibility of hyphenated identities: it assumes that multiculturalism has fostered racism and segregation in those countries that adopted it, and particularly in Britain. The fact that there are 'no immigrants or aristocrats but only French men' is based on the idea that the Republic is one and indivisible as stated in the 1958 Constitution (ibid.).

The same strictly assimilationist perspective informs immigration policies and nationality laws, which in France have traditionally been characterised by a combination of *jus sanguinis* and *jus solis*, where the first grants citizenship to the children of citizens, regardless of where they were born, and the second extends it to all persons born in the national territory (Brubaker, 1992). According to some scholars, the liberal Republican rhetoric and the policies regulating nationality, citizenship and immigration have recently moved towards a more culturally and racially essentialist position (Fassin 2006). This was due to the emergence of right-wing political parties such as the Front National, founded in 1972 by Jean-Marie Le Pen, and to the increasingly strong differentiation between 'commensurably different' and 'incommensurably different' immigrants, and particularly Muslim immigrants (Silverstein 2004). With an increasing tendency towards a racialisation of its citizenship (Blanchard *et al.* 2005), the Republican project of individual and rational citizenship discovered the limits of its 'universal promise' (Fernando, 2009: 385), as shown by the heated debate on the headscarf and the 2005 riots in the peripheries of French cities (Haddad and Balz, 2006). Globalisation, it appears, has determined what Balibar (2004) calls 'the impotence of the omnipotent'.

When defining multiculturalism, scholars distinguish between 'soft multiculturalism' and 'hard multiculturalism': the former is commonly defined as 'a natural extension of democratic values such as tolerance and respect for diversity', whereas the latter is characterised by the emphasis it places on collective identities, the dimension of group belonging and the supremacy of the community over the individual (Borooah and Mangan, 2009: 35; Barry, 1999). Finally, a 'middle view' sees multiculturalism, intended as acknowledgment and toleration of differences and cultural expressions, as the only feasible response to increasing mass migration and to the presence of ethnic minorities within the borders.

Britain, perceived as the multiculturalist country par excellence, follows an interpretation of multiculturalism based on the extension of rights and legal recognition, and even special protection to minority groups and individuals by virtue of their belonging to those groups (Borooah and Mangan, 2009: 35). Historical tradition and national myths play a lesser role in Britain: multi-culturalism is not necessarily seen as deeply linked to a still much debated 'Britishness', although British multi-layered national identity is to a certain extent also based on an anti-racism resulting from a tradition of tolerance and accommodation of difference. Thus negotiations on race relations and the rejection, at least in principle, of racism have been promoted as a distinctive British model of citizenship (Weil and Crowley, 1994: 112; Lewis, 1988). The fact that in Britain the construction of the nation-state did not develop in relation to the integration of immigrants as it did in France, and the fact that the nation 'as a geographical and cultural entity' was unrelated to the construction of the nation as a political entity, does not mean the British model was created 'in a vacuum' (Weil and Crowley, 1994: 113). British traditional attention to 'accommodation' of difference, shown in centuries of political compromise to solve religious conflict, is combined on the one hand with a pragmatic agenda that privileges 'community-based solutions [over] minority issues and, on the other hand, with the liberal idea of keeping racism and race-based controversies out of the political sphere as much as possible' (ibid.).

Albeit partially informed by the liberal idea of equality of citizens, British multiculturalism seems more concerned with the communitarian idea that members of minority groups should be given visibility and space in the public sphere in the name of their belonging to disadvantaged or under-represented ethnic or religious affiliations. In this sense, the conflict outlined in the United States on whether the First Amendment to the Constitution, which advocates freedom of speech, should prevail over the 14th, which protects the right to equal treatment, is solved by the British approach in favour of the second principle (Favell, 1998: 263).

The main criticism addressed to multiculturalism has been that of being based on a dangerous relativism which inevitably leads to the alienation of minorities and to their 'ghettoisation' (Betts, 2002: 9). Moreover, according to its detractors, multiculturalism endangers the unity of society (Rex and Singh, 2003: 4), a concern seemingly shared by British 'public sentiment' (Borooah and Mangan, 2009). Recent debate on the failure of multiculturalism has indeed brought to light a growing concern resulting in a visible change in official policies, as shown by the fact, for instance, that the 2000 multicultural Commission of Multi-Ethnic Britain 'was quickly tempered by the calls for building cohesive communities and a quest for "Britishness"' (Rex and Singh, 2003: 53).

Some scholars and political observers argue that even if multiculturalism and assimilation are often considered irreducibly opposed to each other, France and Britain are actually moving towards a similar approach to inclusion. On the one hand, the French state, following the riots in the banlieue and the claims put forward by its Muslim citizens, has started recognising the need to acknowledge difference, while, on the other hand, British multiculturalism is seemingly moving away from a system that, when applied, ran the risk of creating segregation, towards a system where difference has to be confined to the private sphere (Kymlicka, 1995). However, others think that 'there is no need for convergence' and that indeed France and Britain will retain their antagonistic models based on a liberal and anti-communitarian ideological approach and on a communitarian short-term pragmatism, respectively (Weil and Crowley, 1994: 124).

This overview of the origins of the main models of integration as they have been developed in traditional countries of immigration is meant to provide a general term of comparison for the analysis of the Italian approach to the same issues. It thus represents a starting point and a premise necessary in order to answer the main research questions of this volume, which it is worth restating here: What model, if any, is Italy following in responding to immigration? How does this reaction to otherness influence the redefinition of the very idea of Italianness? The following chapters aim to identify 'the Italian model' and its long-term implications.

1 Italian intellectuals and the 'death of the homeland'

Antagonistic identities in Italy since 1945

1 Introduction

Since the end of World War II and until very recently, there have been only sporadic discussions on Italian identity, and all have been characterised by a general weakness of argument and lack of consistency (Cartocci, 1994; Galli della Loggia, 1996). This silence on the matter led scholars to state that neglect of the themes of the nation and its culture had reached extraordinary proportions by the 1980s, to the extent that the issue of the relation between the nation and the state as well as the political system had been almost completely sidelined by historians (Galli della Loggia, 1996).

This chapter aims to investigate the causes behind the general lack of interest on the part of Italian intellectuals in these issues during the past years as well as to analyse the current state of the debate on the significance and content of a specifically Italian 'national identity'. It will start with the attempt to identify the circumstances that caused a revival of the discussion among Italian intellectuals. It will then consider why a shared feeling of *Italianness*[1] has been judged to be going through a deep crisis.

The chapter will be organised into three separate sections, each examining quite different historical and political issues, which, nonetheless, share the common trait of having triggered various debates on Italianness in the last two decades. The first section will address historical events such as the different interpretations of the Resistance, the military capability of the Italian army during World War II, the role of political parties in post-war Italy and particularly the relationship between the Italian Communist Party with Yugoslavia after the war. The second section will focus on relatively recent internal political issues and will take into account the rise of political actors, such as the Northern League, the longstanding divide between the North and the South of the country, the importance of family belonging and the resilience of political subcultures. A third section will focus specifically on the (largely missing) link between the debate on immigration and that on national identity by outlining the unfolding development of the discussion between Italian intellectuals. This section will question whether and to what extent the arrival of immigrants in the country has determined, or is seen as in need of determining, a renegotiation of the concept of national identity, in order to make its content and meaning more inclusive of the different ethnic groups and cultures. It will try to prove that the debate on the influence of immigration on Italianness has been and still is quite meagre, arising out of occasional diatribes as well as causing bitter controversies, rather than engaging systematically with issues of integration and inclusion. It will suggest that the discussion of the internal factors mentioned and their influence on the (re)construction of an Italian identity contribute to keeping the focus of the debate on internal factors and do not leave space to consider other elements, in this case seemingly external elements such as immigration, which are nevertheless affecting the practices – rather than concepts – of Italianness, patriotism and citizenship.

2 The role and crisis of the intellectual

Before going into the question of Italian intellectuals and their role in the debate on national identity and immigration, it is necessary to reflect, albeit briefly, on the meaning of the term intellectual, in order to make clearer to what category of individuals this chapter is going to refer.

Despite the many attempts to define the nature of intellectuals, the use and meaning of the term today remain controversial and certainly not univocal. That of intellectual represents a concept in permanent evolution and still under scrutiny, as proven by the broad literature on the theme. Originally used as an adjective to contrast intellectual and manual work, the term is tightly linked with the Dreyfus Affair in France, where for the first time it is defined in its modern meaning as an expression referring to an individual or a particular category of individuals. Even though the word had already been used, in Britain, for instance, to describe the poet Byron in 1813 (Williams, 1988: 169), in the Western world of the 19th century it had a different connotation. As a consequence, according to some scholars, such as Jennings and Kemp-Welch (1997: 7), it is not possible to talk about Medieval or Victorian intellectuals in a retrospective way. It is with the Dreyfus Affair that the necessary condition to be an intellectual includes for the first time a call for action – in that case it was the action of writers such as Émile Zola, André Gide and Marcel Proust, who took the responsibility to intervene publicly in political matters.

Scholars tend to agree that the main reference point in the debate on intellectuals is represented by the interpretations of the concept provided by Julian Benda and Antonio Gramsci in 1927 and between 1926 and 1937, respectively (Said, 1994; Jennings and Kemp-Welch, 1997). In his *La trahison des clercs* (1926, The Betrayal of the Intellectuals), Benda delineates the true intellectuals in almost religious terms as not belonging to this world, safe from any involvement in material advantages and practical aims, and looking at scientific and metaphysical thought as the only worthy activities. In this Platonic interpretation, intellectuals[2] are independent individuals who set the standards of superior truths and who never compromise with political power.

In this respect they can be considered 'a tiny band of super-gifted and morally endowed philosopher-Kings who constitute the conscience of mankind' (Benda, 1980: 43). However, despite the lack of attachment to practical goals and political diatribes, Benda's intellectual is not an 'ivory-towered individual [...] devoted to abstruse and obscure subjects', but rather a man (Benda never mentions women as members of the category) driven by his metaphysical passion for truth and justice toward action, which involves defending the weakest in society, criticising established power and fighting unjust authority (Benda, 1980: 52). Only a very limited number of people can be included in the category of intellectuals, as not many are ready to speak the truth in the face of power, being isolated and set apart in order to accomplish courageously the mission to which they are called, which is in constant opposition to the status quo (ibid.).

The definition of intellectuals outlined by Gramsci stands in direct opposition to the one formulated by Benda. The Sardinian philosopher's idea of intellectuals is much more entwined with the real world and the specific political situation of a particular historical time. The first difference with the previous definition consists in the fact that, according to Gramsci, all men are intellectuals, but not all men have in society the function of intellectuals (Gramsci, 1975: 1516). Following Gramsci, one has to recognise his/her own place in society and can contribute to its development in his/her role of intellectual only as an insider, an 'organic' part of a social group at a particular time, from which the expression 'organic intellectual' is derived (ibid.).[3] According to Montefiore, the common trait of the definitions considered until this point is that in order to recognise someone as an intellectual, they all set as criteria two specific characteristics: being autonomous and willing to act, where acting stands for criticising (power), supporting (the victims of injustice), fighting (the status quo) and protecting (the values of justice and truth). In other words an intellectual is 'an incorrigibly independent soul answering to no one', 'anyone who takes a committed interest in the validity and truth of ideas for their own sake' (Montefiore, 1990: 201). As Mannheim puts it, individuals belonging to this category have to be 'free-floating', 'unanchored' and 'unattached' (Mannheim, 1993: 69–80).

However, if all intellectuals have to be independent and willing to act, they are also characterised by a self-awareness and a full understanding of their role within society as required by their duty to 'assimilate [the] point of view and conception of the whole' escaping from personal interests and material aims (Jacoby, 1987: 219–20). The intellectual has to be conscious of his place in society in order to become 'an individual endowed with a faculty for representing, embodying, articulating a message, a view, an attitude, philosophy or opinion to, as well as for, a public', as well as an individual committed to raising embarrassing questions and to fighting against dogmas rather than producing them (Said, 1994: 8). The intellectual's independence from the state comes from their duty to represent issues and people who are 'routinely forgotten' (ibid.: 9). They do so motivated by universal principles such as respect for human rights and love for freedom and justice, but their action is always influenced by the person they are, their experiences and background, and their personal sensibilities. Therefore, Said argues, there is no such thing as a private intellectual, since writing and publishing are actions that gain immediately public relevance and have practical consequences.

Scholars tend to identify in the lack of one of the above-mentioned fundamental characteristics of the intellectual the failure of their 'vocational mission' and therefore the start of a crisis which today is unanimously recognised as the dilemma of contemporary intellectuals. This dilemma can be expressed in the question formulated, among others, by Jennings and Kemp-Welch, 'Are we witnessing the disappearance of the intellectual?' (Jennings and Kemp-Welch, 1997: 12), or, to quote the title of Frank Furedi's book, 'Where have all the intellectuals gone?' (Furedi, 2004). Why are intellectuals considered as going through a crisis that questions their role in contemporary Western societies? In what sense can they be seen as failing to accomplish what Said calls 'their mission'?

According to scholars, the supposed crisis of the intellectuals is linked to the dramatic cultural changes occurring within the academic world and the role played by the media. Gouldner (1979), following Gramsci's work, argues that the old property class has been replaced by 'managers'. In this scenario intellectuals have lost their ability to talk to a broad public and are now trapped in a very specialised language which can only be understood by people working in the same field: 'they are experts addressing other experts in a sort of "lingua franca"' (ibid.: 28–43).

Foucault's claim that the traditional universal intellectual has had his place taken by a specialist who works in a specific discipline but is also able to use his expertise in other, more general fields, stands in opposition to Furedi's perspective on the matter (Foucault, 1981; Said, 1994: 8). Indeed, Furedi blames the transformation of the academic system for the phenomenon of specialisation, which he believes represents the end of the traditional intellectual class. According to him, this involves a growing relativism, mirrored by the modern methods of teaching which place different cultures on the same level, following a post-modern attitude of refusing to recognise the existence of Truth (Furedi, 2004). Following this deconstructive methodology, there are many truths and all of equal dignity, an approach which, according to the scholar, justifies the need to focus on very specialised subjects, and is unable to provide a coherent general idea of the world. Rather, it is aimed at fragmenting any encompassing interpretations and at constructing and reproducing myriad micro-worlds that become the only horizon for each intellectual. In this sense, the intellectual becomes the absolute expert in a specific field and can feel safe from the challenge of addressing anything different from their narrow field of knowledge (Furedi, 2004).

Since the 1940s, to be an intellectual has meant to be a professor, as intellectuals, lost in the universities, started to become interested in tenured employment and therefore governed by bureaucracy (Jacoby, 1987). As Jennings and

Kemp-Welch put it, 'the result has been conformity and mediocrity'. What has thereby been destroyed is not just the 'incorrigibly independent soul answering to no one', but also 'a commitment not simply to a professional or private domain but to a public world' (Jennings and Kemp-Welch, 1997: 14).

Said believes that the only consequence of this shift is that 'what we have now is a missing generation which has been replaced by buttoned up, impossible to understand classroom technicians [...] anxious to please various patrons and agencies [...] not to promote debate but to establish reputations and intimidate non-experts' (Said, 1994: 54). Said therefore agrees with these scholars in identifying specialisation as one of the failures of intellectuals, although he believes that they are exposed also to more dangerous risks, the first of which is what he calls 'professionalism'. With this term the author refers to 'thinking of your work as an intellectual as something you do for a living, between the hours of nine and five with one eye on the clock, and another cocked at what is considered to be proper, professional behaviour [...] making yourself marketable and above all presentable, hence uncontroversial and unpolitical and "objective"' (Said, 1994: 55). The second risk that one runs as an intellectual is political correctness, which forces humanists to think according to norms that 'are supposed to be very sensitive to racism, sexism, and the like, instead of allowing people to debate in what is supposed to be an "open manner"' (Said, 1994: 58).

Finally, the media play a central role in reinforcing this system, as the mass media rely on personality and have the power to decide which voices are heard. Journalists and media magnates today hold the power to set as a new value 'the ability to speak brilliantly on a subject about which one knows absolutely nothing'. In order to survive and be visible, the intellectual has therefore to adapt to the situation and reason no longer in terms of independence but rather in terms of being part of a mechanism, which means having a newspaper column or appearing as much as possible on TV (Jennings and Kemp-Welch, 1997: 14; Debray, 1981).

Since the early 1960s, Jurgen Habermas has written extensively on the role of intellectuals in the public sphere, and on 'visibility' and 'criticism' as characteristics they need in order to shape the reaction of the public they address. Through the analysis of the media and their role in influencing public discussion on issues of general interest, the philosopher reflected on the process of globalisation and fragmentation of information and how they affected participation in the public sphere, and argued in favour of a new understanding of the role of intellectuals in opposition to the reiterated idea of the decline of such public characters. Habermas agrees on the challenges faced by contemporary intellectuals and particularly the revolution in communication strategies triggered by new media such as the Internet. However, albeit seemingly no longer much different from 'clever journalists', intellectuals maintain their role in a public sphere where horizontal communication allows a broader participation. They are still different from media stars and politicians as they are not interested in turning their 'influence' into power and are still characterised by 'the sense of what is lacking and could be otherwise', 'a spark of imagination in conceiving alternatives' and 'a modicum of the courage required for polarising, provoking, and pamphleteering' (Habermas, 1989a, 1989b).

In general, it could be said that with the term 'intellectuals', this chapter refers to individuals who, as a result of their work in a particular field, have gained a sort of recognised moral authority which comes both from their knowledge of certain issues and a capacity to apply that knowledge to a broader analysis of contemporary society. This is a moral authority usually untrammelled by economic and political power or at least not primarily arising from and justified by either. The common characteristic of these intellectuals is their potential ability to influence public opinion on certain themes they choose to debate and their awareness of their power to this effect. In this context, historians, sociologists, philosophers and journalists will be considered intellectuals as far as they seem to have the authority to influence public opinion and the government on certain issues. It is, therefore, possible to look at them more as opinion makers than pure and hardly definable true intellectuals.

Having clarified who exactly this work refers to when addressing intellectuals, it is now possible to enter the question of to what extent and how Italian intellectuals are debating issues revolving around national identity and the impact that immigration has (or is likely to have in the future) on the redefinition of this concept.

3 The revival of the discussion on Italianness

Italian intellectuals' awareness of a supposed crisis of the ideas of the nation and of national identity is a very recent phenomenon. National identity has indeed been neglected by historians for decades, as can be proven, for instance, by an analysis of Federico Chabod's lectures held in Paris in 1950 on the theme of contemporary Italy (Chabod, 1961). In these lectures the crisis of the nation triggered by the war is never mentioned, according to Galli della Loggia, because the author looks at the question from the perspective of a supporter of the Resistance, which was the most common position during those years, and therefore chooses not to provide a conflicting interpretation of the 'civil war nature' of this event (Galli della Loggia, 1996: 19–20). Chabod's attitude, polemically recalled by Galli della Loggia, was shared by the most prominent historians and intellectuals at that time. According to the scholar, they seemed to have removed the question of national identity from public debate and to have ignored it for almost 50 years despite the breadth and depth of a crisis of the idea of nation which led many to feel 'not a nation anymore, never to have been such or, at least, not to have been able to become a nation when it really mattered', which is during the war (ibid.: 18).[4]

The revival of the discussion on Italianness was due to different concerns. A group of historians, journalists and sociologists, including Renzo De Felice, Ernesto Galli della Loggia, Norberto Bobbio, Gian Enrico Rusconi and

Pietro Scoppola, started a debate on the influence of historical events and particularly of the Resistance on the dominant understanding of Italian identity in the early 1990s. Other scholars, especially Giorgio Bocca, Ilvo Diamanti, Mauro Magatti and Roberto Cartocci, focused on the Northern League and how the political party led by Umberto Bossi might influence the shaping of a new feeling of national belonging in direct opposition to Italianness.[5]

In order to explain the renewed interest in themes such as that of the Resistance and the rise to power of new political parties, it is necessary to locate this discussion in the wider context of Italian history and society at the time of the revival of concerns around the idea of national identity. According to Francesca Forno, 'Authors have spoken of the 1990s as the "revolutionary years", referring to the deep crisis that simultaneously involved the political parties, the political class, the institutions and the state' (Forno, 2003: 1). This crisis, investigated by scholars such as Ilvo Diamanti, Leonardo Morlino, Roberto Biorcio and Gianfranco Pasquino, involved a political, historical and social revolution caused by both external and internal factors. At an international level, the main events that contributed to a shake-up of public opinion and to a revival of until then neglected concepts of national belonging and nationalism were mainly represented by the fall of the Berlin Wall in 1989, the war in Yugoslavia in the 1990s and the advent of a united Europe under the increasing pressure of globalisation. As Silvana Patriarca states, 'The interest in national identity comes after a period – in fact almost the whole duration of the Cold War – when the language of national identity and nationalism in Italy were more or less the discursive monopoly of the extreme right. Scholarship ignored the issue, and popular culture developed other interests' (Patriarca, 2001: 21–22). Looking at popular music as a mirror of Italian society, Patriarca recalls, the most recurring theme in the 1990s becomes that of 'la mamma' (the mother), which replaced that of 'la patria' (the homeland) (ibid.: 22).

The conclusion of the Cold War is often seen as the watershed that marks the end of the longstanding opposition between Right and Left based on the perception of the political adversary as absolute evil,[6] and triggered changes in the two political actors whose ideologies most influenced Italian identity after the end of World War II: the Communist Party and the Christian Democratic Party (DC). The consequences on a national level of the fall of the Berlin Wall included the necessity for the Italian Communist Party (PCI) to rethink its own identity, which led to a change of its name into the Partito Democratico della Sinistra[7] (PDS, or Democratic Party of the Left) in 1991, a shift that saw the most extreme wing of the political movement reassert the communist legacy and join minor Left-wing movements in order to form a new party, the Partito della Rifondazione Comunista (PRC, or Communist Refoundation Party) under the leadership of Fausto Bertinotti.[8]

The war in Yugoslavia contributed to increasing fears of a possible dissolution of the Italian nation-state and to facilitating a general revival among intellectuals of the idea of '*homeland*', also linked to the myth of the partisan war. Looking at the collapse of its neighbouring country, Italy started to formulate a new rhetoric of nationalism, while 'most Italian intellectuals took the side of the nation-state and rediscovered the value of a "good" patriotism' (Patriarca, 2001: 23). Finally, the increasing globalisation and the process of European integration contributed 'to the urgency of reflecting on the consequences of the waning of national sovereignty as it has been known so far' (ibid.: 21).

Some intellectuals and scholars, such as Giorgio Bocca (1990, 1998) and Saverio Vertone (1994), believed that Europe represented the only chance Italy had to overcome its problems and particularly the antagonism between the North and the South of the country. They were also convinced that only a European citizenship could succeed where the national state had failed: providing citizens with a common and shared sense of belonging. Others argued that Italy's weak sense of national identity might represent an advantage in order to integrate into a super-national and more inclusive belonging, suggesting the idea that Italy's history and traditions which contributed to turning the country into a natural 'crucible' (crogiolo) of cultures would give it a central role in Europe (Melotti, 2004).

After having briefly mentioned the different external factors that influenced the revival of the debate on national identity, it is also necessary to focus on the internal phenomena that have affected the discussion in the past two decades. The first and main factor is represented by the scandal of mani pulite, literally 'clean hands', a police investigation into political corruption held in the 1990s, which implicated the mafia, the Vatican Bank IOR and the Masonic lodge P2, and which led to the demise of the so-called First Republic, resulting in the disappearance of many parties[9] and in the paralysis of the political system.[10] The feeling of loss and confusion derived from the breakdown of traditional political parties and their related subcultures will be dealt with later in this chapter. Looking at the political consequences of such a downfall, the emergence of new political actors which followed can be seen as a reaction to a situation of widespread instability and uncertainty. This particular political conjuncture was exploited by Umberto Bossi's Lega Nord and Silvio Berlusconi's Forza Italia, to break into the national political scene.

Even though, in order to simplify, we placed the revival of the debate on national identity in the early 1990s, Italian intellectuals themselves seem to have slightly divergent opinions concerning the timing of the rediscovery of the issue of Italianness after a long period of time during which it had been neglected or underestimated. According to Cartocci, it was indeed the beginning of the 1990s that marked the starting point of a new interest in the subject. As he states, 'A long season of amnesia [...] ended once and for all in the late 1980s' (Cartocci, 1994: 9).[11] The scholar dates the first intervention in the debate back to the contributions made by Gian Enrico Rusconi, Pietro Scoppola and Angelo Panebianco to the academic journal *Il Mulino* in 1991 (ibid.),[12] while Rusconi, on the contrary, argues that the national question had already became more acute in public debate in every European country during the 1980s and that this phenomenon was due to the rise of regionalist movements as well as other factors which vary from country to country. In France, for instance, according to the scholar, Le Pen managed to utilise various issues linked to immigration in order to promote what he called 'the priority of national choice'[13] (Rusconi, 1993: 9). In Germany the phenomenon of immigration triggered a discussion on German identity, which led to a xenophobic drift ideologically supported by nationalism. As Rusconi underlines, the main factor that determined the revival of the discussion on national identities was the difficulty of building a politically united Europe (Rusconi, 1993).[14]

In Italy, too, during the first half of the 1980s there seemed to be increased interest in the theme of national identity, marked by the publication of a few books on the subject written by intellectuals such as academic Giulio Bollati (1983), writer and journalist Marcello Veneziani (Veneziani *et al.* 1983) and historian Silvio Lanaro (1988). Nevertheless, these publications did not contribute to opening up a positive and productive debate on the issue but rather had their limit in the fact that they only remarked upon the difficulties of approaching the matter. This debate was short lived: everything was over before the 1990s (Rusconi, 1993: 10).[15] This premature end of the discussion was due to the economic slump and the financial scandals of those years, as indeed that of mani pulite. Under those circumstances, the so-called 'nationalism made in Italy', as Rusconi defined the nationalist pride felt at the time, which had been facilitated by a positive political and cultural conjuncture under the first socialist government, had very little chance of surviving (ibid.). Despite the diversity of opinions concerning the timing of the new debate on national identity in Italy, intellectuals and academics tend to agree that the neglect of the concept of nationality and a general feeling of detachment from the idea of national belonging lasted from World War II until the 1980s, although different scholars attribute greater or lesser importance to the different factors that determined these attitudes.

'We, who were born here, for a long time have chosen not to talk about it anymore. A determined will to remove (such a thought) together with a very bad rhetoric [...] have created a sort of mental block: almost a permanent wound in our self-representation' (Schiavone, 1998: 3).[16] With these words Schiavone opens his work *Italiani senza Italia* (Italians without Italy), and describes the feeling of impotence and detachment from the idea of national belonging experienced by Italian citizens. He pictures them as a people who share a deep sense of mistrust and dissatisfaction, which determines a lack of enthusiasm and perspectives for the future. This feeling of detachment and alienation from national belonging can be explained with, and at the same time can be a symptom of, the phenomenon that Galli della Loggia calls 'morte della patria' (the death of the homeland) (Galli della Loggia, 1996). What does morte della patria mean? What can justify the death of the homeland? Or, in other words, how can the patria die? As Rusconi states in *Se cessiamo di essere una nazione* (If we cease being a nation), 'A nation can cease being such'[17] for a nation is not a fixed and indestructible structure, but rather a fragile social construction made up of shared culture and myths, based on open consensus and reciprocity between citizens. These ties of citizenship, which have to be supported by loyalty and shared experiences and views, represent the institutional structure of 'a nation of citizens' (Rusconi, 1993: 7). The death of the homeland, as Salvatore Satta wrote in *De Profundis* and Galli della Loggia[18] recalls in his *La morte della patria*, is doubtless the most important event that can occur in the life of individuals (Satta, 2003 [1945]: 16; Galli della Loggia, 1996: 3). This is, in their view, what happened to Italy after World War II. A deep feeling of death of the homeland is what anyone who had preserved an idea of the existence of an Italian nation experienced at that time. However, what did determine this 'death of the homeland' and the subsequent disregard of the feeling of national belonging on the part of both intellectuals and ordinary people?

4 Military defeat and the Resistance: the end of a shared memory

Historians Aldo Schiavone, Ernesto Galli della Loggia, Renzo De Felice and Pietro Scoppola, philosopher Norberto Bobbio and political scientist Gian Enrico Rusconi agree, despite their different points of view, on the need to analyse the historical events in which Italy has been involved since World War II in order to understand how the sense of national belonging has developed, or rather has been inhibited in the past, and how this past still contributes to shaping Italian identity. The discussion on the different interpretations of the Resistance, in particular, nowadays represents a point of reference that cannot be disregarded as it constitutes the main focus of intellectuals' reflections. The theme is indeed still very strongly debated and many of the issues currently discussed in Italy are linked more or less directly to the question of national identity as it has been shaped by the different approaches to the Resistance.

The debate on the Resistance and consequently that on Italianness followed three main strands of thought: intellectuals close to the Right focused on the negative aspects of this historical event which, in their view, was a civil war that damaged the sense of national belonging rather than providing the nation with a shared narrative of a common history. These scholars include, indeed, Galli della Loggia, an historian close to the Left at the beginning of his career, who moved towards the Right of the political spectrum, becoming very critical of communism and its legacy. Benito Mussolini's biographer, Renzo De Felice (1929–96), a former student of Federico Chabod, also contributed to the discussion on the Resistance and his views met with heated reactions on the part of scholars who accused him of analysing the dictatorship from the perspective of a supporter.[19]

The main opponent of De Felice's position was Norberto Bobbio (1909–2004), a philosopher, historian and political scientist whose role as an intellectual has been acknowledged nationally and internationally. Bobbio, a member of the Partito d'Azione (Action Party) and traditionally close to anti-Fascist movements, is among those who gave an interpretation of the

Resistance diametrically opposed to that put forward by De Felice. Bobbio, indeed, believed that the struggle against Mussolini represented a central moment in the creation of a national identity.

Finally, the third strand of thought according to which the Resistance and national identity have been discussed has, among its proponents, scholars and intellectuals whose contribution cannot be framed within the two previous categories: among them are Pietro Scoppola and Gian Enrico Rusconi, whose approach towards the debate is characterised by less polemical intents. This is true particularly for Scoppola (1926–2007), an academic and politician elected to Parliament in 1983 in the list of the Democrazia Cristiana, the Italian Christian democratic party, who seemed more interested in finding a compromise between the two opposing interpretations of the events linked to the dictatorship and to the war.

All the intellectuals mentioned above contributed to the revival of the discussion on national identity, publishing in national newspapers close to both the Left and the Right, as well as in more academic journals such as *Il Mulino* and *Limes*. They can be considered intellectuals for their participation in a public debate, which they contributed to creating and shaping, also by echoing the position of other academics less visible in the public sphere, whose voices were confined to academic exchanges.

According to Galli della Loggia (1996), in order to understand the crisis of Italianness it is necessary to go back to the political and military crisis that Italy faced during the war and which led to the defeat of the state to find a plausible explanation for the Italians' feelings of inadequacy and inferiority which determined the progressive failure of a shared sense of national belonging. It is this period of Italian history these scholars look at in order to provide a reason for the so-called disfattismo italiano (Italian defeatism), a widespread mistrust towards the state and a tendency to react to any critical situation with passive resignation[20] (Galli della Loggia, 1996: 8). According to many scholars, defeatism represents a key element in explaining the progressive decline of a shared sense of national belonging. This decline is caused by many interconnected factors such as the attachment to the family rather than to the community/nation which has always been stronger in the South of the country where disfattismo is also deeply rooted.[21]

Going back to the Resistance and its conflicting interpretations, scholars are still involved in exacerbated controversies as to the date on which the homeland died. Different dates, indeed, involve a different explanation of why the concept of homeland came to an end. Intellectuals involved in the discussion agree on the impossibility for Italians of having as a point of reference shared memories and a common perception of their past (Rusconi, 1991, 1993; Galli della Loggia, 1996; Bobbio *et al.* 1996). Nevertheless, the fact that they attribute this outcome to different factors is representative of their deeply divergent points of view on the reasons why Italians cannot share an unambiguous past.

Galli della Loggia thinks that the homeland died at the beginning of the war, when, as he explains through the words of writer Corrado Alvaro, 'A consistent part of Italy wished to be defeated, since the first day of war [...] Solidarity, patriotism and individual responsibility were lost and killed'[22] (Alvaro, 1986: 34–36; Galli della Loggia, 1996: 7–8). He believes that the crisis of the state and its institutions resulted from the military defeat during the war and cannot be directly ascribed to Fascism. What happened in those years was that the political and ethical weakness and inadequacy of the state became suddenly evident and led to an unstoppable loss of the cohesion of the nation. The defeat raised questions about the value of a homeland that was not ready to fight and morally not strong enough to shake off its passivity until the end. As Galli della Loggia argues, ever since Machiavelli the lack of experience and worth of the Italian army have been the main reasons preventing the development in the country of a strong national state (Galli della Loggia, 1996). He quotes Giacomo Leopardi too, who in his *Discorso sopra lo stato presente dei costumi degli Italiani* (1824) argued that a military defeat always triggers a moral crisis which puts into question values of pride and freedom and therefore determines a downfall in self-esteem and faith in the homeland (Leopardi, 1991 [1824]: 129; Galli della Loggia, 1996: 88).

According to Galli della Loggia and even more so according to De Felice, this is why 8 September should be considered the day on which the homeland died (Galli della Loggia, 1996; De Felice, in Bobbio *et al.* 1996).[23] 'I will not start from the 25th of April, but from the 8th of September 1943, the day Eisenhower announced the armistice with Italians. A tragic date for the Italian nation: that is the day the idea of the homeland died'[24] (De Felice, in Bobbio *et al.* 1996: 16). With these words De Felice refers to the feelings of frustration and weariness as well as to the desire for peace on the part of a country where most of the people had believed in the 'Fascist war' (ibid.). Galli della Loggia and De Felice, nonetheless, disagree on the importance of that day, in the sense that, according to Galli della Loggia, it determined a collapse in national pride and therefore the death of the nation, whereas De Felice thinks that it only contributed to highlighting a moral and ethical crisis that most Italians and the nation as a whole had already experienced for years[25] (Galli della Loggia, 1996; De Felice, in Bobbio *et al.* 1996).

De Felice's work aims to show that the Resistance was nothing more than an elitist movement led by small and disorganised groups of people who were perceived by the rest of the Italians as pazzi, fools who wanted to start fighting again when the war was just over (De Felice, in Bobbio *et al.* 1996: 16). He argues that the majority of Italians distanced themselves from the partisan movement after the armistice with the Allies, and remarks upon the existence of a widespread disapproval of it. Other intellectuals refer to attitudes of indifference, rather than hostility, towards the Resistance.

The portrait of the Resistance as a civil war is another contentious issue. First put forward by the leftist historian Claudio Pavone (1991), this interpretation is supported by Galli della Loggia and to a certain extent by Rusconi as well. Galli della Loggia claims that it was even worse than a 'normal' civil war since in that situation there is usually a national winner, whereas in

Italy the only winners were foreigners. According to him, the war between Fascism and the Resistance movement, which was ultimately won by the Allies, did not involve the majority of the population who remained in a so-called grey zone of inactivity and resignation, and who suffered Fascism, the war and the Resistance as they would have suffered an earthquake (Galli della Loggia, 1996: 87; Rusconi, 1993).

A completely different interpretation of the Resistance is provided by left-leaning philosopher Bobbio, who considers 25 April 1945, the day of the liberation, as 'a fundamental date, not only for Italy, but for humankind'[26] (Bobbio, 1996: 19). As it emerges clearly from the exchange between him and De Felice, which in 1996 became a book entitled *Italiani: amici, nemici*,[27] both intellectuals agree that a lack of shared memory is what makes Italy an anomalous country (Bobbio *et al.* 1996). Nevertheless, Bobbio is of the opinion that, as in other European countries such as France or Denmark, the importance of celebrating the liberation should be seen as unproblematic and should not have been questioned in Italy (Bobbio *et al.* 1996: 16). Bobbio recalls that the elitist nature of the Italian Risorgimento did not prevent it from being celebrated for a century:[28] in the same way the fact that the Resistance had been carried out by a minority of citizens does not make it a less important landmark in the history of the country (ibid.).

The philosopher singles out 10 June, the first day of war for Italy, as opposed to 8 September, as a tragic date for the nation which determined the death of a shared feeling of national identity. If De Felice argues that the homeland died the day the armistice was announced and that Italians had wavering opinions on the war depending on which battles were lost or won, Bobbio claims that 'we, a minority, were fully convinced that Italy should lose, but Italians in general were definitely not in favour of entering the war'.[29] Moreover, he adds: 'Except for a few Fascists, there was no popular consensus for the war'[30] (Bobbio, 1996: 19).

The different views in establishing the extent to which Italians took part in the Resistance or opposed it, these clashing interpretations of historical events, have determined the perceived difficulty for Italy to become a 'normal' country, with a normal political Right and political Left, which is what both intellectuals claim to wish for future generations (Bobbio *et al.* 1996). The achievement of this 'dream' of a normal Italy, according to these scholars, depends on the ability and the will of historians to consider all the nuances and differences within such a complex event as the Resistance and the necessity of avoiding univocal interpretations of this phenomenon. According to De Felice, indeed, 'the core of the matter is all here: why has Italy not managed to build a new national awareness on what Italians have really been, rather than on pre-packed reassuring truths and ideological dogmas?'[31] (De Felice, 1996).

Nevertheless, as Rusconi explains, despite the fact that Bobbio and De Felice agree on the need to look at the Resistance from a more neutral perspective, the dialogue between them turned out to be 'rather disappointing

[...] Unless we take this result and the difficulties in the dialogue between the two scholars as the interesting datum on which we can reflect and from which our analysis can start'[32] (Rusconi, in Bobbio *et al.* 1996: 71). Even though they both find it necessary to take into account all the many different interpretations of that historical period, they do not move from their original positions. Bobbio indeed, writing about revisionism, sarcastically states that the idea that historians who criticise Fascism are perceived as moralists, whereas those who criticise anti-Fascist movements are considered good historians or, even better, 'normal' historians, was growing stronger in him (Bobbio, 1996).

On the other hand, the so-called revisionists and some journalists close to the Right insisted that the impossibility of a shared memory based on an unambiguous interpretation of the Resistance was due to the Left's attempt to claim a monopoly on the concept of Italianness. Indeed, according to them, this was nothing different from what Fascism had already attempted to do: 'This had claimed for itself [...] the privilege of representing the idea of the nation [...] the Fascist homeland necessarily was the homeland of the true Italians. [...] Anti-Fascism was believed not to have any other choice than following its enemy's steps, simply claiming for itself the same privilege'[33] (Galli della Loggia, 1996: 32). As a result, such a dichotomy in Italian history, which involved the coexistence of two separate and irreconcilable nations, a *noi diviso* (a divided us),[34] was totally incompatible with the idea of a unitary feeling of national belonging (ibid.: 36). In the author's perspective, the development of a divided nation and of a dual idea of national identity could not have been prevented or avoided in the past, nor could the conflict be solved then (in the 1990s) despite many intellectuals such as Scoppola (1995) believing this to be necessary in the national interest.

According to Galli della Loggia, indeed, this result was implicit in the nature of the Italian Resistance: to overcome Fascism really and develop a new national awareness, the Resistance should have been a stronger movement, whereas Italian partisans did not achieve any real victory against Fascism, something that was instead achieved by the Allies (Galli della Loggia, 1996). The historian believes that among several reasons that prevented the Resistance from embodying national mythology, a major role was played by internal contrasts between different partisan groups on decisive political aspects and the lack of a nationalist ideology. The kind of national identity that emerged after the war was hence not an inclusive identity nor the result of a national struggle for liberation, but rather an elitist belonging linked to a political and moral judgement of what had been right or wrong during those years. In this context, as Rusconi, together with many others, recalls, a majority of people were *attendisti*,[35] that is to say, they passively waited for the end of the war without taking a clear position on it (Rusconi, 1993: 63).[36]

As mentioned above, some intellectuals, such as Rusconi and Scoppola, seek to overcome all the perceived obstacles in constructing a national identity out of an ambiguous and contested meaning of the Resistance, by arguing that those difficulties are part of the past and that, despite them, today it is possible to attribute to the legacy of the Resistance that national and political value it should have had at that time. The Resistance could still provide Italians with a shared memory and a strong and common feeling of national identity (Scoppola, 1995: 52–54). However, Rusconi does not agree with the contents of the common narrative suggested by Scoppola. According to the scholar, Scoppola's justification following which all Italians, even though fighting on different fronts or simply waiting for the end of the war, suffered the same events and shared the same 'will to resist and live' seems to privilege a sociological analysis over an historical investigation and to be too generous in equating 'legitimate strategies of survival on the part of the population'[37] with an active struggle for freedom (Rusconi, in Bobbio *et al.* 1996: 81–82). This positive judgement, Rusconi claims, is attributed too easily by scholars such as Scoppola to the behaviour of the Catholic hierarchy, which was actually ambiguous in its stance or merely aimed at its own survival (ibid.). Scoppola's point of view is entwined with a Catholic ethics according to which 'tragedies would turn people into better human beings'[38] (Scoppola, 1995; Rusconi, in Bobbio *et al.* 1996: 89). Galli della Loggia agrees with Rusconi and underlines that, actually, the common experience suffered as individuals of losing a war and having the country occupied by foreigners does not necessarily involve any particular moral harmony and shared understanding (Galli della Loggia, 1996). Nonetheless, Rusconi also polemises with Galli della Loggia and his rejection of the value and the inheritance of the Resistance due to its internal contradiction and lack of nationalistic ideology. He believes that it is indeed possible to find a common past in those events but only in the solidarity which characterised Italians at that time, rather than the fact that regardless of the side they took, all of them went through the same difficult times (Rusconi, in Bobbio *et al.* 1996).

5 The ambiguity of political parties after the war

Scoppola's attempt to reconcile divergent experiences and different attitudes to the Resistance into a shared Italian identity does not take into account the fact that the Resistance was not the only factor that contributed to creating what many intellectuals consider an unbridgeable rift between contrasting interpretations of the meaning of Italianness. Among the other historical events that, according to some intellectuals, determined the impossibility of constructing a shared feeling of national belonging after the war is the manner in which the PCI dealt with the cession of Venezia Giulia to Tito's Yugoslavia.[39] In his *La morte della patria*, Galli della Loggia, having explained the Resistance movement's aim to claim for itself the right to represent the whole country, focuses on the role that the PCI had in this controversial issue and on its attempt to build a nation by trying to alienate a part of it. The author reacts to those intellectuals who advocate the need for a lowest common denominator which can heal the wound of a divided memory and provide Italians with a powerful and convincing narrative of shared history and national belonging, by underlining the many factors that contributed to the division, among them the fact that the PCI did not oppose but rather facilitated Tito's claims on Istria and the city of Trieste (Galli della Loggia, 1996). He finds the reasons for such an attitude in the myth of Yugoslavian partisan war as well as the PCI's internationalist ideology[40] and rejection of nationalism as a concept linked to Fascism.

The relationship between the PCI and Yugoslavia,[41] investigated by many scholars and more recently by Roberto Gualtieri (2006), played, in the eyes of a number of intellectuals, a pivotal role in the fragmentation of Italian identity after World War II. They believe that in taking position on matters of international interest the party always stood on the side of the foreigners, as long as they had a communist tradition, and often promoted solutions that were deeply 'anti-Italian' and against the Italian interest (Galli della Loggia, 1996: 61). The fact that the PCI decided to stand for Yugoslavia in the dispute about the Venezia Giulia clearly created a tension between the party and the local non-communist resistance movements. Moreover, the fact that the PCI usually supported other countries, such as the Soviet Union, more than Italy because ideologically dependent on them, contributed to developing a sense of inferiority and subalternity, which seems to remain a trait of the Italian character. This attitude, this ideological and moral dependence on foreign countries, contributed to developing among Italians a deep feeling of 'transformism', which weakened the already weak sense of national pride as well as that of national will, and determined the spread of a general attitude of indifference and resignation, particularly in the South of the country.

Writing in 1945, Guglielmo Giannini (founder of the Movimento dell'Uomo Qualunque) tried to foresee the consequences that the renunciation, for instance of Veneto, would have had and how it could have affected the *folla* (masses). His answer to the question 'What would happen to the masses?' is 'Nothing',[42] this meaning that people would have been indifferent. Therefore he concluded that if there is something mortal in this world, it is the idea of homeland (Giannini, 2002: 12; Galli della Loggia, 1996: 112).

According to authors such as Schiavone (1998), the end of strong political ideologies was a further cause for people's detachment from a shared sense of national identity. For decades, indeed, political parties had provided Italians with a strong sense of belonging, and despite the fact that this belonging was based on the mutual exclusion and alienation of opposing interpretations of Italianness, it was not questioned by its members, who tended to consider that belonging was the only possible national identity. Schiavone, rather than focusing on the fact that political parties created antagonistic perceptions and experiences of the same country, prefers to argue that the Italian Republic was based on highly influential political parties (the DC and PCI), which in turn represented a precondition and not a consequence for the formation of the nation-state. Therefore, as soon as the crisis of political parties broke out, especially in the early 1990s with the involvement of the judiciary and the end of the DC's supremacy, its most immediate consequence was widespread feelings of bewilderment among the citizens, and of a loss of identification with specific political ideologies, namely the Catholic and communist ones. Schiavone seems to believe that a common identity based on political belonging, even though involving the exclusion and the denial of a considerable part of the country that embraced an opposing membership, was nevertheless a valid means to participation in an Italian identity.

6 The influence of political factors on the Italian debate on national identity

Among the several political factors that contributed to the revival of the discussion on Italian national identity, the rise of the Northern League doubtlessly is the most influential. During the 1990s, sociologists, political scientists and journalists, such as Ilvo Diamanti, Roberto Biorcio, Renato Mannheimer, Mauro Magatti and Roberto Cartocci, urged by spreading concerns about the rise to power of this new political actor, started a debate on the theme with the intent of outlining the reasons, the geography and the consequences of the electoral success of this party, founded in 1991 as a result of the coalition of different autonomist movements. This chapter does not have as its focus a detailed analysis of the origins of the Northern League or an exhaustive account of the party's position on national identity and immigration. It rather aims to provide a brief overview of the influence that this party has had through its ideology upon the idea of Italian national belonging and how its appearance on the political arena has opened a debate on alternative identities. A more in-depth analysis of the party's role in shaping a much more exclusionary understanding of 'national identity' and citizenship at the time when immigration started to gather pace will be carried out in Chapter 3.

The Northern League seemed to outline a completely novel definition of Italian identity, whereas the post-war parties tended to support traditional, though 'partial', interpretations of national belonging. This section will attempt to argue that Italian intellectuals identify a close connection between the crisis of the feeling of attachment to the nation discussed above and the success of the alternative construction of national community developed and popularised by the Northern League. As a result, they adopted inward-looking perspectives which involved, once again, revisiting historical events and 'failures' considered crucial fault lines.

Intellectuals' analyses of the factors that led to the electoral success of the Northern League in 1992 started from a shared acknowledgement of the deep crisis Italy had experienced since the 1980s. This crisis, among other things, triggered a questioning of the legitimacy and the efficiency of the institutions and of a renewed polarisation between the North and the South of the country. As Cartocci explains, 'we started then to reflect more systematically than in the past on the weaknesses of our democratic culture, on the origins of such weaknesses and even[43] on the meaning of our national identity'[44] (Cartocci, 1994: 9).

According to other scholars, instead, the increasing number of autonomist movements, affecting not only Italy but many other countries such as Britain, Belgium, Spain and Canada, represents a general trend of the 1990s. This resulted from social tensions which triggered a debate all around the world on 'the ethnic question' after years in which historical nationalisms had provided many countries with strong homogeneous collective identities (Melucci and Diani, 1992; Magatti, 1998).

According to Magatti, traditional belongings based on ethnic 'archaic' identities can be rediscovered today (writing in the late 1990s) in developed countries for two different reasons. On the one hand, this tendency can be motivated by the fact that when the values and the institutions of a civic national culture begin to be questioned for different reasons, not least globalisation, national solidarity finds an antagonist in primordial groups based on blood ties or on an unconditional adhesion to values, which weaken the loyalty toward the nation-state (Magatti, 1998: 16). On the other hand, this 'ethnic revival' can be justified as a mechanism, typical of modern societies, which aims to recreate a new sense of collective identity and a feeling of common belonging rather than to rediscover traditional cultural points of reference. It answers people's need to feel part of a whole and to create a relatively safe environment which can contribute to controlling the growing anxiety caused by globalisation and global integration: 'In this perspective what matters is not the objective elements, and being or not being a member of an ethnic group actually becomes a voluntary option'[45] (ibid.: 17). Magatti argues that the ethnic revival does not necessarily involve a new awareness of one's own traditional identity; often it rather invents identities where they do not exist (ibid.: 17). The so-called 'imagined communities' become real following a process of social construction (Gellner, 1983). Despite differing interpretations of the ethnic revival, the two theories described above concur that the emergence of a feeling of belonging in order to build a new ethnic identity is a social, cultural and political process. Besides a process of reinvention of 'old' identities, the ethnic revival also created a considerable number of completely new ones (Rusconi, 1993; Magatti, 1998). These new identities became the vehicle of social conflict: ethnic identity then turns into a means for political mobilisation, which polemically emphasises differentiation, contraposition, antagonism and discrimination (Magatti, 1998: 21; Bell, 1993). The self-attribution of an ethnic identity turns out to be 'a strategic resource to achieve something or to deny something to somebody else'[46] (Magatti, 1998: 20).[47]

The rise of the Northern League, therefore, led various intellectuals to revisit the issue of a weak national identity in terms of the internal divide between North and South. The only solution to overcome this divide requires, according to them, a new emphasis upon a common past and shared narratives. They became concerned with identifying the actors who should develop and tell the country a convincing story of a common past. Rusconi admits that it is not easy to say who should have the responsibility to tell 'a common story made not only of literature, weapons and blood, but also of work and shared struggles, of migration and internal mixing,[48] which created links that cannot be cut without wounding the historical identity of all Italians both from the North and from the South'[49] (Rusconi, 1993: 14). According to the scholar, it is not possible, in Italy as elsewhere, to achieve a civic feeling of belonging without rebuilding a shared memory, at the same time 'critical and united' (ibid.). Rusconi also questions how far back in national history it is necessary to go in order to tell this story and decides, once again, that it has to start from Fascism and the Resistance, which is an opinion shared by many other scholars, as has already been discussed.

7 The role of political subcultures in the Northern League's rise to power

The intellectuals' search for the underlying causes of the rise and success of a secessionist party such as the Northern League led them to focus on the role of political subcultures in promoting and codifying internal barriers to shared values and a common identity.

The concept of a 'political subculture' indicates the power and antagonism against the liberal state of socialist and Catholic movements (Pizzorno, 1966; Sivini, 1971). The so-called red and white subcultures are characterised by their influence on electoral behaviour, in the case of Italy since the second half of the 20th century. Traditionally defined in relation to their geographical distribution (Caciagli, 1988), political subcultures express the complex elements of a local political system and the relation between this political system, culture and economic development (Trigilia, 1981). As Caciagli explains, culture is not only based on opinions and attitudes, but also on ideas and values, symbols and norms, myths and rites, real and repeated and, finally, structures and institutions operating in a specific geographical environment and in an historical context (Caciagli, 1988). While scholars such as Messina (2001) view the red and white subcultures as actors putting forward different and opposing interpretations of politics, others such as Trigilia (1981) see them as variants of the same model.

The crisis of the Italian political system in the early 1990s was mirrored, if not anticipated, by a decline of both political subcultures due to globalisation and industrial expansion as well as the downfall of the communist and Christian democratic parties, which marked the end of the narratives and myths that had made possible an identification with one of the subcultures and its territory (Caciagli, 1995). The weakening of traditional subcultures left space for the emergence of new territorial identities put forward by the so-called 'leagues', the autonomous movements which in 1991 merged into the Northern League (ibid.).

The scholars involved in the debate on the Northern League, such as Roberto Cartocci, Mauro Magatti and especially Roberto Biorcio and Ilvo Diamanti, have investigated the reasons why the party's presence is concentrated in specific areas of Northern Italy (Cartocci, 1994; Magatti, 1998; Biorcio, 1997; Diamanti, 1996). In their view, historical political parties such as the PCI and the DC played a central role in supplying citizens with a sense of identification: they indeed always worked as narrators of those tales that have been defined as fundamental for the formation of a national identity based on common views and shared memories (Rusconi, 1991). They provided citizens with a strong sense of belonging based on well-defined ideologies and symbols, which facilitated a complete and unquestioning identification and integration within equally well-defined political subcultures as well as unquestioning trust expressed through the voto di appartenenza (literally 'vote of belonging'), a vote based on shared values and views rather than on the rational consideration of a balance between benefits and costs. This is why the downfall of traditional political parties represented a loss for Italians, which undermined their feelings of national belonging and left them utterly bewildered (Schiavone, 1998). The crisis of the DC,[50] due to the scandals linked with the era of mani pulite, and the transformation undertaken by Italian society since the 1980s, described by Cartocci and Magatti as secularised and individualistic, made it possible for the Northern League to dominate a geographical area that had traditionally been governed by political, economic and social actors close to the Catholic Church and embedded in the 'white' subculture (Cartocci, 1994; Diamanti, 1996; Magatti, 1998).[51]

The interpretation of political subcultures as positive vehicles of identification was questioned by authors such as De Felice, Galli della Loggia, Cartocci and Magatti, who argued rather that they provided alternative interpretations of the idea of the 'good life', contributing to delegitimising shared identities[52] (Galli della Loggia, 1996; Cartocci, 1994, Magatti, 1998). As already underlined in the section on the influence of historical factors in the debate on national identity, Galli della Loggia actually accused the PCI of attempting to alienate identities different from the communist one by postulating that the communist identity was tantamount to Italian identity (Galli della Loggia, 1996). Cartocci also argued that political subcultures did not necessarily represent an opportunity for a common belonging but rather often represented an obstacle for the achievement of such a sense of belonging as they narrowed and limited the horizons of a more inclusive identification (Cartocci, 1994: 68).[53] The author took as an example the opposing interpretations of the Resistance. These antagonistic points of view on past events prevented Italy from being founded on unitary and shared values and from turning feelings of trust and loyalty toward the state and the nation itself into a civil religion (Cartocci, 1994).[54] On the contrary, the failure of Italian institutions to create a cult of the state or at least a widespread attitude of respect and trust towards it made the Italian nation more vulnerable to charges of illegitimacy, motivated by the attempt of one of the 'nations' within the nation to alienate the others.

According to Cartocci and Magatti, political subcultures had therefore contributed to underlining the division within the country and were not able to overcome internal conflicts and particularly the one between the North and the South, since the value of solidarity has always been seen as internal to each subculture rather than transversal and cross-cutting (Cartocci, 1994; Magatti, 1998). As a result of the opposing identities they supported, traditional subcultures inspired an exasperated version of 'localism', which made it easier for the Northern League to find its space in the political arena. The same authors also recognised that the Catholic subculture can be seen, to a certain extent, as supportive of a unitary identity. Nonetheless, the Catholic Church's stance for national unity was carried out through the use of a 'rhetoric of solidarity', which, according to Cartocci, relies on the idea of Catholic moral duty, rather than on the construction of common narratives and memories. Here, what is important to highlight is how, according to intellectuals, the rise of the Northern League is quite closely linked with the Italian state's inability to tell its citizens a common narrative in order to promote and sustain a strong feeling of belonging.

The debate on the Northern League is particularly complex and still in progress, which is why it is necessary to specify that the analysis carried out in this chapter does not represent a systematic or an exhaustive investigation, but rather a general outline of the perspectives from which the phenomenon has been analysed. It is also intended to provide a further explanation of the perceived difficulty that Italy has always had and still has in building a strong sense of belonging based on a common past and a shared memory, as well as to show that intellectuals are attempting to counteract the identity construction work carried out by the Northern League with a strong emphasis on the need for a new national narrative, which is able to strengthen territorial ties and North-South solidarity. In this way some intellectuals and opinion makers openly acknowledge the need to revisit current narratives of Italianness, constructing powerful stories of internal unity and solidarity which stretch back to the past and forward into the future. Yet these same intellectuals do not appear to comprise the inclusion (or even the exclusion) of immigrants in their vision of a renewed sense of national identity. It is precisely the absence of the issue of immigration from recent and current debates upon, and need for, a strong Italian national identity that will be examined in the next sections.

8 The debate on the influence of immigration on Italian identity

The analysis of the historical and political factors that have influenced the discussion on Italian identity carried out until this point aimed to show which topics and issues Italian intellectuals have been debating and popularising. Acknowledging their inclination to analyse 'internal issues' contributes to providing a first, albeit partial, explanation for the lack of interest on their part in those aspects perceived by them as 'external factors', above all immigration. Without denying the importance of the political and historical factors taken into account until this point, it seems appropriate to argue here that this seemingly external phenomenon, immigration, has in time come to represent an important challenge for the future of the country and particularly for a redefinition of the meaning of national identity. This aspect of the debate on Italianness, however, only emerges in the public sphere through separate individual interventions, occasional and usually polemical in nature.

As Melotti[55] explains, the current Italian political and ideological discourse on the impact of immigration is characterised by exacerbated tones and heated polemics. During the early 1980s, some intellectuals engaged in the debate on immigration and suggested ways to address this – at that time new – phenomenon: a new model of society based on what they defined as 'social integration', which involved the protection of immigrants' identity (Melotti, 2004: 162). This solution was soon replaced by what the author refers to as a naive and questionable idea of multicultural society, which was supposed to solve every problem all of a sudden, according to intellectuals such as Ferrarotti, Ghirelli and Macioti, who formulated it and advocated that the main result of promoting such a society would consist of a 'cultural enrichment' (ibid.). As some journalists such as Giorgio Bocca and Gad Lerner state, many other scholars closed their eyes in the face of a complex situation and attributed all the problems linked to immigration to the supposed racism of Italians (Bocca, 1998; Lerner, 1989; Melotti, 2004: 162). Melotti thinks that although serious episodes of racism have happened in Italy, analysing Italians' xenophobic behaviour as some authors such as Balbo and Manconi do, does not help to build a strong debate in the country on the impact of the massive arrivals of people with different cultural and ethnic origins. Moreover, he argues that these academics, in focusing on the Italians' presumed racism, did nothing more than apply French key concepts of racism to the Italian case. Explanations that were suited to the French situation have been 'slavishly repeated' by these intellectuals, whereas, according to Melotti, these models of interpretation are not only questionable, but can even be misleading if applied to the Italian context (Melotti, 2004: 163).[56]

Clearly, Melotti's polemical account of the debate shows that he does not agree with the idea that multiculturalism can solve the issues raised by immigration. However, despite his criticism of such a position and although he considers this discussion unhelpful in addressing the phenomenon of immigration, he does not engage with other perspectives, nor does he add anything new to the debate. Melotti also focuses on Italian identity and its perceived weakness, attributing it to numerous and strongly interconnected reasons. The first reason he mentions is related to an internal factor: the role of political subcultures, which he, in common with many of his colleagues, believes to have fostered a sense of mistrust in, and even rejection of, the state (Melotti, 2004: 169). The second reason is linked with immigration, but rather than engaging with the challenges that it poses to Italian society today, Melotti embarks on a long digression on the origins of Italians' suspicion towards foreigners, going as far as listing the attempt of the Turkish Mehmet Ali Agca to kill Pope John Paul II in 1981, and the song of the river Piave with its verse 'Va fuori d'Italia, va fuori straniero' (Leave Italy, leave you foreigner) (Melotti, 2004: 172).[57]

Even though Melotti's analysis has ambitious intents, its limit is that it focuses very much on the concept of racism, despite its criticism of the same attitude in other authors, as well as in being as inward-looking as the other perspectives previously examined. Moreover, the scholar focuses on the justification of racist or exclusionary attitudes that date back to World War I, rather than addressing the new issues raised by the foreign presence within the country. Finally, and more importantly, despite the fact that he reflects on both national identity and immigration, he never links the two and does not reflect on the influence that the latter has or might have on the redefinition of Italianness. Nevertheless, Melotti's work does provide a general overview, even if it is not exhaustive, of the manner in which intellectuals have participated in both debates, while supplying a number of valid reasons for the weakness of this debate.

Rusconi's analysis of immigration is fairly isolated.[58] The scholar starts his examination of immigration and citizenship by stating that one of the most important consequences of the creation of the nation-state is the resulting equivalence between citizenship and nationality as part of contemporary culture. As he argues, asking a foreigner what nationality they belong to and of which country they are a citizen is not something spontaneous, since it is not so evident that the two things – nationality and citizenship – are different and separate concepts. The nation-state attributes to its citizens political rights granted by citizenship, at the same moment that it provides them with a nationality. Nevertheless, the concept of nationality also works as a limit which, for instance, prevents the automatic granting of the same rights to citizens belonging to another nation, even if the latter is an ally and the relationship between the two nations is particularly good (Rusconi, 1993). According to Rusconi, the relatively new necessity to distinguish between and keep separate the idea of nation and that of citizenship comes from two different and recent phenomena. He identifies the first with the imminent (at the time of Rusconi's writing) introduction of European citizenship. The second phenomenon is linked with the presence of immigrants 'who benefit or aspire to benefit from a number of civil, social and even political rights, such as citizenship of the country of immigration, which they are allowed to apply for even choosing (or being forced) to retain a foreign nationality'[59] (Rusconi, 1993: 167).

Rusconi bases his ideas on a primarily structural difference between immigration in Europe in the past compared to today. The first significant aspect is that, in the past, immigrants have been invited to some European countries in order to satisfy the need for a workforce during a period of economic boom, whereas immigration has been officially discouraged in Europe since the 1970s.[60] The second is that in the past immigrants tended to arrive almost entirely from other European countries, whereas since the second half of the 1960s they have started coming from outside Europe, and especially from

Africa and Asia, which meant that they are defined by 'cultures, life-style and "colour" visibly "different"' (Rusconi, 1993: 168). Rusconi states: 'At this stage the collective perception of immigration as a threat at a European level could not be avoided, and neither could the awakening of a deep anxiety which led to xenophobic attitudes and racist violence. [...] The majority of European population has no clear idea of the economic consequences of immigration: do immigrants determine a fall in work opportunities or do they take up jobs left vacant by the locals?'[61] (Rusconi, 1993: 168–69).

This type of worry has been used as a means to justify xenophobic intolerance. Nonetheless, the author suspects these anxieties to be mere instruments for giving already existing prejudice and fears a rational basis, instead of being the cause of these prejudices. For the first time in European history, a considerable number of citizens have come into contact with populations of different ethnic origins and cultures. Racism in its traditional form, which until the 1940s was culturally accepted[62] and even encouraged, has now been rejected. Nonetheless, the idea that immigration contributes to the degeneration of society and the environment, which citizens try to protect, is presented as an undeniable fact: 'It is not a coincidence that immigration is catalogued (and experienced) as a sort of new social illness, alongside (and comparable to) unemployment, organised crime or pollution (when it is not seen as a sum of all these problems)'[63] (Rusconi, 1993: 169).

According to Rusconi, this last interpretation of immigration very frequently represents the ground on which political parties compete with each other: from Jean-Marie Le Pen's Front National in France to Jörg Haider's Freedon Party in Austria, it contributes to reinforcing xenophobic movements. In Italy, too, political actors such as the Northern League exploited latent racist feelings and anxieties transforming them into political claims. The result of these irrational worries as well as the action of such political parties is that the focus of the discourse on immigration is no longer on how to deal with this trend but rather on how to make the boundaries impenetrable. While all European countries agree on the urgency of finding adequate means to stop irregular immigration, they do not seem to have a common strategy on anything else such as, for instance, the granting of civil rights or free circulation within Europe for regular immigrants. Different governments react in different ways to immigrants' requests and produce distinct laws on citizenship, education, work and religion, to the extent that these strictly national responses to immigration could represent one of the issues that the (future) European Union (EU) (will) find more difficult to face in a unitary way (Rusconi, 1993: 168–73).[64]

Although the premises of Rusconi's analysis are the denunciation of the lack of discussion on the impact of immigration on national identity, the critique of the position that intellectuals are assuming within the debate and the weakness of their arguments, he does not focus upon the meaning of Italianness which immigration will (or already has) inevitably put into question, as it has done in other European countries. Nevertheless, he does examine how this relatively new phenomenon will influence the responses to immigrants' particular claims and the definition of a new citizenship, which for the first time, in his view, has to be unattached and independent from the concept of nationality. Even though he does not go further in discussing how Italianness might (or indeed ought to) change, other than becoming detached from the idea of citizenship, Rusconi represents one of the few (isolated) voices in the Italian debate on the subject of national identity in connection with immigration, and his analysis attempts to provide definitions of concepts such as solidarity, rational choice versus spontaneous belonging, and indeed the difference between nationality and citizenship.

9 Italian journalists and philosophers: the polemical and the unheard

Currently there are very few journalists taking part in a debate characterised, as we saw, by isolated positions and occasional polemical exchanges. The only journalist who has systematically discussed immigration and its impact on Italian society and culture during the period that is being taken into account here, is Magdi Allam. Allam, once a moderate[65] Muslim intellectual writing for *Corriere della Sera*, recently found himself at the centre of a heated debate when he converted to Catholicism and chose a new middle name (Cristiano), which he used to sign his editorials against Islam. Allam focuses almost exclusively on Muslim immigration[66] and mainly advocates the necessity of regulating the dialogue between Muslim leaders and the Italian government. He believes, indeed, that the most extremist Muslim representatives should not be allowed to take part in any dialogue with Italian institutions. He also thinks that Italians should value and recognise their historical origins as Catholics, which should never be neglected. Catholicism has to be considered a secularised religion today but, nevertheless, the journalist argues, it is vital not to underestimate the importance of this religion in order to understand who Italians are today and how the state and citizens should react to Muslim claims. Allam has also written about the crisis of the multicultural model adopted by the Netherlands, which, according to him, has recently proven an inadequate means to address problems posed by immigration, especially since the assassination of film director Theo Van Gogh in 2004 (Allam, 2004). The journalist believes that the only way that Muslims can live in Italy is by accepting the rules of the state and recognising the values shared by the citizens which underpin their national identity (Allam, 2005).

Allam warns of the dangers of dual identities and different systems of education, and argues, for instance, that Muslim schools[67] should not be allowed in Italy, as they do not contribute to the integration of immigrants but instead create obstacles to this (Allam, 2006a, 2006b). He believes that fundamentalism must not be given a place in Italian society and that the state should not enter into dialogue with any fundamentalist Muslim leaders. Although Allam focuses on immigration and its impact on identity, he, as well as many others, proceeds in his analysis to consider how the identity of immigrants has to change in order for them to assimilate or integrate into

Italian society. He does not focus on how the collective understanding of Italian identity might need to change and become more pluralist under the influence of, in this case, Muslim immigration. On the contrary, he offers constant warnings on the risk of Italians being Islamised by the most extremist part of the Muslim community, which, according to him, is planning to replace the state's laws with its own rules based on religion.[68] It can be said that Allam is one of the very few who have provided a link between immigration and the meaning of identity, and yet he has done so by advocating not a more pluralist and inclusionary understanding of national belonging, but rather the revival of an organic and exclusionary sense of community.

One of the very rare occasions in which intellectuals have been involved in a public discussion on immigration in the national newspapers is when, on 29 September 2001, the editor of *Corriere della Sera*, Ferruccio De Bortoli, published Oriana Fallaci's article entitled 'La rabbia e l'orgoglio' (Rage and Pride), written on the same day as the terrorist attacks on the United States.[69] Fallaci's intervention cannot be considered a contribution to an intellectual debate since it was conceived primarily as an uncompromising statement of her strong personal position on what she calls 'the conquest of Italy on the part of Muslims', and not as the start of an open debate, as proven by the fact that the writer was not interested in addressing the controversy that her article raised. Moreover, the reactions to Fallaci's article and book cannot be considered part of a proper debate on immigration either, since, despite showing strong opposition to Fallaci's views, they were quite similar in style and register. Despite its huge impact on national public opinion and the fact that some intellectuals, such as political scientist Giovanni Sartori and writer Dacia Maraini, tried to engage with what Fallaci had expressed in her article, most of the reactions aimed to undermine the journalist by accusing her of being out of her mind, as well as old and ill, rather than attempting to reject her radical ideas. Intellectuals and journalists did not consider this episode an incentive to open a systematic discussion on immigration, but instead ignored it. To a certain extent, even Maraini and Sartori fell into the trap of not being able to steer the discussion away from Fallaci's populist and offensive register.[70]

The fact that only a few journalists have been mentioned here does not intend to indicate that the whole category is neglecting the theme of immigration. On the contrary, since the 1990s national newspapers have regularly covered the issue. The decision to mention only a few is due to two factors. The first is that most journalists who deal with immigration write about single, specific episodes and particularly focus on the most sensational and emotionally striking cases, while not really keen to carry on more in-depth reportages, providing broader or more reflexive interpretations of the phenomenon or problematising it and looking at it from different perspectives: immigrants, indeed, make it into the news only when it is crime news.[71] The second reason is that those writing about specific episodes usually do so without engaging in a wider debate and their voices do not play a significant role in the public discussion on the theme. In this respect, they can hardly be defined as intellectuals or opinion makers in the sense that has been previously explained.

The same can be said of other intellectuals, who, however, cannot be considered public intellectuals for they do not take part in public debates: Italian philosophers. There are indeed a number of political philosophers who worked or are working on concepts such as tolerance, integration, inclusion and dialogue, even though they do not refer to the sense of national belonging or contextualise their reflection within the Italian case. If Italian journalists write about too-specific episodes linked with the foreign presence in the national territory, most philosophers have the opposite problem, for they abstract from specific cases with the result that their voices do not appear to find a space in the public arena, nor influence in any way Italian political and social life. However, it is still worth just briefly mentioning their work, which could potentially have an impact in the ongoing discussion on Italianness if contextualised or reflected upon and applied to concrete issues by intellectuals more involved in popular debates.

Anna Elisabetta Galeotti, for instance, has examined the idea of tolerance and its different meanings from both perfectionist liberal and neutralist liberal perspectives (Galeotti, 1994). As a case study, she discussed the controversial 'affaire du foulard',[72] but her analysis of concepts such as identity and autonomy did not lead her to examine Italian identity or its relation to ethnic and religious difference.

Similarly, in her book *Tolleranza*, Maria Laura Lanzillo addresses the notion of tolerance and the interpretation of the concept provided by philosophers such as Hobbes, Locke, Hume and Voltaire, without analysing the meaning that tolerance[73] has today or the development of multiculturalism in contemporary democracies (Lanzillo, 2001). Norberto Bobbio, too, focused on the relation between equality and freedom as premises for a democratic society as well as on the concept of citizenship, but despite this analysis, he considered globalisation and technological change as the challenges that the nation-state and national identity have to face, to a larger extent than immigration (Bobbio, 1995).

A philosopher who has worked on identity in a context that can be applied to the concept of difference with reference to multicultural societies, and who advocates the necessity of finding harmony in the coexistence of difference is Ermanno Bencivenga. His work, *Oltre la tolleranza* (Beyond Tolerance), examines the different definitions of the concept that philosophers have developed in the past, and elaborates a new idea of the ego being capable of facing the challenges posed by difference in contemporary Western societies (Bencivenga, 1992). Bencivenga argues that modern societies seem to deal with political issues in an irrational manner. Their irrationality consists in devising solutions to new problems and challenges, which are limited and short-termist, as they do not look to the future and do not take into consideration their long-term consequences.[74]

The exclusion of such stimulating thoughts on otherness and pluralism from public debates suffered by Italian philosophers is due, as already anticipated, to their 'specialisation' and the language they use to address specific issues, that lingua franca typical of academics, which contributes to their isolation and prevents their voices from being heard in the public sphere. Finally, their exclusion is also reinforced by the media system, which, as stated earlier, 'relies on personality' capable of addressing a general public of non-specialists. In this sense, an obscure language as well as a limited audience and absence from the media, all contribute to create a filter, which keeps the philosophers' voices away from the public sphere and therefore, from a pragmatic perspective, makes them 'irrelevant' in the already weak debate described above.

10 Conclusions

This first chapter started with an acknowledgement of a general lack of interest and participation on the part of academics, journalists and philosophers in the discussion on the relation between immigration and Italianness. It recalled how the concept of national belonging has been widely discussed again in the 1990s, after 50 years during which it has been almost entirely neglected, and indicated the main historical and political factors analysed and popularised by intellectuals, particularly the conflicting interpretations of the Resistance and the rise to power of the Northern League.

This interest on the 'internal phenomenon' has provided an, albeit partial, explanation for the pushing to the margins of a relatively (at the time) new phenomenon – immigration – which is deeply linked to the transformations that the concept of national identity is likely to go through in the imminent future. Intellectuals who have been taking part in the different but related debates analysed in this chapter tend to identify in the lack of shared and authoritative 'narratives' the reason for a failure in building an unambiguous and strong Italian identity. This is a failure that they seem to attribute unanimously to the state and its institutions. Despite the fact that the majority of intellectuals agree that Italy lacks common symbols and values indispensable for a feeling of solidarity capable to keep the nation together, and despite their agreement on attributing this failure to the state, none of them identifies the actors who nowadays should be telling this common story. They do believe that someone should have the responsibility to do so, but, as Rusconi puts it, it is hard to say who should or could play this role. Interestingly, none of them even mentions the possibility of attributing this responsibility to their own category or to individuals who are part of that category. The fact that intellectuals seemingly do not invest themselves with this responsibility of storytelling could imply that their role within our society is going through a crisis. Despite this being a concern in contemporary Western societies, the detailed analysis of the discussion of the Resistance and the role of political parties after the war, carried out in the first section of this chapter, shows that intellectuals can take quite radical positions on certain issues and have an impact on public opinion. Therefore, the lack of interest and participation in a debate on immigration has to be attributed to factors other than a crisis of the role of intellectuals in our society today. Or, at least, this crisis did not prevent them from taking upon themselves a role of leadership in central matters linked with identity other than immigration.

Their influence on the perception of the Resistance is indeed huge and public opinion on the subject is shaped mostly by their interventions and the ideas they advocate. Moreover, their taking a position on the matter also influences the way in which the state looks at it, as proven by several political choices such as the creation of a national commemoration, the 'Festa della Repubblica', established in July 2000, and of the Museum of the Resistance opened in July 2002, and the way in which they are entwined with the interventions of Italian intellectuals. The commemoration day for those killed by the Nazis at the Fosse Ardeatine on 24 March 1944 promoted by intellectuals close to the DS represents another clear example of the influence of intellectuals on the state on matters linked to national identity and shared memories.

The case of the analysis of the Northern League is slightly more complex, since sociologists, political scientists and journalists have discussed it systematically, but privileging some aspects and often neglecting others. Indeed, at that stage (in the 1990s) they seem to take into account only the reasons for the rise to power of the party and the means it used to succeed, and not the type of national identity it was building; nor did they seem to address the consequences that this new identity, characterised by being profoundly exclusionary, would have on both the general sense of national belonging experienced by citizens and the role and consequences of immigrants' presence in the country. A more detailed outline of the new imagined community and national identity constructed by the League and its effects on public opinion and on the state's policies toward immigration will be carried out in more depth in Chapter 3, focusing specifically on these aspects.

This chapter also attempted to identify the reasons why intellectuals seem to avoid considering immigration in a systematic and non-episodic manner. A possible reason could be their acceptance of the dominant interpretation of immigration as a temporary phenomenon rather than an increasingly permanent trend. This would explain why they only consider single episodes without developing any broader analysis or clear position on the matter in general in order to provide long-term solutions or models of integration. This attitude is not characteristic only of intellectuals but, as the final chapter of this work will try to argue, is typical of the political system too, and is reinforced by the media system. It also has to be said that the analysis carried out in this chapter only concerns the revival of the debate as it developed in the 1990s and does not take into account more recent discussions on the meaning of Italianness. With the 150th anniversary of Unification on 17 March 2013, a wide number of books have been published on the issue and various celebrations and events have taken place throughout the country. The developments in the discussion on national belonging today and a comparison with the issues taken into account until this point will be the main subject of the final chapter of this book.

Moving from the causes to the consequences of the weakness of the intellectuals' role in the debate on national identity and immigration, one of the aims of this study will be to analyse the effects of this lack of contribution upon the political sphere and the state's decision making as well as public opinion in general. The first outcome of such a lack of participation in the public sphere consists in their inability to influence the state's decisions on the matter, especially by comparison with other actors taking part in the debate, such as the Northern League and, to a certain extent, the Catholic Church.

The effect upon public opinion and citizens of the absence of most prominent intellectuals from the debate on immigration is quite complex since, as mentioned above, some of the works of philosophers and thinkers are not accessible by the majority of people. This is for different reasons, particularly the language in which they are expressed and their theoretical nature, as well as filtering mechanisms exerted by the media. Consequently, the voices that could be heard the most have been those that have adopted an aggressive and uncompromising tone. The case of Oriana Fallaci is representative of this situation.

As a result of the intellectuals' silence, these aggressive positions have reinforced a growing anxiety towards immigration and therefore indirectly provided the state with a widespread consensus for its restrictive policies towards the newly arrived, based on the need to prevent any further arrival, rather than facing it with a long-term and well thought-out strategy. Moreover, the intellectuals' absence from the public discussion on the theme and their lack of interest in being the subjects who tell the national 'narrative' to the country, determines a shift of power towards those actors that have engaged in the debate by putting forward their own (aggressive and exclusionary) narratives while presenting their ideas as objective and a-problematic, as this work will try to prove in the following chapters.

Notes

1 Italianità in Italian.
2 Among these intellectuals the author locates philosophers such as Spinoza (1632–77) and Voltaire (1694–1778).
3 In this sense, Gramsci's definition and his faith in the working class is close to Brzozowski's idea of intellectuals (Brzozowski, 1910; Walicki, 1989: 176–98).
4 '[D]i non essere più una nazione, o di non esserlo mai stati, o di non essere stati capaci di esserlo quando solo e per davvero contava.'
5 Only later, just before the 150th anniversary of Unification, do we see the flourishing of a number of publications on the (often contested) meaning of the Risorgimento (Unification) and its impact on the building of a specific feeling of national belonging, as we shall see in Chapter 5.
6 In fact, the polemical opposition between these two 'ideas of the world' is still in place today, as it emerges when one looks at the use of the term 'communist' (referred to political opponent, magistrates and members of civil society) on the part of Silvio Berlusconi and its allies/supporters. The same can be said about the term 'Fascist', used frequently to de-legitimise political contenders but also holders

of different opinions in everyday conversations. On this subject see: Anon. 'Berlusconi a sorpresa a Ballarò. Mills? I giudici sono comunisti', *La Repubblica*, 27 October 2009; Anon. 'Berlusconi: "I comunisti ci sono e vogliono farmi fuori attraverso la magistratura"', *Il fatto quotidiano*, 5 January 2011; Bracalini Paolo, 'Ora comunista è un insulto per gli ex comunisti', *Il Giornale*, 7 Janaury 2011.

7 Under the leadership of Achille Occhetto.

8 Further changes within the PDS occurred in 1998, with the change of the party name into DS (Democratici di Sinistra), and later, in 2004 when the DS, Margherita (Daisy), the Socialisti Democratici Italiani (Italian Democratic Socialists) and the Republicans formed a new coalition (Ulivo, or Olive Tree) under the leadership of Romano Prodi. Finally, the birth of the PD (Democratic Party) in 2007 marked the fusion of the different movements into a single party.

9 The parties most involved in the scandal were the Christian Democratic Party and the Socialist Party, whose leader, Bettino Craxi, became a symbol of political corruption and chose to leave Italy (where years in jail awaited him) for Tunisia, where he lived until his death in 2000.

10 The mani pulite case exploded after a period already characterised by political and financial scandals such as the collapse of the Banco Ambrosiano. The death of the bank's President Roberto Calvi (whose body was founded hanging under Blackfriars Bridge in London on 18 June 1982) still represents an unresolved mystery of Italian political history.

11 'Una lunga stagione di rimozioni, di inadempienze e di imprevidenze è definitivamente tramontata con la fine degli anni 80.'

12 The three articles were entitled: 'Se l'identità italiana non è più motivo di solidarismo' (If Italian identity is no longer a reason for solidarity) (Rusconi 1991); 'Una incerta cittadinanza italiana' (An uncertain Italian citizenship) (Scoppola 1991); and 'Representation without Taxation' (Panebianco 1991).

13 '[L]a priorità della scelta nazionale.'

14 What is interesting in Rusconi's approach is the fact that despite comparing the Italian situation to that of other countries where the debate on national identity was strictly related to that on immigration, the author does not pause to reflect on the impact that immigration to Italy might have on Italianness. He rather focuses on Europe and European integration as a key factor in order to explore the feeling of national belonging. This is already a first sign of an attitude quite common amongst intellectuals which we shall explore in more detail later on.

15 '[T]utto però è finito [...] tra la fine degli anni ottanta e i primi novanta.'

16 'Noi che vi siamo nati, preferiamo da tempo non parlarne più. Un'ostinata volontà di rimuovere, e poi troppa cattiva retorica, seguita da un eccesso del suo contrario – abitudini coltivate con eguale talento – hanno creato una specie di blocco mentale: quasi una lesione permanente nella rappresentazione di noi stessi.'

17 'Una nazione può cessare d'esserlo.'

18 Galli della Loggia seems to hold a sort of monopoly on the concept of 'death of the homeland', to which he devoted most of his studies. However, the concept had already been explored by Renzo De Felice a year earlier (1995). Even if not labelled as 'morte della patria', the same concepts of the gap between the idea of the state and that of the nation and of the decline of such ideas as related to patriotism had been discussed by Gentile (1982). As the historian explains, 'That book had several reviews, although nobody paid attention [to the issue mentioned above] despite the fact that [the book] anticipated by a decade the various discussions on the "death of the homeland". That must mean that the theme was not of interest for intellectuals back then' (Gentile 2003a: 36).

19 De Felice, among all intellectuals, is the one who has been more exposed to the charge of being a supporter of Mussolini, and for this reason his work has often been discredited or polemically contested. His student, the historian Emilio

Gentile, has recently explained in the book interview *Italiani senza padre. Intervista sul Risorgimento* (Gentile 2003a: 90–93) how superficial this judgement is. Gentile himself has often been considered as the 'traditore', the rebel student who had rejected De Felice's interpretation of Fascism. (For a more detailed account of De Felice's work and public role, also see Gentile 2003b.)

20 Defeatism had been studied before by other scholars, who tend to explain it with reference to the Fascist period. See Morgan, P., 'The Trash who are Obstacles in Our Way: the Italian Fascist Party at the Point of Totalitarian Lift Off, 1930–31', *The English Historical Review*, Vol. CXXVII, No. 525 (2012); Wilcox, V., '"Weeping Tears of Blood": Exploring Italian Soldiers' Emotions in the First World War', *Modern Italy*, Vol. 17, No. 2 (2012).

21 On family and blood ties as the foundations of the nation, see also Banti, A.M., *La nazione del Risorgimento. Parentela santità e onore alle origini dell'Italia unita* (2000) Torino: Einaudi; Banti, A.M. and Ginsgborg, P. (eds), 'Per una nuova storia del Risorgimento', in *Storia d'Italia, Annali, 22, Il Risorgimento* (2007) Torino: Einaudi, xxiii–xli.

22 'Gran parte d'Italia si augurò dal primo giorno della guerra la disfatta. [...] La solidarietà e il patriottismo e il senso della responsabilità individuale, andavano disperse e uccise.'

23 As Pavone states, 'even today, considering the 8th of September as a tragedy or the beginning of a process of liberation represents the dividing line between two opposite interpretations (of the war and the Resistance)' (Pavone, 1991: 36).

24 'Non parto dal 25 Aprile, ma dall'8 Settembre, il giorno in cui Eisenhower annunciò l'armistizio con gli Italiani. Data tragica della nazione italiana: quel giorno è l'idea di patria che muore.'

25 In a more recent contribution, Emilio Gentile stated that the decline of a shared idea of 'patria' had begun much earlier than 8 September. The historian believes that the death of the homeland dates back to a period that he locates between 1912 and the advent of Mussolini, and which coincided with the 'ideologisation of the nation'. With this expression Gentile refers to the fragmentation of the idea of the nation and the delegitimisation of opponents' interpretation of the idea of 'patria', presented as the 'anti-nation' tout court (Gentile, 2003a). Gentile also sees the claim on the part of a section of the Italian society (from the Catholics to the socialists) to incarnate the only true Italy as the inheritance of Risorgimento, an attitude further reinforced by Fascism. The common characteristic of these 'views of the world' was, indeed, that of holding the exclusive monopoly of Italianness. Mussolini, for instance, believed that anti-Fascists were simply anti-Italians. An example of this attitude is that attributed by Galli della Loggia to the Left. On this theme, see also Gentile, 1982.

26 '[U]na data fondamentale non solo per l'Italia ma per l'umanità.'

27 'Italians: friends and enemies'. The book also includes a contribution by Rusconi.

28 As the analysis of the celebrations for the anniversaries of Unification will show, the shared attachment to that historical event is anything but a-problematic. Many scholars argue that there was no enthusiasm for the state-organised celebrations and that these events and mass participation were nothing but empty collective rituals.

29 'Noi, una minoranza, eravamo pienamente convinti che l'Italia dovesse perdere ma gli Italiani nel loro complesso non erano certamente favorevoli all'entrata in guerra.'

30 'Eccetto per qualche fascista non c'è stato nessun consenso popolare per la guerra.'

31 '[I]l nocciolo della questione sta tutto qui: come mai l'Italia non è riuscita a fondare una nuova coscienza nazionale, invece che su verità di comodo e su dogmi ideologici, su quello che gli Italiani nel bene e nel male sono stati?'

32 '[P]iuttosto deludente [...] A meno di non prendere proprio questo risultato e le difficoltà di comunicazione tra i due studiosi come il dato interessante su cui riflettere e da cui prendere avvio.'

33 'Questo aveva reclamato per sé […] il privilegio di rappresentare l'idea di nazione […] la patria fascista era obbligatoriamente la patria dei veri Italiani. […] L'antifascismo credette di non avere altra scelta che imitare il suo avversario, soltanto reclamando per sé il privilegio.'

34 This definition is taken from the title of Remo Bodei's (1998) book *Il noi diviso*.

35 From the verb 'attendere', to wait.

36 However, many other scholars argue that citizens' participation in the Resistance can only be appreciated when compared to the involvement of German or even French citizens in anti-fascist movements.

37 '[L]egittime strategie di sopravvivenza della popolazione.'

38 '[L]e disgrazie renderebbero gli uomini migliori.'

39 The key issue is more generally the supposed lack of loyalty towards Italy on the part of the PCI, resulting from its strong relation with Moscow. On the cession of Trieste to Yugoslavia, see: Pagani, 2004; Udina, 1979.

40 This internationalism was also reinforced by the inheritance of Roman imperialism as well as by the influence of the Catholic Church.

41 A broad literature on the relationship between the PCI and Yugoslavia/the USSR is available today (see, for instance, Galeazzi, 2005). The revisionist historians cited in this chapter, Galli della Loggia above all, tend to focus on these international relations while being oblivious to the fact that the relations between the DC and the USA were equally strong (on this subject see, Formigoni, 1996; Del Pero, 2011).

42 'Cosa accadrebbe per la folla?' 'Nulla.'

43 The word 'even' ('persino' in the Italian version) highlights the novelty of an approach that would take into account the issue of 'national identity'.

44 'Si è così cominciato a interrogarsi con maggiore sistematicità rispetto al passato sulle insufficienze della nostra cultura democratica, sulle origini di queste debolezze e persino sul senso della nostra identità nazionale.'

45 'In questa visione non contano tanto gli element oggettivi e l'essere o no membro di un gruppo etnico diventa in ultima istanza un'opzione volontaria.'

46 '[U]na risorsa strategica per ottenere qualcosa o per negare qualcosa a qualcun altro.'

47 According to this interpretation, an important factor that contributed to the growing of autonomist movements is linked to the expected impact of their claims on the allocation of resources and on access to non-material benefits as well.

48 It is important to note that when he mentions 'migration' and 'internal mixing', Rusconi is still referring to Italians' emigration abroad or to internal migratory waves from the South to the North of the country, whereas the arrival of foreigners to Italy is completely overlooked at this stage. In 1993 Italy had already faced the two 'Albanian crises' and public opinion had started manifesting a high level of anxiety about the new arrivals. However, although national newspapers and opinion makers had begun to discuss this relatively new phenomenon, the debate on immigration had not yet started overlapping with the debate on Italianness. The two discussions will remain separate for a while longer and it would not be incorrect to say that, to a certain extent, this was still the case until recently. As Chapter 4, on the Italian legislation on citizenship and immigration, will show, the attention of the institutions and of political parties is still quite oriented towards the protection of the rights of Italian expats rather than on the integration of foreigners into Italy.

49 '[U]na storia di comunanza fatta non solo di letteratura, di armi e di sangue, ma di lavoro e fatiche comuni, di migrazione e rimescolamenti interni da cui si sono prodotti legami che non possono essere spezzati senza ferire l'identità storica di tutti gli italiani del nord come del sud.'

50 The authors neglect the fact that the DC was not the only party hard hit by the mani pulite investigation, which also deeply affected the Socialist Party (PSI) and the PCI.

51 See Chapter 3 on the exploitation, on the part of the Northern League, of the Catholic rhetoric in order to attract or consolidate electoral consensus.

52 De Felice attributed to the DC and the PCI a direct responsibility in the decline of nationalism, weakened, according to the historian, by socialist Marxist internationalism and Catholic universalism, respectively (Gentile, 2003a: 97).

53 According to some scholars, if Fascism had contributed to fostering mass partici-pation, after the collapse of the regime, such adhesion to political movements simply migrated into the two main parties (DC and PCI), marking the passage from the era of 'nationalistic patriotism' to that of 'party patriotism', an expression used by Mario Ferrara in 1947 to indicate the coincidence of the concept of the party with that of homeland (Gentile, 2003a: 61).

54 It is interesting to compare this position with Gentile's idea that the lack of civil religion in Italy is due to the presence within the national territory of the Vatican. Indeed, according to the scholar, a civil religion can only flourish where there is no dominant Church. In the case of Italy it could either coincide with the dominant religion (and therefore it would not be a proper 'civil' religion) or could emerge in contrast with the national religion. Moreover, Gentile (2001), as many others, believes that, given the universal aspiration of the Catholic Church, it would be impossible for it to work as a civil religion without being fragmented into different religions linked to different nations. On the relation between the process of nation building and religion in Italian Risorgimento, see: Traniello, 2012.

55 Despite a certain criticism that will be addressed here of Melotti's work, the author represents a point of reference in the reconstruction of the interventions on immi-gration put forward in the public sphere, as not only does he take part in the debate itself but he also appears to be one of the few intellectuals to reflect sys-tematically on the chronology of the discussion and to take stock of the debate in progress.

56 Melotti, however, does not further explain this statement or in what sense/which aspects of the French 'framework' could be misleading if applied to Italy.

57 The song 'The legend of the Piave' is an Italian patriotic song which narrates the battle of Solstice (1918) between the Italian and the Austro-Hungarian armies, a fundamental battle for Italy in World War I. All four strophes end with the word 'straniero' (foreigner). On the relation between Italian history and patriotic songs, see also: Franzina, 1996; Pivato, 2002.

58 This isolation, however, is limited to the intellectual's role in the debate on immi-gration, whereas his interventions in the discussion on Italianness are well known and find a central space in the public exchange between intellectuals on the matter.

59 '[C]he godono o aspirano a godere alcuni diritti civili, sociali e persino politici di cittadinanza del paese di insediamento pur mantenendo (volontariamente o coattivamente) una nazionalità straniera.'

60 However, this is true only for Northern European countries, whereas immigration to Italy had not yet become 'visible' in the 1970s. Moreover, even today, when it is actually true that immigration is generally discouraged, the case of Italy is still more complex. As we shall see in Chapter 3, the Northern League's rhetoric on immigration is highly ambiguous precisely because it combines strategic anti-immigration statements with an ever-growing demand on the part of the territory for an increasing workforce.

61 'A questo punto la percezione collettiva dell'intero fenomeno migratorio non poteva non assumere in Europa toni di allarme sociale, con la mobilitazione di paure profonde che ha portato a veri e propri comportamenti xenofobi e vio-lenze razziste [...] La maggior parte della popolazione europea non ha le idee

chiare sulle conseguenze economiche della immigrazione: gli immigrati creano disoccupazione oppure coprono posti abbandonati dagli autoctoni?'

62 And even 'institutionalised' under Fascism (see the racial laws of 1938).

63 'Non è un caso che nell'immagine pubblica l'immigrazione è catalogata (e vissuta) come una nuova specie di patologia sociale, da accostare alla disoccupazione, alla criminalità organizzata o all'inquinamento (quando addirittura non è vista come somma di queste patologie).'

64 More recently the EU has started putting forward proposals for common policies, although these seem to be more oriented towards a limitation of the phenomenon and the sanctioning of those countries which for their geographical position represent the weak fronts of 'fortress Europe'.

65 Allam's position has recently began to radicalise to the point that today it would not be possible to define him as 'moderate'. The last polemical move of the intellectual has been that of announcing he was officially leaving the Catholic Church because of its soft take on issues linked with Islam. In particular, the announcement was made after Pope Francis's speech on inter-religious dialogue and his words of opening towards the Muslims who share with Christians the faith in one God. (On Pope Francis's speech to the diplomatic corps, see: Ingrao, 2013; Anon. 2012a; or in English, Davies, 2013.)

66 The confusion between the status of immigrant and that of Muslim often leads many to use the two terms as interchangeable. This is true of Allam but also of some members of the Catholic Church, as we shall see in Chapter 2.

67 The debate on Muslim schools spans from 2005 to today. For different perspectives on the issue, see: Anon. 2005a, 2006; Vernizzi, 2011.

68 This concern is also shared by some representatives of the Catholic Church, as well as by other intellectuals, for instance the journalist and writer Oriana Fallaci.

69 The article later became a book (Fallaci, 2001b). The book, translated and sold in 16 countries, had a huge impact on national and international public opinion.

70 On the responses to Fallaci, see the following articles, all published in *Corriere della Sera*: Sartori, 2001; Maraini, 2001; Zincone, 2001.

71 On the media and the representation of immigrants, see Belluati *et al.* 1995.

72 The affaire du foulard exploded in France in 1989 when three Muslim female students were expelled from a secondary school in Creil following their refusal to remove their headscarves, judged as incompatible with the laïcité of French state schools.

73 As Galeotti and Lanzillo themselves recognise, the concept of tolerance itself is very problematic, as it implies the superiority of a group over another which has to be 'tolerated' and configures therefore an asymmetric relation between mainstream societies and the 'other' within.

74 An exception in terms of his presence in the public sphere is represented by Giovanni Sartori, who can probably be considered more of a political scientist than a political philosopher. Sartori has written extensively on pluralism, otherness and democracy. His articles often appear in the national press. Particularly relevant in this context is his book *Pluralismo, multiculturalismo e estranei. Saggio sulla società multietnica* (Sartori 2000b).

2 The Catholic Church and the debate on identity and immigration

One can fight the Church, persecute it, make deals with it, but one cannot ignore the Church: this is a fact that finds confirmation in nineteen centuries of history.[1]

1 Introduction

While analysing the political factors that contributed to creating an Italian identity, the previous chapter focused, among other things, on the influence of political subcultures in shaping national belonging. It examined the 'white' subculture, linked with the Catholic Church, in order to verify how influential it has been in building a strong – although, according to some scholars, partial – sense of *Italianness*. This chapter aims to consider in more depth the role of the Church in the context of the wider debate on national identity and immigration. The main research questions that will be addressed here can be formulated as follows: What is the Church's official position on the issues of identity and immigration and what model of citizenship, if any, is it putting forward? Has there been any change in its attitude towards minority ethnic and religious identities? If so, is the Church reacting to matters of law and order following widespread feelings of uncertainty and anxiety among ordinary citizens, often reinforced by the media, or is it reacting to immigration in order to reassert its capability of attracting consensus, which its own representatives often define as declining, at least in terms of active participation? Finally, how does the Church position itself with regard to the state or, in other words, to what extent does the Catholic world interfere with institutional approaches to diversity and how does it outline the role the state should have in the managing of the social consequences of the growing influx of foreigners into the country?

In order to accomplish this task, this chapter will start from a general overview of the debate on religion and politics in Western democracies as it has developed since the 1980s. It will deal with the specific case of Italy and provide a brief account of the relationship between the Catholic Church and the Italian State. It will then focus on the main ecclesiastic documents, encyclicals, pastoral notes, guidelines from the Italian Episcopal Conference (CEI) released on the two subjects since the Second Vatican Council. Finally, the chapter will take into account a number of more controversial documents and particularly the pastoral notes *La città di San Petronio nel terzo millennio*[2] and *Nota sull'espressione 'chiese sorelle'*,[3] written in 2000 by Cardinal Giacomo Biffi, at that time archbishop of Bologna and the then Cardinal Joseph Ratzinger, respectively. By placing such documents, which raised concern amongst observers and opinion makers, within the wider context of the Italian political and social scenario, it will attempt to provide a fairly exhaustive picture of the ecclesiastic role in the development of a public debate on the issues of diversity, minority identities, immigrants' rights, inter-religious dialogue, and the links between national identity and culture/religion. Following this, the reactions of different groups and individuals to these pastoral notes will be analysed. First of all the response of various Catholic representatives will be taken into account, showing that the Church's position on the matter became more radical after 2000. This section will also highlight how within the Church there are different if not opposing positions on the issue, where the main opposition pits the Pope and the hierarchy[4] on one side and Catholic voluntary associations as well as a few individual parish priests close to anti-globalisation movements on the other.

This chapter will also compare and contrast the documents approved by John Paul II, such as the *Dominus Iesus*, written by Joseph Ratzinger, with other documents that represent personal positions and have not been officially commented on by the Pope, such as indeed Cardinal Giacomo Biffi's pastoral note. The analysis will also be extended to sermons and speeches by ordinary priests who either disagreed with the pastoral note or praised Biffi for it, as well as the reaction of Italian journalists, politicians and opinion makers to the same document. Finally the reactions of the representatives of other religions, and particularly those from the Muslim community, will be analysed.

The main aim of this work is to address the circumstances surrounding, and the strategies and the means adopted by the Church to open the debate on immigration, looking both at its public discourse on the issue and its influence on the state's policy making in this field. It will argue that the positions taken by Church representatives on the everyday 'emergencies' linked with the arrival of immigrants in the country often represent a pretext for reasserting the importance of certain values. In this sense, the debate on immigration contributes to constructing a highly visible space in which to develop a broader dialogue – a concept that in the official documents of the Church very often overlaps with that of evangelisation, as will be explained in more detail – on a subject related to immigration, but closer to the interests and needs of the Church: the identity of Italians as Catholics and, as a consequence, the necessity to defend and protect this traditional identity against its potential detractors.

The analysis of the above-mentioned documents and the reactions to them will try to prove four main points. First, it will stress the distance between the rhetoric of inclusion of Catholics living abroad and the lack of attention devoted to non-Catholics in Catholic countries and in Italy in particular.

Second, as already stated, it will be argued that the debate on immigration has been 'exploited' by the Catholic Church to remark upon the need for a stronger feeling of national belonging strictly linked with Italy's 'Catholic origins'. In this sense the issue of immigration worked as an opportunity to reassert the importance of Catholicism in Italian history and in the nation-building process as well as the supremacy of Christian values vis-à-vis both alternative ideas of the good life and a much-feared growing relativism. Third, this chapter will assess the strategy followed by the Church to achieve national relevance and go beyond the boundaries of an internal Catholic reflection. This strategy consists in claiming for itself a right to freedom of speech which, according to the Church, is not yet guaranteed by the state. This right to express ideas also includes the right and duty on the part of the Church not only to put forward a particular view of the good life but also that of intervening in the public sphere by suggesting to the state how to react to issues raised by the presence of immigrants in the country. In this respect, the Church assumes a dual and contradictory role: on the one hand, it intervenes in matters related to public administration such as law and order, while on the other hand, it officially denies its responsibility in making decisions in this sphere, on the basis that it is not its duty to deal with such issues. As a result, the Church constantly engages in polemics and discussions on immigration, going as far as suggesting practical solutions to deal with this phenomenon, but at the same time it promotes a rhetoric of political disengagement.

Finally, this chapter will explore the concept of rationality and how it has been used to justify certain statements and radical positions on immigration and on the superiority of Catholic values. In particular, it will focus on the assumption that all human beings provided with common sense are Catholics. This is an idea reinforced by various representatives of the Church, such as Cardinal Biffi, throughout the debate on immigration. One of the aims of this chapter is to unveil the dynamics of such statements to show how they are often based on authority rather than on rationality, justified by an old tradition so unquestioned for centuries as to become self-evident. It will show how misleading this syllogism can be, as it uses as interchangeable terms deeply different concepts such as those of nationality, citizenship and religious belonging, with the result of providing a picture of Italians, where, for instance, Muslims are referred to as immigrants or foreigners, neglecting the fact that many of them are actually Italian citizens. The main argument that will be put forward in the concluding remarks is that the Church has contributed to promoting an original model of identity and citizenship based on the concept of 'selective solidarity', while seemingly outlining a model of a state where the concepts of religious and national belonging conflate and coincide. It will also be suggested that this approach to the phenomenon and the double role played by the Church as a point of reference for Italians and as a victim of new enemies contribute to reinforcing the citizens' growing anxieties towards immigration and provide the state with a general consensus for its restrictive policies towards the arrival of both legal and illegal immigrants to the country.

2 The general debate on religion and its impact on politics

The post-modern era, usually defined against the concepts of globalisation, mobility and secularism, has often been presented as characterised by the decline of traditional common values based on moral judgement. Such common values have supposedly been replaced for decades by new sets of criteria capable of enabling an interpretation of the world based on the tangible progress achieved in the fields of economy and science, and detached from any belief, faith or spirituality, which have been relegated to the individual's private sphere. Social scientists' argument, popular in the 1960s, that modernisation, urbanisation, education and scientific advancement would determine the spread of secularisation (Sahliyeh, 1990) started being questioned in the 1980s, when a new awareness of the importance of religion started to resurface, a phenomenon that has been explained with a number of factors, from the economic crises to the distinction between Church attendance (declining) and traditional identities (still very much rooted in Christianity in Europe) and, perhaps more interestingly, to Churches' reactions to such decline and to their adaptation strategies, put forward in order to survive in a secularised world (Berger, 1999).[5]

Nowadays a growing number of scholars, regardless of their position vis-à-vis the secularisation theory, would agree with Jacini's concern about the impossibility of neglecting the role of the Catholic Church and more in general of religion, in the analysis of Western contemporary societies and the mechanisms and common patterns according to which they work and develop. As Jelen and Chandler explain, scholarly research has shown in over a decade that religion is an important source of political attitudes. 'Indeed a number of analysts have suggested that the West in general and the United States in particular, are in the midst of a "culture war" ... in which religiously based values supplant economic interests as the basis for political conflict and mobilization' (Jelen and Chandler, 1996: 142, citing various other authors – see note 6 for detail). Academics and opinion makers have argued and still argue today that religion represents a fundamental factor in any debate concerning democracy, political participation and the construction of identity. Studied from different perspectives and disciplines, ranging from religious and cultural studies to international relations, from social and welfare studies to transnational migration studies, religion has emerged as an important factor in order to explain not only the nature of conflict in contemporary societies, but also the construction of national, multiple and collective identities, the behaviour of political parties and social movements, the process of inclusion and exclusion, attitudes towards European citizenship and the reactions to, and critique of, modernity and post-modernity. This section aims to outline briefly the state of the debate on these issues and the general conclusions that academics have drawn from their analysis of religion and its impact on identity and politics. This broader picture of the role of 'Churches' in national and international political life will provide a general background for the analysis of a specific case study: that of the Italian-based Catholic Church and its role in the public discussion on national identity and immigration. Indeed, despite the fact that most of the studies on the role of religion in our democracies come from the US debate on the issue and draw their conclusions from the empirical studies conducted in the United States, the theoretical framework they contributed to build can well be applied to the rest of the Western world, including Italy.[6]

The revival of interest in the dilemmas linked to morality and beliefs was triggered by a general acknowledgment on the part of scholars that histori-cally religion has greatly contributed to the emergence and differentiation of modern nation-states and their capacity to grant citizenship and representa-tion as well as to mobilise participation in political choices. The intellectuals who are taking part in the debate tend to focus on the process through which traditional religions have redefined themselves in the post-modern era, how they have shaped a new (political) message in order to maintain, increase or regain support, and the extent of their influence on local, national and super-national politics. This renewed awareness of the need to analyse institutiona-lised forms of belief and their engagement in filling the vacuum left by the current dominance of economic values (Jelen and Chandler, 1996) has brought scholars to investigate the links between secularised or civil religion in the era of globalisation and the process of identity building (Cochran, 1998; Seidler, 1986). Indeed, the central question of these studies – 'how does religion react to modernity?' (Seidler, 1986) – implies a broader investigation of themes related to group identity (Leege and Kellstedt, 1993); religion as an interest group (Wilcox *et al.* 1993; Warner, 2000), capable of mobilising people at a local level (Greenberg, 2000); the ability/inability of religious groups to foster trust and horizontal links (La Porta *et al.* 1997); and finally, their role in enabling citizens to sustain multiple identities as transnational migrants who take the Church as the trait d'union between their homeland and the host country (Voye, 1999).

Moreover, these recent investigations into the role of religion in democratic societies have extended to looking at its impact on politics and its relationship with international, national and local governments. This analysis revolves around a fundamental double question which scholars have formulated as follows: 'Are there distinctive contributions that religion can make to political discourse?' and 'Are there special reasons for limiting religions' role in political discourse?' (Jelen and Segers, 1998: ix).

Regardless of the different answers given by researchers to this inquiry, the questions themselves already imply the acknowledgement that religion mat-ters in politics and it matters in the making and breaking of alliances with political parties, therefore representing a central factor in the dynamics of allocating power to competing political actors (Warner, 2000: 17). This is why another field of scholarly investigation is represented by the behaviour of political parties, and particularly European Christian Democratic Parties, and their need to compromise with religion to gain the consensus of a considerable sector of society (Cochran, 1998). Indeed, as Warner (2000) argues by quoting Antonio Gramsci,[7] religion does not formally differ from other ideologies and therefore deserves an accurate analysis of its representation in politics and its place in the competition between different actors to gain visibility and space in the public sphere. Indeed, religion, similarly to other ideologies, 'provides an interpretative map of the world, a system for evaluating the justice and distributive schemes as well as ethical and behavioural codes to follow' (Warner, 2000: 17). Acknowledging this implies the recognition of religious organizations and particularly the Catholic Church as a 'strategic, calculating and influence-maximizing organization' (ibid.).

Scholars seem to agree that 'there is little doubt that, historically, religion was a major organizing system in the emergence of modern nation states', even though it has often been neglected by historians and sociologists who, for a long time, seemed to identify the nation with its geographical position and the common history and language of its people (Hornsby-Smith, 1999: 172). Nevertheless, 'it has generally been recognised that a major component in culture has been the dominant religion, its institutional arrangements, its relationship with the state and with the social and political elites, rituals of memory and celebration, its values and moral beliefs system and so on' (ibid.). As Cochran argues, referring to the United States but also to the West in general, 'whatever one might think in the abstract about the desirability of religious commitment in political life, the concrete fact of American history demonstrates that the issue was settled generations ago. Like it or not. Americans are religious people. Religion has played a major role in the chief development of our history' (Cochran, 1998: x). The scholar recalls the exchange between Jelen and Segers on the legitimacy and utility of US institutions and the role of religion in recognising and promoting such authorities, all issues which revolve around the concept of 'civil religion'.[8]

The core of the question, therefore, is investigating whether democratic societies need religion in order to survive or can find a social 'glue' in other common beliefs and dominant ideologies. In other words, scholars discuss the possibility for a nation to be secular and yet find unity and national cohesion in a different set of traditions and myths. Some authors, such as Segers, seem to reject the possibility of a society detached from religion and its values, whereas others, as indeed Jelen, believe in the alternative of 'secular creed foundation'. However, both recognise the actual great influence of the Christian Churches and organisations upon public debate on themes such as those of 'abortion, gay rights and sexually explicit content in television, movies and music, and on the Internet'. Both scholars also recognise that these discussions and the Church's support of certain political parties have often determined the results of US elections, not rarely achieved through the exploitation of themes linked to family values perceived today to be under the constant challenge of different lifestyles (Jelen and Segers, 1998: xi).

Regardless of the different answers these authors give to the dilemma on whether the foundations of a nation's culture rely on 'firm moral ground' derived from religion or rather on individual choices and progressive forces of cultural change, both acknowledge that the discussion about the public role of religion necessarily opens a debate on the idea of identity and national belonging. As Cochran argues, religion can contribute to a democratic dialogue, which is why, according to him, political actors 'must tolerate beliefs and practices that diverge from their own, even those they find deeply offensive' (Cochran, 1998: xvi). Moreover, they also have to be ready to accept religious arguments in public debate, and it is their duty to counterbalance them using 'arguments and ideas that everyone can understand and at least potentially accept, otherwise they will never be able to persuade anyone'. Finally, they must be willing to compromise rather than to radicalise their own positions (ibid.). The difficulty in communication between the two spheres depends also on the language they use to convey their messages: the specific unique vocabulary of the Church and a publicly accessible language that the state has to use to address citizens (ibid.).

The new element in the dialogue between Jelen and Segers consists in opening the way to another 'dilemma' linked to religion: that of language and its accessibility to common individuals and the gap between trust and rational choice, which has been analysed by many other scholars while attempting to set the necessary conditions following which religions and Churches can be given a role in the political arena. For religious groups seeking visibility in the public sphere, Cochran seems to advocate an internal democratic discourse. Indeed, 'political actors will not take particularly seriously monolithic communities without internal freedom that seek a place at a pluralistic table'. Another condition for inclusion in the public arena is again linked to language and prescribes the need for Churches and religious groups to abandon their specific terms and theological references for a 'neutral language' typical of a public open dialogue. However, this is a neutrality that Cochran defines as 'impossible', showing a rather common lack of faith in the Churches' ability to transform and adapt in order to gain respect in politics (Cochran, 1998: xvi).

A great contribution to the academic debate on the increasingly relevant issue of the 'neutrality' of religious language has emerged from Jurgen Habermas's answer to Rawls's position on the place of religion in the public sphere, and from the studies on the related concept of 'translation'. According to the German philosopher, indeed, religious discourse can find a space in the public arena for it contributes to amplifying the nuances of opinions and public arguments, although a main condition is posed to its legitimation: that such discourse undertakes a process of 'universalising translation'[9] (Habermas, 1989a), where the terms indicate the process of developing arguments rooted in personal beliefs through rational argumentation, the two interlocutors following a reciprocal effort to reach consensus or at least common understanding of the positions at stake (Lingua, 2010).

A clear example of the influence of religion in the public sphere can be found in the field of international affairs, whereby processes of identity building are involved, as proven by relatively recent studies on the concept of

European citizenship. Scholars such as Hornsby-Smith (1999), Voye (1999), Boswell (1994), Nelsen, Guth and Fraser (2001), and Schlesinger and Foret (2006), who have investigated the attitude of mainstream religions towards Europe, have come to the conclusion that it is possible to group European religions under three dominant dichotomies: Northern Protestantism vs. Southern Catholicism, Western Catholicism vs. Eastern Orthodoxy, and Christian Europe vs. Muslim Turkey. They agree on the fact that Catholicism has played a fundamental role in the process of European integration.[10] Indeed, the Catholic Church inspired the attitude of Christian democratic parties,[11] whose values are traditionally based on 'integration, compromise, accommodation and pluralism', as proven by their positive response to the project of a monetary union (Hanley, 1994: 2). According to the outcomes of studies conducted since the late 1980s, Christian democratic parties more than others have shown explicit support for a supranational identity and seen 'European integration as a means to overcome nationalism' (ibid.: 8). The same scholars argue that, on the contrary, Protestant countries are usually Eurosceptic and more interested in the affirmation of national and regional identities (Voye, 1999: 281). Moreover, they perceive a strong differentiation between the Church and the state as desirable (Willaime, 1995: 320; Voye, 1999: 281). As Voye recalls, among the first 12 countries that joined the EU, seven were quasi-exclusively Catholic (Voye, 1999: 281). Vincent goes as far as to say that even the EU flag with its stars reminds Europeans of their Catholic origins since it is a clear reference to the veil of the Virgin Mary (Vincent, 1993: 79). The Catholic Church's interest in the European project has been welcomed by political forces working for its realisation as it offers, as an alternative to a purely economic union, that of a Europe unified by religion and therefore 'clearly different' from the Arabic and Muslim world (as proven by the difficulties of allowing Turkey to join the 'Christian club') (Voye, 1999: 280). In this respect, both the Church and national political parties are in the ideal position to pursue their particular aims while publicly being perceived as committed – as Voye puts it – 'to giving a soul to Europe' (ibid.).

Regarding the impact of religions on national and international affairs, moreover, scholars seem to agree on the fact that the Catholic Church, as well as many other Churches, can be considered an interest group.[12] Studying these interest groups involves an analysis of the process of identity building they promote in order to be successful, which means retaining a central role in societies characterised by growing secularism and globalisation. Indeed, as Warner recalls, after World War II, the Catholic Church faced the challenge of establishing itself again in the new democratic nation-states. In order to do so, it necessarily had to form alliances with political parties. Following this strategy, the Catholic Church behaved as 'an interest group whose actions can be modelled as if it were a firm in a market seeking a supplier of goods' (Warner, 2000: 4). Forming or breaking an alliance depends on how successful the Church is in pleasing its followers and obtaining benefits for them and for itself (ibid.). In this sense, the Church becomes a representative of a particular subgroup in society that needs a connection to political parties in order to be represented in the public sphere, a sort of 'transmission belt', which passes the requests of citizens to the political system (Eldersveld, 1964; Lawson, 1980; Becker, 1983; Zeigler, 1985; Warner, 2000). Alternatively, as Panebianco explains, Churches create their own parties, as in the case of the Catholic Church and the Italian Christian Democratic Party, which is 'a party born from the direct will of religious institutions'[13] (Panebianco, 1992: 229). The concept upon which all scholars insist is that interest groups 'provide an important link between the government and the governed' (Thomas, 1993: 1), and that the struggle in which the Church is involved is mainly aimed at confirming and reinforcing its 'monopoly of power' (Warner, 2000: 21).

In order better to understand the power of the Church in national and international politics, researchers have then started applying theories used to analyse group identity and interest groups to religious organisations, coming to generally similar conclusions regarding group identification and features. Tajfel (1981) argues that there are two main characteristics typical of group identification: an awareness of membership and psychological attachment to the group, whereas those who feel attached to the group and its values but do not see themselves as members can be considered as exhibiting group sympathy (Conover, 1986). According to Wilcox, Jelen and Leege (1993), group consciousness includes different factors that scholars have classified as follows: group identification; power discontent ('the belief that your group has less power than it deserves'); system blaming ('the belief that your group is disadvantaged by the system and does not deserve its subordinate position'); and orientation toward collective action (Wilcox *et al.* 1993: 72; Miller *et al.* 1980, 1981; Gurin, 1985; Klein, 1984; Cook, 1989).

Other scholars have analysed 'polarized group affect', the affinity towards members of one's own group and hostility towards members of different groups: both attitudes and group consciousness determine a more active political participation on the part of members (Wilcox *et al.* 1993: 72). This is why the analysis of group-related attitudes is of central importance in understanding politics, as religious groups help citizens to make political choices, particularly on specific policies and on the candidates to be elected. In other words, religious groups strongly influence both their members' political behaviour and the electoral results, as well as the reactions and strategies developed by political parties to gain or maintain their power (ibid.). Moreover, the study of 'polarized group affect' contributes to explain how an 'enemy' is much needed in order to build a well-defined group identity. According to the literature on the theme, it appears that precisely for this reason, members of minority religions seem to be more committed to the group and more keen to act in its name and defence.

This datum finds confirmation in scholarly investigations of Catholicism, which emerges as more effective in inculcating values when it is not the mainstream religion: Catholics in non-Catholic countries prove more faithful to conservative values and show a much higher level of church attendance than those living in Catholic countries. The same can be said of minority

religions in Catholic countries, which seemingly attract more practising followers than they do in countries where they represent the mainstream religion
(Jelen and Wilcox, 2002). In other words, attachment to the group is inversely
proportional to the power of that group and a stronger attachment to the
group is justified by the struggle on the part of minority religions to emerge
and gain visibility in the public sphere. As a result, 'competition between
religious dominations has a positive effect on religious involvement and,
conversely, [...] religious monopolies tend to inhibit personal religiosity'
(ibid.: 72). This is why Catholics in Protestant countries exhibit higher levels
of religious observance than where they are the majority as, for instance, in
Italy.[14] The relationship between religion and the state is also determined by
the power of a particular religion: indeed, where it is dominant it will tend to
support the state and contribute to reinforcing citizens' trust in the institutions,
whereas if it represents a minority competing with more powerful religious
antagonists it will show a critical attitude towards the state (ibid.).

In a similar way, analysing the relationship between religious groups and the
national state, only this time looking at the issue from the opposite perspective
and taking as a point of reference governments and democratic institutions, it
can be said that the control the state exerts on religions is inversely proportional to its power: the weaker and more politically unsure of itself a state is,
the more 'it will attempt to maximize the scope of political control over
ecclesiastic affairs' (Vallier, 1971: 16). Moreover, the greater this political
control is, the more the Church will be 'fashioned to serve political ends' and
the less the state will prove capable of developing a secular theory of political
legitimacy. In this sense, according to Vallier, nations that are closer to the
Vatican and have a clear separation between the state and the Church 'provide
the Holy See and its transnational units the greatest possibilities for influence'
(ibid.: 16–18).

This relationship between mainstream religions and nation-states under-
took substantial changes after World War II: the Church, having been forced
to give up temporal powers and having lost its control on political affairs,
reshaped its own role within national boundaries and in international affairs
while gaining more freedom to assert its views on controversial issues and
ethical problems. Having realised that the days of political alliance and overlapping interests had gone for good, it started looking for new allies, which it
found in other Christian religions (Vallier, 1971: 18): 'Through this process
the Church has moved up in the hierarchy of social control towards a systematic position as a global pastor' (ibid.: 22–23). In this sense, it managed to
reinforce its power rather than surrender to its evident decline while gaining
increasingly stronger support from citizens whose trust in the institutions was
being weakened by religion itself.

Indeed, as Putnam (1993) argues, hierarchical religions, while attracting
people's support, damage the development of horizontal ties of solidarity and
trust. This theory, aimed at proving 'strong negative association between trust
and strong hierarchical religions', particularly fits the case of Catholic

countries, and Italy above the others (La Porta *et al.*, 1997: 333–38). While weakening citizens' trust in national institutions, Catholicism also has the effect of mobilising people at a local level, both in a negative sense, as for instance to show discontent with the institutions, and in a positive sense, building stronger connections within the group and increased commitment to it (Greenberg, 2000: 377–94). At the same time, the Church reinforces its own power at an international level since, as proven by many studies on transnational migration, it represents a point of reference for individuals who relocate themselves in a new country but keep strong connections with their homeland, or at least feel part of both their country of origin and the new place where they work and live. Indeed, religious identities and practices also enable migrants to sustain membership in multiple locations. This is made possible not only by the links the Catholic Church holds with its institutions in other countries[15] but also by the similarity of membership required for the two groups, which give migrants a sense of continuity and often represent their only chance of integrating (Levitt, 2003: 847–73).

Voye (1999), Warner (2000), Cochran (1998), Jelen and Segers (1998) agree on this interpretation of religious groups and particularly Catholic institutions as organisations that had to reconsider their role and put themselves forward as supposedly impartial experts in practical ethical issues and on their great impact on decision making, especially vis-à-vis weak political actors and governments. With the shift from a codified and institutionalised public morality to a more individualistic attitude, according to which choice is relegated to the private sphere and to the ethics of individuals, the Catholic Church, as well as other Churches and religious groups, presents itself as a 'neutral consultant' in the field of ethics in post-modern societies. In the 1990s, indeed, representatives of the Church in Europe started becoming opinion makers and points of reference for states unable to make decisions on controversial matters (Warner, 2000; Vallier, 1971; Jelen and Segers, 1998). Even more importantly, this shift and requalification of religion took place without any intervention or opposition on the part of governments and mass media, which rather portrayed the phenomenon as natural. To achieve this new status the Church had to change substantially: it presented itself as de-dogmatised and was more careful about the language it employed to express ideas and put forward solutions to controversial questions, as for instance referring more often to human rights rather than to the 'laws of God' (Warner, 2000: 278). As a result, contemporary societies have to deal with the paradox of Catholic representatives acting as influential members of consultative committees on ethical dilemmas which are supposed to offer disinterested and neutral opinions on questions of central importance for the Church. Warner warns of the impossibility for the Church to play such a role, since it implies taking a distance from its own set of values and its particular idea of the world. She also calls into question the role of the media, which have failed to denounce, or indeed even to acknowledge, the existence of such a deep contradiction (Warner, 2000: 278).

The different aspects of the debate on the role of religion in contemporary democratic societies and its relationship with national and international politics summarised in this section provide a general background for a further analysis of the Italian case and particularly of the role of the Catholic Church in the debate on Italianness and immigration. As this chapter will try to prove, if on the one hand the scenario described above seems to apply perfectly to the Italian case, on the other hand Italy can be considered a special case precisely because of its geographical and historical closeness to the Holy See, a factor accounting for the high interference on the part of the Church in politics and vice versa. This peculiar relationship between the Vatican and the Italian state is the focus of the following section of this chapter.

3 Universal aspiration and its formal limits: the relationship between state and Church

The adjective Catholic comes from the Greek *katholikos*, which means universal.[16] The Church, by proclaiming itself Catholic, claims a universal power that 'concerns all men, the entire mankind', 'the whole universe', 'that penetrates all sciences and disciplines; that extends to the most diverse branches of knowledge'.[17] 'The Church is Catholic in two ways. It is Catholic because of Christ's presence […] It is Catholic for it is sent by Christ on a mission, which addresses the totality of humankind: all men are called to become the new people of God. For this reason these people, while being one and united, must extend towards the entire word in all centuries, in order to fulfill the intention of the will of God, who at the beginning created human nature and who wants to gather together his children who were lost' (CEI, 2003: III, art. 830, 831). How can this universal aspiration free from temporal and geographical limitations be reconciled with the autonomy and independence of particular sovereign secular states? Or, in other words, how can a universal Church whose territory is geographically incorporated in a foreign country exert its universal influence? This section will address the special relationship between the Catholic Church and the Italian state in order to provide a political and historical explanation for the recurring interference in the administration of Italian internal affairs, and in this case immigration policies, on the part of the Church.

Before addressing the specific case of the Italian state and its official relationship with the Catholic Church, it is necessary briefly to take into account more generally the connections between secular nation-states and Churches operating within the same national boundaries. According to Ferrari (2006), a state needs to possess two characteristics in order to be defined as secular. First, it must guarantee 'individual religious freedom, which means the irrelevance of one's religious convictions with regard to the enjoyment of political and civil rights' and it must prohibit the discrimination of those who have beliefs different from the mainstream. Second, there must be a distinction between state and Church, based on the autonomy of minority religions and the lack of interference on the part of the Church, a reversible principle which also establishes the independence of the state from any form of religion. The latter cannot have any role in legitimising a power, which has to be based on citizens' will.

This independence is today guaranteed to Western democracies despite the fact that in certain countries, such as Britain, Denmark and Norway, the heads of State (i.e. royal families) have to profess a certain religion, since members of government and representative of the opposition are free to be atheists or followers of minority religions without this implying any 'diminution of their civil and political rights' (ibid.: 11–12; Davis, 2000). Ferrari, referring to Warnink (2001) and Robbers (2001), explains that the autonomy of the state and the Church in European countries is established with the Constitutional Charters and with specific agreements or 'concordats' stipulated by the representatives of the state and those of recognised religious minorities (Ferrari, 2006: 12).[18] Amid the limits now outlined it is possible to maintain that 'the secular state' constitutes a model of organisation of relations between religion and politics that is widely shared in European countries, beyond the legal superstructures still hinging on the existence of concordats, state Churches or dominant religions. Within this picture the presence of Muslim communities constitutes a dual challenge: on the one hand for the Muslims themselves who have to find a means of integration in a reality (the secular state) that is culturally alien to many of them, and on the other, for the Europeans who have to understand how far the secularity of the state can go in integrating this alternative idea of the good life (ibid.). Given this premise and leaving aside momentarily the 'challenge' of European Muslim integration, which will be addressed later on in this chapter, the specific case of Italy and its peculiar relationship with the Roman Catholic Church can now be addressed,[19] as it emerges from the official agreements signed by representatives of the two institutions.

This peculiar relationship is formally regulated by the Lateran Pacts signed in February 1929 by a representative of the Pope, Cardinal Pietro Gasparri,[20] and the then Prime Minister Benito Mussolini. If until then the saying 'a free Church in a free state'[21] had vaguely established the duties and the rights of the two powers, the Lateran Pacts ratified in detail the separation of and the relation between these two entities. After decades of disputes following the taking of Rome in 1870 and various attempts to resolve the tensions between the Papacy and the newly born Italian state, such as the Act of Guarantees in 1871,[22] the Lateran Pacts[23] gave to the Holy See absolute and visible independence, allowing it to become an autonomous territory on which the Pope could exert full sovereignty, which marked the official birth of the Vatican State. Moreover, the agreement confirmed that the Roman Catholic religion was the only official state religion, as already documented in the first article of the Statuto Albertino.[24] The pact also granted the Church some privileges concerning the citizens of the Vatican State, the immovable property of the Holy See and tax exemptions. Finally, it involved a conspicuous assignment of shares[25] as compensation for the annexation of a relevant part of the Holy See's territory by the Italian State. The agreement, denominated 'Concordat', also regulated the relation between Church and state, recognised the validity of religious marriages, and the power of the Sacred Roman Rota[26] to annul them, and granted the teaching of Catholic religion in Italian schools at every level of the educational system.

After the war, following a process promoted by the Christian Democratic Party and supported by a Communist Party worried about the possible class and ideological clashes that could further weaken the newly born Italian Republic, the regulations of the Lateran Pacts were included in the Republican Constitution (1948), whose article 7 establishes that 'The State and the Catholic Church, each in its own order, shall be independent and sovereign [...] their relations shall be regulated by the Lateran Pacts [and] amendments to the Pacts accepted by both parties shall not require proceedings to revise the Constitution'. Moreover, article 8 states that: 'All religious creeds shall be equally free before the law [...] religious creeds other than Catholicism shall have the right to organize in accordance with their own statutes, in so far these are not incompatible with the Italian legal order [and] their relations with the State shall be determined by the law on the basis of agreements with their respective representatives.' A long process of consultation between the Italian state and the Vatican for a revision of the Lateran Pacts, started in 1969, resulted in 1984 in a new 'Concordat',[27] which on the one hand affirmed citizens' right to freedom of religion and the independence of the Catholic Church, and on the other hand abolished the compulsory weekly hour of religion in the school syllabus as well as the state's stipend to the clergy. Moreover, according to the 'Additional protocol', a sort of appendix to the 'Concordat', 'the principle established with the Lateran Pacts that the Catholic religion is the only state religion is no longer in force'.[28] The discussion on a possible further revision of the Lateran Pacts, pushed forward by certain political representatives, is still ongoing today and causing tension between the political system and the CEI,[29] which in 2005 reacted vehemently to what Monsignor Betori called 'the paper bullets', referring to the pressure coming from the press and the government for a definitive closure of the Vatican question.[30]

The complex relationship between Church and state in Italy cannot be fully understood without taking into account, albeit briefly, the role of the Italian Christian Democratic Party. The fact that the DC has been the major political actor in the Italian political scenario, taking part in more than 50 governments since the 1940s,[31] has led scholars to identify its political action with a direct emanation of the Church's will and strategies (Francis, 1992). However, the shaping of relations between the two powers appears to be far more complex than that: if on the one hand Catholicism played a prominent role in shaping parties agenda and policies, on the other hand the reliance of political issues, relating to matters of lifestyle or bio-ethical dilemmas such as human fertility and euthanasia, emerging in a context whereby the state is perceived as weak, 'contribute significantly to defining in religious terms the nature of the state and Italian society' (Donovan, 2003: 96).

As time does not allow for a more in-depth analysis of the relationship between the DC and the Church in Italy, such multi-layered interaction can be framed within a schematic division into three main phases: the era of support, the years of non-alignment and the phase of 'neutrality'.[32] Under Pope Pius XII (1939–58), at the peak of its direct involvement in politics, the Church actively supported the DC, with the Pope and members of the Catholic hierarchy intervening during different electoral campaigns directly or through their voluntary networks and associations,[33] or encouraging parish priests to speak from the pulpit (Wertman, 1982: 87) and presenting the action of voting as a duty. If until the 1970s (and particularly during the 1950s) the state was identified by its critics with the DC and generally perceived as a 'clerical one'[34] (Donovan, 2003: 98), the referendums on divorce (1974) and abortion (1981) marked a watershed in the perception of the DC and its political stability while being interpreted by public opinion and the Church itself as a neat defeat for the Catholic world (ibid.: 99; Francis, 1992; Wertman, 1982). As Francis (1992: 786) explains: 'In Vatican circles, the defeats were viewed as strengthening the case for rebuilding the Church in Italy and distancing the Church from the Christian Democratic Party.' This phase of transition coincided with growing disaffection on the part of citizens towards established parties which culminated in the 1990s with the collapse of the First Republic, following the corruption scandal of Tangentopoli. The Church, aware of the growing criticism investing the political world and concerned about being associated with the DC started distancing itself from the party and following a new strategy aimed at presenting itself as 'neutral' (Donovan, 2003: 95), a phase which marked a shift in the priorities of the Vatican and CEI from political to cultural Christian unity (ibid.: 107) and moved the focus of Church's agenda towards moral matters and ethical issues (Ceccarini, 2009: 180).

Scholars seem to agree on choosing 1995 as the year in which the strategy of neutrality was 'officially' pursued, a date that also marked a shift in the role played in the Italian political scenario by the CEI. The relevance of this shift and that of the increasing degree of separation between the Vatican and CEI vis-à-vis Italian political affairs, acquires particular relevance in the understanding of the – only apparent – contradictions in the Church's responses to the issues of immigration and national identity, as it will emerge in the next section of this chapter. If the Catholic Church has always been involved in the state's politics, as proven by the so-called 'vademecum' written in 2003 by the then Cardinal Ratzinger in order to give Italian members of Parliament (MPs) instructions on which laws and measures discussed by the Parliament were to be considered ethical and which not[35] (Provenza, 2003), such an interventionist approach has recently moved to a different level, whereby the Vatican and CEI have started to include issues such as immigration in the number of 'delicate matters', for they entail a reflection on concepts and values that are crucial for the Church. The latter has indeed exploited the debate on immigration to give prominence to concepts of identity and otherness, thereby promoting a firm defence of what it calls 'the rights of the individual', including the right not to restrict religious beliefs to the private sphere.

The consolidation of this 'neutrality' on the one hand contributed to the strengthening of the secularisation process while, on the other hand, forcing the Church, now deprived of a stable political ally, to address directly 'the state, the parties and public opinion' in order to reassert its leadership (Donovan, 2003: 96). In this sense, the Church has moved its discourse 'from the party to the pulpit' (Kalyvas, 1996, quoted in Ceccarini, 2009: 177), becoming a proper lobby capable of bringing together the Catholics of the Right (teo-con) and those of the Left (teo-dem) and establishing itself as the most powerful extra-Parliamentary actor of the Italian political scene. This transformation, which sheds light on the peculiarity of the Italian case, was made possible by a series of factors, from the crisis of traditional mass parties to the internal fragmentation of the Left, even though the main reason for such a radical change is represented by the role played in this phase by the CEI and its most prominent representative, Cardinal Camillo Ruini,[36] who was allowed far more visibility and power in 2005, with the advent of Benedict XVI's papacy. As Ceccarini (2009: 181) explains, Ratzinger, already Prefect of the Congregation for the Doctrine of the Faith, was more interested in Italian domestic affairs than John Paul II and therefore worked to reinforce the relationship between the Vatican and the Italian bishops. This strategy was based on the attempt to turn Italy, perceived as the ideal starting point to begin the fight against ongoing global secularisation, into a sort of 'laboratory', an 'export model' for the re-Christianisation of Europe.[37]

Since 2008, an increasingly strong continuity between the Church and the Right has been established, a continuity that resulted in the overlapping of the 'fundamental values' promoted by specific political parties, for instance Berlusconi's Forza Italia, and the Church (Ceccarini, 2009: 187). This closeness, profoundly relevant in the Italian political scenario, assumes even more importance in light of the fact that the Church is the most trusted institution in Italy. Opinion polls, indeed, show that only the Church and the police have survived the increasingly clear disillusionment of Italians towards national institutions[38] (Diamanti, 2014; Ceccarini, 2009). This says a lot about the legitimation of the Church's rhetoric and its role in shaping public opinion as well as the attempt of mainstream parties to align with such rhetoric or to be perceived by the public as close to the Church, facilitating at the same time the legitimation of the Church's claim for a place and visibility in the public sphere. Such strategy for the winning of a place in the public arena cannot be regarded as an independent action on the part of the CEI, but has to be considered as operated in agreement with the Vatican (Ceccarini, 2009: 180). To be added to this picture are the public endorsements of members of the Catholic hierarchy for Right-wing parties, as, indeed, in the case of Ruini's support for Forza Italia and Berlusconi (Donovan, 2003: 103).

This 'special relationship' has allowed the Church to play a double role: on the one hand the Vatican has repeatedly put forward a rhetoric of disengagement from politics, judged to be a competence of the state, whereas the addresses of the Church's universal discourse cannot be limited to Italians; on the other hand, it actively influenced Italian politics (through direct interventions by CEI members or through Catholic interest groups). This contradiction, as we shall see, explains the discrepancies between the Vatican position on immigration and minority religions as expressed in official documents addressed to all Catholics in the world, and the less welcoming interventions on the same matters addressed to Italian public opinion and political representatives. This alliance between Church and politics, which has become normal and therefore generally accepted by public opinion, has had the effect of contributing to build political identities on moral values (Ceccarini, 2009).

The Catholic universal discourse on identity and otherness

This section will address the sometimes contradictory interventions on the part of the Catholic Church in the discussion on immigration. When did the Church start considering this issue as relevant and feel it had a duty to have a say in it? Where does this interest originate? Or, to put it differently, when did immigration begin to matter to the Church? The answer to this last question varies greatly depending on whether one considers the official documents of the universal Church[39] or the documents destined for a specifically Italian public. In the first case, indeed, the Church can be considered a pioneer of discourses on otherness, an expression that includes both ethnic and religious difference; in the second case its concern on national identity and immigration to Italy reflects the delays and the difficulties, already mentioned in the Introduction of this book, that have characterised the political debate on the theme. Moreover, the case of Italy, often used as an example, contributes to reinforce the idea of a country that works as a model to export.

Rather than following a strict chronological order, this section will start with some brief considerations on the central concepts related to otherness addressed by the Church since the 1960s, in an attempt to provide a map of a constellation of key issues, which can be helpful to understand the elements of continuity and those of rupture with tradition in the more controversial documents. This first step in the analysis will focus in particular on the following issues: migration, minority religions, models of integration, Truth, evangelisation, dialogue, atheism, secularisation, national identity and freedom of religious choice. It is important to clarify that what will be taken into account in the analysis of concepts, such as those of dialogue and evangelisation, are their political implications and the impact of the Vatican's interpretation of them onto the Italian public debate on identity and otherness, and that this investigation does not aim to provide any insight into the theological aspects of them.

The awareness on the part of the Church of the challenges posed by migration, considered a non-temporary and non-reversible phenomenon, has been recorded for the first time in a systematic way[40] in ecclesial documents during the preparation for the Second Vatican Council. Looking at documents such as the Constitution *Gaudium et Spes*, the Decrees *Christus Dominus*, *Apostolica Actuositatem* and *Ad Gentes* can give the impression that human mobility was not a prior concern for the Church, since not much space in them is devoted to the Pastoral for Migrants, which is only mentioned in brief passages. However, as with most Conciliar documents, the texts mentioned above underwent radical cuts before being officially approved. As De Paolis (2005) suggests, the analysis of the Conciliar preparatory documents (*Acta*) in their integral version, can contribute to clarify the intentions and the reflections behind the final decrees and encyclicals and provide a more articulated account on the Church's position on the aforementioned issues.

The first interesting datum that emerges from both preparatory and final documents is that the subjects, the recipients of the pastoral care on which all texts focus, are the 'emigrants', those who work on ships and other means of transport, tourists and all categories of people that chose or were forced to move.[41] The main concern for the Church back then, therefore, was the spiritual, moral and social life of emigrants, who, by leaving their country of origin, faced a number of risks, the most dangerous of all being the interaction with non-religious populations or individuals and the loss of their faith. This challenge, aggravated by the distance from home and the process of adaptation to the culture of the country of arrival emerges clearly in the preliminary schemes for the *Christus Dominus*, where the idea of assimilation seen as a (negative) model of inclusion is mentioned for the first time. This datum acquires relevance if compared to the Vatican position on the assimilation of immigrants that features on more recent documents. For decades, indeed, the ecclesial documents seem to focus exclusively on Catholics living and working or temporarily residing in countries where Catholicism is not the mainstream religion and, to a certain extent, this is still the case today.[42]

The definition of the migrant revolves around the concern for those who have no access to spiritual guide and pastoral care, or at least not in their language; this explains why most documents group together 'economic migrants', travellers, refugees and, in certain cases, tourists.[43] A crucial aspect of these first documents in the light of the importance of the Italian case and the power of CEI in matters related to identity and migration is the fact that such need for individual care of the 'Catholics with no parish' is transferred to the bishops and their national Conferences,[44] which have to follow the norms and proceedings indicated by the Roman Curia. Before addressing the issues related to the conditions of the migrants, it is necessary to highlight that the migrants the Conciliar and post-Conciliar documents refer to are exclusively Catholics who have already been baptised, and that only recently has the Church been forced by current debates to deal with the presence of non-Catholic migrants and in particular of Muslim foreigners. The 'jurisdiction' on the latter, however, is external to the Commission for the Pastoral Care of Migrants as it resides within the Congregation for the Evangelisation of Peoples (Sabbarese, in De Paolis 2005). This specification is relevant in this context for it exposes the relation between dialogue and evangelisation which is crucial in the Church's documents on migration.

Summarising the position of the Church on a number of issues related to migration is not an easy task. However, it can be said that in general the

Church seems concerned with a number of recurrent matters and – given that each document retraces and expands on the guidelines of the previous documents – that these themes resurface in most documents while not much is added to the picture each time. This means that if one considers the changes in migration patterns and in the presence of minority religions in Europe, the Church has been moving quite slowly in acknowledging them and reacting to them. The documents are clear for what concerns any form of discrimination or racism, which the Church rejects and actively fights:[45] immigrants who have been baptised cannot be considered foreigners as they are part of 'the family of God'.[46] They need to be granted a set of rights, from the right to be reunited with their families[47] to equal treatment in the workplace to, more importantly, the right to maintain their own culture and faith.[48] The Church clearly condemns any forced absorption of minorities into the mainstream culture. Several documents refer directly to the models of assimilation (which can never be forced upon migrants),[49] integration (recommended but only if voluntarily chosen by the minority),[50] pluralism (as a matter of fact that characterises contemporary societies),[51] and multiculturalism (which poses to Catholics a series of challenges).[52]

On the one hand multiculturalism can prevent the discrimination of migrants, on the other hand the risks of plural societies are many and insidious. The Church seems particularly concerned with the spreading of secularised cultures,[53] cultural and religious relativism, agnosticism,[54] atheism,[55] social alienation[56] and ghettoisation.[57] If the pastoral care of migrants is a duty of the Church, the state should operate to grant migrants access to education, social housing and to put them in the condition of preserving their identity.[58]

The state should also decide on the number of migrants allowed in its territory, a choice which should result from considerations on the economic and social need of the host nation and from the aim of granting an internal balance, which is to say making sure that no minority culture can represent a threat for the local community while, at the same time, governments should enact legislation to promote respect and sanction discrimination.[59] The Church is also called to contribute to this mission, as laws are not enough to prevent racism.[60] In the Church's discourse on human mobility, as it has been said, the migrants are traditionally intended as Catholics who had to move to a different region or country. When addressing the immigrant rather than the emigrant, the documents put the foreign presence in relation with the many diasporas of Catholics, and Italians in particular. The Church has always spoken of foreigners from a sociological perspective, based on the general assumption derived from its doctrine, that immigrants have to be considered as brothers to be welcomed and supported in the name of an unconditional love and Christian charity. However, this perspective, based on the idea that 'nobody is a foreigner within the Church',[61] unveils the selective nature of the Church's solidarity, which emerges more clearly when the documents refer to the presence of foreigners of faith different from the Catholic, and namely Muslims, who are by far the minority that poses more challenges to the Church's spirit of charity.

The theme featured for the first time in the encyclical *Nostra Aetate* (1965) in which the respect of the Church towards religions different from the Catholic is openly stated.[62] The part of the document devoted to Islam[63] starts from the admission on the part of the Church of its own past mistakes in the relations with the 'Muslim brothers'.[64] The document highlights the common aspects of Christianity and Islam, such as the searching for God and peace, prayer and the sincere disposition towards the Truth, while neglecting the pillars (two out of five) of Islam that are not compatible with Christian values, such as the pilgrimage to Mecca, omitted in the text.[65] Citing the words of the *Nostra Aetate* (2): 'The Catholic Church does not reject anything of what is good and saint[ly] in these [different] religions' as they reflect 'a ray of that Truth which enlightens all men.'[66] In other words, the other religions are considered 'partial revelations',[67] having a 'preparatory function' for the reception of the Gospel: the tension towards God indeed is seen as a first step in the process of knowledge, albeit it is insufficient for salvation.[68] If the Holy Spirit acts on every human being, the difference between Christians and people of other faiths is the (lack of) 'awareness' of the source of salvation.[69] The Truth that emerges from the Church's documents is one which cannot accept compromises, which has to be universal and absolute[70] and therefore needs to be spread through evangelisation[71] that addresses the whole of mankind. The attitude of the Church towards Muslims is one of 'dialogue', even though this dialogue, which does not imply giving up Truth,[72] seems to coincide with evangelisation, as its main aim is that of converting the interlocutors to the Gospel. The main obstacle to the dialogue, which while allowing non-Christians to evolve in their faith[73] contributes to reinforcing Christian identity,[74] is represented by religious relativism,[75] the main cause for the 'de-Christianisation' of cultures.[76] The concept of 'culture', threatened by relativism[77] – also called religious indifferentism, agnosticism and atheism – seemingly overlaps with that of 'Christianity', while the term is used as a synonym of 'national identity'.

Following the documents, religious indifferentism and Islam appear as two sides of the same coin, both being reinforced by globalisation and internationalisation[78] and both representing a challenge to the preservation of mainstream/local cultures and identities. Moreover, they both concur to altering the 'cultural balance' made of shared values rooted in language, habits and traditions linked to the nation and tied with the feeling of belonging to the motherland.[79] The Church seems aware of the danger of being charged with nationalism[80] (De Paolis, 2005) and colonialisms,[81] which it condemns, albeit often in relation to the case of non-Catholic countries where citizens who convert to Catholicism are deprived of their civil rights.[82]

4 From Ratzinger to Biffi: a comparative analysis of the Catholic Church's interventions on identity and immigration

Through a comparative analysis, this section will take into account the main documents, which represent a sort of turning point in the debate on

Italianness and immigration. In looking at the chronology of their publication, the main characteristic that emerges at a first glance is the fact that the most controversial of them, which had a stronger impact on public opinion, were all written in the few months between June and September 2000. Indeed, Cardinal Ratzinger's *Nota sull'espressione 'chiese sorelle'*[83] was approved by Pope John Paul II on 9 June 2000 and published on 30 June 2000. Similarly, another document signed by the then prefect of the Congregation for the Doctrine of the Faith, entitled *Dominus Iesus*,[84] was dated 6 August and published on 5 September of the same year. Another crucial document, which contributed to opening a strong debate on immigration, was written in the same month and sent to parishes on 13 August: the pastoral note *La città di San Petronio nel terzo millennio*,[85] authored by Cardinal Giacomo Biffi, archbishop of Bologna. These three documents, and particularly the *Dominus Iesus* and Biffi's note, represent to a certain degree a turn in the Church's attitude towards immigration, from that general goodwill based on traditional Christian charity towards a much more political and utilitarian attitude, which this work will refer to as 'rational selection' (as opposed to 'natural selection').

The analysis of these texts will be followed by a brief overview of several interventions and proposals, which were put forward by individual parish priests as well as by important members of the hierarchy immediately after the initial heated discussion derived from Biffi's intervention. Although the latter can be considered the cause of the 'scandal', it seems appropriate here to follow the actual chronology in order to address a central question: why were all documents published in 2000? Why one after the other, within a period of three months? Finally, what impact have they had and are they still having on the debate on identity and immigration in Italy?

The *Nota sull'espressione 'chiese sorelle'*, written by Ratzinger as head of the Congregation for the Doctrine of the Faith, had the precise aim of clarifying the meaning of the expression 'sister Churches', and to remove the ambiguities of the common usage of the term in official documents. As the cardinal recalls, the term, originally used in official documents to describe the dialogue between the Catholic and the Orthodox Churches, had become part of a common language to indicate the relationship between them. Nevertheless, the author argues, 'unfortunately more recently the employment of such expression has been extended in certain publication by a number of theologians [...] to indicate on the one hand the Catholic Church and on the other hand the Orthodox Church, inducing the idea that in reality there is not only one Church of Christ, but that this only Church will be re-established only following the reconciliation between the two sister Churches'[86] (Ratzinger, 2000a). Subsequently, the term 'sister Churches' began to be applied also to the Anglican and other non-Catholic Churches. Therefore, this document, approved by Pope John Paul II on 9 June 2000, was meant not only to denounce the use of this expression with a meaning deeply different from its original one, but also to clarify the need for an official intervention to regulate – or better, ban – this recent use, particularly in official ecclesial documents. This apparently purely theological specification can be considered as much more politically significant if linked to the other documents mentioned above, and in this sense it can be seen as a first step towards a more articulated strategy in addressing the debate on identity and the role of religion. This is confirmed by the register of the *Dominus Iesus* and Biffi's pastoral note, which followed after a few months and concurred to reinforce the still veiled message of an intrinsic superiority of the Catholic Church.

The incipit of the *Dominus Iesus*, extracted from Mark's Gospel, opens with a reminder of the Church's universal mission of bringing the Gospel to every single human being in the world and of distinguishing between those who will listen to it and those who will not as 'those who will believe[.] and will be saved' and 'those who will not believe and will be condemned'[87] (Ratzinger, 2000b: §16, 15–16). This exquisitely doctrinal statement reveals its political inclination in an attempt to establish which attitude the Church should adopt towards those who do not believe. The Church, Ratzinger writes, looks with sincere respect at those 'ways to behave and live', those doctrines that, however different from the Catholic, reflect a 'ray of that truth which enlightens all men'. Moreover, as the cardinal states, announcing this Truth involves practising an inter-religious dialogue whose aim is to enrich and get to know each participant while responding to the Truth and respecting freedom (ibid.: §2). In less than a page, Ratzinger established a double premise: first, to define vaguely the other religions as 'lifestyles', in this sense almost referring to them as arbitrary choices among different options; second, to frame them as a sort of partial derivation from a superior Truth, a ray descending from a single origin and later on simply as 'contemporary cultural needs'[88] (ibid.: §3).

According to Ratzinger, the most appropriate means to deal with these ways of life is through a dialogue considered the only possible communication in a world threatened by relativistic theories, aimed at justifying religious pluralism not only *de facto* but also *de jure*. In other words, the cardinal is arguing that even if the coexistence of different beliefs in contemporary democracies is undeniable, and therefore should be recognised, it cannot be explained, even less justified in its principles, which is to say it cannot have a normative value (Ratzinger, 2000b: §4). In order to stem and correct this growing relativism according to which no revelation can be the true one, it is necessary to reassert the definitive and complete character of the Catholic universal revelation (ibid.: §§5–6). Here the cardinal introduces for the first time that concept of rationality and intelligence which turned out to be so controversial in his Regensburg lecture, held on 12 December 2006.[89] Indeed, he goes as far as to say that Catholicism allows people to reach the Truth through the use of 'coherent intelligence',[90] whereas 'the other religions consist of a mixture of experience and thoughts based on the wisdom of men who are on a search for a Truth, which has not yet found a clear confirmation. In this search they can only rely on God's magnanimity in partially revealing himself through a still confused and erroneous perception'[91] (ibid.: §§7–8).

In this sense, the uniqueness and unity of the Catholic religion cannot be questioned but only accepted in its evidence (Ratzinger, 2000b: §16). As a consequence, Ratzinger concludes, the Church cannot be considered the sum of the different Churches, nor can the idea of the absence of a unified Church be accepted and compensated by a common search for it (ibid.: §19). To put it differently, this means that despite the genuine attitude of the other Churches, it is not possible to neglect the fact that their faith comes from various mistakes, if not from superstition, and in this sense they (the different faiths) represent an obstacle rather than a way to salvation (ibid.: §21). In this respect the dialogue can be seen as an attempt to bring salvation to those who are excluded from it. This dialogue has to be based on an equal dignity of the different interlocutors, even though this equality refers to the individuals, that is to say, the subjects who carry the beliefs, and not to the specific content of those beliefs (ibid.: §22). The document's conclusion specifies that only when this unity is complete, can it be affirmed that 'You are neither strangers nor guests, but rather co-citizens of the saints and relatives of God'[92] (ibid.: §23). I would argue that the choice of terms such as 'foreigner' as opposed to 'citizen', albeit borrowed from the language of the doctrine, is not a random one but rather expresses a specific political concern on the part of the Church and not only the need for a doctrinal specification.

This is confirmed by the speech given by Cardinal Ratzinger on 5 September, the day on which his *Dominus Iesus* was presented to the press. At the press conference, Ratzinger was even clearer in his reference to such words. First of all, he reminded the audience of how often nowadays people tend to assume that different religions represent diverse ways to salvation: this attitude 'can be defined, without running any risk of being contradicted, as relativism'[93] (Ratzinger, 2000c). According to the cardinal, relativism, defined as the prevalent attitude in the contemporary Western world, is often justified on a theological basis with the impossibility of receiving a full and clear divine revelation. This relativistic attitude towards the Truth becomes, therefore, a justification for a widespread religious pluralism according to which what is true for an individual could not be true for others. In this respect, the idea of a universal and binding Truth promoted by the Church is often mistaken by non-Catholics for a sort of fundamentalism, an attack on the spirit of the modern age and a threat to tolerance and freedom (ibid.). As we shall see later, this view, shared by other representatives of the Catholic hierarchy, is of central importance in the Church's claim for visibility and freedom of speech as well as for its rhetoric of victimisation.

Going back to the text, Ratzinger laments that the meaning of the term 'dialogue' itself is therefore erroneously intended and distorted from the original one established by the Second Vatican Council, since in its everyday use the term does not signify a mission aimed at conversion, a way to find the Truth, but rather becomes 'the essence of the relativistic dogma, the opposite of conversion'[94] (Ratzinger, 2000b: 1). As the cardinal argues, according to the dominant relativistic thought, the 'dialogue' is nowadays intended as the attitude of putting different beliefs on the same level, so that everything assumes the same importance and dignity, being at the same time relative. This (erroneous and dangerous) kind of dialogue is invoked by the advocates of pluralism to promote collaboration and integration between different religious positions (ibid.).

Not only does Ratzinger criticise this attitude for its false premises, but he goes as far as to argue that as long as relativism is seen as a 'philosophy of humanity',[95] capable of guaranteeing tolerance and democracy within our societies, it will have as its first result 'further marginalis[ing] those who insist on defending Christian identity and its claim of universal Truth'[96] (Ratzinger, 2000b: 2). As will be argued later on, this statement represents a fundamental first step towards the strategy that the Church has been developing in order to reassert its own role in the country: a strategy based on the presumption that the Catholic Church has today become a victim, a minority, and therefore has to be protected and supported by the state. To make his message even clearer, Ratzinger defines the growing criticism directed at Catholic Church's aspiration to an absolute and definitive Truth as 'a false concept of tolerance'[97] (ibid.). Moreover, he claims that the idea of tolerance as an expression of freedom of conscience, thought and religion, as re-asserted in the *Dominus Iesus*, has indeed been defended and promoted by the Second Vatican Council and has always been a fundamental ethical position in the Christian belief, in this way affirming the Catholic origins of this value. Nonetheless, according to him, this principle of respect for freedom has today been manipulated and extended to the content of what is tolerated, thereby assuming that different religions, lifestyles and views of the world have equal dignity and neglecting the existence of an objective Truth. In this respect, tolerance means renouncing the Truth, which is, indeed, today perceived as a secondary and irrelevant issue. As a consequence, the cardinal states, faith and superstition, experience and illusion cannot be distinguished (ibid.).

Finally, without a search for the Truth, the recognition of other religions itself becomes contradictory, as it is not based upon clear criteria of discernment when judging what is positive and what is negative or when distinguishing between a superstition and a religion (Ratzinger, 2000b). One might question how such criteria could be formulated, since it seems clear that the Church would wish to promote a particular idea of the Truth, which would most probably be seen as unacceptable and arbitrary by those who do not share the same views or faith. Here, Ratzinger does not engage more openly with a definition, which is, however, already implicit in the document and seemingly based on rationality.

Ratzinger's speech for the presentation of his *Dominus Iesus* follows the same path as the document itself in its opening, with a declaration of respect for different religions, followed by a core of theological and ideological clarifications, which represent the main message, and a conclusion that reaffirms the initial reassurance about the Church's respect and positive disposition towards different beliefs. Nonetheless, just before reasserting this attitude towards the end of both his speech and document, in order to leave the reader with the impression of a constructive process of mutual understanding, Ratzinger shoots his last arrow: 'Everything that is good in the other religion [...] has to be acknowledged and valued [...] the seeds of Logos are scattered everywhere. However, we cannot close our eyes to the mistakes and the deceptions of the other religions'[98] (Ratzinger, 2000b: 2). This is why, he concludes, the Catholic Church's esteem and respect for other religions cannot lessen the originality and uniqueness of the Christian revelation, and therefore cannot put a stop to the Church's mission of evangelisation (ibid.). Once again, the choice of the word 'deceptions' (inganni), which has quite strong connotations, implying conspiracy or voluntary disguise rather than just an erroneous interpretation, does not seem to have been a random choice.

The *Dominus Iesus* had been presented as a general theological reflection, addressing both the whole Catholic community and non-Catholics in explaining the Church's attitude towards the other religions. It was written in a formal technical language, which made its polemical and practical implications remain quite implicit. On the contrary, the pastoral note *La città di San Petronio nel terzo millennio*, authored by Cardinal Giacomo Biffi, written on 13 September 2000, a week after Ratzinger's document, begins by addressing a limited audience (the people of Bologna and more precisely 'the believers'[99]) and a precise issue (the roots of these citizens' Christian identity), while its polemical intent is quite clear from the beginning.

The document opens with a call to the people of Bologna for a stronger awareness of the privilege of belonging to this city and the sense of pride this belonging requires. In the section entitled 'A Christian face',[100] Biffi introduces a long reflection upon the city of Bologna aimed at justifying the pride citizens should feel in considering themselves part of a town that was born and has developed in a culture deeply influenced by Catholicism and shaped by the Church's enterprise (Biffi, 2000: §7). The author then embarks on a sort of review of all the historical sites and monuments of Bologna, which represent a symbol and a product of this Catholic culture: the shrine of the Madonna di San Luca, the Church of San Petronio, icon of unity of aims and values as opposed to the two towers as symbols of conflict and civil wars, the cathedral, Santo Stefano, and even the arcades, typical of Bologna's architecture (ibid.: §§9–17). This overview of places linked to Catholicism ends with a 'concluding remark'[101] on what Biffi defines as the historical truth that, unfortunately, the new generations are forced to ignore, which is that in the whole peninsula and not only in this city, the public works that represent Italy in the world, the statues and buildings that still today are symbolic of Italians' adhesion to traditional Christian values, were commissioned by the Church (ibid.: §18).

Characteristic traits of Bologna, according to Biffi, are also the love for science, intellectual curiosity and a determination to fight ignorance and backwardness. Moreover, the people of Bologna are also well known – or so the bishops seems to believe – for their attitude and capacity to investigate things in depth in order to identify the 'final aim' that grants life a precise meaning (Biffi, 2000: §25). The city, the cardinal states, is renowned for its renewed faith in God, which represents the source of beauty, brotherhood and health in the region, and which takes a concrete form in the many institutions created within the city to support the poor and the marginalised (ibid.: §33).

Despite this glorious past and world fame, however, Biffi also pauses to reflect on the 'undeniable drop of tension',[102] intended as a spiritual and ethical relaxation – occurring not only in Bologna but in the rest of the world as well (Biffi, 2000: §24). The city, he states, seems to have lost its traditional attachment to those ancient values on which its civilisation was built, an issue which leads to the need to identify what he calls 'the difficult challenges of our times'.[103] To these challenges the city should react not with panic or alarmism, but rather by asking itself how to preserve its own identity (ibid.: §36). To what challenges does Biffi refer?

The archbishop specifies that two main causes can be identified in order to explain the moral decadence of our societies: 'The challenges, which are already looming upon us are mainly two: the growing influx of people coming to us from countries that are far away and different and the spreading of a non-Christian culture amongst Christian populations'[104] (Biffi, 2000: §36). The last statement opens the way to a section of the pastoral note entitled 'The matter of immigration',[105] which can be considered almost as a separate document for two reasons: first, because its register is very different from the rest of the text; and second, because it constitutes the most controversial part of the document and the main source for the discussion on immigration on a more practical level on the part of the Church. It is therefore worth analysing this section in more depth.

In the first paragraph ('A surprise'[106]), Biffi states that first of all it is necessary to acknowledge that the massive arrival of immigrants in the country has been a surprise for 'all of us', where 'us' means both the Church and the state. According to him, the latter seems lost and unable to deal with the situation rationally; nonetheless, the Church too has been caught unprepared and despite its efforts to alleviate the discomfort and privations of the newly arrived, it has not proven until now capable of developing a common practical and less abstract position on the matter. Indeed, the generic solidarity and the importance of evangelical charity – despite their being both legitimate principles and a duty for the Church – have proven more well meaning than useful since acting in the name of such solidarity and charity does not allow for dealing properly with the real complexity of the 'problem' (Biffi, 2000: §37). Nevertheless, the cardinal argues that solving social issues such as that of immigration is not a duty of the Catholic Church, whose members should not feel guilty for not having the strength to deal with it and to put forward practical solutions. Charging the Church with such a responsibility and expecting it to confront these 'problems' would be a sign of an intolerable 'fundamentalism',[107] since its mission is rather that of spreading the Gospel and following 'the duty of love';[108] this mission can be accompanied by but not replaced with any charitable action (ibid.).

According to Biffi, the Christian duty of proselytising implies as a precondition an inclination towards an open and sincere dialogue, even though evangelisation can never be limited to such a dialogue. The one outlined by the cardinal is a dialogue that can be supported by an objective knowledge of different positions and views, but which can be considered fulfilled only when it has managed to bring the knowledge of Christ to 'those amongst our brothers, who haplessly have not yet benefited from it'[109] (Biffi, 2000: §§38–40). From Biffi's perspective, the fact that this evangelical mission does not tolerate any deliberate exclusion of addressees and has therefore to be universal, is something which should never be neglected. Catholics are called upon to provide an answer to this 'indeclinable responsibility they have towards all the newly arrived'[110] (Muslims included), a duty mitigated by their awareness of possessing a truth that is 'absolutely incomparable with the – albeit valuable – glimmer [of truth] provided by various religions and Islam'[111] (ibid.: §40). Moreover, Biffi remarks upon the duty already discussed in the *Dominus Iesus,* of behaving towards immigrants with Christian charity, which means helping them to reach the knowledge of the Truth 'according to their concrete capabilities'[112] (ibid.: §41).

Having established these general premises based on Christian values and duties and an explicit call for differentiation in the state's and the Church's respective roles in relation to immigration, in the section entitled 'A realistic approach'[113] Biffi seemingly leaves to one side the theoretical aspect of the issue and begins to address it at a more practical level. This paragraph opens with the consideration that in dealing with the variegated phenomenon of immigration, Christian communities cannot avoid considering and judging differently specific individuals and groups in order realistically to react to them in the most appropriate way (Biffi, 2000: §42). At this point the cardinal engages in a more detailed analysis of the different cases, starting with Catholic immigrants: they – regardless of the language they speak and the colour of their skin – have to be treated in a way that makes them feel that 'within the Church there are no strangers';[114] they have to be welcomed and considered as brothers, part of the same family. Moreover, when they are part of a large group they should be encouraged to preserve their particular Catholic tradition, which will be regarded with 'affectionate attention'[115] (ibid.).

Biffi goes as far as to set out a sort of regulatory plan on practical issues in order to clear the way of possible misunderstandings and avoid contradictory responses on the part of the Church. In particular, he clarifies, the members of the ancient Oriental Church will have to be considered with respect and, despite their not yet complete harmony with the Roman Catholic Church, they should occasionally be allowed to use Catholic churches to celebrate their rites. Nonetheless, the attitude towards non-Christians, who have to be 'loved and, as far as possible, assisted in their needs',[116] has to follow the rules already established by CEI in 1993, which is that in order to avoid a dangerous confusion, they cannot be granted the use of churches, or places commonly used for activities connected to the Catholic cult (Biffi, 2000: §42; CEI, 1993)

The following section of the pastoral note, entitled 'General remark',[117] is the most specific and detailed, since it addresses 'the desirable behaviour of the state'[118] and of its representatives towards immigration. It contains the most unequivocal statement on – according to the cardinal – the most appropriate means to deal with the issue, which later on became the focus of a heated debate and which is today often recalled as one of the very few seemingly rational criteria set out in order to answer the questions posed by the arrival of immigrants in the country. Here Biffi states: 'The criteria for the admission of immigrants cannot respond solely to economic or welfare-related principles [...] it is necessary to deal in a serious way with saving the identity of the nation',[119] since Italy is not an uninhabited, deserted land with no history and living traditions, or cultural and spiritual features, to be populated indiscriminately as if it did not have a heritage and civilisation that need to be preserved (Biffi, 2000: §43). In Biffi's view, in order to build a peaceful coexistence, if not a desirable integration, the state must take into account that the immigrants' conditions at the start of the process are not equally favourable: in other words they are not equal, which is a fact that the representatives of Italian institutions should never neglect (ibid.). Moreover, the document explains, the newly arrived should be urged to familiarise with the traditions and identity of the 'specific culture'[120] in to which they want to integrate (ibid.).

Paragraph 44 addresses specific themes in even more detail and can be seen as the most controversial in the whole document. Here, indeed, the archbishop embarks on an analysis of the case of Muslim immigrants, arguing that: 'the case of Muslims has to be treated with particular care. They follow a different diet [...] different holidays, they have a family law incompatible with ours, a view on women very distant from ours (to the extent that they allow and practise polygamy). Above all they have a deeply extreme view of public life, whereby the perfect overlapping of religion and politics is part of their faith [...] even though before imposing their views they wait until they are powerful enough to prevail.'[121] To conclude, the cardinal states, the role of the Church is that of evangelising, whereas it is the state – every modern Western state – which has to develop a political strategy to manage the phenomenon (Biffi, 2000: §44).

Before bringing the focus back to the city of Bologna, Biffi concludes this more polemical part of the document with a short section concerning Catholicism as the historical national religion in order to remind his addressees that even though Catholicism is no longer the official state religion, it is nevertheless the historic religion of the Italian nation as well as the source of its identity and past greatness. Therefore, according to him, it is absolutely inadequate to compare it to other religions or 'cultural views'. Moreover, he argues that a democracy which grants minorities a respect that damages the majority or does not imply an equal respect for what represents a tradition, is a very peculiar democracy. He goes further to mention as an example of 'substantial intolerance'[122] the case of those schools where the crucifixes[123] have been removed following the request of citizens who have faiths other than Catholicism (Biffi, 2000: §45).

The bishop then briefly mentions the other challenges typical of contemporary societies: immigration, indeed, is not the only issue they have to deal with. First in his list comes the spreading of a culture that even though not hostile to Catholicism, does not take it into account (and does not refer to it) in establishing its principles: this is the case of the prevailing scientific thought orientated towards functional goals rather than concerned with a search for the Truth. At the same time, the growing globalisation at a social and economic level is destined to produce a state of deep alienation, while the developing sector of media and communications grants space and visibility to a culture based on superficial perceptions that pay scarce attention to individuals, their historic memory and their capacity to invest in long-term projects. The degeneration of our society, mirrored for instance by the difficulties faced by institutions such as the family, has to be ascribed, in the author's view, to men's aspiration to a 'freedom without Truth'[124] – that is to say, not rooted on 'true' values, which above all damages the dignity of human beings. Nevertheless, Biffi adds that not everything linked with modernity has to be considered as evil: in his view it is necessary to distinguish what can be accepted and what must not. The criterion for this distinction should never be political, as politics aims to find a compromise and stipulate agreements; it should rather be based on faithfulness towards an immutable Truth as well as on 'our identity as believers'[125] (Biffi, 2000: §§47–48).

Biffi's main point, briefly mentioned earlier, becomes clear at this point, when he states that Italian contemporary society seems to be led by mere 'opinions', often antagonistic to the Catholic view of the good life, since they look upon Catholicism with hatred. What the archbishop finds surprising in this scenario is the fact that the Church's representatives do not seem to be concerned, or even aware, of this process. When the cardinal anticipates the outcome of this trend in the relatively short term, he seems quite convinced that 'Europe is either going back to being Christian or it is destined to become Muslim':[126] no matter what direction it takes, the 'culture of emptiness'[127] – Biffi never calls it relativism as Ratzinger does – has no chance of prevailing. Indeed, a culture indifferent to values will not survive the ideological assault of Islam: the latter can only be defeated by a return to 'the origins' and therefore necessarily to traditional Christian foundations (Biffi, 2000: §52). Despite the general rhetoric of disengagement used by the Catholic hierarchy to remark upon the need to distinguish between the role of the state and that of the Church in dealing with immigration, Biffi does put forward practical solutions that the Italian State should enforce to deal with this phenomenon, such as, for example, the utilitarian idea that the state should operate according to what here will be defined as a 'selective solidarity' based on the 'rational' selection and therefore giving the priority to Catholic immigrants, who are easier to assimilate.

Before taking into account the reactions to these documents on the part of other members of the Church, as well as of representatives of other religions, it is worth analysing the similarities and differences between Ratzinger's

Dominus Iesus and Biffi's pastoral note, as well as the points they each try to make. As stated earlier, Ratzinger's and Biffi's positions on the foreign presence in the country are not the first interventions on the matter of immigration coming from the Church. Even though several pastoral notes had been written and published in the past, for instance by the CEI, these previous documents only remarked upon the traditional concept of Christian charity, and looked at the issue from a general doctrinal point of view, according to which immigrants had to be considered as the new poor, which the Church and Catholic individuals had the duty to love, welcome and, when possible, support. To a certain extent, Ratzinger's *Dominus Iesus* and Biffi's *La città di San Petronio nel terzo millennio*, represent a turning point in the message of the Church. Indeed, despite the fact that the idea of Christian love still represents a point of reference in the Church's attitude towards immigrants, this attitude is clearly informed by an intrinsic superiority of Catholicism, which makes Ratzinger state that 'Catholics cannot even be tempted by Islam' (Ratzinger, 2000a).

Moreover, for the first time the Church not only comments upon this supposed superiority but goes so far as to put forward practical solutions to these 'challenges of our times' (Biffi, 2000), questioning, among other things, the role that the state should play in dealing with the issue. Although written in different styles and aiming to achieve different objectives, the core of ideas expressed in the *Dominus Iesus* and Biffi's pastoral note overlap and often coincide. They both consider different religions as 'ways of life' resulting from empirical experience and erroneous thoughts, whereas Catholicism is seen as the only religion capable of reaching the Truth through a rational process, using intelligence rather than superstition or common sense.

Regarding the criteria that the two representatives of the Church consider adequate to judge other beliefs, Ratzinger advocates that only the principle of Truth – rationality – represents a means to defeat contemporary relativism, while Biffi, even though agreeing on the principle of Truth, focuses more on a practical/utilitarian criterion to regulate relations with people who have different ideas of the good life. Both believe that the common characteristic that can promote and facilitate integration on the part of immigrants and the prerequisite to welcome them can only be Catholicism. The choice of Catholicism as the only solution to matters related to immigration is based on a common syllogism which both Ratzinger and Biffi construct, which has as its premise the fact that 'every man provided with logic and rationality sees the Truth and therefore is Catholic', and ends with the seemingly logical conclusion that 'every Italian is Catholic'. In Biffi's case the privileged treatment accorded to Catholic immigrants not only follows the principle of Truth but is also based on the practical distinction between peoples who are easy to assimilate and others who are judged to be impossible to assimilate, such as, for instance, Muslims.

Both Ratzinger and Biffi consider relativism as a sort of false tolerance, since they believe that tolerance coming from passive acceptance of different ideas of the good life is based on a fundamental mistake: the idea that different views have the same dignity and therefore nothing is absolute, as well as the fact that tolerance is extended not only to the individuals who hold a particular belief but also the content of that belief, whereas the only tolerance that remains faithful to the principle of Truth is a tolerance towards individuals.

Finally, they both agree that the Church has the right to accomplish its mission, which consists in proselytising: only after a sincere conversion is it possible to become a member of the Church and – this is a recurrent message in the cardinals' documents – 'within the Church nobody is a foreigner'. Recognising the superiority of Catholicism and becoming part of the Church seems to be the only way immigrants can shift from being 'others', foreigners, to becoming citizens, part of the Catholic family. The concept of the Catholic family, interestingly enough, seems to conflate and coincide with that of the nation, since not being a foreigner and therefore being Italian coincides with being Catholic, following a transitive property of the above-mentioned syllogism which 'proves' that every Italian is Catholic and is aimed at granting Italian citizenship to every Catholic.

On 18 April 2005, during the Missa pro eligendo Romano Pontefice, Ratzinger advocated that a clear and strong faith and an open belonging to the Catholic Church are today seen as a sign of fundamentalism, whereas a spreading relativism seems to be judged as the only appropriate attitude in this era in which people let themselves easily shift from one doctrine to another as the wind changes. This ironical statement already contains implicitly the claim for a stronger freedom of expression on the part of the Catholic Church, which implies a critique of the concept of political correctness, particularly when referring to the Muslim community (*De Magistris*, 2005).

While both authors tend erroneously to identify all Muslims with immigrants, Biffi, whose language is surely sharper than Ratzinger's, does not hesitate to depict Muslims as conspirators who are plotting to impose their religion on Europe, a mission that will only be revealed when they have enough power to prevail. This view, as we shall see in Chapter 3, is shared by the members of parties such as the Northern League, which exploited this image to make the call to public opinion for the preservation of a threatened Italianness more effective.

5 The first reactions to Biffi's pastoral note

On 6 September 2000, a day after Ratzinger's press conference on the *Dominus Iesus*, and a week before the release of Biffi's pastoral note, a letter by Catholic priest and politician Don Gianni Baget Bozzo to the Northern League leader Umberto Bossi was published in the League's newspaper, *La Padania*. Although it could be seen as a personal request to Bossi, the letter is central to the discussion on Islam as it indirectly asks to make the 'natural' alliance between the Church and the Northern League more institutionalised. Indeed, Baget Bozzo started by reminding Bossi of the role the League plays in defending Italian traditional identity, which is nowadays threatened by Islam. According to him, the threat is due to the fact that Islam is supported in our societies by political actors who, despite having diverse aims, see it as a minor evil. The reference is both to non-Catholics who consider Islam almost as a symbol of secularism (probably because of its fight against traditional Catholic symbols such as the crucifix), and to Catholics themselves who seem ready to give up their religion for a new faith, which consists in an unconditional love for the others (Baget Bozzo, 2000).

These two perspectives are, according to Baget Bozzo, vitiated by the same mistake: they consider individual Muslims rather than focus on their beliefs, which – the priest claims – constitutes the real problem. In the concluding part of his letter, he addresses the Catholic representatives for their misinterpretation of Christian charity, the only consequence of which will consist, in his view, in a growing power of Islam within Western countries. This, he insists, is a scenario made plausible if not very probable by the Church itself and its choice to grant Muslims places for their 'cult' without realising that 'every place given to them becomes a territory of Islam': a situation that will inevitably cause a deep, incurable fracture in Italian society (Baget Bozzo, 2000). Despite being similar in tone and content, Baget Bozzo's letter to Bossi cannot be seen as a reaction to Biffi's pastoral note which was presented to the press a week later. Nevertheless, this intervention can be considered as part of that movement, internal to the Catholic Church, which has seemingly identified immigration as the cause of the decline that Italian society is supposedly going through. This movement produced not only isolated official documents but a lively debate which was mirrored in interviews, sermons and seminars such as the one organised by pro-immigrant association 'Migrantes' on 30 September 2000, where the main speaker was Cardinal Biffi, determined, once again, to remark upon the ideas already expressed in his pastoral note.[128]

Interestingly, however, the first reaction to the *Dominus Iesus* and to *La città di San Petronio nel terzo millennio* did not come from the Church: neither Pope John Paul II nor other members of the Catholic hierarchy intervened either to criticise or praise them, at least until a more immediate reaction had come from the press and from the representatives of other religions. Both documents would probably have remained part of an internal discussion if Italian newspapers, including Catholic ones, had not reported extensively on them. The general impression in analysing these articles is a lack of moderate stances, as all interventions, both for and against Biffi, seem quite radical. Questioned by journalists immediately after the archbishop's press conference, most of the Church's representatives seemed strongly to support Biffi. Monsignor Alfredo Maria Garsia, head of the CEI Commission for immigration, praised the rational criteria elaborated by Biffi to allow immigrants into the country. A similar position was adopted by Don Oreste Benzi, Cardinal Angelo Sodano, then secretary of the Vatican State, and Monsignor Francesco Gioia, former secretary for the Council for the Pastoral Care of Migrants and Itinerant People. The latter, quoting from the 1998 pastoral note 'La Chiesa di fronte al razzismo. Per una società più fraterna' (CEI, 1989), focused on the need for social justice which is today threatened by certain minorities' attempts to impose their idea of the good life on a weaker majority (Anon. 2000c).

If these first interventions were aimed at supporting Biffi's document without entering into the details of its contents, a more theoretical debate started in the pages of the periodical *L'Espresso* on 28 September and developed until the first week of October. Throughout this period, the main newspapers addressed the contents of Biffi's note and its ideological orientation while the Pope, without commenting on Biffi's ideas, gave a series of speeches aimed at promoting the dialogue between different cultures, and the then Prime Minister Romano Prodi took part in the opening of a new Sikh temple near Reggio Emilia.

Giovanni Sartori, a political scientist, writer and columnist for *Corriere della Sera*, opened the debate from the pages of *L'Espresso*. In his articles, Sartori explained that his first reaction, when interviewed immediately after Biffi's press conference, was to take a distance from the bishop's words. Nonetheless, having read the whole document, the author reconsidered his own position while reflecting on how 'an intelligent faith is close to and agrees with the intelligence of reason'[129] (Sartori, 2000). Despite their different preoccupations and priorities – the good religion for Biffi and the good society for Sartori – the latter agrees with the idea that the state cannot distinguish between immigrants to welcome and immigrants to reject using criteria exclusively based on economic convenience or welfare requirements. Moreover, he agrees with the idea that the main problem with immigration is the presence of Muslims among the newly arrived. With specific reference to centre-left MP Livia Turco's negative reaction to Biffi's list of irreconcilable differences between 'us' and 'them', and her call for the need to remember not only what divides but also what unifies people with different beliefs, Sartori reminded Turco that the word 'Islam' means subjection and that the Arabic word for freedom – homayai – only expresses a condition of non-slavery. According to him, Biffi's depiction of a future scenario in which Islam will prevail is correct (Sartori, 2000). Finally, Sartori concluded that Biffi was one of the few who followed an ethic of responsibility, a morality that takes into account the consequences of our choices, whereas many, Pope John Paul II among others, base their judgements on an ethic of principles according to which what really counts is the intention, and unexpected or negative results can be ignored (ibid.).

On 1 October, Stefano Andini (2000) in his article for *L'Avvenire*, argued that Biffi's intervention unveiled worries and thoughts which were already implicit and shared by political parties as well as common citizens, and that the archbishop had managed to raise his voice against a spreading hypocrisy. According to him, Biffi was not stepping back from the Church's traditional message of Christian charity but was simply addressing a real situation. It was not by chance, Andini stated, that this position was shared by intellectuals such as Sartori himself, Ernesto Galli della Loggia and journalist Giuliano Ferrara who had never been particularly close to the official position of the Church. Moreover, he believed that the Muslim community would have protested against this document not because it was concerned about its members' integration into Italian society but rather because it could represent an obstacle to its claim for more 'privileges', which it was at that time discussing with the government.

After a few days, two articles signed by Leonardo Zega and Jenner Meletti, published in the mainstream newspapers *La Stampa* and *La Repubblica*, respectively, focused on the impossibility of obtaining the views of any representative of the Church on *La città di San Petronio nel terzo millennio*. After the first public reaction immediately after the press conference, the Catholic hierarchy seemingly stepped back and refused to comment on the polemic and debate raised by the document, insisting that the ones under scrutiny had to be considered an internal discussion. However, they seemed generally to support their 'colleague' Biffi, often inviting the journalists to read the document with more attention in order to realise that it represented a message of love rather than hatred towards 'the other' (Zega, 2000; Meletti, 2000).

While very few cardinals, bishops and parish priests, as reported by Zega and Meletti, accepted to be interviewed on the subject and none of them accepted any of the many invitations to participate in TV programmes during the days following Biffi's press conference, John Paul II decided to speak. This decision was interesting as it came when the discussion was still very heated, which is what led many to think he wanted to give his followers a clear direction. However, on 1 October, during the Sunday Angelus, the Pope talked about Ratzinger's *Dominus Iesus* rather than Biffi's pastoral note, despite the fact that the controversy at that time was mainly about Biffi's view. Contrary to expectations, the Pope never mentioned the bishop's pastoral note: instead, John Paul II proved more interested in trying to explain the real meaning of Ratzinger's thought. Considering Catholicism the only religion capable of reaching the Truth as superior to all other creeds, he stated, does not imply an arrogant and discriminatory attitude towards different faiths, towards which the Church maintains the respect and love that have always been fundamental in its doctrine. Moreover, the Pope remarked upon the importance of keeping the dialogue with the others as open and sincere as it had been during the few days in September when representatives of different Churches and states met in Lisbon with the aim of promoting an inter-religious dialogue (Anon. 2000h, 2000c).

The day after Biffi's press conference on his pastoral note, *La Padania* published an unsigned article on the document, which summarised the bishop's thought and focused on the need for the state to deal with the situation without attributing an inadequate responsibility to the Church, as well as on the Church's right to distinguish between its doctrine, based on the already mentioned Christian love for the other, and the issues linked to social justice that had to be dealt with by the government. *La Padania* insisted on defending Biffi's statement that, 'in the end one should recognise and openly state that the only citizens to whom the right of cultural freedom is denied are, indeed, the Catholics'[130] (Anon., 2000a). This polemical statement, which was later remarked upon by other members of the Catholic hierarchy, represents a key concept in the debate on immigration and a clear demand on the part of the Church and the League for more space for religion in the public sphere, a demand of recognition and compensation for the lack of visibility, which is traditionally put forward by minorities reacting to past discriminations.

Even though the first reactions of other Church members to Ratzinger's and Biffi's documents tended to be in favour of the opinions they expressed,[131] these positions did not represent the Church as a whole. It rather seems that even though most of the higher members of the Catholic hierarchy supported 'their colleagues', nevertheless many priests who worked with Catholic associations were critical of these interventions. However, the reaction of these individuals was not immediate, probably because they were not encouraged to speak up by the media, which were more interested in the authoritative views of important members of the Catholic hierarchy. An exception in this case is represented by Don Vitaliano Della Sala, a young priest in the parish of Sant'Angelo della Scala, close to the social centres and the Seattle anti-global movement, who took Biffi to court for incitement to racial hatred. According to Della Sala, Biffi's statements resulted from a deep ignorance of immigrants' conditions of life in Italy, as well as on a need to build or preserve a particular identity on the basis of a constant struggle against an enemy, which in the past was communism and today was represented by immigration and particularly Muslim immigration. According to the priest, the Church's opinion on issues relating to both legal and illegal immigrants was quite homogeneous and his voice represented a rupture and relatively isolated position in the Catholic mainstream position (Anon. 2000d).

Della Sala's reaction was the strongest, even when compared to that of representatives of other religions such as the Waldensian theologian Paolo Ricca and the leaders of the Muslim community of Bologna, Altounji M. Radwan and Daniele Parracino. Ricca had intervened on Ratzinger's *Nota sull'espressione 'Chiese sorelle'* the day after it was released, but did not comment on Biffi's document, which was published a week later; nor did he express his opinion later on, when the discussion became of central interest in the media. This quiet reaction can be plausibly explained by the fact that immigration was not the main concern of the Waldensian community, since most of its members are Italian, and therefore did not perceive themselves as the target of the document. In his response to Ratzinger's note as well as to the *Dominus Iesus*, Ricca defined them as standing in open contradiction to the spirit of the Second Vatican Council which, according to him, 'Rome' seemed to have forgotten. Moreover, he embarked on a critique of the doctrinal contents of the document and claimed the right to define the Waldensian community as a Church, basing this right on a brief analysis of the Gospel (Ricca, 2000).

More concerned with the issue of immigration was the declaration of Pallavicini, leader of the CO.RE.IS,[132] who remarked upon the dialogue developed with Italian institutions and firmly hoped that documents such as those published in September with their insistence on the superiority of Catholicism and the danger of immigration would not interfere with the ongoing process of mutual understanding between the Italian state and the CO.RE.IS. Despite the quiet tone of his reply and his intention to keep the dialogue open, Pallavicini underlined the confusion and contradiction in Biffi's use of terms such as Muslim and immigrants, which were not necessarily synonymous. This was evident in his own case, since he is the first Italian Muslim citizen. Moreover, the CO.RE.IS claimed that the Church's novel attitude towards other religions was in open and clear contradiction to the message in favour of a dialogue given by Pope John Paul II in 1986 during the inter-religious meeting in Assisi (CO.RE.IS, 2000).

In a similar fashion, the Muslim community of the city of Bologna called for a stop to the controversy which, as they stated, they themselves were not interested in fomenting. They rather took their chance to thank Prime Minister Romano Prodi and Minister for Social Solidarity Livia Turco for their support for the Muslim cause (Anon. 2000e, 2000f). Indeed, Prodi and Turco were among the few politicians who, immediately after the publication of Biffi's pastoral note, intervened to reassert the laity of the state as a fundamental trait of contemporary democracies in general and of Italy in particular. Romano Prodi intervened in the debate the day after Biffi had criticised, among other things, those Catholics who held positions of leadership in the country. The cardinal had attacked them for their lack of commitment in supporting their Church and their attitude of ignoring what, in his view, was happening in Italy, which he summed up as a condition whereby 'practising Catholicism in Italy has become impossible'[133] (Anon. 2000f).

Prodi never mentioned Biffi directly while taking part in a ceremony for the opening of a Sikh temple in Novellara, not far from Bologna, on 1 October 2000. He rather referred to Cardinal Carlo Maria Martini, whose position on immigration was diametrically opposed to Biffi's. Indeed Prodi, quoting Martini, remarked upon the importance of values such as difference, coexistence and pluralism, and stated that 'a society that is not plural and multiethnic is destined to fall back on itself'[134] (Anon. 2000g). Moreover, Prodi stated that in Europe all citizens have the same rights, regardless of their condition as immigrants, as long as they respect the law: thus Italy could be the home of everyone who worked for an 'harmonic coexistence', as Martini defined it. The opening of the Sikh temple – with the participation of a representative of the Muslim community, Professor Mahmoud Salem Elsheilch – had also been an occasion to talk about the law on freedom of religion presented by Prodi on 3 July 1997 and under Parliament's scrutiny at that time.

After this first outburst, the Catholic representatives waited for the situation to calm down before intervening again. It is interesting to note that the whole discussion started suddenly, developed vehemently with a crossfire of articles, press conferences, counter-reactions, and declined quietly all within a period of two weeks, after which things seemed to be back to normal and the 'incident' forgotten, albeit only apparently, if one considers the impact it had on the subsequent debate on identity and immigration.

The obvious question concerns the reasons why all the documents that created the controversy were written in the same month and why, after the first reactions aimed at denouncing this 'clash of civilisations', the debate faded away. There are two main logical answers to this question. First, the origin of the whole discussion was without doubt Ratzinger's *Dominus Iesus*, which opened a new era for the Church, as it became less concerned with 'political correctness' and more determined to raise its voice, a determination probably facilitated by the spreading awareness of a progressive decline of Catholicism, as openly recognised by both Ratzinger and Biffi. Moreover, Ratzinger's point of view, which has always been decisive for the Church's official positions on certain issues, started to emerge more openly, despite being seemingly far from the Pope's perspective on the same themes. I argue that what made it possible for Ratzinger to speak in the way he did about the superiority of the Catholic Church was precisely his awareness of the role of John Paul II as the paladin of dialogue between different religions. The idea of brotherhood promoted by the Pope through inter-religious meetings and marches, and his interpretation of difference as enriching and, not least, his personality and attitude towards his followers made it easier for Ratzinger to use a different tone. It could be said that it is precisely because of this more open attitude towards immigration that Ratzinger could take a different role in the debate.

It also has to be said that the Church has always relied on Ratzinger's knowledge and theological rigour in the redefinition of the Catholic doctrine and its adjustment to different historical and political times. In a certain sense, the cardinal's cold and rational approach was moderated by the Pope's personal charisma. It could be said that Ratzinger's intervention gave an indication of how the Church's position on certain issues would have been much more radical if he had been the Pope, as confirmed after his ascension to the papal throne, which exposed to what extent he was more interested in Italian affairs than his predecessor.

A second hypothesis to explain why the debate exploded so suddenly in the autumn of 2000, and faded just as rapidly a few months later, can be linked to the fact that 2000 was the Jubilee year, and therefore an important occasion for the Church to celebrate Catholicism and somehow re-launch it. As proven by the documents previously analysed, the Catholic hierarchy seemed aware of a progressive 'drop of tension', as Biffi defined it, meaning a decline, at least in terms of active participation of the believers. The Jubilee could then represent, or ought to represent, a chance to remind Italians of their Catholic origins and their natural and traditional belonging to Christianity.

This call for a return to tradition was based on different strategies. As mentioned above, if Wojtyla's role as Pope was that of the father (or the grandfather as he had been defined during the various World Youth Days), Ratzinger had the more difficult role of the theologian, whose duty was that of clearing away theoretical misunderstanding and clarifying the implications of the dogma, regardless of the consequences this 'mission' could bring. Ratzinger's speech can be seen as part of this strategy, which often seems to be based on a constant warning of the danger represented by the 'other'. In this sense, as the rebel parish priest who spoke against Biffi argued, the Church always had to define itself against an enemy, previously communism and today immigration.

To conclude, despite the turn in the Church's rhetoric on otherness, and despite the lack of open criticism of Biffi's pastoral note and Ratzinger's *Dominus Iesus*, a brief overview of the post-2000 interventions on immigration on the part of the Church shows that both Pope John Paul II and representatives of the CEI Pastoral for Migrants have maintained their traditional attitude of openness towards the newly arrived. In November 2004, indeed, Bishop Lino Bortolo Belotti, president of the Commissione Episcopale per le Migrazioni, authored the official message for the 91st World Youth Day: 'Il mondo come casa: dalla diffidenza all'accoglienza.' The document established for the first time the link between Italian emigration since 1914 and the arrival of 'thousands of men, women, children ready to embark on expensive and dangerous journeys to reach the "Garden of Eden they had dreamt about": Europe'.[135] Citing the Gospel, it remarked upon the need to look at the immigrant 'with benevolence, sympathy, as a neighbour, as a human being and therefore as a carrier of values and enrichment, not as a stranger, a potential enemy, as the law seems to look at him/her or as a trouble to be pushed away, but as a member of a united family'.[136]

Leaving aside for a moment the criticism directed at the laws on immigration, what is interesting in this document is that it seemed to focus on specific categories of immigrants, among them those of Roma and Sinti, 'often objects of contempt'.[137] However, it referred exclusively to those immigrants who are only temporarily present in the territory as, for instance, people working in local fairs and circuses or on cruise ships. In this sense, despite the welcoming spirit behind the document, grouping the Roma and the Sinti with other groups characterised by a nomadic lifestyle seems quite a superficial generalisation, since the presence of Roma and Sinti communities in Italy dates back as far as the 13th century and many of them are Italian citizens, and therefore they cannot be compared to temporary migrants. Moreover, if Roma and Sinti have often been at the centre of heated debates on 'the other', this has not been the case for the other categories taken into account by the CEI. Grouping together these very different categories of migrants under the label of 'temporary' only has the effect of promoting tolerance for those who are simply passing through the country, who incidentally are far less discriminated against than those who decide to settle permanently in Italy. As the next chapter will show, the immigrants who are looked at with suspicion and who are marginalised more within Italian society are those perceived as a threat precisely because of their intention to settle in the country for good.

This mechanism of temporary sympathy or tolerance for passer-by immigrants has proven quite dangerous, as for instance in the case of Albanians, welcomed upon their arrival and discriminated against once it became clear that they intended to stay and start a new life in Italy. In this sense, even if the document signed by Belotti explicitly encouraged Italians to welcome these immigrants and therefore implicitly distanced itself from positions such as those expressed by Biffi and Ratzinger, somehow it plays with a fake problem, and therefore can be considered as more welcoming only in its intentions and its general rhetoric. Moreover, even if it seemed to protect Roma and Sinti, it actually does not do them a favour as it presents them as temporary and therefore to be temporarily welcomed rather than methodically integrated. In this sense, these immigrants have to be loved and treated according to Christian charity in everyday life but no debate is opened on their long-term presence and need/right to integrate. It should also be added that migrants of Muslim faith were not mentioned in these more recent documents.

The case of Pope John Paul II is quite different and provides an example of that welcoming rhetoric based on the importance of the dialogue, which allowed Ratzinger to assume a more radical position, as mentioned earlier. John Paul II intervened officially on the theme of immigration in 2004, with a message written for the World Day of the Migrant and the Refugee. The document focuses on the integration of the newly arrived, intended not as an assimilation, which neglects the specific cultural identity of the immigrants, nor as a marginalisation, which could lead to a situation of apartheid. According to Pope John Paul II, integration is 'knowing the others more in depth. It is a long-term process, aimed at constructing societies and cultures [...] The migrants, within this process, are committed to taking the necessary step leading to social inclusion, such as learning the language and adapting to the laws and the rules in the workplace, in order to avoid the creation of an exacerbated diversity'[138] (John Paul II, 2004).

The document also remarks upon the conflicts created by the coexistence of different identities, which can only be resolved by finding the 'just balance between the respect for one's own identity and the recognition of the identity of the others'.[139] The solution put forward by the Polish Pope was that of promoting an open dialogue 'between people of different cultures in a context of pluralism which goes beyond mere tolerance to reach a feeling of sympathy'.[140] Finally, the Pope agreed with Ratzinger's belief that 'In order to be coherent with themselves, Christians cannot give up their mission to spread the Gospel to all human beings (Mark 15,15). They have to do that, clearly, respecting other people's conscience'[141] (John Paul II, 2004).

To a certain extent, the new position of the Church on the issue of immigration, marked by Ratzinger's *Dominus Iesus* and Biffi's pastoral note, set an important precedent and contributed to legitimising an exclusionary rhetoric later exploited by Right-wing political parties such as the Northern League.

However, it is not possible to consider the Church as a united front lined up against immigration. Solidarity and openness towards immigrants have been expressed occasionally by institutions such as the CEI and by the Pope himself even after 2000, regardless of the fact that they were occasionally overshadowed in the debate by the more radical anti-immigrant interventions.

6 Conclusions

The analysis of the interventions on the part of the Catholic hierarchy in the debate on immigration shows a new trend in the Church's attitude towards the newly arrived. For decades and until 2000 the Church's reaction towards immigrants had always been inspired by Christian charity, according to which others had to be loved, welcomed and possibly helped in their needs, an official position noted in the documents and pastoral notes on immigration written until the end of the 1990s. Ratzinger's *Dominus Iesus* and Biffi's pastoral note represent a dramatic turn in the Church's rhetoric on identity and immigration.

Through the account of the transformation undertaken by mainstream religions since the late 1980s, this chapter has tried to frame this new attitude within the struggle of Churches seeking to overcome an acknowledged decline and (re)gain power. In the case of the Italian Catholic Church, the first step in this new strategy was to claim for recognition of Catholicism as superior to other beliefs, which are defined as mere 'ways of life' based on empirical experience or, even worse, simply superstition. The documents analysed argue that every human being provided with rationality necessarily has to be Catholic. Despite the fact that the syllogism is based on a non-demonstrable and non-self-evident premise, the final equation identifies all Italians with Catholics. The battle fought by the Church becomes then a battle that has to be supported by the whole nation, since, according to Cardinal Biffi and Cardinal Ratzinger, it is not only the Church but Italian identity as well which is threatened.

Both Ratzinger and Biffi argue that the only duty of the Church is evangelisation: this process of enlightenment, they claim, is today made particularly difficult, if not impossible, by the 'false tolerance' typical of our societies. The idea that different interpretations of the good life can be attributed equal value results in an aggressive attitude on the part of non-Catholic individuals and groups towards the Church. Hence the latter is portrayed as a victim and the only subject to which the right of freedom of speech is denied or whose freedom of expression is defined by others as totalitarian and intolerant. Having redefined itself against the other, the Muslim enemy, and its role as a victim, the Church appropriates the strategy typical of traditional minorities, which consists in a dual demand to the state for a positive freedom (being given more space in the public sphere), and a negative one (denying other groups the same right). According to the literature on identity and otherness, minorities claim protection from the state in the name of past discrimination.

The Church, in a diametrically opposite way, carries on these requests in the name of its glorious role in the past of the country. At a time when it seems to be struggling against an openly recognised decline in popularity, Islam is invoked to gain visibility and confirm a privileged role within the country.

Despite the fact that the Church's main interest is not the arrival of foreigners with different cultures and religions, its contribution to the debate on immigration is of central importance. In filling the gaps left in the public discussion by the lack of participation of Italian intellectuals and by the still confused position of the political class, the Church emerged as a leading voice on the theme, as can be proven by the analysis of its interventions, particularly during the autumn of 2000, the year of the Jubilee. In this sense, it followed a mechanism which, in the last three decades, all mainstream religious groups in Europe and the United States have followed – namely, presenting themselves as 'global pastors', neutral state consultants on ethical matters, which now also include immigration. In order to acquire this new role and start a dialogue with the government, the Catholic Church has developed new communication strategies, based on a language and rhetoric which privilege terms linked with human rights rather than the Gospel.

As this chapter tried to prove, despite its acknowledgement of the need to distinguish between its own responsibilities and those of the state, the Church also put forward practical solutions to deal with the situation, proving very influential in the state's decision making in matters related to immigration, particularly since Ratzinger's ascent to the papal throne. Although controversial, 'rational selection', based on Catholicism as a guarantee for a smoother assimilation, promoted by Biffi, represents one of the few clear and coherent criteria set until now. While enabling a rhetoric of disengagement, the Church seemingly aims to replace the state by granting immigrants citizenship, following a principle of 'selective solidarity' according to which all immigrants have to be loved but only those who are ready to abandon their own religious identity to embrace Catholicism can become Italian.

However, it is important to remark upon the fact that what is new in these documents is the rhetoric of victimhood and the Church's internal division, whereas in terms of signs of doctrinal coherence with previous official documents issued since the Second Vatican Council, the difference is not that striking. The documents of the Church, as already mentioned, are characterised by their incorporation of principle established in previous encyclicals, pastoral letters and speeches. This is the case of the views on the relationship between dialogue and evangelisation, or the key issue of reciprocity in granting foreigners freedom of religion. In this sense, the 'revolution' consists in the change of linguistic register and rhetoric strategy.

The same can be said of the difference between the approach to the issue of immigration and religious diversity of Pope John Paul II and Pope Benedict XVI. If it is true that the two pontiffs were closer than appeared to be the case in terms of doctrine, it is also clear that their ability to communicate, their interpretations of solidarity and Christian love – at least as they emerge from their public discourses – seem profoundly different and were perceived as such by public opinion. This difference could well be ascribed to the diverse roles that Pope John Paul II and his 'guardian of the doctrine' played, the former as the father of all Catholics, an old and ill father, and the latter as the intransigent warden of the Truth.

The interest of Ratzinger in Italian affairs, which can be read as a joint attempt of the cardinal and the Italian bishops to turn Italy into an export model of Catholicism is, nonetheless, rather clear. As the perspective chosen to discuss the interpretation of the ideas of identity and otherness in this book is one that heavily relies on the importance of rhetoric and discourse as means employed to shape both 'reality' and public perception of such reality, the impact of this rhetoric, regardless of the intentions of the actors who put it forward, cannot be ignored. As will be argued in the last chapter of this book, the Church's strategy and language have been borrowed and exploited by the Northern League, which probably represents the only other strong voice in the contemporary debate on immigration. As a consequence, the Church's response to immigration, based on a recurrent use of terms such as foreigner and citizen, Catholic and Italian, Muslim and immigrant, as well as its constructed dual role as victim, but also as a point of reference for the country, indirectly contributed to increase public anxiety and shared concerns. Such influence has to be understood within the political convergence between the CEI and the Italian Right, which has been illustrated above.

If Biffi represents an exception – a significant exception, as the archbishop's document was the one that featured most prominently in the national media – then it can be argued that even in its most uncontroversial documents on Islam, the Church does not seem to have gone far from the idea of a society organised in concentric circles, as described in the *Nostra Aetate*. Here, indeed, Catholics occupy the inner circle, surrounded by Christians and, progressively departing from the core, by Jews and, last, by Muslims, placed in the outside circle. The documents analysed seem to suggest that the only principle according to which it is possible to move closer to the 'family of God' and be included in that core represented by Catholics/Italians and the only means to no longer be a 'foreigner' is still conversion to Catholicism. This can be considered the case at least during the period taken into account here. The effect of Benedict XVI's resignation as Pope and the influence on the debate under scrutiny of the election of Jorge Mario Bergoglio in 2013 will be addressed in the last chapter of this book.

Notes

1 From a speech given by Stefano Jacini, member of the Italian Constituent Assembly, during the discussion on the Constitution and in particular on article 5 regarding the inclusion of the Lateran Pacts in the text (14 March 1947).
2 'The city of Saint Petronius in the third millennium.'
3 'Pastoral note on the expression "sister Churches".'

4 With the exception of a few distinguished Catholic personalities such as Cardinal Carlo Maria Martini, archbishop of Milan, and Dionigi Tettamanzi, secretary of the CEI.

5 Religious institutions, according to Berger, can react to modernity/secularisation by employing two alternative strategies: rejection, for instance through religious revolution, or indeed adaptation, for instance by creating religious subcultures (Berger, 1999: 4).

6 For what concerns the role of religion in Western democracies, the United States and Europe are generally seen as paradigms of the two main models of relationship between Churches and the state. The main object of debate is which of the two models (the United States where the religious and political spheres often overlap or even influence and legitimate each other, and Europe, with all the different degrees of secularisation, in most cases seen as an ideal and hard-to-reach objective) represents the exception. On this issue see Taylor, 2007; Hayes, 1995; Hammond *et al.* 1994; Kellstedt *et al.*, 1994. On the dialogue on the resurgence of religion in Europe between scholars who think that the process of secularisation is still holding in the old continent and those who argue that religiosity is back at the forefront, see: Chirico, 1985; Shupe, 1990; Berger, 1999; Norris and Inglehart, 2004.

7 Gramsci, 1971: 312–13. For a better understanding of Gramsci's interpretation of religion as an ideology as well as a means for rebellion, see: Billings, 1990; Kertzer, 1980; Fulton, 1987.

8 On civil religion, see: Bellah, R.N., *The Broken Covenant: American Civil Religion in Time of Trial* (1975) Chicago, IL: University of Chicago Press; Coleman, J.A., 'Civil Religion', *Sociology of Religion*, Vol. 31, No. 2 (1970): 67–77; Davie, 2011; Westerlund, 1996. In Italian: Bottoni, 2000; Paganini and Tortarolo, 2004; Rusconi, 1999. For an historical overview of the concept of civil religion, see Gentile, 2007.

9 On Habermas's discussion of Rawls in relation to the role of religious views in the public sphere, see Lingua, 2010.

10 See also: Marks and Wilson, 2000; Nelsen *et al.* 2001; Durand, 2002.

11 On the rise and impact of Christian democratic parties, see: Fogarty and Dame, 1957; Hanley, 1996; Kalyvas, 1996, 1998; Van Hecke and Gerard, 2004; Durand, 2013.

12 For a definition of interest groups, their role in policy making and their influence on public opinion, see: Berry, 1997; Cigler and Loomis, 2011; Kollman, 1998.

13 Panebianco's direct cause-effect link between the Church's will and the creation of the DC in Italy is controversial, and is rejected by a number of scholars who believe the connection to be much more subtle. For instance, see Giovagnoli, 1996. For a more detailed analysis of the factors accounting for the relations between the Church's agenda and the rise in fortunes/decline of the Italian Christian Democratic Party, see Allum, 1997.

14 Applying this interpretative model to Italy would also imply an acknowledgment of the deeper internal cohesion and orthodoxy of minority religions such as, indeed, Islam.

15 As we shall see later on in this chapter, the number of ecclesiastical documents devoted to the theme of pastoral care for Catholics living in non-Catholic countries is representative of the importance of the issue for the Catholic hierarchy.

16 As Kalyvas (1998: 299–300) explains, 'Universalistic appeal has always been a primary concern for the church, and indeed the contention that "The Church cannot become a party because it is common to everyone" was included in the 1890 papal encyclical *Sapientiae Christianae*'. However, it has to be noted that such theoretical disengagement from direct interventions in politics does not reflect the current strategy of the Italian Church, which has intervened on several occasions in a number of political and social issues, as this chapter will show.

17 Source: *Dizionario Garzanti Linguistica*, Universale, 2005.

18 For what concerns recognition of minority religions in Italy on the part of the state, agreements have been signed with the Jewish community in 1987, with the Orthodox Christian metropolitan in Venice in 1991, with the Baptists in 1994, and with the Italian Buddhists and Jehovah's Witnesses in 2000. In 2002 a Parliament discussion was introduced with the aim of finding an agreement with the Italian Muslim community as well (Donovan, 2003: 103).

19 For a more detailed description of the state-Church relationship in Italy, see: Margiotta Broglio, 1991, 1996; Acerbi, 2003. On the issue of relations between the Church and the 'political community' according to Canon Law, see Dalla Torre, 1996.

20 Secretary of state for the Holy See, a role corresponding to that held in Italy by the minister of foreign affairs.

21 In Italian, 'libera Chiesa in libero stato'.

22 The Act of Guarantee was aimed at finding a compromise on the unresolved 'Roman question'. It recognized the Pope's independence granting him the rights of a sovereign, such as immunity from arrest and trial and the allocation of diplomatic representatives. Regarding territorial ownership, the Pope retained the Vatican and Lateran palaces in Rome as well as Castel Gandolfo. Even though part of these properties was located within the Italian State, they were all exempted from taxes. The Pope was also offered compensation for the loss of the lands now under the jurisdiction of the Italian State. Pius IX rejected the offer and proclaimed himself a 'political prisoner'. The *non expedit*, the prohibition for Catholics to take part in the election, was launched for the same year and repeated in 1874, becoming official and 'permanent' in 1886 (Clark, 2008: 103).

23 A different matter is that of informal agreements between the Church and Italian governments, such as the Gentiloni agreement. The expression 'Gentiloni pact' refers to the secret deal between Italian Prime Minister Giovanni Giolitti and President of the Catholic Electoral Union Ottorino Gentiloni. Its substantially pragmatic aim was that of contrasting the Socialist Party in general elections. Giolitti's liberal candidates were granted the support of Catholic voters in return for their backing of Catholic policies, with the result of granting liberals a large majority in Parliament. The ban on Catholic voting was hence lifted by the Church. On the embarrassment and the political consequences that followed once the pact had been revealed, after the elections, see: Cotta, 1992; Coppa, 1967.

24 Article 1 of the Statuto Albertino enacted on 4 March 1848 and destined to last until 1944–46 established that Catholic religion was 'the only state religion'. Ten days later, on 14 March 1848, the 'Statuto Fondamentale del governo temporale degli Stati della Chiesa' was issued by Pope Pius IX, which provided for the Catholic religion to be the necessary condition to be granted political rights by the state.

25 '[T]itoli azionari.'

26 One of the three tribunals of the Catholic Church (1910 *New Catholic Dictionary*, www.studylight.org/dic/ncd/view.cgi?n=8831). See Dalla Torre, 2013.

27 See: Bolgiani, 2009; De Franciscis, 1989; Spotts and Wieser, 1986.

28 Law 25 March 1985/121, 'Modificazioni al Concordato lateranense dell'11 Febbraio 1929 tra la Repubblica Italiana e la Santa Sede'.

29 The Italian Episcopal Conference, a permanent assembly of Italian bishops, was founded in 1972. See Sguazzardo, P., 'I cinquant'anni della Conferenza Episcopale Italiana: alle origini di una storia. Nota sulla relazione tenuta dal prof. Andrea Riccardi in occasione della XLIX Assemblea generale della CEI', *Rassegna di Teologia*, Vol. 43 (2002): 881–91.

30 On the controversy related to a further revision of the Concordat, see the exchange between MP Enrico Boselli and CEI representatives Archbishop Giuseppe Betori and Cardinal Camillo Ruini. The heated discussion revolved around the role of the Church in the political and social life of the country. On the one hand the Church's hierarchy claimed the right of letting the 'civil nature' of Catholicism emerge

within Italian society; on the other hand many MPs argued that the interference of the Church in Italian matters was unacceptable and had not manifested itself to the same degree in any other European country, thus turning the case of Italy into an anomaly (Anon. 'La Chiesa e la proposta di revisione dei Patti Lateranensi. "Sul Concordato la discussione è chiusa"', *Corriere della Sera*, 16 November 2005; Meli, 2005). Right from the immediate aftermath of the agreement of 1984, the CEI claimed it was excluded from the negotiation and its representatives argued that fundamental issues were left out of the agreement, particularly the promotion of the values of life, family and the protection of the territory and its culture (CEI, 'Dichiarazione sull'accordo di revisione del Concordato lateranense', 18 febbraio 1984, *Enchiridion della Conferenza Episcopale Italiana*, Vol. 3 (1980–85), Bologna, EDB, 1989: 931). Moreover, immediately after the signature of the agreement, the CEI expressed its doubts on the form (a concordat) chosen to regulate the relations between the Church and an increasingly plural Italian State (see Margiotta Broglio, F., 'Modifiche degli articoli 7, 8, 19 della costituzione e prospettive di revisione del concordato lateranense', in *Individuo, gruppi, confessioni religiose nello stato democratico. Atti del Convegno nazionale di diritto ecclesiastico, Siena 30 novembre–2 dicembre 1972* (1973) Milano: Giuffrè, 1027–43, cited in Astorri, 2004).

31 As Furlong (1996: 59–60) explains, the success of the Christian Democratic Party, which 'provided every Prime Minister from December 1945 to June 1981 and several thereafter' was not exclusively due to the – nevertheless fundamental – close relationship with the Vatican, but also to the support of the Allies aimed at fighting the communist threat and to another factor which emerged later on in Italian political history: 'the state participation system led by state holding companies IRI and ENI, the Fund for Southern Development (Cassa per il Mezzogiorno) and the uncontrolled extension of state-supported occupational pension schemes'. Donovan (2003: 101) also argues that the DC, far from being the 'long arm' of the Church, was shown in the early days of the Republic to be independent from direct clerical and papal influence, as proven by its strategical political alliances, which included coalitions with the Marxist parties and with the lay parties (for instance, Liberals and Social Democrats). According to the scholar, amid the lack of strict dependence of the DC from the Church, the relationship between the two was still visible and the party later on was to become much more ambiguous in this sense, at least until the 1970s. Others, such as Pace (1995), have written of the supposed Christian political unity as a myth. On the Italian DC, see also: Cappadocia, 1961; Piretti, 1995.

32 For an historical account of the impact of Catholicism on Italian civil society since the 1950s, see Impagliazzo, 2004.

33 For instance, *Azione cattolica*.

34 This interpretation, however, does not take into account the 'red' (communist) subculture also dominant in Italy.

35 Another example is the pastoral note on non-negotiable values discussed at the CEI Permanent Commission in March 2006 and addressed to Italian MPs (Ceccarini, 2009: 190).

36 Ruini was elected general secretary of the CEI in 1986 and served as its president from 2001 to 2007.

37 This strategy proved successful as other Episcopal Conferences in countries such as Spain and Portugal started looking at the Italian case as a point of reference and following the example of the Italian bishops, for instance organising public rallies and demonstrations to promote the value of the traditional family and against the granting of rights to homosexuals. On this issue, see Magister, 2007.

38 In the case of the police, such trust seems to be rooted in the growing anxieties relating to criminality and immigration (Diamanti, 2014).

39 On the difference between a variety of documents (legal documents, pastoral notes, encyclicals), see De Paolis, 2005.

40 Formally, the first document is the Constitution *Exul Familia*, published in 1952 by Pius XII, which is part of the Canon Law and the importance of which resides in its normative and historical approach. The Constitution, which represents the first collection of laws aimed at dealing with human mobility, also retraces the Church's past fragmentary interventions on single issues related to the migration of Christians at a time, the aftermath of World War II, when migratory movements had started to grow again. The limit of the Constitution was that it focused almost exclusively on the role of missionaries and priests abroad (Sabbarese, in De Paolis, 2005).

41 Decree *Christus Dominus*, 28 October 1965, N. 18.

42 It should also be noted that for a long time the term 'migration' referred to internal migration. This shows how much the cardinals who authored these documents had in mind the case of Italy, which, between the 1950s and the 1970s, has witnessed a conspicuous movement of people from the South to the North of its territory. The same thing can be said about a number of texts that refer to multiculturalism and the discrimination of migrants, where both allude to the difficulties faced by Southerners working in the more industrialised North. For an example of the norms regulating internal migration, see: Acta et documenta, Series II, Vol. II, Part III: 729–31.

43 Acta synodalia, Vol. II, Part IV: 811–19. The original text lists the following categories: 'Homines quamplurimi, sive singuli sive turmatim, per annum, animi relaxionis vel rusticationis vel sanitatis curandae causa, suas domos ad tempus relinquere solent, externas civitates aut montes aut marium lacuumque oras petitur' (816).

44 Acta synodalia, Vol. III, Part IV: 140; Part VI: 169. On the issue of the relation between the Universal Church and local churches dealing with migrants, see De Paolis, 2005; Corecco, 1987.

45 Declaration *Nostra Aetate*, 28 October 1965, §5; John Paul II, Message for the Day of the Migrant and the Refugee *Nella Chiesa nessuno è straniero*, 25 July 1995, Par. 4; Pontificio consiglio per la giustizia e per la pace, *La Chiesa di fronte al razzismo*, 3 November 1988, §§1, 8.

46 John Paul II, encyclical *Laborem Exercens*, 14 September 1981; Pontificio Consiglio per la Pastorale dei Migranti e degli Itineranti, 'Chiesa e mobilità umana', 26 May 1978, Part II: §1.

47 John Paul II, Speech for the World Day of Migrants, 'Gravi, dolorose e complesse le condizioni le condizioni delle famiglie coinvolte nella dura situazione dell'emigrante', 15 August 1986.

48 Pontificio Consiglio della Pastorale per i Migranti e gli Itineranti, 'Chiesa e mobilità umana', 26 May 1978.

49 Ibid.

50 John Paul II, Speech for the World Day of the Pastoral for Migrants, 'La Chiesa testimone e promotrice dell'integrazione dei migranti', 17 October 1985.

51 Commissione teologica internazionale, 'Fede e inculturazione', 8 October 1988, §1; 'Il Cristianesimo e le religioni', 30 September 1996, §1.

52 John Paul II, Message for World Peace Day, 'Dialogo tra le culture per una civiltà dell'amore e della pace', 1 January 2001, §8.

53 Pontificio Consiglio della Cultura, 'Per una pastorale della cultura', 23 May 1999, §21.

54 John Paul II, Opening speech for the IV General Episcopal Conference of Latin-American Bishops, 'Nuova evangelizzazione, promozione umana, cultura cristiana: Gesù Cristo ieri, oggi e domani', 12 October 1992, §22.

55 John Paul II, 'Fede, speranza e carità nella prospettiva del dialogo religioso', 29 November 2000, §9.

56 'Chiesa e mobilità umana', §5.

57 'La Chiesa testimone e promotrice dell'integrazione dei migranti', 17 October 1985, §4.

58 'Gravi, dolorose e complesse le condizioni delle famiglie coinvolte nella dura situazione dell'emigrante', §3.

59 'La Chiesa di fronte al razzismo', Part IV: 29; encyclical *Pacem in Terris*, 11 April 1963.

60 Episcopal Commission for Migration and Tourism, 'Ero forestiero e mi avete ospitato', 4 October 1993, Part I: 10.

61 John Paul II, 'Nella Chiesa nessuno è straniero e la Chiesa non è straniera a nessun uomo e in nessun luogo', 25 July 1995, §3.

62 The fact that Islam is addressed in this encyclical depends on the pressure coming from a number of members of the Second Vatican Council who believed that if the relation with the Jewish had been addressed, the same had to be done for Muslims.

63 To be more precise, it should be said that the dialogue the Church aims to build has its interlocutors in individuals of the Muslim religion, whereas Islam is never mentioned.

64 See also John Paul II, 'Operatori di pace nel pensiero e nell'azione, con la mente e col cuore, rivolti all'unità dell'intera famiglia umana', 27 October 1986.

65 See also John Paul II, 'Lo spirito di Dio e "i semi di verità" presenti nelle religioni non cristiane', 9 September 1998, §1.

66 This attitude to recognise the 'common values' expressed in the *Nostra Aetate*, features also in *Ad Gentes* and *Lumen Gentium*; its importance is also stated in more recent documents, such as, for instance, that published by the Pontificio Concilio per il dialogo religioso on 19 May 1991, entitled 'Dialogo e annuncio' (§§16–17).

67 See also, John Paul II, 'Fede, speranza e carità nella prospettiva del dialogo religioso', 2000.

68 Salvation can only be achieved through the sacraments. The principle of the 'Extra Ecclesia nulla salus' (literally, 'there cannot be salvation outside the Church') is a fundamental pillar of Catholicism. The *Dominus Iesus*, witten in 2000 by Cardinal Joseph Ratzinger, remarks on this concept as we shall see in detail in the next section of this chapter.

69 'Dialogo e annuncio', 19 May 1991, §§28–31.

70 John Paul II, encyclicals *Fides et ratio*, 14 September 1998.

71 Paul VI, Apostolic exhortations *Evangelii Nuntiandi*, 8 December 1975.

72 'Il Cristianesimo e le religioni', 30 September 1996. On the relation between Truth and dialogue, see also the encyclical *Ecclesiam suam*, 6 August 1964.

73 On the concept of 'enculturation', see: 'Per una pastorale della cultura', 23 May 1999, I: 2–5; and *Ecclesia in Africa*, 14 September 1995; the encyclical *Redemptoris mission*, 7 December 1990, §52.

74 'Dialogo e annuncio', C: 42. On the dialogue as a 'preparatio evangelica', see 'Fede e inculturazione', 8 October 1988.

75 Commissione teologica internazionale, 'Fede e inculturazione', 8 October 1988, III: 14; encyclical *Centesimus annus*, 1 May 1991, §21.

76 'Per una pastorale della cultura.'

77 'La Chiesa di fronte al razzismo.'

78 'Dialogo e annuncio.'

79 John Paul II, Message for World Peace Day, 'Dialogo tra le culture per una civiltà dell'amore e della pace', 1 January 2001, §14.

80 'Chiesa e mobilità umana', Part I: 2.

81 John Paul II, speech for the World Congress on Migration, 'Migrazioni: l'impegno della Chiesa', 15 March 1979, §1; on the difference between evangelisation and colonialism, see 'La Chiesa di fronte al razzismo'.

82 'La Chiesa di fronte al razzismo', §11.

83 In English, 'Note on the expression "sister Churches"'.

84 Dichiarazione circa l'unicità e l'universalità salvifica di Gesù Cristo e della Chiesa.

85 In English, 'The city of Saint Petronius in the third millennium'.
86 '[P]urtroppo recentemente l'uso di tale espressione è stato esteso in certe pub-
   blicazioni e da alcuni teologi […] per indicare la Chiesa cattolica da un lato e la
   Chiesa ortodossa dall'altro, inducendo a pensare che nella realtà non esisterebbe
   l'unica Chiesa di Cristo, ma essa potrà essere di nuovo ristabilita a seguito della
   riconciliazione tra le due chiese sorelle.'
87 '[C]hi crederà […] e sarà salvo', and 'chi non crederà e sarà condannato'.
88 '[E]sigenze culturali contemporanee.'
89 The protest arose from the following quotation extracted from *Dialogue Held with
   a Certain Persian, the Worthy Mouterizes, in Ankara of Galatia*, written by Manuel
   II Paleologus in 1931: 'Show me just what Muhammad brought that was new and
   there you will find things only evil and inhuman, such as his command to spread
   by the sword the faith he preached.' To the supposed violence of Islam, Ratzinger
   opposed the rationality, the 'coherent intelligence' as a means to reach the Truth.
90 '[C]oerente intelligenza.'
91 '[…] la credenza nelle altre religioni è quell'insieme di esperienza e di pensiero,
   che costituiscono i tesori umani di saggezza e di religiosità, che l'uomo nella sua
   ricerca della verità ha ideato e messo in atto nel suo riferimento al Divino e
   all'Assoluto.'
92 'Non siete più stranieri nè ospiti, ma siete concittadini dei santi e familiari di Dio.'
93 '[S]i può definire, senza timore di essere smentiti, relativismo.'
94 '[L]'essenza del dogma relativista, l'opposto della conversione.'
95 '[F]ilosofia dell'umanità.'
96 '[M]arginalizzare ulteriormente chi si ostina nella difesa della identità cristiana e
   nella sua pretesa di diffondere la verità universale.'
97 '[U]n falso concetto di tolleranza.'
98 'Tutto ciò che di vero e buono esiste nelle religioni […] va riconosciuto e valo-
   rizzato. […] I semi del Logos sono sparsi ovunque. Ma non si possono chiudere
   gli occhi sugli errori e inganni che sono presenti nelle religioni.'
99 '[I] credenti.'
100 'Un volto cristiano.'
101 '[O]sservazione conclusiva.'
102 '[I]nnegabile calo di tensione.'
103 '[L]e difficili sfide del nostro tempo.'
104 'Le sfide che già ci sovrastano sono principalmente due: il crescente afflusso di
    genti che vengono a noi da paesi lontani e diversi e il diffondersi di una cultura
    non cristiana tra le popolazioni cristiane.'
105 'La questione dell'immigrazione.'
106 'Una sorpresa.'
107 '[I]ntegralismo.'
108 '[I]l comando dell'amore.'
109 '[Q]uei nostri fratelli, che sventuratamente ancora non ne sono beneficiati.'
110 '[I]ndeclinabile responsabilità che essi hanno nei confronti di tutti i nuovi arrivati.'
111 '[A]ssolutamente inconfrontabile con i pur preziosi barlumi offerti dalle varie reli-
    gioni e dall'Islam.'
112 '[S]econdo le loro concrete possibilità.'
113 'Un approccio realistico.'
114 '[A]ll'interno della Chiesa non ci sono stranieri.'
115 '[A]ffettuosa attenzione.'
116 '[A]mati e, per quanto è possibile aiutati nelle loro necessità.'
117 'Considerazione generale.'
118 '[I]l comportamento auspicabile dello stato.'

119 'I criteri per ammettere gli immigrati non possono essere solamente economici e previdenziali. [...] Occorre che ci si preoccupi seriamente di salvare l'identità della nazione.'

120 '[P]eculiare umanità.'

121 '[I]l caso dei musulmani va trattato con una particolare attenzione. Essi hanno una forma di alimentazione diversa [...] un diverso giorno festivo, un diritto di famiglia incompatibile col nostro, una concezione della donna lontanissima dalla nostra (fino ad ammettere e a praticare la poligamia). Soprattutto hanno una visione rigorosamente integralista della vita pubblica, sicché la perfetta immedesimazione tra religione e politica fa parte della loro fede [...] anche se di solito a farla valere aspettano prudentemente di diventare preponderanti.'

122 '[I]ntolleranza sostanziale.'

123 On the crucifix controversy in Italy see the judgment on the case of Lautsi and Others vs. Italy (Application no. 30814/06), European Court of Human Rights, Grand Chamber, 18 March 2011, www.uniroma2.it/didattica/Ecclesiastico/deposito/Esempi_di_pronunzie.pdf (accessed 7 April 2014).

124 '[L]ibertà senza verità.'

125 '[L]a nostra identità di credenti.'

126 'L'Europa o ridiventerà cristiana o diventerà musulmana.'

127 '[C]ultura del niente.'

128 What remains to be assessed is the choice on the part of the Caritas Migrantes association, well known for the spiritual and material assistance it provides for migrants, to invite Biffi as a guest to speak at their conference.

129 '[U]na fede intelligente sia vicina e conciliabile con la intelligenza della ragione.'

130 '[A]lla fine vogliamo avere il coraggio di dire che gli unici che non hanno la libertà culturale sono i cattolici.'

131 See Anon. 2000b.

132 Comunità religiosa islamica, or Italian Muslim community.

133 '[È] impossibile praticare il cristianesimo in Italia.'

134 '[U]na società che non sia pluralistica e multietnica [...] è destinata a chiudersi.'

135 '[M]igliaia di uomini, donne, bambini pronti ad affrontare viaggi costosi e pericolosi per raggiungere il "sognato paradiso terrestre" delle terre europee' (Commissione episcopale per le migrazioni e il turismo, 'Il mondo come una casa: dalla diffidenza all'accoglienza', 21 November 2004, 1).

136 '[C]on benevolenza, con simpatia, come vicino, come persona umana quindi portatrice di valori e ricchezze, non come straniero, non come potenziale nemico, come sembra guardarlo la legge, o come incomodo da allontanare, ma come membro di un'unica grande famiglia' ('Il mondo come una casa: dalla diffidenza all'accoglienza', 21 November 2004, 1).

137 '[S]pesso oggetto di scherno.'

138 '[U]na maggiore conoscenza di ciascuno. E'un processo prolungato che mira a formare società e culture [...] Il migrante, in tale processo, è impegnato a compiere i passi necessari all'inclusione sociale, quali l'apprendimento della lingua nazionale e il proprio adeguamento alle leggi e alle esigenze del lavoro, così da evitare il crearsi di una differenza esasperata.'

139 '[G]iusto equilibrio tra il rispetto dell'identità propria e il riconoscimento di quella altrui.'

140 '[F]ra uomini di culture diverse in un contesto di pluralismo che vada oltre la semplice tolleranza e giunga alla simpatia.'

141 'Se coerenti con se stessi i Cristiani non possono poi rinunciare a predicare il Vangelo di Cristo ad ogni creatura (cfr Mark15,15). Lo devono fare, ovviamente, nel rispetto della coscienza altrui.'

3 The Northern League and the debate on identity and immigration

1 Introduction

The rise to power of the leghe autonomiste and particularly that of the Northern League can be seen as the most significant change in the political scenario of post-war Italy. Since the early 1990s, the leagues have marked a season of new political and electoral trends within Italian society. Their success can be attributed mainly to their ability to interpret, from a new perspective, political issues based on the traditional conflicts within the country: from the North–South divide, to the public versus private debate, to the lack of communication between civil society and political parties (Diamanti, 1993: vii).

Since its advent on the national political scene, countless definitions of the Northern League have been formulated in the attempt to explain its origins as well as the conditions that made possible its progressive and often unexpected rise to power. From a condition of the soul, to an expression of thoughts already discussed in every Northern family before the League's advent, to a movement of rupture, to an anti-party protest, the League and the many leagues incorporated into it, with their contradictions and changes of strategy, have been investigated in depth by scholars such as Biorcio (1997), Diamanti (1993, 1996), Tambini (2001), Cartocci (1994), Cento Bull and Gilbert (2001), Albertazzi (2006, 2007) and others.

This work does not intend to engage with the now extensive literature on the several factors that brought the League to national attention, its origins and electoral growth, nor does it aim to investigate its ideology in exhaustive terms. It will only mention the conditions under which the party was created, the implications of its electoral success and its main interests in order to provide a general background for the analysis of a specific issue deriving from its position on identity: that of immigration. The investigation of the League's perspective on immigration and (sub)national identity requires an analysis of the central values on which these positions are based, and of the rhetoric used to put these views forward in the national debate. This chapter will start with a brief account of the origins and rise to power of autonomist leagues in the 1980s and their merger into a unitary party a decade later. It will then investigate the shifts in aims and strategy of the Northern League, particularly since the invention of Padania, and its influence in the ongoing process of identity building in the Northern regions of the country. While leaving aside a more detailed analysis of the League's electoral results and its transformations, the chapter will summarise the different definitions of the party provided by scholars, focusing particularly on the theoretical and pragmatic reasons for its distinctive attitude to immigration. It will also ask whether this attitude has changed since the advent to power of the League as well as the reasons behind this hypothetical shift.

In order to provide a clear picture of how the phenomenon of immigration is perceived by the party's leader and its followers, the chapter will take as a case study the interviews, editorials and letters for the most part extracted from articles published in the party's daily newspaper, *La Padania*, between 2006 and 2009, with a particular focus on 2007.[1] It will then introduce its ambiguous relationship with the Church, arguing that both actors pay particular attention to certain key concepts such as those of freedom of speech, solidarity, multiculturalism, integration and traditional identities, while sharing an original rhetoric based in both cases on the critique of what they perceive as the supposed hypocrisy resulting from political correctness. Despite what this chapter will define as a conflictual and often opportunistic relationship, and despite a radical difference in their declared aims, these two political actors, albeit moved by diverse concerns, contribute in different ways to influencing the state reactions towards immigration, as this analysis will attempt to prove.

This investigation shows how, despite the leghisti's constant reassurance that they are not racist and that they support values such as solidarity, the message that their interventions conveys seems to go in the opposite direction: it appears that the League influenced, if not inspired, the government's restrictive policies towards immigration and even more that it created a public which, moved by irrational fears, demands such measures. Finally, and most importantly, this work intends to frame the attitude of the Northern League to immigration into a theoretical model, which will be referred to as an 'institutionalised state of exception'. This interpretation will stress the immigrant's resignation to a status of 'permanent transitoriness' and a role as *homo sacer* as the only condition for being at least temporarily tolerated (integration is not even contemplated) following a process in which they have no control, while assessing the consequence of this highly exclusionary model of citizenship.

2 Ethnic identities in the era of globalisation

At the time of its first appearance on the national political scene, in the late 1980s, the Northern League was seen by opinion makers and political opponents as a marginal movement with scarce influence on the electorate, and was often neglected, if not ridiculed, as a folkloristic manifestation of local demands and mostly irrelevant for the majority of the country. When, in the early 1990s, it became clear that the new party was gaining visibility and had the power and the popular support to influence Italian political life, scholars such as Ilvo Diamanti and Roberto Biorcio started warning the political class of the danger of underestimating this ambitious and unconventional new political contender.

In his *La Lega. Geografia, storia e sociologia di un nuovo soggetto politico* (1993), Diamanti, a pioneer in this field, stated that the topic of the rise to power of the Northern League was still relatively obscure. Moreover, he argued, the attitude of other parties' representatives and that of opinion makers, who often underestimated the role of this 'movement of rupture', did not contribute to opening a debate on a phenomenon that would have soon emerged as absolutely unique (Diamanti, 1993). A decade later, scholars such as Tambini (2001) and Cachafeiro (2002) also remarked upon the need to consider the Northern League as a complex and nuanced political phenomenon in terms of origins, electoral growth and aims. According to them, an accurate analysis of the party had to start from the acknowledgment of the fact that Umberto Bossi's League is not a single-aim party but is rather characterised by multiple objectives which keep changing and developing constantly.

As scholars recall, the 1970s were characterised by the decline of those social movements that, a decade earlier, had contributed to promoting the values of community, solidarity and civil consciousness. New claims started to emerge from the ashes of that 'grand egalitarian utopia',[2] which had marked a period of commitment towards communitarian shared ideals (De Luna, 1994: 24). This decline opened a new season of less ideologically oriented claims, which had their roots in individualistic and mainly material interests. In post-industrial Italy, the fragmentation and decentralisation of the main industries had brought about a shift from a unitary representation of workers, for instance in opposition to factory owners, towards a more pluralistic scenario in which 'uniqueness was replaced by plurality, concentration by dispersion'[3] (ibid.).

The crisis faced by industrial committees, workers' associations, women and proletarian movements marked the end of the traditional opposition between genders as well as between work and capital, which had provided until then a clear means of representation and had contributed to shaping recognisable and socially accepted – albeit antagonistic – identities. Social conflicts stopped becoming politicised, while politics began to aim at finding legitimation in itself and its mechanisms. According to De Luna, this passage from solidarity to selfishness can only be explained by referring to the categories of 'victory' and 'defeat', since the movements emerging in the 1980s would not have had a chance to prevail without sweeping away those that had preceded them. It was in these circumstances that the fluxes of communication were interrupted, ideas started losing fluidity and became stiff and entrapped in fixed schemes leaving space for the widespread distrust and selfishness that became 'common practice' in the 1980s and particularly after the fall of the Berlin Wall in 1989, which officially marked the decline of communism and one of its main agents in Europe: the Italian Communist Party (PCI).

If the crisis of Italian post-industrial society and the decline of the Communist Party in the late 1980s is of central importance to explain the loss of identification with a community and/or a social class, and the fracture between the social and political spheres, scholars also looked to the other Italian mass party – the DC, the Italian Christian Democratic Party – in order to explain the origins of this new era of selfishness and individualism. Cachafeiro (2002), Diamanti (1993) and Cartocci (1994) consider the role that the DC played in the crumbling of the Italian party system, and the subsequent loss of identity and feeling of bewilderment on the part of citizens, which acquires particular relevance in light of the fact that the Northern League has proven more successful in those regions where the 'white subculture' was traditionally stronger. Even though the level of trust in traditional mass parties in Italy seemed to remain stable during the 1980s, this was quite a fragile equilibrium based on the attitude of voters to grant parties a 'voto di appartenenza' – that is to say, a vote motivated by the belonging to a well-defined group and by the adherence to specific values traditionally promoted by a party characterised by a strong ideology. This type of vote was destined to be replaced by the so-called 'voto di scambio', an instrumental and volatile vote granted to a party on the basis of possible advantages deriving from it, whereas a vote based on free choice on the part of citizens fully informed on the different options and free from ideological prejudices represents a 'voto di opinione' (Cartocci, 1994: 91; Parisi and Pasquino, 1977: 215–39).

The final blow to the already troubled Italian party system arrived in 1992 with the 'clean hands' police investigation into parties' corruption, which, as already mentioned, resulted in the disappearance of mainstream political parties and, in the end, of the First Republic.

The 1980s were characterised by radical protest by the core regions of Northern Italy demanding to be recognised as 'different' and 'special' on the basis of their ethnic specificity, a request which left scholars 'puzzled' (Cachafeiro, 2002: 45). Indeed, as Cachafeiro explains, there is academic agreement on two facts: that the North cannot be considered ethnically homogeneous, and that a protest such as that which took place in those years did not come from peripheral areas of the country as might have been expected, but from the more economically advanced regions of Piedmont, Veneto and Lombardy (ibid.: 46).

Since the 1960s, indeed, the rapid economic growth and the extent of state intervention in social matters put the need to organise more functional local governments at the centre of public discussion, a debate which led to the creation of 'ordinary regions'[4] (Romanelli, 1995). Putnam (1993), Cachafeiro (2002) and Kitschelt (1997) agree in identifying the creation of partially independent local governments as the reason for the protest of Northern regions seeking recognition as special, despite their internal lack of ethnic and cultural diversity. The only linguistic minorities in Italy are represented by the German-speaking population of south Tyrol, the French-speaking inhabitants of Valle D'Aosta and the Slavic minority groups who live close to the border with the former Yugoslavia.

Nevertheless, the protection of a linguistic idiom supposedly shared by most regions in the North of the country seemingly represented the main concern of these new movements, whose ideology combined Ethnism and 'Third Worldism', defined as 'political discourse of internal colonialism in European states' (Cachafeiro, 2002: 46). Since the late 1970s, this rhetoric of internal colonialism and Third Worldism, based on the concepts of oppression and victimhood exploited by the League, had become a common means to put forward claims of independence and self-determination in many other European countries, following the process of decolonisation of the 1960s (ibid.: 58).

Even though the creation of 'ordinary regions' is clearly not the only or indeed the main reason behind the birth of these movements, it nevertheless contributed to stress on the importance of territory as a means to gain recognition and show antagonism and disillusionment towards the political system. The concept of territory as a source of identity is indeed of central importance in providing an explanation for a new type of local identity based upon specific interests within a local economic and social context. Moreover, it also contributes to the shaping of an 'anti-identity', as it allows members to distinguish between them and the other, the enemy: in the case of Italy, this dichotomy historically applied to the North–South divide and to the difficult relationship between the centre and the periphery. In this respect, nationalism, federalism, regionalism and other theoretical models to define identity come precisely from these diverse interpretations of the idea of territory (Diamanti, 1993: 14).

According to Diamanti, the Northern League has been able to manipulate the ambiguity of the idea of territory in order to achieve its own goals. In his view, the party managed to translate all its claims into territorial issues, from fiscal federalism, to the opposition to traditional political parties, from the call for protection of a linguistic/cultural minority to the anti-immigrant rhetoric (Diamanti, 1993: 6). Moreover, the League became visible at a time that marked in all European countries the passage from traditional to modern societies, a process characterised by two main trends: secularisation and globalisation. This shift was often connoted by the tension between a set of dichotomies representing old and new values and ways of interpreting life.

The first antagonistic attitudes are those of 'individualism' as opposed to 'localism': in this sense the local dimension of life and the close ties with the family work as a '"filter" through which external "modernising" cultural and social influences are mitigated and even neutralised' (Cento Bull, 2000: 11). Moreover, the new political and social climate in some Northern provinces of the country also contributed to creating a new model of associationism, characterised by horizontal connections established through rational choice rather than resulting from ascriptive characteristics. Secularisation played a central role in this tense process of modernisation since religious values usually linked to conservative, non-liberal attitudes started being challenged by secularist values typical of modern societies, characterised by those individualist attitudes held responsible, for instance, for the demise of the DC. According to Cento Bull, while in Europe 'administratively unitary states [...] developed class-based cleavages in the course of the industrialisation process, but also shed locally- and regionally-based subcultures, in Italy the traditional sub-culture weakened but did not disappear in the post-war period' (ibid.: 12).

If the voting behaviour in traditional societies was determined by the orientation of family and friends and bounded to loyalty towards a precise set of values and a well-defined sense of belonging, in modern societies the vote is supposedly freed from these constrictions and based on the rational choice of individuals. Finally, in modern societies the voting behaviour is also supposedly not influenced by the different territorial and/or class political subcultures (ibid.). However, the non-linear pattern of modernisation in the areas previously dominated by the white subculture can also explain the rise to power of a new type of territorial party following the demise of Christian democracy.

3 From local movement to national party: a brief account of the League's rise to power

While most scholars start their investigations into leghismo from the first electoral successes of the Northern League in the early 1990s, others, and particularly Cachafeiro (2002) and Diamanti (1993), include in their accounts different local protest movements, which were born at least a decade before Bossi's League, in order to show where the latter originates as well as which elements of its predecessors it dropped and which it retained. The rise to power of the political actor that established itself as the third national political party in the 2008 elections (Battaglia, 2008) has its roots in the many leagues and movements which started claiming recognition by and independence from the Italian state in the 1970s. Back in those days, many much more fragmented and less structured leagues voiced local protests in peripheral areas of Northern Italy. Ethno-territorial political claims started emerging from the contradiction represented by the core regions' resentment towards the state due to their perceived economic marginalisation. Ethnicity, even invented, became then a 'principle of legitimacy for the acquisition of rights in the Italian state' (Cachafeiro, 2002: 47).

This new trend in Italian politics arose from a European ethnic wave of political mobilisation which took off in the late 1960s and kept growing in the following decade, creating a 'category of practice' – namely that of self-determination based on ethnic difference – which provided European sub-regions with a relevant criterion to put forward claims of 'speciality' (Cachafeiro, 2002). Born already as a movement in the 1950s, Ethnism grew increasingly popular in the 1960s and 1970s, which saw a renewed interest in national minorities and the creation of institutions such as CIEMEN (Centro Internazionale Escarrè per la Minoranze Etniche e Nazionali), aimed at granting representation to those groups that perceived themselves as 'colonised' by the nation-states emerging from World War II. Particularly, the Liga

Veneta, 'the mother of all leagues', as its leader Franco Rocchetta defined it, represents the precursor of this new trend in Italian regional politics, as it was the first to organise itself as a movement in the 1970s, and later on as a party, and to give the general dissatisfaction of Northern industrial areas a more structured form. As Cachafeiro (2002: 58) explains, in the 1980s in the region of Veneto economic transformation took place in parallel with a profound change in politics as well. After two decades of industrial growth which had reshaped the urban landscape of the area, the region became a highly productive zone strongly oriented towards a new economy based on exports, at the same time as the crisis experienced by traditional mass parties in the area started becoming increasingly evident.

Veneto, in particular, had always been a stronghold of the DC and, consequently, of the Catholic Church and its subculture. Not only did the Venetian leaders of the DC lose their privileged roles within the party at a national level (Pansa, 1986) but the growing process of secularisation of Italian society also contributed to the erosion of loyalty towards the old party and to the rise to power of the Liga Veneta, officially born in 1980 (Diamanti, 1993).

At the same time, the spontaneous movements of protest in Piedmont, where the first autonomist claims date back to the early 1950s, started converging into a more structured organisation claiming recognition of ethnic difference: the Movimento Autonomista Rinascita Piemontèisa (later Union Piemontèisa) was born in 1980 under the leadership of Roberto Gremmo. In Lombardy the protest underwent the same process and the Lega Autonomista Lombarda, destined to rise to the national political scene under the leadership of Umberto Bossi, was officially launched in 1980–81. The leagues merged into the Lega Nord per l'Indipendenza della Padania in 1991, following a heated internal competition to secure leadership, a battle won by Bossi, who in the 1992 general elections brought the party to the forefront of Italian national politics, turning it into the fourth political force within the country.[5]

Moving from the chronology of the development of the leagues to the analysis of the geography of the vote, scholars seem to agree on the fact that the Northern League has proven more successful in achieving electoral consensus in the industrial districts of those Northern regions, whose economy is based on family-run factories and small industries, and where the DC had traditionally been the most powerful party in terms of support and identification. In his analysis of voting patterns in Northern provinces, Diamanti identified three main areas of influence: the first coincides with the provinces of Piedmont, such as Turin, Vercelli and Cuneo; the second is represented by the core of Veneto and included Vicenza, Treviso and Verona; while the third area covers northern Lombardy with the cities of Bergamo, Varese and Como. Considering these areas, the sphere of influence of the leagues included all the Northern regions, with the exception of the cities of Milan and Pavia, where its presence was not yet significant (Diamanti, 1993: 30).[6]

An analysis of the electoral trends shows a certain continuity and internal consistency to the extent that the leagues' uniform presence in these territories resulted in the creation of a new subculture comparable to the red/communist one and the white/Christian democratic one that were prevalent until the late 1980s. The League succeeded in creating a strong feeling of belonging shared by a considerable number of citizens within the boundaries of the regions mentioned above. Moreover, this new subculture seemed not only to replace the white one but to show a high degree of continuity with it, a fact confirmed by the increasing electoral decline of the DC in the areas of growth of the Northern League (Diamanti, 1993: 35). It was the beginning of the 'green shirts era'.

4 A racist party?

Until today there have been many attempts to define the Northern League and to channel its claims, contradictions, changes of strategy and shifts in priorities into a coherent interpretation. If scholars such as Cachafeiro and Diamanti identified ethno-regionalism and nationalism as the most appropriate framework to understand the early days of the movement, others such as Biorcio (1997) and Diani (1996) focused more on the anti-system instances of what they saw primarily as a populist party.[7] Besides the various definitions, Bossi's party has generally been labelled as racist by political opponents and opinion makers: whether interpreted according to the theoretical frameworks of populism or ethno-regionalism or nationalism, all these definitions have generally been associated with a fundamental xenophobic attitude. The recurrent use of provocative, rude, grammatically incorrect and not at all politically correct language,[8] the 'spectacular headlines' on national newspapers (Albertazzi, 2006: 23) contributed to spreading the idea that being *leghista* involved, among other things, a rejection of 'the other'. This meant Southerners in the first instance and then foreign immigrants, but also gays, drug addicts, and generally anyone leading an alternative lifestyle, described as a 'weak' member of society.

Two of the characteristics attributed to the party are particularly significant for the analysis of the League's position on the issues of identity and otherness. The first is the concept of territory and its role in creating what De Winter and Tursan (1998) call 'an exclusive group identity', albeit an invented one (Cento Bull and Gilbert, 2001: 56). The second is the category of nationalism applied to the League by scholars such as Tambini (2001) and Melucci (1985) and, particularly, nationalism intended as a political strategy, a performative way of doing politics (Tambini, 2001: 9), rather than an analytical concept or, in other words, an inauthentic posture functional to the achievement of specific goals (Breuilly, 1992; Brubaker, 1992). Both interpretations can prove useful to understand the role and authenticity of the party's discourse on immigration vis-à-vis identity, and the shift in the definition of the latter during the last decade, as the section on editorials from *La Padania* will show.

Moreover, even though establishing whether the League can be defined as racist is not the aim of this investigation, the question becomes significant when we try to understand what role this intolerance plays in the construction of a specific model of citizenship. In other words, the League's controversial statements and restrictive measures put forward to deal with immigration will be taken into account to establish whether they contribute to the creation of a particular idea of the state, peculiar to the Northern League, and how this hypothetical idea might respond to the foreign presence within the country. The following examples of unconventional or politically incorrect interventions, which can be easily considered racist, can provide the first elements to unveil the League's sometimes implicit definition of identity as it emerges from its opposition to the otherness personified by immigrants.

It is possible to describe the linguistic code used by leghisti as layered like an onion, with the more institutionalised and politically correct statements and speeches given in official circumstances working as a superior layer, which envelops a core of progressively stronger messages. Many examples of the latter have been reported on by journalist Gian Antonio Stella in his *Dio Po – Gli uomini che fecero la Padania* (1996), a collection of interviews and interventions on the part of members and MPs in which they manifested an open intolerance towards 'ethnicities' or 'races' grouped together as different from the Padana.

The leghisti's main object of denigration has traditionally been those whom they define as terroni, a term derived from the word terra (soil), coined to describe in pejorative terms those employed in agriculture, and generically referring to Southerners. In this sense, the term terrone works as a synonym for lazy, backward, dirty, Mafioso and ignorant. In fact, it sums up all the characteristics that have in time come to be associated with the concept of 'Southernness'. From the slogan 'Kill the Southerners, save millions'[9] used in a meeting in Chioggia on 15 September 1996, to recurrent statements such as 'The North has got one single problem: Southerners',[10] the League has always identified non-Northerners as 'a problem', if not 'a plague' for 'our society', the latter referring to the North, to what is often called 'our home' (casa nostra) (Stella, 1996: 2, 34). A reason for the resentment of the people of the North towards Southerners consists in the privileges the latter are supposedly granted by the state and by their 'massive' presence in public administration. In this sense, the protest arises from the perception of a double difference: a cultural/ethnic incompatibility and a difference in attitude on the part of the state towards Southerners and Northerners, based on the systematic discrimination against Northerners in the distribution of resources.

The words of Gipo Farassino, founder of the autonomist group Union Piemontèisa and later Northern League member, exemplify Northerners' attitude towards non-Padani: 'We have been colonised. I live in Turin and I cannot speak the local dialect in a shop because the shop owner is a Southerner ... They ask you: speak Italian, please [...] Can you not see it? At the cinema they [the actors] speak Neapolitan ... think of Troisi [a Neapolitan actor very popular in Italy]'.[11] Not only is the North perceived as 'invaded' or 'colonised', but Southerners themselves, according to many leghisti, do not recognise themselves as Italians but rather keep as a point of reference their regional origins. Again quoting Farassino: 'Have you ever heard anyone saying "I am Italian"? No, they say: I am Calabrian, I am Sicilian ... we are not attached to a nation but to a region [...] A multiethnic state cannot exist. You can keep it together with the weapons, but sooner or later people will react.'[12] What is interesting in this statement is the fact that the impossibility of keeping together without coercion a multiethnic state is referred to as a state in which Southerners represent the 'foreign' component: a state whose multiethnic character is determined by the presence of fellow Italians classified as non-Padani. As the analysis of more recent debates on multiculturalism will show, Southerners seem to have now been replaced by non-Italian immigrants in this rhetoric against a pluralistic state. This does not mean that Southerners have smoothly managed to integrate into the North of the country, but they are not the main concern of the Northern League today. In this sense, if Southern identity has been essentialised in fixed stereotypes and exploited in order to built an alternative identity and provide Padani with a sense of belonging, after the invention of Padania the League's rhetoric on identity started focusing on the new 'other': the 'extracomunitario'.

As Balbo and Manconi (1993: 18–19) explain in their *Razzismi: Un Vocabolario*, the word 'immigrant' stresses the 'otherness' of different people who share a common status characterised by their travelling, their suffering and their memories of the country of origin, which overlooks their internal differences (whether they are men or women, black or Asian, their different traditions, languages and history of their homelands). The term 'extracomunitario',[13] however, which only exists in Italian and does not translate into other languages, puts the stress on Europe, on its citizens' shared identity rather than on the people it refers to and aims to describe. In this sense, while still seeing immigrants as being 'extra', 'outside' and therefore excluded, it contributes to reinforcing the feeling of belonging to a European identity 'that until not many years ago was completely alien' to those who now exploit it to preserve the status quo of 'fortress Europe' (ibid.).[14]

The following statements collected by Stella in a series of interviews are symptomatic of the fact that despite not having completely replaced the terroni, the extracomunitari have nonetheless become the centre of the League's concern. As the journalist Stella recalls, Northern League MP Mario Borghezio has often stated that immigrants should be washed, put on a military plane (and not on civil planes as they would rape the air hostesses) and sent back to their countries. The only contact that the true leghista is allowed to have with foreigners and of which he can be proud is seemingly sexual intercourse, often used to prove the lack of racism of any sort among the party members. In this respect, Borghezio proudly recalls episodes of sex tourism involving black women[15] referred to as a 'local product', while embarking on a complicated differentiation between migrant women in Italy, all labelled as prostitutes,[16] and black women abroad, a language which represents quite a contradiction for a man who became well known for his violent call for the repression of the 'immoral habits' (costumi corrotti) of the citizens of Turin and for advocating the need to use plastic bullets against black people. Paradoxically, the MP defines himself as non-racist and, on the contrary, as interested in different cultures as supposedly proven by his anti-colonial positions (Stella, 1996: 39). He instead classifies as the worst form of racism the employment of black people in the domestic sector on the part of those who publicly speak against immigration (ibid.: 43).

The apparent contradiction in these racist statements is that they are often expressed precisely to reject the charges of racism or to address the same accusation at the Italian state. In this sense, Borghezio's opinion, expressed through the use of anti-colonialist rhetoric, that the true racists are those who employ immigrants or delude them with the perspective of an easier life is shared by many leghisti and is recurrent in the speeches of the League's leader himself. This sense of 'solidarity' and anti-colonialism, based on the idea that cultures need to be protected from foreign invasion and rooted in the ideology of the Nouvelle Droite,[17] does not prevent Bossi from referring to immigrants of African origin as 'bingo bongo' or from suggesting opening fire against immigrants' boats that disembark in Italy.

The latter suggestion was followed more recently by Northern League representative – now party secretary – Matteo Salvini's idea to segregate immigrants on different train coaches from those reserved for Italians (Anon. 2009b). Despite the general acknowledgment of the party's 'institutionalised intolerance', some scholars who analysed the phenomenon of the Lega in its early days tend to classify it as non-racist, or at least as not primarily centred on a xenophobic ideology. In rejecting the idea of the Northern League as a purely racist organisation, authors such as Balbo and Manconi refer to the classical definitions of racism resulting from academic research on the subject. It is now worth looking briefly at this literature on the theme to understand better not only where the idea that the League is or is not racist originates, but also whether any of the attitudes described by scholars in the field emerge in the party anti-immigration rhetoric and actions, which will be taken into account later on when analysing the editorials from *La Padania*. More importantly, what sort of model is the party constructing in its almost schizophrenic attempt to reconcile a public rejection of the charges of racism, a response to the demand for a new workforce by the Northern economy and its followers' more or less explicit rejection of the 'other'?

5 Beyond traditional racism

Academic investigation of racism has produced a broad literature on a subject that is still under scrutiny and defined as in constant transformation. As Goldberg (1993) states, any definition of racism has to be based on empirical observation and result from its diverse manifestations in everyday life and therefore cannot be formulated a priori, at a purely theoretical level, as detached from the reality in which it manifests itself. Scholars such as Miles and Brown (2003: 3), while agreeing on the idea of racism as a concept in continuous transformation, are concerned with the fact that a 'Wittgensteinian argument' like the one put forward by Goldberg, needs to be counterbalanced by a political imperative according to which there must be consensus on what racism is in order to define it as politically or morally unacceptable. In the absence of such a clear definition, according to the authors, any opposition to racism becomes meaningless and any analysis of the subject is invalidated. They believe that if too broad a definition of the term, as for instance 'everyone is racist', would result in racist attitudes escaping censure as a mere 'product of cultural determinism or an expression of human nature'; an excessively narrow definition of the concept would allow racism to acquire a certain degree of legitimacy, as in the case of 'racial hierarchy' theories that, since the 1950s, have been used by nation-states to label their ideologies as nationalist rather than racist.

If there seems to be consensus among scholars on the idea that racism is not a static phenomenon,[18] the same thing cannot be said on the use of the term 'race'. The concept is considered by them as necessary today in order to draw the boundary between legal and illegal behaviour[19] and to provide victims with laws aimed at protecting them. In this sense the concept of racial groups is the price to be paid for a law against indirect discrimination (Miles and Brown, 2003: 4; Banton, 1996). Moreover, the importance of 'racialised consciousness' among oppressed groups who find their own identity by virtue of being socially discriminated against for their 'inferior' race has to be further stressed, for the term 'race' is used by minorities as a symbol of their status, their suffering and their history, as shown by pre-colonial African or modern African-American history (Banton, 1996).

As Balbo and Manconi recall, since 1951 the United Nations Educational, Scientific and Cultural Organization (UNESCO) has been arguing the case for abolishing the term 'race' and replacing it with 'ethnic group'. Nonetheless, the authors believe that the idea of racism is clearly already quite ambiguous and difficult to define, and that therefore the concept has to be explored and constantly redefined in order to prevent its opposite – anti-racism – from becoming equally meaningless and unclear. In other words, they argue that only by reaching consensus on what racism is and by acknowledging its presence in our societies is it possible to react to it in a strong way.[20] If we cannot talk about 'invented races', which do not exist, then it becomes impossible to react to the attitude classified as 'racism'. Racist attitudes can only be firmly opposed if recognised as a fundamental problem, a clear enemy easily identifiable (Balbo and Manconi, 1993: 10).

The authors believe that the problem that European countries are facing in their attempt to fight racism originates from an erroneous interpretation of the phenomenon. Particularly, they blame the media for a distorted representation of the issue: in other words, according to them, the question to be asked is not whether an individual, a group or a place, are racist, as the answer to these questions can only be positive if the individual, the group, the citizens of a specific place openly declare their racism with a verbal statement or with an active oppression or segregation of those they consider 'inferior' (Balbo and Manconi, 1993). Moreover, they insist on the risk implicit in using the 'classic' conception of racism in order to establish who falls into the category of racist. Indeed, not only can there be racism even in the absence of openly racist claims, but also the idea of a racism based on the biological and physical superiority of a group does not represent the main trend in contemporary societies, where racism manifests itself in different, more subtle and more ambiguous ways.

What is being tackled here is the issue of a grey zone in which racism originates and grows without being recognised as such, which is precisely the case of the Northern League. Indeed, even though its ideology does not seem to be centred on biological difference, nonetheless it contributes to cultivating a xenophobic attitude, while providing a justification for inner fears linked to 'the other' within Italian society (Cento Bull, 2000; Zaslove, 2004: 103). Since the 1990s academics seem to have abandoned the traditional belief typical of the 1930s and 1940s that racism is based on the physical distinctiveness of its victims, as made self-evident by the impossibility, for instance, of distinguishing a Bosnian Muslim from a Bosnian Serb, which, nonetheless, has not prevented the eruption of one of the 'worst genocides of the second half of the twentieth century' in the political and civil sphere (Miles and Brown, 2003: 6).

Recent investigations of racism have also tried to cover the moral aspect of the issue by trying to answer a fundamental question: Why is racism wrong? The studies of Bonnett (2000) and King (2000), among others, have attempted to show the dangers implicit in this ideology and its everyday manifestations. Taguieff (1995) polemically dismisses the moral distinction between good and evil as closer to the category used by medieval Christian theology than to scientific discourse in order to stress the importance of analysing the issue at a political level rather than in its moral implications. Many scholars agree with the idea that the political issues linked with racism are much more significant in our societies than a moral judgement on it, and argue that what really matters is its effect on contemporary societies and the possible (political) answers to deal with it, a belief that comes from the acknowledgment of the fact that, since the 1980s, political parties in many European countries have started to demand legitimisation and public recognition for racist claims not very different from those put forwards by Fascist ideologies in the 1930s (Miles and Brown, 2003: 15).

Driven by the same preoccupation, authors such as Turner *et al.* (1984) have formulated a more political definition of racism, purely based on the distribution of resources and access to basic rights, by stating that the term 'racism' identifies a system of distribution of power according to which certain groups are given access whereas others are systematically excluded from benefiting from it. The different types of racism as they have been outlined and classified by scholars in the last two decades include: additional racism, competitive racism and cultural racism.[21] Additional racism results from 'adding' a physical, ethnic or cultural difference to a factor of social fears, and is linked to pre-existing feelings of anxiety due to perceived threats of, for instance, crimes against property or the person, drug dealing, fears of spreading illnesses and viruses, and of other behaviour considered 'irregular' or different.

Be the threat imaginary or real, the common reaction is always that of finding somebody responsible for it outside the community: the guilt has to be placed onto a subject who can be easily identified as different, following a psychological mechanism that seeks to take immediate distance from the 'deviant behaviour' (Balbo and Manconi, 1993: 62–66). This attempt to 'rationalise' fears and intolerance works according to a standard process: the first step consists in putting an emphasis on the 'criminal act', second comes the description of immigrants' lives as 'miserable' and socially stigmatised, and finally the neglect of immigrants' everyday life, which includes their families, their jobs, their social networks. By simplifying their existence and reducing it to an act perceived as deviant, this mechanism contributes to the creation of stereotypes and to the classification of a specific group as significant only in terms of public security (ibid.).

The second type of racism is based on the defence of the territory and its resources: it arises from the idea that immigrants represent potential competitors in the allocation of resources such as transport, accommodation, health system and jobs. It is characterised by the battle for 'space', be it a square, a street, a train station, and the fear that allowing different groups to occupy it, even though temporarily, will result in the exclusion of citizens from those areas and will determine a loss of control on the part of the community. The struggle not to lose territory has as its first consequence the creation of 'areas of segregation', ghettos where the weakest groups contend with each other for 'the space conquered at the expense of the locals'[22] (Balbo and Manconi, 1993: 66–74). Finally, cultural racism originates from the attempt to preserve and protect from external threats a set of values, a precise view of the world and a lifestyle, and from the rejection of different cultures and ideas of the good life. The interpretation of immigration as a threat results in a series of fixed answers to the phenomenon: according to the Federazione giovanile comunisti italiani (FGCI, or Italian Communist Youth Federation) survey carried out in Milan in the early 1990s,[23] when asked whether immigrants could be considered 'normal' citizens, a high percentage of Italians answered 'as long as they respect the rules of our society'. The ambiguity of this answer lies in the fact that it does not discriminate between breaking the law and simply living according to values, religions and traditions different from mainstream ones.

As the section on the editorials of *La Padania* will highlight, in the case of the Northern League all three categories of racism mentioned above seem to play a role in the construction of a generally intolerant attitude: from the control of territory to the supposed superiority of Padanian culture over different sets of values, from the simplification of immigrants' private lives to linking their presence with fears of security and public order. In this sense, this interpretation of 'the other' as a threat represents the premise for the development of an exclusionary model of citizenship aimed at the systematic marginalisation of foreigners.

6 The invention of Padania and a new exclusionary identity

In identifying the invention of Padania with the beginning of a new era in the Northern League's political response to immigration and in the creation of a new exclusionary identity, this work follows the interpretation offered by Cento Bull and Gilbert in *The Lega Nord and the Northern Question in Italian Politics* (2001). The scholars argue that if the ethno-regionalism developed by the party in order to provide Northerners with a shared identity could until 1996 be considered a mere 'invention', later on downplayed by the leader himself, the advent of Padania determined a growing concern on the part of the League with the dangers implicit in a multiethnic state, on which it declared war. The writings of party ideologue Gilberto Oneto, and particularly *L'invenzione della Padania* (1997), prove that the creation of the new nation, characterised by the re-exhumation of a set of symbols and rituals relating to the North's Celtic ancestors,[24] represents a key moment in the League's strategy and a central concept in the redefinition of its claims. Following Oneto (1997: 11), 'Padania really exists, from a geographic, linguistic, cultural and economic point of view [...] its citizens have fought in order to re-affirm their own national identity. There is no need to invent anything that already exists. To invent means to redefine, recover, go back to, rediscover'.[25]

The important element in Oneto's definition of the new nation consists in the claim that a constructed national identity was imposed by Fascism on people to whom it denied the right of self-determination, a point that assumes particular relevance in light of both the party's more recent exploitation of the concept of a common Italian national identity as a means to reject immigrants and the rhetoric of victimhood that justifies such an exclusionary approach towards 'the other', as the analysis of the more recent debate will show.

Until the invention of Padania, the recurrent references to a fake Unification, to a systematic colonisation of the North on the part of the central state, and to the 'cultural cleansing' of what was described as a minority within the country, were mainly directed at reinforcing – through a rhetoric based on victimhood – a still weak unitary Northern identity, as it emerges, for instance, from Bossi's programmatic declarations contained in his *La rivoluzione*, written with journalist Daniele Vimercati in 1993. At that point, the future Padania was presented as a 'land of conquest' (terra di conquista) and its people as a minority group whose different identity was not acknowledged by the state (Bossi and Vimercati, 1993: 24).

According to Cachafeiro (2002: 103–4), 'The fabrication of a united North incorporated also a diverse and multicultural North. Sameness within the North also encompasses diversity. Lega politicians from Lombardy, Veneto and Piedmont assert the differences within the North but downplay their political relevance'. This common identity was founded on the sameness of 'race', traditions, language and culture. Ethnicity was not the only criterion for territorial distinctiveness: since the 1990s, Bossi has rejected this 'simplistic' interpretation and has begun to include 'economic identity' in the characteristics shared by Northerners. While the differences between Northern regions were considered minimal and irrelevant in this phase, those between the North and the South were instead described as fundamental: the enemy that nationalistic groups desperately need in order to reassert their own identity was clearly identified in the Southerner and in the central state.

Until 1996 there is indeed still no sign of the new threat of the 'extracomunitario': the party priorities seem to follow the traditional path already established in the programmes of the various regional leagues, such as the document *Superare lo Stato centralizzato*, the official manifesto of the Lega Lombarda published in 1983. The document consists of a 13-point list of programmatic declarations, which include the battle against the central state for the allocation of resources, the autonomist project, the weak presence of Northerners in the public administration, the protection of traditional values and culture from external attacks and the federalist revolution[26] (Bossi, 1996).

Since 1996, however, the League has been getting closer to the positions typical of the New Right, particularly on the politics of identity and immigration, while increasingly directing its interests towards 'multiculturalism, American capitalism, European integration and the "other", a phase characterised by a "profound cultural pessimism"' (Cento Bull and Gilbert, 2001: 127). A comparison between the pamphlet cited above and other documents published by the Northern League since 1996, and particularly *Padania, identità e società multirazziale*,[27] shows how radically the attitude towards immigration has changed. The pamphlet argues that immigration from outside Europe is sustained if not promoted by a combination of forces such as global capitalism and the international Left which contribute to presenting it as a spontaneous and irreversible trend. The promotion of a multicultural society based on an individualistic and cosmopolitan view of citizens is supported by minority powers, which are, however, 'hegemonic' in the cultural sphere, and therefore will inevitably bring about the destruction of local and territorial identities if not opposed by citizens' aspiration to independence and self-determination.[28]

The document identifies five main points which correspond to as many strategies to protect this identity from the threat posed by immigration. It starts from the refusal to grant the vote to foreigners, who can never feel part of the community and feel a sense of duty towards the state, followed by the struggle to 'save the specificity of our people' and the need to give Padanians priority in the social services.[29] It also states the necessity to start a 'polite request for the return of non-EU foreigners to their homes', while the last measure consists in a call for more investment in the agriculture of non-European countries in order to provide their citizens with 'a dignified alternative' to migration (Mussa, 1998; Cento Bull and Gilbert, 2001: 128–29). The key elements of the party's current anti-immigration discourse, such as that of 'internal multiculturalism', the link between immigration and crime, the right of the locals to protect their territory, the rhetoric of the invasion and the rejection of the charge of racism,[30] which will be analysed in the following section of this chapter, emerge for the first time in a structured way in this document.

To summarise the main elements of this shift in the Northern League's strategy and ideology, it can be said that in the early days the party's discourse on identity was much more focused on the 'us' component rather than on the external 'them'. Southerners, as the 'other', played a role functional to the construction of a rhetoric based on victimhood used to gain autonomy from a tyrannical state. With the invention of Padania, however, the focus shifted from 'us' to 'them', the immigrants, perceived not only as competitors in the allocation of resources but also as carrying an inner cultural and ethnic difference absolutely incompatible with Northerners' values and 'inevitably' resulting in a clash of civilisations. At this point, immigrants not only started being presented as dangerous for (potentially) stealing job opportunities but also for the 'invented' fixed characteristics attributed to them by leghisti, such as, for instance, their supposed intention of colonising Padania and Italy and imposing their own ideas of the good life.

Until the 1990s, the League's rhetoric on identity and otherness was seemingly based on the instrumental concepts of tolerance (towards the others as long as they stayed in their countries) and solidarity (towards its own people first of all and then to the 'others', following a long-distance charitable approach to the Third World), always put forward with the double aim of rejecting the charge of racism and building bridges with the Catholic Church. However, more recently the party has launched several campaigns against immigration which leave no room for doubt. With the invention of Padania and the outline of an increasingly more exclusionary identity, the party lifted the veil on an implicit but nonetheless substantial paradox. On the one hand, the Lega seemingly rejects the immigrants who are much needed in the local economy of the North, as recently shown by Andall (2009) in her analysis of the demand/offer ratio in selected Italian provinces. On the other hand, the party employs a rhetoric of closure which entraps immigrants into fixed stereotypes and prevents them from integrating by making their presence significant only in terms of public order and security. In other words, while they have to be employed in order to maintain the local economy in a healthy state, they are denied the most basic civil rights, from the vote to housing, while at the same time they are made scapegoats[31] for the North's problems, from criminality to pollution, from the decay of the cities to the growing fears linked to globalisation[32] and secularisation.

Through the analysis of the Lega's more recent positions on immigration, the next section will try to show not only how foreigners are perceived by the Padani but also what long-term model of society the party is putting forward in reacting to the phenomenon. As anticipated in the Introduction, this is a model of an 'institutionalised state of exception' based on the idea that the only way to 'tolerate' the foreign presence within not only the North but the country as a whole, is to keep the newly arrived in a permanent state of precarious and temporary inhabitancy.

7 The League's anti-immigrant rhetoric

Through the analysis of articles, interviews and editorials published in *La Padania*, this section will provide a more detailed account of the party's position on immigration and the idea of an original, alternative identity behind it. It will try to show how the more exclusionary turn in the rhetoric on otherness since the invention of Padania has become increasingly more radical and how such a shift translates into a battle fought on different fronts: from cultural and ideologically oriented discrimination to practical/everyday marginalisation of the immigrants. The aim of this analysis follows the same rationale as the previous chapter in establishing whether the League, in reacting to the foreign presence within the North of the country, is putting forward a specific or alternative model of citizenship.

The general impression in reading the interventions, articles, editorials and interviews appearing in *La Padania*, the party newspaper founded by Umberto Bossi in 1996,[33] is that they seem to follow a common pattern and be centred on two main issues presented as deeply linked to each other: namely, law and order, and immigration. The discussion of these subjects involves the recurrent use of a predictable and fixed rhetoric based on the concepts of identity and otherness. The inner tension between the 'us' and 'them' poles is conveyed through the creation of an atmosphere of tension and fear resulting from a precise communication strategy based on social alarmism. This rhetoric is sustained and brought into force by the use of terms such as alarm, battle, emergency, peril, risk, terrorism, criminality, security, explosion, catastrophe, tragedy, suspicion, violence, colonization, invasion, Islamisation and similar. It is indeed in these terms that the party addresses the issue of what is an open 'us' versus 'them' conflict, expressed by the opposition of two sets of contrasting stereotyped identities.

The first of these includes the values of culture, right to self-determination, nation, West, Christianity, truth, homeland, (our) people, tradition, rule of the state. The second one, which refers to immigrants, includes the terms clandestine, (those) people, extremism, terrorism, Islam, Chinese mafia, (Islamic) propaganda, Islamic state, state within the state, gypsies, guests, foreigners. The issues that concern the party are both ideological and practical: from the impossibility of building a multiethnic society to social housing and the supposed discrimination of Padanian families, just to mention a few examples. Throughout the years, the measures put forward by the League as adequate to solve these conflicts can be summarised with two recurrent slogans: 'zero tolerance' (tolleranza zero), and 'iron fist' (pugno di ferro) (Carcano, 2006).

The identitarian rhetoric emerges as a key element in the party's public discourse: Padanian identity, and more recently and quite surprisingly Italian identity, features in most of the articles, almost invariably referred to as 'lost' or 'threatened' and therefore needing to be rediscovered and emphasised. The titles of the articles are representative of this feeling of loss and fear and the consequent call for the defence of an oppressed or denied sense of belonging.[34]

However, even though the expression 'la nostra identità' is recurrent in these interventions, this identity is always defined exclusively in negative terms, which is to say in relation to the events and circumstances that put it at risk. If in the early days of the League the supposedly common language, the economic and cultural environment, the local dimension of belonging and the Lutheran work ethics were presented as the essence of Northern identity, the more recent definitions acquire a meaning only in opposition to 'otherness', following a common mechanism in the construction of all collective identities. The concepts of 'roots' (radici) and belonging to the territory still play a central role in the current debate, as does the idea of 'our people' (nostra gente) committed to the protection of this identity and to the autonomy of the new nation and its values (Polli, 2009). However, the focus has shifted towards the external element to the extent that, occasionally, Padanian identity appears to consist precisely of this commitment to fight to preserve the status quo, in this claim for freedom and in the reaffirmation of the concept that the North is 'our home' (casa nostra) (Cota, 2009). This explains why, in order to provide a broader and more meaningful description on 'Padanian-ness', it is important to analyse it in relation to the perceived threats that are supposedly endangering it.

Starting from factors resulting from the current international conjuncture, a supposed threat accounting for the rising level of anxiety in the North is identified by the party in globalisation, understood as a pervasive phenomenon, which penetrates not only the economic but also the cultural, political and social spheres. A globalised society is one in which the differences are levelled and people behave according to the same social principles all around the globe. To this 'utopian multi-racial society' the League opposes the preservation of differences, which also implies a 'sincere respect' for alternative ideas of the good life, as long as they are put into practice in the countries in which they developed. When addressing the 'issue of immigration', this differentialist approach[35] advocates the need to give priority to immigrants who are easier to assimilate, while targeting Muslim immigrants as the least desirable[36] (Bassi, 2007b; Ferrari, 2007), as they represent a double threat as terrorists and as enemies of Christianity.[37] It is not only the people who are perceived as threatened but also the territory and its peculiar traditions. Interestingly enough, Catholicism is seen as a necessary counterpart to overcome the growing relativism and the announced Islamisation of the nation (Bassi, 2007c).

As argued by Bossi in a speech given in Cà San Marco in 2006,[38] 'The individual, having once cut off the tie with his own land and stock, becomes a stateless person, rootless like a tree at the mercy of the wind blown by the globalist power [...] Nations are not like water, which can be mixed with other elements randomly. Nations can hardly be mixed together. People always go back to their own roots'.[39] When the links with the homeland weaken, 'nations [...] run the risk of being erased':[40] annihilation and colonisation are the inevitable consequences of giving up the constant struggle aimed at 'retaining the control over our own land'.[41]

This objective can only be pursued, according to the Lega's rhetoric, through a twofold strategy: on one side by proactively promoting cultural initiatives, such as the creation of the official Federalist Foundation promoted by MP Roberto Maroni and launched in June 2007 with the aim of 'giving space, at a theoretical level as well as through concrete actions, to all those expressions of federalist and identitarian cultures in Padania and beyond'[42] (Poli, 2007); and on the other side with an aggressive attack directed at what is perceived as the ultimate and most dangerous challenge to the survival of traditional identities: immigration and particularly Muslim immigration.

The issue of immigration is presented by the League through a discourse centred on an apocalyptic interpretation of 'our future' that links it to a series of risks and catastrophes deriving from the arrival of foreigners to the country. This is why, according to the party, it is necessary to react first of all by sending out a 'cry for help' (grido d'allarme), a 'cultural alarm' (allarme culturale) and a 'terrorism alert' (allarme terrorismo) (Gibelli, 2007g; Mirabile, 2007a) in order to attract the attention of what is portrayed as an invasion (Montanari, 2007a), a national emergency (Garavaglia, 2007), which threatens 'the future of our children' (Gallizzi, 2007).

The future as imagined in these articles is anything but rosy since it will involve a long phase of decline which has already started and will result in a new Islamic Nazi-Fascism (Montanari, 2007a, 2007b; Boiocchi, 2007). This warning cry directed at spreading awareness among the people of the fact that any reaction to the phenomenon other than rejection, and particularly the 'fake welcoming attitude'[43] hypocritically put forward by the Italian Left, is dangerous, is considered by the League's representatives almost as a moral duty (Gibelli, 2007g; Iezzi, 2007b).

The annihilation of the people heralded by a significant number of articles is presented as the consequence of an ongoing war between the state in its local institutions on one side and 'ethnic groups who do not want to integrate' and who benefit from a set of privileges, such as the right to vote, that the central government intend to grant them to the disadvantage of the national and local communities, which end up paying the price for this lack of rules. Among the rules that should be respected there is the main principle established with the 'Bossi-Fini law', which strictly ties immigration to work permits as well as the systematic police inspections of mosques, dismissed as mere 'fake places of cult', cover-up used to spread Islamic propaganda. The ruling class currently in power (at that time a centre-left coalition) has to be held morally responsible for the problems experienced by Northerners since its ignorance and private interests have turned Italy into a land of conquest. In general, it can be said that immigration is believed to be aggravating an already 'explosive' situation, a delicate phase that the country (interestingly enough the point of reference here is the old nation) and the entire world are facing and which corresponds to a loss of traditional Christianity values, rooted, for instance, in the central role of the family as well as the community, as this analysis will show.

There appear to be three main targets in the League's anti-immigrant campaign: the Chinese, the Romanians and all Muslims. The title of an article written by the Northern League's MP Stefano Stefani and published on September 2007 seems to go to the heart of the problem, namely 'Us, them and law and order'.[44] 'Crime is crime', Stefani argues, implying that there cannot be any justification for it and demanding adequate punishment. These three groups, the first two characterised by a nationality and the third by religious belonging, seem to be the crucial ones in the League's battle, which is carried out on two different levels. On the one hand, these immigrants, grouped under the indistinct definition of 'questa gente', represent a problem for law and order in Northern Italian cities; on the other hand, a fundamental issue with their presence is the clash of civilizations, ideas of life, religious and cultural differences, considered as absolutely incompatible with the valori leghisti (Montanari, 2007b).

Generally speaking, the references to daily violence and crime are rather vague: the facts are recalled quite superficially, as are the data on official surveys and investigations on the links between immigration and criminality. When referring to the police's and secret service's reports, the articles employ ambiguous language: 'according to a recent report'; 'in the light of what has recently happened in Perugia'; 'as confirmed by the secret service the situation relating to terrorism is rather delicate'; 'the words of the head of the police should alarm us'.[45] This strategy, while avoiding statistics, numbers and details, leaves unquestioned the existence of a strict relation between illegal immigration and problems of law and order, while referring to a supposed constantly growing number of crimes perpetrated by foreigners. Such crimes are often mentioned in the opening or at the very end of the articles or interviews, serving a double function: on the one hand they justify at the beginning the strong opinions expressed in the core of the article, while on the other hand they leave the reader with this image of immigrants as criminals and therefore with a last feeling of concern and fear.[46]

Apart from these more or less generic references to intelligence reports confirming and backing the concerns linked to the arrival of 'these people', the alarmism is also 'justified' through the recollection of some specific problems such a Chinatown revolt in Milan (Stucchi, 2007); the results of the investigations into the terrorist cells in Perugia, Turin and Cremona (Grimoldi, 2007; Indini, 2007a); the link between Islam and the new BR (Red Brigades) in an anti-American struggle (Cota, 2007); the assassination of a couple in Treviso (Garavaglia, 2007); the hijacking of a bus (the article does not mention when and where this happened) (Gibelli, 2007c); the removal of the crucifix in Mangialli hospital in Milan (Gibelli, 2007b); the release of 'il Rom della strage', Marco Ahmetovic, who killed a group of friends in a drunken car accident (Bassi, 2007e); the Reggiani killing[47] (Roselli, 2007).

Not only are these episodes described with little detail but they are just mentioned in passing while analysing more general and more ideological issues that the authors of the articles aim to push at the centre of the political debate. This impression seems to be confirmed by the fact that other crimes, which happened at the same time, are not reported at all, as if the impact of a few symbolic ones on public opinion constantly reminded of the them could be enough to justify the need for a broader discussion on immigration or, better, for a more decisive strategy to prevent and stop new arrivals in the country. Moreover, the articles contribute to crystallising immigrants' identities, with the result that certain groups will be indissolubly associated with a specific threat. In this sense, the Chinese are essentially Mafiosi and represent unfair competitors in the local economy. As reported by Borghezio at the EU Parliament, 'the Chinese mafia is today extremely powerful. Over the years it has developed anticipating the challenges of globalisation and getting ready to face them. It represents enemy number one for our future: it is the most organised – and therefore the most dangerous – criminal group'[48] (Gallizzi, 2007). For this reason it cannot be ignored by politicians who, instead, often choose simply to turn their heads away. He mentioned an unspecified 'Chinatown revolt' in Milan to argue that the Chinese community in the city is blackmailing the state, which has shown its weakness and its incapability to respond adequately. Moreover, Borghezio remarked upon what he presented as a shared belief among the party members, that 'these Chinese groups tend not to integrate as they ought to; on the contrary they are inclined to build a different state within the state', which they fund through a series of illegal activities such as the smuggling of 'clandestines' across Italian borders[49] (ibid.). What is interesting here is the fact that the MP, speaking on behalf of his party, concludes his intervention by repeating that the battle against the Chinese power has to be considered the first priority.

The first priority seems also to be that of dealing with the Muslim community, as clearly emerges from a number of interventions on the subject appearing in *La Padania* in the years under scrutiny and beyond. Muslim immigrants feature in most of these articles and their presence in Padania and Italy is constantly portrayed as a 'bomb ready to explode' (bomba pronta a esplodere), a 'bomb on our heads' (bomba sulla nostra testa) (Cota, 2007), a 'time bomb' (bomba a orologeria) (Gibelli, 2007e). The party's representatives seem to be primarily concerned with the risk linked to terrorism, an anxiety based on the assumption that Muslim organisations are connected to the new BR and are ready to join their battle against America and the West (Cota, 2007). They see in the Left's laissez-faire attitude and their proposal for a new law on freedom of religion a way to open the doors to the Islamisation of 'our society' (Montanari, 2007b). The mosques are nothing but places used to protect 'extremists or terrorists, which are the same thing' (Mirabile, 2007a; Gazzotti, 2007; Iezzi, 2009), and in this respect they are a clear example of how the project of integration has ultimately failed as much as any attempt to build a multicultural society in countries such as the UK (Gibelli, 2007a).

Indeed, mosques contribute to creating ghettos, which in time become a 'cradle of Islamic terrorism' used for recruiting new members and planning attacks[50] (Gibelli, 2007e; Girardin, 2009), and therefore should be closely monitored if not closed tout court (Polli, 2007b). These 'centre of terror' (centrali del terrore) operations hide and protect people who have been trained to think that 'prevaricating Westerners is a duty for every good Muslim',[51] a message that has become clear since the terrorist attacks on the United States on 11 September 2001 and the subsequent bombings in Madrid and London (Indini, 2007a). A number of vaguely mentioned reports from Carabinieri and the secret services warn that Italy is going to be the next target of Islamist terrorist attacks (Iezzi, 2009), a threat which cannot take anyone by surprise, since 'Islam has never proven to be moderate'[52] (Indini, 2007a), and its followers have never committed themselves to comply with the laws and duties required by their country of arrival (ibid.). Islam, the articles argue, does not contemplate any exception to its fixed and unquestionable ideology (pensiero unico): 'Too many people, behind the cover-up of seeking employment or further education, are actually here to recruit and train persons ready to attack any time soon. The threat of terrorism, even through the employment of weapons of mass destruction, is increasingly strong'[53] (Gibelli, 2007e).

The threat of terrorist attacks is not the only concern of the League: 'This is a proper clash of civilizations. Against us, against freedom and democracy in favour of religious totalitarianism and against human reason'[54] (Gibelli, 2007e). To this challenge, which includes the physical occupation of 'our squares' (Garibaldi, 2007c), only the League seems to be ready to react, emerging as the 'the last bastion [baluardo] arresting the invasion' (Montanari, 2007a), a role shared with its youth movement, committed to the respect of Padanian laws and traditions against the burqua and faithful to the principle that 'everyone is the master in his own land'[55] (Lega Nord, 2004).

Besides the clash of civilizations, the party seems concerned with a number of practical issues that arise from the foreign presence. If in the case of Muslims a clear issue is the request to remove the crucifixes from public spaces[56] (Gibelli, 2007b), other 'problems' concerning all immigrants and their requests have proven central to the League's rhetoric. Examples include the question of social housing, which should be assigned to Italians first of all, whereas the 'extracomunitari' should not be given the right to be included on the waiting lists. As proudly announced in 2005 on the party youth's website, 'Thanks to the Northern League there will not be only Muhammed on the waiting list for social housing'.[57] This position is in line with the League's commitment to defend the territory, its squares, streets and neighbourhoods. Moreover, immigrants should not be given the right to vote, even after a certain number of years of continued residence in the country, a position presented as diametrically opposed to that of the Left, and consequently perceived as the primary cause of the problems linked to immigration.

To conclude this overview on immigration, it can be said that there seem to be a number of practical reasons for the rejection of immigrants. Most are summarised in a sort of manifesto,[58] published in 2004, which explains that these are of an economic, social, and health and safety nature. At the economic level, it is argued that employing foreign labour at low salaries will end up damaging the local economy and make it less competitive with the rest of Europe while triggering the discontent of natives. At a social level, it states that Padanians and Italians are not ready for the changes brought about by immigrants, and that these alternative lifestyles represent trauma for an otherwise homogeneous (Christian/European) society.[59]

This is why the League declares itself ready to contribute to helping the disadvantaged nations in their own territory, a strategy which, as we shall see, plays an important role in the construction of a mono-directional, long-distance solidarity. Moreover, the document remarks upon the fact that granting medical care to everybody without distinguishing between the locals and the immigrants (above all illegal immigrants) is not fair to the citizens who pay taxes and contribute to the economic growth of the country.

Finally, the pamphlet expresses a request of central importance to the party: namely, that immigrants should be dealt with at a local level. This request is often put forward as the ultimate solution and is reinforced by the League's project of a federal state, which is presented as the best form of state also in responding to the challenge of immigration.[60] However, while working on the project of a federal state, the party has also put forward a number of measures to confront 'the other', which will only be mentioned in passing here, as they will be the subject of Chapter 4, dealing with the laws passed by different governments. One of these measures, suggested as a partial solution, is that of taking immigrants' fingerprints in order to have more control over their identity and their movements (Maccanti, 2007). The range of initiatives is broad and stretches from the idea of using the navy to prevent the arrivals (and if necessary bomb the ships), to the call for public demonstrations against immigration in the squares of Padania, to more folkloristic threats such as the 'pig day' (maiale day) planned by MP Calderoli, which consists of 'profaning' with pig manure the building site destined for a mosque (Pandini, 2007). This is not dissimilar to the MP's public statement on his plans to 'celebrate' the beginning of Ramadan by eating pork ribs (ibid.).

The interventions of the Lega's representatives are reinforced through the use of military metaphors, which include the terms 'war' (guerra), 'barricades' (barricate), 'trench' (trincea), 'battle' (battaglia) and 'fight' (lotta). However, as mentioned above, while the main battleground sees the League fighting its number one enemy, the immigrants, the party also carries on another offensive against an internal adversary, namely the Left, which it holds responsible for the national emergency, often perceived as resulting from an ideologically oriented response or an opportunistic attitude aimed at attracting immigrants' consensus.

The League was most critical while in opposition, suggesting that such protest had the twofold aim of attacking immigration while undermining its political adversaries' credibility in dealing with the situation. The party accuses la sinistra of acting in the name of false tolerance merely aimed at achieving electoral results, for instance by suggesting immigrants be allowed to vote in general elections after five years of residence in Italy. It accuses left-wing parties of looking at the issue of immigration through the 'rose-coloured' lenses of an ideology based on a fake buonismo (Gibelli, 2007h; Roselli, 2007).

In this sense, according to Bossi and his followers, it is this political class that should be recognised as racist, since it deludes people with the dream of a better life and a series of promises that the country, at the moment, is unable to fulfil (Montanari, 2007c; Mirabile, 2007b). With its attitude of openness and optimism, the centre-left coalition has shown the immigrants that 'the door is open', that illegal immigrants will not be punished but, on the contrary, will be looked after (Polli, 2007b; Carcano, 2007). Such an irresponsible attitude has had as its first result that of institutionalising the clandestine presence within the country (Iezzi, 2007c). The leftist intelligentsia is presented as trapped in political correctness and driven by the aim of proving the irrationality of citizens' legitimate concerns in order to achieve an electoral consensus. Once again the citizens' life, homeland and culture are put at risk by those – the 'real Taliban' – who insist on presenting 'security' as a false problem (Garibaldi, 2007b; Baldi, 2009; Gibelli, 2007f).

In arguing that the real racism is by its political opponents, the Northern League's representatives attempt not only to discredit the Left but also to prove that their party cannot be perceived as racist, since it does not promise things that it cannot grant. The party's resentment towards the Left is also due to the fact that the Left, too, has opted for a zero-tolerance attitude and has demanded the expulsion of all Roma in times of crisis, such as after Reggiani's killing[61] (Roselli, 2007). As Rosselli wrote in *La Padania*, 'Once they were tolerant, now they all act as sheriffs. But when things like this happen in the North nobody does anything about them. They are racists in reverse'[62] (ibid.). The latter accusation refers to the belief that despite being themselves the true racists, left-wing politicians played the race card to the disadvantage of the leghisti. According to the League's representatives, this is a clear sign that they were right and that, in dealing with immigration, political parties should not compromise, since the only possible solution to the 'problem' is that of expelling even the communitarians (Montanari, 2007c) and preventing new arrivals tout court (Garibaldi, 2007c). Alternatively, the immigrants can go and live 'in the towns governed by the Left, where they know they will welcomed [...] the main matter is not even what sort of policies should be enforced since the issue is that these people should not enter the country at all as we are unable to absorb such groups in terms of providing employment for them. Not to mention the fact that they do not show any will to integrate with us'[63] (Mirabile, 2007c).

The constant references to a delicate economic phase and to the difficulties met by Padanians themselves to find jobs contribute to justifying in rational terms the party's complete rejection of immigrants even as workers, while showing the failure and incoherence of the Left and its double responsibility in turning the immigrants into victims and triggering episodes of intolerance. Indeed, the leghisti believe that the citizens' occasionally violent reactions towards the newly arrived can be explained by the fact that they are 'fed up' (stufi) with the situation and with being denied the right to self-determination, which can be summarised in the well-known formula 'master in our own home'[64] (Cota, 2009).

The case of Romanians is emblematic of both this idea that Italians must react if they want to be in control of their territory and of the conflict with the Left. Slogans such as 'If we get back in government, out with the Romanians'[65] (Roselli, 2007) were used in the League's electoral campaigns to gain a broader consensus. If Chinese and Muslim immigrants are tied to their fixed identity as Mafiosi and terrorists, the case of Romanians is even more controversial. Most of the time simply labelled as 'gypsies' (zingari), they are denied any recognition of their identity and internal difference in terms of ethnic, cultural, national and religious belonging. The common trait under which they are grouped together is that of their nomadic lifestyle, while no distinction is made between non-nomadic Romanians, Roma and Sinti of other nationalities, including Italian. Indeed, despite the fact that many of them are Italian and have been so for centuries, they represent the ultimate 'foreigner' and the essential criminal.

Their innate difference is expressed through a series of stereotypes, such as that 'stealing does not mean for gypsies what it means for us'[66] (Gibelli, 2007g), which is to say that theft is part of their culture. Their presence is linked with an increasing criminality and particularly with a rise in episodes of theft, child kidnapping and all sorts of not clearly defined 'heinous crimes' committed in the immediate proximity of their camps. This is why the mayors of the North demand the power to deal with them at a local level, with the aim of forbidding their presence within their cities and sending them to build their barracks in areas ruled by the 'more tolerant' Left (Gibelli, 2007g; Roselli, 2007).

Perceived as seeking to exploit a state that they do not recognise and to live by stealing what they did not work for, they represent the last 'other', the most marginalised community (Gibelli, 2007g; Roselli, 2007). The idea that Italians have the right to control and protect their territory justifies the increasing violence against immigrants, actions that occasionally are not only legitimised but even triggered by some among the League's most extreme representatives. While 'decriminalising' such violent episodes, the party follows a double strategy in order to present itself as non-racist: on the one hand it remarks upon the idea that Italians (not only Padanians) are the real victims and those discriminated against as they cannot set the rules and be in power in their own 'home', while on the other hand, it reminds its detractors of the fact that solidarity represents a central value of the Lega's political thought. According to this rhetoric of victimhood, not only are leghisti unfairly considered racist, but they are also denied the right to freedom of expression, since every time they make public their position on immigration they are classified as intolerant.

The paradigmatic example exploited to prove this is the case of the arrest in Brussels of European MP Borghezio following his demonstration outside the Parliament wearing an anti-Islam tee-shirt in September 2007. The party commented on the episode, omitting to mention the many incidents involving verbal violence against immigrants whose protagonists were never sanctioned, by stating that in Europe as much as in Italy people are denied the right to express their ideas in a peaceful way (Boiocchi, 2007). As a result, according to them, they have become the ultimate victims, to whom the most basic civil rights are denied, while the need to be politically correct brings about para-doxical situations such as that of removing the crucifix from classrooms in order not to offend Muslim pupils and families (Gibelli, 2007b, 2007d; Montanari, 2007a). This last case is considered emblematic of a clear dis-crimination against Italian citizens together with a series of other situations, such as, for instance, the fact that they have to pay taxes to fund the Lam-pedusa CPT (Centro di permanenza temporanea, or Centre of Temporary Stay),[67] where immigrants arriving in Italy illegally via sea are kept until they are identified and repatriated, and also pay for people who, having escaped from the CTP, will also 'steal from their houses'. Another example is that of tourists who travel on planes that also take on board illegal immigrants who need to be repatriated. Both examples are used here to show how Italians are the true victims (Polledri and Maraventano, 2007).

If the groups of immigrants mentioned until now share the common char-acteristic of being plotters planning to exploit the state without respecting it, others are, according to the party's rhetoric, those who need its solidarity. Whenever the League is accused of being racist, its leader and followers are keen to remind their detractors of the several initiatives and foundations that see them committed to providing relief and support for disadvantaged popula-tions in their own countries. Such philanthropic actions are carried out in the name of an immutable principle: 'let's help them to help themselves', or 'let's help them in their own home(lands)'[68] (Bossi, 2009). This principle, derived from the party's anti-colonial belief that people have the right to be sovereign in their own countries, is aimed at demanding the same attitude of respect for Ita-lian citizens. The anti-immigrant rhetoric of the articles published in *La Padania* is often mitigated by the claim that Umanitaria Padania or Co.Pa (Cooperazione Padana) have always been active in offering support to countries such as Somalia, Serbia, Romania, Eritrea, Bulgaria and others (Mariani, 2006). These initiatives, as well as those of the voluntary association interestingly named 'peace warriors' (Guerrieri della pace), are usually only mentioned to prove a more general point – that the Northern League is not racist – whereas in none of the articles examined is it possible to find details of what exactly has been done and by which organisation in each country. The point here is clearly that of showing how the party's political action takes into account the value of solidarity. A brief analysis of the latter, in relation to the concept of Christian charity, is useful in order to understand better how both the League's defini- tion of (national) identity and the relationship with the Catholic Church have changed in the last decade and more precisely since the Muslim presence within the country has taken centre stage in the debate on immigration.

8 The League and the Catholic Church, selective and long-distance solidarity

Following Oneto, 'Solidarity and love for thy neighbour surely are two of the Christian duties, which are part of our culture but to which, nonetheless, should be devoted a number of observations: first of all the neighbour (the word itself says it all) is a person who is close to us, a relative, a member of the family. Our true neighbour is he who belongs to our ancient community and he who has signed with us a social and even institutional contract. After that, if there is more left, we can turn our attention towards the others, but this extension [of care and attention] cannot be intended as a duty of the community'[69] (Oneto, 2004). Despite the fact that Oneto, to a certain extent, takes a distance from the Christian idea of an indiscriminate universal soli- darity, it is important here to remember that the Catholic Church itself has recently moved towards a more restrictive idea of the concept, as proven, for instance, by the CEI guidelines examined in Chapter 2 – a shift that here is measured more in terms of the impact that certain positions of individual Catholic representatives on religious difference have had on the Italian public debate on the matter, rather than on the real intentions or global strategy of the Church as a whole.

What is interesting in the Northern League's rhetoric on solidarity is the fact that it also stresses the need for a common Christian identity that needs to be protected from the Islamisation of the country (Indini, 2007a). In this sense, the endangered identity that the party is committed to save from external threats becomes one primarily characterised by its Catholicism and, even more interestingly, a national one. In other words, when referring to a dying culture, threatened by the arrival of immigrants, the League has recently extended this identity to all Italians, using the terms 'Italian' and 'Catholic' or 'Christian' as interchangeable. In this respect, by taking back the streets of Padania to demonstrate against immigration in an attempt to pro- tect Italian identity, the League is also 'taking the squares to rescue the Christians'[70] (Gibelli, 2007d). Another common challenge presented to both the Church and the political party is what this latter defines as 'this laicism which mortifies us'.[71] Secularism is associated by the League with political correctness: both attitudes, used in the attempt not to offend cultures different from 'ours', force Italians to deny or reject the historical Catholic traditions that inform national identity (Gibelli, 2007b).

Solidarity, in the Lega's rhetoric, has to be reciprocal and dialogue is only possible with those countries that show respect for this identity – a theme, that of reciprocity, which also features prominently in the ecclesial documents on identity and otherness.[72] In this sense, Italy and the West in general should fight for their rights not only at home but also abroad, in countries such as Saudi Arabia or Pakistan, where Catholics are discriminated against because of their religion, are not free to wear religious symbols or celebrate mass even in private, and lose their jobs for the same reason (Maroni *et al.* 2007). Intolerance towards Catholicism is considered a substantial 'intolerance towards our culture', against 'a rediscovered identity that surely cannot be exchanged with a pacifism that sacrifices the truth'[73] (ibid.). Once again the concept of truth and the identification of religious belonging with the national character have proven central ideas of the Church's position on multi-faith and multicultural societies. While accusing Islam of being intolerant in its claim to be the only true religion, the League presents Catholicism in the same terms (ibid.). The parallel with the attitude of the Catholic Church in this respect is too striking not to assume that the League is actually borrowing its (most problematic) rhetoric to put forward its claims, occasionally even quoting Pope Benedict XVI, following a strategy aimed at turning Padania's war against immigration into a common battle for Christianity and Italian national identity, and therefore significant to the whole country and the West in general.[74] Both political actors – albeit in different terms and degrees – put forward a definition of the concept of solidarity based on the idea of reciprocity, and directed primarily at selected groups that are perceived as easier to assimilate, while considering the case of Muslim immigrants as the ultimate other: in the case of the Lega as the enemy within, and in the case of the Church as the most dangerous challenge Christianity is facing, certainly the most difficult, if not impossible, group of foreigners to integrate.

Despite the recurrent references to a new definition of Italian Catholic identity, the League has not entirely resolved its difficult relationship with the Church. The latter is still, after all, the political actor most critical of the legislative measures put forward by the party to deal with immigration, which members of the Catholic hierarchy have often described as racist and unacceptable, as for instance after the approval of the so-called 'security package' (pacchetto sicurezza) and the introduction of the 'crime of illegal entry' (reato di clandestinità) (Anon. 2009f). However, this relationship has deeply changed in the last decade, and the two powers are today closer than ever before, as can be proven by looking at the first hostile exchange of views between the two in the early 1990s.[75]

This link between the Church and the League has often been overlooked or minimised by scholars. As Moia (1997: 5) recalls, academics were quite surprised when 'a survey commissioned in the Department of Sociology of the Università Cattolica by the Christian Democratic Party revealed that the majority of the Northern League supporters were young, wealthy, self-employed and had voted until then for the DC. The most worrying result of the investigation was, according to the researchers, the fact that more than two thirds of those interviewed defined themselves as practising Catholics. A statement which indicated a belonging [to Catholicism] incompatible with the support given to an "autonomist utopia" characterised by a strong racist attitude, social egoism, lack of solidarity' (ibid.). Scholars' bewilderment was justified by years of difficult relationships between the Church and the Lega, during which the party had on several occasions tried to win Catholic support while at the same time provoking the Church and more or less directly challenging its power.

The document *Ripartire dal popolo*, written in 1991 by Irene Pivetti[76] to prove that her party was committed to the values of family and solidarity, was aimed at overcoming the rejection on the part of the Church of what its representatives perceived as an intolerant political actor with whom they were not willing to engage in dialogue (Moia, 1997). The League's second attempt to gain legitimacy came in December of the same year, when the Catholic hierarchy officially recognised the Republics of Slovenia and Croatia, a move based on the acknowledgement of people's right to self-determination. The news was immediately reported in *Autonomia Lombarda*, the Lega Lombarda newspaper, in an article which underlined how the same opinion could apply to the Padanian case and how this position could be interpreted as a sign that after years of suspicion the Church's attitude towards the party and its idea of federalism, initially considered 'parochial' and 'xenophobic', was eventually changing (Moia, 1997: 131).

In 1992, the scandal of 'mani pulite' played a double role in this relationship, contributing on the one hand to uniting the Church and the League to stand against the traditional political parties while, on the other hand, giving Bossi's party a pretext to attack the Catholic hierarchy for its connivance with the old DC, deeply involved in the scandals (Pivetti, 1992). At that time, Moia (1997: 42) recalls, the time of the opening of the Church to the League was not yet at hand. The Church started recognising the party when it became significant in terms of electoral results in the 1996 elections: since then many Catholic representatives, such as Cardinals Martini and Ruini and Como Bishop Maggiolini, have started to reconsider their previous opinion of the party and acknowledge the presence of the League (Moia, 1997). In general, what Moioli said in 1991 about this relationship can still be considered valid today: 'the Church's intransigent rejection of leghismo'[77] is inversely proportional to the Church's participation in politics. In other words, the less the single representatives are active in the political arena, the more they criticise Bossi's party (Moioli, 1991: 131).

This pattern seems to confirm an element that emerged in the previous chapter from the analysis of the role of the Church in the debate on immigration: the higher the position Catholic representatives occupy in the Church's hierarchy, the more they show concern for the phenomenon. This is particularly true when the debate on immigration focuses on Muslim foreigners. Even though it is also necessary to state once again that it not possible to consider the most prominent representatives of the Catholic hierarchy as a united front, the well-known exceptions in this sense being represented by

Cardinal Carlo Maria Martini and Cardinal Dionigi Tettamanzi particularly on immigration concerns, on the issue of Islam and Muslims in Italy, the Church and the League seem to agree more than the Church would admit, at least until recently, when the ascent to the papal throne of Francis reshuffled the cards, as we shall see in the last chapter of this book. To simplify, it could be said that the Church works on two different levels. On the one hand its hierarchy officially condemns anything the League expresses in politically incorrect terms and anything that can be seen by public opinion as racist, insisting instead on the values of dialogue and mutual understanding. On the other hand, it takes part in controversial initiatives as long as they are justified by some sort of pseudo-intellectual premise, as happened, for instance, when priest Don Baget Bozzo and Cardinal Giacomo Biffi gave a speech during a demonstration against immigration, organised by the League, to celebrate the anniversary of the battle of Lepanto in 1571 as a definitive moment of victory over Islam on the part of Christianity (Guolo, 2004). The presence of Catholic representatives at a demonstration that had the double aim of reaffirming the supremacy of Christianity and protecting its values from Muslim assault was not commented on either by the Pope or by any other member of the hierarchy. This is not the only occasion on which representatives of the League and of the Church have stood united against Islam: another example is the participation of some Church members at the demonstration against a project for the construction of a mosque in Lodi (Anon. 2002b). Leaving aside the different reasons behind the League's and the Church's response to Muslim immigration, it can be said that what clearly emerges as their common concern is the threat it poses to a traditional and Catholic Italian national identity. In this sense, by turning the struggle for the North into a struggle for the nation and for Christianity, the League set out on a path already taken by the Church in its attempt to link its own decline with that of the nation. It is quite clear that this shift in the relationship between the two powers was purely instrumental and centred only on the identification of the enemy rather than in the strategies to defeat it. Finally, both powers are more concerned with achieving their own goals – whether this means (re)gaining a declining support or obtaining privileges in the allocation of resources – than with immigration. Nevertheless, they both contributed to shaping the state's reaction to immigration as well as creating two models of integration and citizenship which had a significant impact on public discourses on identity and otherness.

9 The immigrant as a homo sacer and the permanent state of exception

As the analysis of the articles published in *La Padania* has tried to show, the general concerns related to immigration put forward by the Northern League as well as the shifts and the turning points in a rhetoric on identity and otherness, over the years have determined the outlining of an original and very exclusionary idea of coexistence of different lifestyles and ideas of the good life characterised by an attitude of closure and diffidence towards the newly arrived. Many of the traits defined by scholars as typical of different types of racism are evident in the Lega's political thought: from territorial to competitive racism. Above all, what seems significant here is the articulation typical of additional racism featuring clearly in the party's political discourse, characterised by the need to provide intolerant attitudes with a rational justification articulated in three main phases: the constant comments on criminality and their exaggeration; the representation of immigrants' lives as miserable; and the total neglect of their everyday lives or the private dimensions of their lives. These are all factors that clearly inform the League discourse on immigration. As the review of the League's articles tried to show, the process through which foreigners acquire relevance in the national media merely in relation to their being 'criminal' or a threat, is characterised by the vagueness of the information provided, the tendency to 'employ easy-to-use news', a warning conveyed in a dramatic way[78] (Albertazzi, 2007: 335), and through language that relies on 'assumptions' and 'probabilities', which have as their first result the triggering of irrational and often unjustified fears among the public.

These worries of local society, regardless of how distant they are from an objective interpretation of the situation, become then the 'reality', according to a mechanism described by scholars such as Dal Lago as 'feeding on itself' (autopoietico).[79] Since the 1990s, he explains, the canovaccio, the scheme followed by the newspapers when referring to immigration, has been a fixed one, characterised by three phases: a direct threat to the locals on the part of immigrants, the protest of the locals, the arrival of the police and the (only temporary) relief for the locals, destined to last only the brief period of time between different 'assaults' or crimes (Dal Lago, 2004: 73).

In the case of the League, it can be said that this last phase of relief does not feature in the discourse on immigration, as the fear is exacerbated to a level where the threat is presented as constant and the crimes committed as increasing in number and brutality.[80] This mechanism is nothing more than 'empty tautology', since it is the very action of sending out an alarm which 'proves' the fact it is denouncing: in other words, the process of providing definitions of reality works according to a mechanism in which if citizens define a situation as real, then its consequences became real (Dal Lago, 2004).[81]

As classic studies[82] on the auto-produced construction of reality have shown, subjective definitions of a situation become real, and therefore objective, particularly when they are related to delicate aspects such as the fear of a perceived enemy. This particular way of 'manufacturing' reality is reinforced by the generally accepted idea that the victim has the right to be the first to provide a definition of the situation, which inevitably will influence the following definitions (Dal Lago, 2004: 74). By exploiting the change in the paradigm used to provide these definitions, determined by the crisis of the 1990s, the Northern League has managed to turn 'fear' into a means to shape public opinion and gain support (ibid.: 77).

Another classic mechanism that assumes particular relevance in the party's rhetoric consists in the 'victimisation' of the aggressor and in transferring the blame onto the real victims (Dal Lago, 2004: 63). In this sense, by presenting themselves as discriminated against in not being granted freedom of expression and in being sanctioned for their racism, the party's representatives can turn the immigrants into the perpetrators and portray them as not only aggressive and unwilling to accept 'Italian' (Catholic) values, but also as the direct cause of the leghisti's marginalisation in their own territory. Taking this process a step further, it then becomes clear that the status of victim and the frustration of the locals can be used, and indeed have been used, to justify episodes of violence against the immigrants, rendered the target of an 'acceptable' or 'understandable' intolerance.

By making the extracomunitarians significant to the political life of the country only in virtue of the crimes they commit or are 'naturally inclined' to commit and preventing them from acquiring any role but scapegoat in the public sphere, the League turns the immigrant into a homo sacer, as Agamben describes. In his *Homo Sacer: Sovereign Power and Bare Life* (1998), the philosopher analyses the classical definitions of sovereignty and citizenship in the attempt to describe phenomena such as Fascism and the Holocaust. Through the categories of rule, example and exception, and inclusion and exclusion, Agamben defines the homo sacer as the 'exception' (from the Latin *ex capere*, to take outside). The homo sacer represents an exception as he is banned from society and all his rights are revoked; his life is crystallised in a condition in which he can be killed without his killers being sanctioned but he cannot be sacrificed in a ritual. His is a 'human life […] included in the juridical order solely in the form of its exclusion (that is, of its capacity to be killed)' (Agamben, 1998: 8). In this sense, his figure is symmetrical to that of the sovereign in his being inside and outside the law at the same time.

Agamben distinguishes between human beings' 'bare life' (zoe) and 'bios' (qualified life and therefore also and mainly political life), and argues that the homo sacer is considered simply as bare life and is not recognised in the political sphere. To a certain extent, he represents the limit, indeed the exception, essential to set the rule: he is excluded from the good life only achievable though politics while existing as a body that cannot reach a 'life worth being lived' in the only possible way, which is through the state and therefore through recognition by the sovereign (namely the law). This bare life that characterises the homo sacer, according to Agamben, is 'a life that as such is exposed to a violence without precedent in the most profane and banal ways' (Agamben, 1998: 114). The bare life 'expresses precisely both life's subjection to a power over death and life's irreparable exposure in the relation of abandonment' (ibid.: 83). Here lies the paradox of the condition of the homo sacer: he can be recognised by society precisely and only for his being just bare life and precluded from acquiring political relevance. In this sense, the law that decides on the exclusion at the same time gives the individual an identity. This identity consists in being the exception, outside the society and the law and for this reason 'included in it' as what is different from the norm, what citizens can measure their inclusion against.

Immigrants, by occupying the bottom level in the work sector, have traditionally contributed to elevating the status of those locals who used to be 'the last' in the social ladder and therefore have also made it possible for Italians to acquire a new and more desirable role within society and to build a new confidence and feeling of achievement. In this sense, to a certain extent immigrants were included in the receiving society as their status was different in degree but not in substance from that of the natives, as in the case of Southerners who had migrated to the North and who, despite initial discrimination, found in the factories and in the workers' struggle a means to integrate.

On the contrary, the homo sacer's presence is not considered to be of the same nature as that of citizens. Not only is he not significant as a term of comparison in the judgement of what is to be successful or integrated, but he simply is not part of that social ladder and therefore has no chance to move up and to be included or to integrate. The homo sacer is he who does not belong: this condition is permanent as it constitutes precisely the essence, the nature that characterises that human being and his category. The homo sacer cannot escape his destiny of exclusion as this does not depend on his actions or intentions/desires but is determined by birth.

Similarly, the immigrant, illegal and legal, is excluded from taking part in the political life and from access to civil rights, while, at the same time, he becomes part of the society as 'the exception', the bare life, and can be included in it only in virtue of this status as 'other'. This means that the concession to enter the country can be granted only as a temporary situation, precarious and subject to a law that the immigrant can neither contribute to formulating, nor challenge. Immigrants are allowed to interact with the community only as living signs of the boundary between the inside and the outside. Their life is in the hands of the sovereign as he can decide on their 'life' and 'death', which is their being temporarily accepted or permanently/temporarily excluded, whereas the option of being permanently accepted is not contemplated.

As Agamben argues, we live in a society where the state of exception is increasingly common and can be extended indefinitely according to the will of the sovereign, or, in other words, of the law and of those who have the power of formulating and enforcing it. In this sense, the Northern League, with its influence in state decision making on the issue of immigration and for its actual 'being' the state can be seen as the sovereign who has the power to decide on the life and death of the immigrant. Life here does not coincide with rights: the premise for this comparison between the immigrant and the homo sacer is that they have neither rights nor the chance to change their status. Life means instead the temporary concession/permission to live in the country until circumstances, or laws created by the sovereign, change.

What is important here is also the fact that with the immigrant being outside the law, the sovereign does not need to justify rationally or to explain the shifts or sudden turns in its strategy of government and therefore, applying this to the situation of immigrants, also in regulating their presence within the country. The practical implications of this mechanism, whereby immigrants can be granted a temporary and revocable right to live in the country or expelled from the territory on the basis of a new disposition or new laws, will be analysed in the next chapter, which will focus on the legislation on immigration.

An example of arbitrary decisions on the part of the sovereign in this respect is the exploitation of an ambiguous presentation of the offer/demand ratio in the work sector, coupled with a stereotyped interpretation of immigrants' identities and incompatibility with the national character. This is the case of the so-called 'badanti', the domestic workers, mainly women, whose role has been often and again recently discussed with reference to their being much needed in an ageing society in which women's productive and reproductive roles have become difficult to reconcile. The League's position on the subject has been one of support for the regularisation of more female immigrants but strictly limited to those employed to look after the elderly. These new sanatorie have been presented by the party as una tantum – exceptional measures. In this sense, those who are allowed to enter the country will benefit from an exception to the rule (no more immigrants) that can be revoked, extended or suspended at any time by the sovereign, and therefore represents a typical case of precariousness. Conversely, the party's rhetoric against the regularisation of male immigrants is justified by the idea of a saturated job market that does not take into account the real needs of the country and is based on the stereotypical idea that immigrants steal locals' jobs and make the economy weaker and less competitive. This position exposes the League's split between the public discourse aimed at gaining electoral success and the real demand for an immigrant workforce on the part of the factories of the North. In its manifest contradiction, this purely strategic attitude can be labelled as 'simulative politics' in the meaning given to the expression by Blühdorn (2007) and Cento Bull (2009), as Chapter 4 will argue.

I would define the model put forward by the League as an alternative to a multiculturalism destined to fail as an 'institutionalised state of exception', which means a state under permanent 'exceptional' circumstances related to an internal crisis and to an external threat. The expression clearly represents a contradiction in terms, since to make an exception means 'not to treat someone or something according to the usual rules'. If the exception is permanent, it becomes the rule, hence the logic gap: in this way the perceived internal and external challenges, turned into reality by the definition of them provided by political actors, media and public opinion, are exploited to turn exceptional, una tantum, reversible measures put forward to deal with immigration into 'normality'.

This model of state is based on a hybrid between an identitarian and a repressive/legalitarian approach to otherness. On the one hand, a 'strong identitarianism' is based on the fear that 'the presence of immigrants will alter the national culture and may consequently pursue a strategy of limiting and screening immigration flows and citizenship, with a strong preference for immigrants of national origin or […] culturally homogeneous', an attitude that often leads to xenophobic and racist positions (Zincone, 2006: 5). On the other hand, the legalitarian approach aims mainly to 'suppress crime and terrorism by the immigrants', a position in theory shared by all parties, with different degrees of tolerance of crimes, and in the case of the League with a 'zero tolerance' level (ibid.). This model of state implies the subscription to a unidirectional social contract, which demands complete fulfilment of requirements and commitment to determined values on the part of immigrants and strict respect for a set of duties. At the same time immigrants have no access to civil rights and to resources, from visibility in the public sphere to freedom of religion and expression, to the vote and down to accommodation, welfare system and safe working conditions.

In the classic definitions provided by thinkers such as Hobbes and Locke, the social contract is based on the balance between what the individual loses (part of his freedom) and what he gains (mainly protection). In the model outlined by Locke, the citizen has the right to withdraw from the contract (by killing the sovereign) when the state does not fulfil its role and cannot guarantee three main rights: property, freedom and security (Locke, 1988 [1689]). The immigrant does not have such rights, because by signing the contract they are simply agreeing to fulfil a set of duties but are not being granted any right apart from being temporarily allowed to enter the country.

The type of state developed by the League resembles more Hobbes's Leviathan (2009 [1651]) in the principle that there cannot be any sort of rebellion against the sovereign: the 'citizen' cannot be freed from his status of subjection, since the king cannot do any wrong. He is the law and his actions set the rule: by acting, he provides definitions of what is right and what is wrong. Applying this paradigm to the 'state of exception', what is interesting is the fact that the permanent state of threat and emergency allows the sovereign to change the rules without warning and suddenly if necessary, whenever citizens' security is perceived to be at risk. In this sense, the immigrant confirms his position as an outsider: since he is not a citizen, the state does not have a duty to protect him.

10 Conclusions

The analysis conducted until this point was aimed at describing what model of state the Northern League has put forward in its attempts to react to immigration while also explaining how the position of the party on the matter has shifted since the invention of Padania and how increasingly strict is has become recently. Several interesting changes have occurred since the early days of the party. First, the aggressive rhetoric directed at Southerners and the central state has faded, leaving room for the invective against the new enemy: the 'extracomunitario'. Until the creation of the new nation, the so-called terroni represented the main 'problem' for the North in terms of allocation of resources that should be distributed to Padani in the first place, and in terms of an undesired 'multiethnic state' in which they represented the 'other'. By exploiting the 'difficult' coexistence of different ideas of the good life, crystallised in fixed dichotomies, the League aimed to achieve independence or some degree of autonomy from Rome. Padanians were portrayed as victims on whom Fascism had imposed a fake' national identity, which did not respect their ethnic and cultural diversity. Europe was seen as a role model to whom the new nation aspired to belong and under which it hoped to see its independence recognised and protected. In terms of shared values and economic perspectives, it was much closer to Padania than Italy. Southern immigrants within the territory were confined to the lower rung of the social ladder, perceived as difficult to integrate and therefore isolated, albeit somehow included de facto.

Since the invention of Padania and following the increasing significance of foreign arrivals in the public debate, the League has started using a catastrophist rhetoric in order to create the new enemy, a mechanism intensified by a feared Muslim 'invasion'. It can be said that the Southerners' integration (albeit not complete) has improved since this shift of focus on the part of the League, which brought about a new definition of national identity which for the first time referred to the old nation and to its shared Christian values. As shown in the section on the relationship between the League and the Church, this was quite a dramatic change in strategy. Immigrants who are allowed to enter the country are segregated at the bottom level of society and do not have guarantees that they will be able to remain 'in'. They have no civil rights and no voice in the public sphere, but are necessary for two reasons: first, because they are much needed in the work sector, and second, because the party still needs a 'scapegoat' to fuel its political action. However, their presence, visible only in circumstances that link them to criminality, is a revocable concession rather than a right, a condition that turns them into homines sacri. Illegal immigrants, but often also regular immigrants, are confined to an external orbit from which they can gain no access to the country: these are the generic 'extracomunitari', Roma, Albanians, and mainly Muslims. There is no space for these foreigners, who are essentially depicted as carrying a fixed identity attributed to all members of that particular ethnic or religious background.

The most 'revolutionary' change in this new model is that the borders of Padania have come to coincide with those of Italy: the old internal division seems to have been forgotten in the name of the need to make the issue of immigration and the perceived threat significant at a national level. In this sense, the party takes a path already taken by the Church in presenting Italian national identity and Christian values as coinciding and, therefore, both under attack. As a result, all Italians, no matter whether Northerners or Southerners, are supposed to share the same anxiety towards the new arrivals and are called to form a united front in order to 'save' their common identity and shared territory. In the case of the Northern League, this strategy could also be justified by the attempt to gain support in areas of the country where it had not had electoral success.

The League, as much as the Catholic Church, uses as a means to convey its message a rhetoric based on victimhood, following the process described above, according to which transferring the blame onto the victims contributes to legitimising and making more objective a subjective and arbitrary 'definition' of the situation. The two political actors have developed original interpretations of the concept of solidarity which to a certain extent overlap: if the Church puts forward a 'selective solidarity', only directed at those perceived as holding similar values or as easier to assimilate, thus excluding mainly the Muslims, the League's approach invokes a long-distance solidarity aimed at helping people as long as they stay in their own country. Both powers consider helping first their own people as the more adequate criterion to discriminate between those who can be 'saved' or granted temporary entrance and those who will be 'condemned' or 'permanently excluded' (in both cases represented by Muslims).

Emphasising the main difference between the Church's and the League's attitudes in this respect can help to explain better the models they outline. While in the paternalistic quasi-theocratic state developed by the Church everybody can theoretically and potentially become 'a member of the family' as long as they give up their religious identity and embrace Catholicism, in the case of the League such access does not depend on the willingness of the immigrants to accept and recognise different values, including the mainstream religion. On the one hand, by erasing their past and accepting to be enlightened by the truth, immigrants can be recognised by the Church as equal and become automatically Italian. On the other hand, in the case of the Lega, as mentioned above, immigrants' will to integrate, to subscribe to a different set of values and forget their origins, is not enough for them to be granted access. Their exclusion is decided at birth, particularly if they come from countries or religious backgrounds perceived as intrinsically adverse to the West. Moreover, while it can be said that, albeit extremely strict, the assimilation rule imposed by the Church is crystal clear, the same cannot be said of the model set by the political party, since, as already stated, the complete lack of regulation is the result of a permanent state of exception, which means chaos and impossibility for the outsider to take action in order to integrate.

The Northern League's political discourse on immigration, reinforced and legitimised through the exploitation of the language of a Church that, despite its unquestionable decline, still represents one of the most trusted institutions in Italy, has a dramatically strong influence both in legitimising the state's exclusionary and restrictive policy making and in shaping a public opinion whose perception of the 'emergency' as real has been shaped by the party's rhetoric.

The changes in the Lega strategy on immigration and in its identity politics are important mainly for the consequences they have on state policy as well as on the progressively significant role of extreme positions in public discourse on the issue of 'diversity'. The main result of this strategy of rejection is the 'mainstreaming of fear', the normalisation of an extremely exclusionary rhetoric, which were once the prerogative of extreme-right parties and which have today become a stable feature of centre-right mainstream parties. This process of institutionalisation will be addressed in detail in the last chapter of this book, which will also take into account the recent scandals involving Bossi and his family, which brought about a change of leadership – Roberto Maroni first and Matteo Salvini more recently – which, as will be argued, has contributed to radicalise further the positions of party representatives and supporters vis-à-vis 'otherness' and immigration in particular.

Notes

1 Since 2007, the party's rhetoric on identity and otherness begins to radicalise. This is also the crucial phase in which the endangered identity in need of protection is presented as national and Catholic, rather than exclusively linked to Padania.
2 '[G]rande utopia egalitaria.'
3 '[L]'unicità viene sostituita dalla pluralità, la concentrazione dalla disseminazione.'
4 On the regions with a special status, see: Ciarlo, 2000; Olivetti, 2002; Nevola, 2003; Putnam *et al.*, 1993; Putnam *et al.* 1983; Desideri and Santantonio, 1996.
5 In the 1992 elections the League gained 8.7 per cent of the vote, and 8.4 per cent in the following general elections of 1994, when the party ran within the centre-right coalition led by Berlusconi.
6 On how the geography of the vote for the DC and the Northern League has changed since the end of the First Republic, see Diamanti, 2009.
7 More recently Wood (2009) and Albertazzi (2006) have also written about the League as a party exhibiting a set of distinctive traits typical of populism. As classical studies (Canovan, 1981; Taggart, 2000) explain, populism is characterised by indicators such as a high degree of identification with the leader, an aggressive exclusionary rhetoric, which finds its main target in immigrants and Muslim foreigners and nationals, constant references to traditional values and national myths, the interpretation of religious culture as a sign and a guarantee of national sameness, a call for the protection of a supposedly threatened homogeneous national identity, the construction of 'imagined communities' to be achieved through secession or devolution, and the challenging of the established political order. On populism in Italy, see: Tarchi, 2003; Biorcio, 2007.
8 See Iacopini and Bianchi, 1994.
9 'Ammazza i terroni, risparmia i milioni.'
10 'Il Nord ha solo un problema: i terroni.'
11 'Siamo colonizzati. Vivo a Torino e non posso parlare torinese in un negozio perchè il bottegaio è meridionale […] Ti dicono: per favore parli in italiano […] Ma non lo vede? Al cinema si parla napoletano, a teatro in napoletano, in tivù napoletano […] pensi a Troisi' (Farassino, quoted in Stella, 1996: 59).
12 'Ha mai sentito un italiano dire "sono italiano"? No, dicono: sono calabrese, sono siciliano […] non siamo fedeli a una nazione ma a una regione […] Uno stato multietnico non può esistere, puoi tenerlo assieme per un pò con la forza delle armi, ma prima o poi c'è la reazione' (Farassino, quoted in Stella, 1996: 46).
13 Literally, 'excluded from the community'.
14 On the shift in the Lega's perception of Europe and the EU, see: Wood, 2009; Albertazzi, 2007; Huysseune, 2010.
15 The expression used by Borghezio – 'le negre' – accounts for the League's aggressive, provocative and ultimately racist language.
16 '[L]e bruttone nigeriane che battono qui da noi.'

17 On the roots of the fear of invasion in the ideology of the Nouvelle Droite, see Zaslove, 2004.
18 See Wetherell and Potter, 1992.
19 Banton, 1996.
20 Other scholars believe in the importance of taking a distance from the idea that the use of these 'invented races' is necessary in order to achieve justice. Amongst them, see Gilroy, 2000: 52.
21 Respectively 'razzismo addizionale', 'razzismo concorrenziale', and 'razzismo culturale' (Balbo and Manconi, 1993).
22 '[L]o spazio vinto ai locali.'
23 Cited in Balbo and Manconi (1993: 75).
24 On the role of the Celtic past in the party's rhetoric, see: Hague *et al.* 2005; Destro, 1997. On the Lega's folkloristic collective rituals as means of political propaganda (even when the use of the past contradicts more authoritative academic sources), see Albertazzi, 2006: 25.
25 'La Padania esiste geograficamente, etnicamente, linguisticamente, culturalmente ed economicamente [...] i suoi cittadini hanno lottato per affermare la propria identità nazionale. Non c'è bisogno di inventare qualcosa (la Padania) che esiste già. Inventare così significa ridefinire, ritrovare, ritornare a, riscoprire.'
26 On federalism and regionalism in the Northern League public discourse, see: Roux, 2008; Cento Bull, 1999; Agnew, 1995; Keating and Wilson, 2010; McDonnell, 2006.
27 Padania, identity and multiracial society (1998), authored by Giorgio Mussa, then the League's adviser on foreign policy.
28 'L'immigrazione extracomunitaria viene favorita e sostenuta da un insieme di forze – minoritarie ma egemoni dal punto di vista culturale ed economico – che la presentano come un fenomeno "spontaneo e irreversibile" verso il quale non è possibile opporsi' (Mussa, 1998).
29 See also Zaslove, 2004: 108.
30 'L'immigrazione extracomunitaria in Padania ed in Italia, favorita da uno stato corrotto ed inefficiente, sta assumendo le proporzioni di una vera e propria invasione [...] Allarmismo ed esagerazione? Niente affatto [...] Di fronte alle ridicole accuse di razzismo che vengono lanciate contro i patrioti che si oppongono alla distruzione del proprio popolo bisogna ribadire con forza il sacrosanto diritto della nostra gente a mantenere e difendere la propria identità etnico-culturale e religiosa ed a non essere ridotta, in prospettiva, ad una minoranza residuale sulla propria terra. Certamente bisogna rivendicare il diritto di essere padroni a casa propria.'
31 On the immigrant as a scapegoat, see Zaslove, 2004: 103.
32 Regarding the League's discourse on globalisation, see Wood, 2009.
33 The party also has a radio station (Radio Padania) and a TV channel (Tele Padania), which started broadcasting in 1997 and 1998, respectively.
34 'L'Emilia riscopre la sua identità' (Iezzi, 2007a). 'Aiutiamo le nostre genti a riappropriarsi delle loro identità' (Polli, 2007a). 'Difendiamo la nostra terra dal furto della nostra identità' (Alessandri, 2007). 'Manifestare per difendere la nostra identità' (Bassi, 2007a).
35 On Bossi's paradoxical egalitarianism, see Spectorowski, 2003.
36 In this sense, the categories of immigrants that have to be given priority in the process of integration correspond to the groups perceived as easier to assimilate from a cultural point of view: Catholics, Europeans, and second- and third-generation migrants descending from Italians emigrated abroad (Zaslove, 2004: 105). This specification is particularly important as it shows, on the one hand, the overlapping of the League's discourse with the position of a number of members of the Catholic hierarchy, Cardinal Biffi above all, while, on the other hand, it contributes to clarifying the rationale behind the orientation of the Italian legislation

on citizenship towards the so-called 'Italians abroad', to whom it grants priority over the (even second-generation) immigrants already living in Italy, as Chapter 4 will show. Such a 'priority list' also acquires relevance as it exposes an idea of a Europe that, albeit still implicitly, appears to be founded on religious and cultural homogeneity.

37 Concerning the Lega's perception of Muslims as terrorists and as a threat to Christian identity, see Diamanti, 2000, quoted in Wood, 2009: 172.

38 'Fino alla nostra libertà' (Bossi, 2006).

39 'L'individuo reciso da ogni legame con la propria terra e stirpe diventa così uno sradicato apolide, un albero senza radici e resistenza, in balìa del vento del potere mondialista [...] I popoli non sono come l'acqua che si può mescolare a piacere. I popoli si mescolano con difficoltà. Gli uomini tornano sempre alle loro radici' (Bossi, 2006).

40 '[U]n popolo [...] rischia l'annullamento' (Bossi, 2006).

41 '[T]enerci casa nostra' (Bossi, 2006).

42 '[D]are voce, sia sul piano teorico che su quello dell'azione concreta, a tutte quelle espressioni della cultura federalista e identitaria in Padania e non solo.'

43 The original term used in Italian is 'buonismo'.

44 Stefani, S., 'Noi, loro e la sicurezza', *La Padania*, September 2007.

45 '[S]econdo un recente rapporto, "recenti indagini", "alla luce di quanto recente-memte avvenuto a Perugia", "come confermato dai servizi segreti, la situazione sul fronte terrorismo è particolarmente delicata", "le parole del capo della polizia ci devono allarmare".'

46 See, for instance, Bassi, 2007d.

47 Giovanna Reggiani, aged 47, was raped and beaten up on 30 October 2007, in Rome, by a 24-year-old Romanian citizen, Romulus Nicolae Mailat, living in the Tor di Quinto 'campo nomadi', the transient campgrounds next to the station. The woman died in hospital 24 hours later. Mailat was sentenced to 29 years in prison. See: Anon. 2007a, 2007c, 2008b.

48 'La mafia cinese oggi è molto potente. Nel corso degli anni ha fatto un salto di qualità attrezzandosi addirittura in anticipo per le sfide della globalizzazione. Rappresenta il pericolo numero uno per il nostro futuro: è l'associazione mafiosa meglio organizzata e dunque più pericolosa.'

49 '[Q]ueste comunità cinesi tendono a non integrarsi come dovrebbero, ma a costru-ire uno stato nello stato.'

50 'Culla di terrorismo islamico.'

51 'È compito di ogni buon mussulmano prevaricare gli occidentali.'

52 '[L]'Islam non ha mai dimostrato di essere moderato.'

53 'C'è troppa gente che con la scusa di una ricerca del lavoro e per motivi di studio costruisce e addestra figure pronte a colpire in ogni momento. E la minaccia ter-roristica anche in armi di distruzione di massa è sempre più forte.'

54 'Questa è un'autentica guerra di civiltà. Contro di noi, contro la libertà e la democrazia a favore dell'assolutismo religioso e contro la ragione umana.' This interpretation recalls that of some representatives of the Church and Ratzinger's Regesburg lecture mentioned in the previous chapter. It is not easy to establish whether the League has once again borrowed another controversial aspect of the Church's discourse in order to legitimise the dichotomy Catholicism/reason versus Islam/superstition.

55 '[F]edeli al concetto di "ognuno padrone a casa sua".'

56 The case that triggered the debate in Italy was that of Muslim citizen Ali Smith, who demanded the removal of the crucifix from his children's classroom in a school in Ofena. In 2003 the Court of L'Aquila ruled that the request be accepted on the part of the school. Despite the media exposure of the controversy, this was not the first case in which the Supreme Court had deliberated on a crucifix being removed

from a public space. In March 2000, with the deliberation number 2925, it closed a controversy started in 1994 on the refusal of an Italian school teacher, Marcello Montagnana, to vote in a classroom used as a polling station where a crucifix was displayed.

57 'Grazie alla Lega finalmente non ci saranno solo Muhammed nelle graduatorie per le case popolari' (Lega Nord, 2005).

58 Veronesi, 2004. The Lega Nord manifesto, authored by Angelo Veronesi, was first published in *La Settimana di Saronno* on 9 June 2004, and later advertised on the Lega Nord and Giovani Padani websites.

59 See Bossi's discourse on the impact of globalisation on the ruin of Christian identity, cited in Wood, 2009: 171. On the homogeneity of the European nations as based on Christian roots, see Zaslove, 2004: 109.

60 On the devolution and decentralisation of power in relation to matters of immigration and the supposed demagogy behind the proposal on the part of the Left to grant immigrants the right to vote in local elections, see Indini, 2007b; Garibaldi, 2007b, 2007c.

61 The mayor was then Walter Veltroni (PD – Democratic Party), who demanded extraordinary measures to deal with the Roma and Sinti of the capital and argued that 'before the inclusion of Romania into the EU, Rome was the safest city in the world' (see Anon. 2007b).

62 'Prima buonisti, ora sceriffi. Ma quando queste cose succedono al Nord nessuno a Roma ha mai mosso un dito. Sono razzisti al contrario.'

63 'Nei comuni di centro sinistra dove sanno di essere accolti con buonismo e tolleranza [...] la questione principale non è neanche che tipo di politiche attuare perché il problema è che queste persone non devono neanche entrare nel paese perché non abbiamo la possibilità di assorbire queste comunità in termini di lavoro. Senza parlare del fatto che loro non hanno nessuna volontà e intenzione di integrarsi con noi.'

64 On the discrimination of Italians to the advantage of foreigners, social networks and particularly Facebook offer a vast repertoire of posters and cartoons.

65 'Se torniamo al governo via i Romeni.'

66 'Il furto per i nomadi non ha lo stesso significato che ha per noi.'

67 Later renamed CIE (Centre of identification and expulsion).

68 'Aiutiamoli ad aiutarsi' or 'aiutiamoli a casa loro.'

69 'La solidarietà e l'amore per il prossimo rientrano sicuramente fra i doveri cristiani che sono parte della nostra cultura, ma che meritano alcune considerazioni: innanzitutto il prossimo (lo dice la parola) è chi ci è prossimo, vicino, parente, famigliare. Il nostro prossimo vero è chi appartiene alla nostra comunità antica e chi ha sottoscritto con noi un contratto sociale, anche istituzionale. Poi, se ne avanza, ci si dedica agli altri, ma questa estensione non può essere intesa come un dovere comunitario.'

70 '[I]n piazza per salvare i cristiani.'

71 '[Q]uesto laicismo che ci mortifica.'

72 On the concept of reciprocity in the ecclesial documents, see: John Paul II, 'Post-Synodal Apostolic Exhortation *Ecclesia in Africa*', 14 September 1995, §58.

73 '[I]ntolleranza verso la nostra cultura', 'una ritrovata identità che non può certo essere barattata con il pacifismo a scapito della verità.'

74 Gibelli, 2007b.

75 On the shift from the League's pagan rites to the promotion of Christian values and the alignment with the Church on an anti-Islamic position, see Albertazzi, 2006: 32.

76 Journalist, Northern League MP and later (1994–96) president of the Chamber of Deputies.

77 '[L]'intransigente avversione della Chiesa al leghismo.'

78 Writing in 2007, Albertazzi claims that 'at the moment there is little interest in opposing immigrants on religious grounds', but 'there are signs that this might indeed happen' (342). This is clearly the case today, as Chapter 5 will show particularly in the case of religious difference.

79 The etymology of the term comes from the Greek αυτό (*auto*, meaning 'self') and ποίησις (*poiesis*, meaning 'creation'). The expression indicates a system that reproduces itself starting from its own elements or, literally, through self-creation.

80 On the link between immigration and crime in the leghisti's perception, see Zaslove, 2004: 102.

81 On the issue of the Lega's use of the media or the party itself featuring in the national media, see Biorcio, 2003.

82 See Goffman, 1981.

4   The Italian legislation on immigration

1 Introduction

Public debates on immigration have emerged in many Western European countries since the 1950s and have influenced the domestic policies and integration models put forward by the different nation-states. Italy has been affected by similar debates considerably later, for historical and political reasons addressed in the Introduction and Chapter 1 of this book. The development of the legislation aimed at regulating the phenomenon followed a similar path, being formulated at different stages only since the late 1980s. Before then, given the general attitude towards immigration, perceived as generally non-problematic by both the political class and public opinion, Italy relied on the pre-existent Fascist laws to regulate the phenomenon. As previously argued, the revival of discussions on national identity among intellectuals and in the media, which started at the same time, did not take into account, among the various challenges faced by a supposedly weak sense of national belonging in search of a renewal, the growing number of arrivals, at least until as late as the early 1990s, and even then only marginally.

Until the late 1980s, the Italian legislation on immigration was mainly characterised by occasional ad hoc measures aimed at regulating the job market in a protectionist way. Even after Italy began to become aware of its transformation from a country of emigration into a country of immigration, the state lacked a long-term vision and a clear and coherent approach to the phenomenon. Through the analysis of the history and the development of the Italian legislation on immigration, this chapter will argue that to a certain extent this is still the case today. The previous chapters have shown how the discussion on the theme has shifted from the perception of the other as 'picturesque' and in need of help towards an interpretation of the foreigner as a threat to the culture and security of the nation. This chapter will address the processes according to which such a turn in the common understanding of the phenomenon has translated into the state's reaction to the foreign presence vis-à-vis the issues of labour and citizenship. At a time when immigration is increasingly portrayed as causing a clash of civilisations, symbols such as the crucifix have become emblematic of a war of values, and there is growing talk of an 'invasion' of foreign people intentioned to conquer Italy, this chapter will provide an account of the transition from a generic disposition to welcome the newcomers to an institutionalised and often bipartisan emphasis upon exclusion. Taking into account the economic and social changes that have occurred in the last three decades, as well as the political discourse on immigration, this chapter will analyse the Italian legislation, the institutions and political actors responsible for the various laws, and finally the more restrictive policies put forward by parties such as the Northern League, as part of what will be defined as a 'simulative' type of politics. The constraints imposed by the EU and communitarian laws as well as the open criticism of supranational institutions towards the Italian approach to immigration will also be considered.

Starting with the polemics on the issue between centre-right and centre-left coalitions, already broadly illustrated, this chapter will also aim to explain the role of many social groups, which have contributed to containing and limiting the impact of strong ideological or merely utilitarian positions on the actual making of the laws. It will account for the apparent lack of noticeable differences – practical and ideological – in the measures passed by different governments until 2008 and the consequent general tendency to focus on protecting the borders rather than promoting integration. In addressing the question of whether Italy is following any existing model in dealing with immigration or whether it is, on the contrary, elaborating an original interpretation and new solutions, the formulation and enforcement of the selected measures will be contextualised by addressing the various social, economic and cultural changes as well as the different migratory waves that have occurred in the period of time under scrutiny.

Finally, the chapter will assess the influence of the interpretations of national identity and immigration put forward by the Church and the League upon the policies introduced and implemented by the various governments. The analysis will take into account four possible hypotheses: 1 the laws increasingly reflect the model of integration put forward by the Northern League; 2 the laws fit into the model suggested by the Church; 3 the laws represent either a combination of the two models or, rather, an original model, different from those suggested by the political actors taken into account; or 4 they express a complete lack of strategic vision and do not form a coherent model but are on the contrary ad hoc measures emerging as responses to specific and temporary emergencies.

2 The pre-1990s legislation: 'immigration without politics'

The first significant, albeit limited in numbers, migratory wave to Italy started in the aftermath of World War II, when groups of foreign students reached the main university cities in search of a better education.[1] Until the late 1960s, however, they arrived mainly from richer European countries such as France, Britain, Switzerland and Germany, while, after 1967, the year of the Greek colonels' *coup d'état*, the number of Greek and Iranian students started to grow, reaching its peak in 1981–82, when foreign students registered at Italian universities amounted to 113,000. The following two decades were characterised by a steady decline in the foreign presence, with 30,790 permits to study in Italy in 2001–02. Such a downturn is mainly due to the recurrent regularisation of irregular immigrants from the late 1980s, which provided an alternative to the requests for study visas. Moreover, in 1990 the Martelli law made it possible to convert a study permit into a work permit and allowed students aged 14 to 18 to join their parents who worked in Italy (Einaudi, 2007: 85).

The second migratory wave consisted of the arrival in the 1960s of women employed in the domestic sector, mainly emigrating from the former colonies and from Catholic countries. Recruited by Catholic associations or agencies which acted as mediators,[2] they tended to arrive with regular permits or with tourism visas and seek regularisation once in the country. Perceived as less visible than the men and somehow less dangerous, they represented the 'invisible' immigrants and faced difficult working conditions due to a lack of regulation of the domestic sector. The economic boom of those years and the weakness of the welfare state[3] contributed to an increase in the request for this type of worker as well as in the applications to regularise those already employed but still irregular (Einaudi, 2007: 86; Colombo and Sciortino, 2004: 54; Andall, 2000; Parrenas, 2001).

If the presence of the badanti[4] never raised concern – even today it is considered deeply different from the arrival of male immigrants – and went almost unnoticed, a different reaction was directed towards Tunisian workers who, since 1968, had started travelling to eastern Sicily following Italians who were returning to the country after years of emigration and were first employed on the island as farm workers and, since the mid-1970s, in fishing and agriculture (Colombo and Sciortino, 2004: 54). These were the first migrants to be almost immediately accused of being a threat to the public order and targeted by spontaneous anti-immigrant groups who demanded their expulsion. The fourth and last pre-1990s migratory wave took place between 1961 and 1989 and was mainly directed at the industrial sector. It became 'recognised' or problematic, albeit not systematically addressed, in the late 1970s, when growing unemployment (with peaks of 10.3 per cent in the South[5]) started causing general resentment towards the newly arrived. This particular wave of arrivals triggered the debate on 'competition' and 'complementarity'[6] in the work sector: for the first time the discussion revolved around whether these immigrants were stealing the jobs of the locals or were rather taking up jobs that the locals refused to do, as can be proven by an analysis of the newspapers of the time (Einaudi, 2007: 86–89).

If until 1989 it was still possible to monitor the numbers and identify the nationalities of the newly arrived, from the early 1990s this became rather difficult, if not impossible, as illegal immigration grew while the presence of foreign workers increased in almost all sectors of the Italian economy, following events such as the fall of the Berlin Wall, the conflict in Yugoslavia and the Albanian crises. The number of visas increased dramatically in concomitance with the so-called sanatorie, the amnesties employed to regularise illegal migrants in 1986, 1990, and later in 1995, 1998, 2000, 2002 and 2008, determining a lower presence of irregular stays. By then the rise of the Northern League and the exacerbation of the discussion on the issue had contributed to place immigration at centre stage in the political debate.

Interestingly, the first measure to regulate the influx was put forward by the Ministry of Labour and Social Security,[7] which, acting as the Ministry of the Interior,[8] indirectly established the first guidelines of a migratory policy. The ministerial memorandum No. 51 of 4 December 1963[9] for the first time introduced a link between legal entry into the country and possession of a valid work contract, stating that only those previously authorised by the ULP, the Local Recruitment Office,[10] to work in Italy could apply for a visa. Such employment could only be granted to foreigners after ascertaining that there were no Italians ready or qualified to take that job. These job permits could be renewed for a maximum of 12 months, while the right to live in the country could be revoked if the contract expired or ceased (Bonini, 1987: 105; Einaudi, 2007: 99).

This measure, regularly neglected in the debates on the legislation on immigration, is particularly interesting when compared to the so-called Bossi-Fini law,[11] bitterly criticised by the Left and often perceived as a dramatic U-turn in policy making. A comparison between the memorandum and Law 189 of 2002 later on in this chapter will highlight the fact that the 'protectionist' approach, centred on the regulation of the work sector, has always featured in the Italian response to immigration. The main consequence of this particular memorandum was that of confining an important part of the labour force to a situation of illegality, whether that means workers entering the country illegally, finding a job and then pretending to apply for one from abroad or simply immigrants being recruited to work in the black economy.

The formulation and implementation of the 1963 measure was not preceded or accompanied by a political or cultural debate on immigration and therefore was not influenced by any particular ideologically oriented interpretation of the foreign presence within the labour sector, but rather represented an attempt – albeit not much articulated – to control the job market, as well as a response to the first manifestations of intolerance on the part of Italian workers towards their foreign counterparts. Often such tensions resulted in the expulsion of the so-called 'fake tourist' (falso turista) – the expression referring to those who had entered the country with a tourist visa and never left after it expired.[12]

Soon after this first partial measure, immigration began to be tackled – yet again indirectly – through a series of measures, discussed and passed between 1973 and 1990, aimed at making it increasingly difficult for foreign students to apply to Italian universities, a trend broken only in 1998 with the Turco-Napolitano law,[13] which removed some of the obstacles erected by the previous laws (Musaragno, 2001). The main consequence of this repressive trend, with only the exception of women working in the domestic sector who regularly benefited from ad hoc measures since the first sanatoria of 17 December 1979, was that the new waves of immigrants were destined to remain illegal, particularly after the block of entries in 1982 (Horniziel, 1990: 110).[14]

In this first phase characterised by attempted reforms, mainly aimed at protecting the internal job market while strengthening the economy, immigration was somehow depoliticised or not yet seen as relevant at a national level: it was, following Einaudi's definition, an 'immigration without politics'. During this period, trade unions and Catholic associations, such as Caritas, acted as an emergency replacement for an inexistent welfare state and provided immigrants with both material aid and moral support. Leaving aside the specific interests behind the role played by the unions, what matters here is the fact the these two actors contributed to highlight the need for a Parliamentary discussion on immigration and for a more consistent normative approach on the issue. Following this pressure, in 1978, the government led by the then Prime Minister Giulio Andreotti commissioned an inquiry into the state of immigration, which resulted in the first official collection of data carried out by the Interdepartmental Committee for Emigration.[15]

The first practical outcome of the investigation was law No. 943 of 30 December 1986,[16] authored by Christian Democratic MP Franco Foschi, at the time also secretary of the Committee. In the eight years that passed between the publication of the report and the approval of the law, many measures were discussed in Parliament, although none of them ever made it onto the statute books. It can be said that these, generally restrictive, laws by decree proposed during this period were formulated mainly in order to foster the economy, a mechanism that makes sense only when considering that at that point immigration was seen as dangerous for the economic prosperity of the country, whereas feelings of anxiety in relation to a supposed clash of values had not yet emerged. This interpretation appears paradoxical, considering that nowadays immigration, albeit much needed to make the Italian economy more competitive, is considered a threat mainly in 'cultural' terms (Cento Bull, 2009; Andall, 2009). Two statements by the then Minister of the Interior Oscar Luigi Scalfaro, are representative of the pre-1990s occasional debate on the issue, showing, on the one hand, a concern with the impact of new arrivals in the job market and, on the other hand, a much stronger solidarity with the immigrants as human beings. On the former, the minister argued that, 'Italy has no intention of becoming a country of immigration. In this perspective and given the impossibility of sustaining the economic and social price related to the welcoming of a high number of foreign workers, Italy has no intention at all to base its economic development on the importing of a foreign workforce'.[17] Moreover, Scalfaro added:

Italy has a humanitarian tradition adequate to its civilisation: open doors for those who come here in search of freedom or to escape persecution or for those forced into a state of illegality; our understanding equally goes to those who, despite the current lack of job opportunities and economic growth, come to Italy with the aim of working and integrating into a society that they respect. Our doors are open to foster tourism from everywhere in the world, as tourist flows represent a source of economic growth, job opportunities and, not least, a means for mutual enrichment [...] Amid this will to open the doors, unfortunately we need to set a limit in order to avoid abuses and risks.[18]

These arguments are illustrative of the attitude of considering immigration as problematic only with regards to a job market already at risk, and contribute to explaining why the first measures dealing with the subject were mainly, if not exclusively, directed towards the protection of Italian workers, while at the same time showing a high degree of sympathy for the immigrants.

The international agreements on immigration subscribed to by Italy were also centred on the treatment and the rights of the foreign labour force, as outlined, for instance, in the International Labour Organization (ILO) Convention (No. 143), signed in Geneva on 4 June 1975 with the purpose of guaranteeing foreign workers the respect of their basic human rights (article 1). This was the last of a series of international agreements[19] establishing the main principles regulating the working conditions for economic migrants legally employed in the countries that signed the convention. Article 10 contains the most relevant principle, which reads:

> Each Member for which the Convention is in force undertakes to declare and pursue a national policy designed to promote and to guarantee, by methods appropriate to national conditions and practice, equality of opportunity and treatment in respect of employment and occupation, of social security, of trade union and cultural rights and of individual and collective freedoms for persons who as migrant workers or as members of their families are lawfully[20] within its territory.[21]

The convention also provided a definition of the term 'migrant worker' as 'a person who migrates or who has migrated from one country to another in search of employment', a definition which includes 'any person regularly admitted as a migrant worker'.[22] The definition of the migrant exclusively as a worker, dominant in the pre-1990s Italian debate, somehow derived from the Marxist idea according to which immigrants are part of the international proletariat,[23] whose members are citizens of the world, united by their common condition as workers. Similar in its conclusion was the interpretation of the Catholic subculture, expressed by the slogan 'Nobody is a foreigner in my country',[24] which looked at the phenomenon from the perspective of the receiving countries.

There are two interesting factors here. First, that the Church's position, at least for what emerged from the analysis carried out in the previous chapter, has shifted to such an extent that the more recent position is summarised in the recurrent motto according to which 'Nobody is a foreigner *within the Church*'.[25] Second, that despite their deep antagonism, the Marxist and the Catholic subcultures shared at that point a similar will to welcome immigrants, a position based, in the first case, upon the idea that being workers in the first instance and simply human beings in the second instance were the essential and only requirements to be fulfilled in order to be integrated. In the second case, the perspective is reversed and immigrants are perceived as brothers who need to be loved as human beings first, and workers in the second instance, although such interpretation of migration has recently moved towards the idea of religious sameness as the main means of integration.

The fact that until the late 1980s the main political actors involved in a newborn discussion on immigration were international organisations such as the ILO,[26] and national interest groups, such as the unions and the Catholic voluntary associations, sheds some light on the reason why, until the Martelli law (1990), the proposed measures did not contain any reference to security, law and order, or any restrictions and sanctions for illegal immigrants. Before asking what had changed in the late 1990s and what therefore determined the development of increasingly 'punitive' legislation, it is worth looking briefly at law 943 of 1986, mentioned earlier.

Its first article confirms the principles of the ILO Convention, stating that the Italian Republic grants all extracomunitari – this is the first time the word appears in an official document – equal treatment and the same opportunities given to national workers. Moreover, it guarantees access to social services, education and housing while remarking also upon the immigrants' 'right to maintain their own cultural identity'.[27] However, more than a sign of openness and goodwill, this first article has to be read as an acceptance of the international agreements as well as a sign that immigration was not yet perceived to be a threat, whereas the focus of the law is once again the labour sector. Indeed, the main corpus of the law is centred on the formulation of even more detailed rules regulating the relationship between employers and foreign workers: monthly updated lists of workers, the impossibility for employers to employ a worker who is not at the top of such lists and, even more importantly, monthly investigations to ascertain the lack of availability of Italians for those jobs. The main clause in favour of immigrants is the possibility to join a family member regularly employed in the country and the permission for their relatives arriving in Italy to start work themselves after a year of residence. Moreover, the law considers with greater flexibility the case of female migrants working in the domestic sector, since it allows employers to put forward a richiesta nominativa, that is to say, to indicate a specific person rather than having to give employment to the first person on the official list, a concession not extended to male workers. However, as Einaudi puts it:

> The law was [...] based on a reductive interpretation of the immigrants' labour market and at the same time on overly complex mechanisms. It

ignored self-employment and itinerant trade, as well as the request to employ through nominal request an individual whom the employers had personally met or knew already rather than choose randomly from numbers and names that did not mean anything. Moreover, it had to face the relevant issue of Italian economy of migration, which neither law 943/1986 nor any of the subsequent laws managed to resolve: that of the fundamental role played by the informal economy in providing immigrants with a job without allowing them to obtain the legal requirements to apply for a visa.[28]

As stated above, at the time of the implementation of the first law on immigration the phenomenon was still perceived by the political system and public opinion as temporary and the newly arrived were believed to be aiming to reach other countries (Melotti, 1996). However, in 1973, with the oil crisis, it became clear that the expansion of the service sector and the more restrictive policies adopted by European countries that had traditionally encouraged immigration had resulted in a considerable rise in the number of migrants who had chosen Italy. This new trend turned the migratory balance within the country to positive for the first time: at that point Italy was more a country of immigration than one of emigration, as it had traditionally been since Unification.

Not only were European migrants oriented towards Italy as their definitive destination, but for the first time they arrived in considerable numbers from developing countries, pushed by demographic, economic and political factors (Golini and Bonifazi, 1987). This new typology of arrivals was following a general tide of migrants travelling from the East to the West and from the South to the North of the world (Ferrera, 1996). Nonetheless, Italians did not react openly to immigration, despite the fact that the arrivals grew constantly, at least according to a number of census documents[29] – an attitude of openness or probably denial that later triggered internal contradictions and unexpected turns, such as episodes of racism (Paci, 1987) which will be analysed later in this chapter.

The change in the migration pattern, from a situation in which all arrivals could be interpreted as linked to a search for a job, to one in which immigrants arrived in Italy for all sorts of different reasons, moved not only by push factors but also by pull factors, was not addressed through new legislation, nor was the role of illegal immigrants in the black economy (Bonifazi, 1992; Mughini, 2002). Even though the pressure from independent pro-immigrant associations contributed to the development of a relatively welcoming legislation, at least in the intention of those who proposed such measures, the fact that the issue of immigration was approached exclusively from the perspective of the employers and immigrants were considered merely as workers laid a fertile ground for the approval, years later, of restrictive measures which did not encourage a process of integration and, on the contrary, justified exclusionary social attitudes (Zincone, 2006).

3 The 1990s

Until the late 1980s, Italy went through a phase of economical and political stability and even though the crisis – the mani pulite investigation, the end of the First Republic, institutional collapse and social unrest[30] – was around the corner, it had not yet manifested itself. It is in this still peaceful political climate, occasionally shaken by sporadic yet unexpected racist attacks, that a new law was formulated by the then Minister of Justice Claudio Martelli. Law No. 39 of 1990[31] represents the first structural measure to deal with the phenomenon in a broader sense than just in terms of its impact on the economy and on the job market.

The episode that catapulted the issue of immigration onto the newspaper front pages was the assassination of Jerry Masslo in Villa Literno in August 1989. South African refugee Masslo and his fellow co-workers were brutally assaulted by robbers intentioned to steal the money they had saved and which they kept in their house[32] (Magni, 1995: 41; Einaudi, 2007: 141). The death of the refugee, which followed other similar episodes in the Neapolitan area, was interpreted as a racist raid and immediately became the symbol of a political world incapable of dealing with immigration. Anti-racism mass demonstrations were organised during the following days while public opinion, led by non-political organisations, started to demand Parliamentary discussion of a new and more adequate law (Einaudi, 2007: 142).

The struggle against racism dominated the 1980s, reaching such an intensity in the political rhetoric that it was defined by scholars and opinion makers as 'easy anti-racism' (anti-razzismo facile), or 'cultural and political conformism' (conformismo culturale e politico), as Balbo defined it, resulting from dogmatism and a refusal to understand in depth the phenomenon on the part of political parties and Catholic associations, accused of turning the leftist traditional solidarity towards immigrants into an intolerant refusal to address the issue in rational terms (Einaudi, 2007; Sciortino, 1998). The criticism according to which such an anti-racist stance was the product of 'dogmatic ideologies', to a certain extent contributed to delegitimise the position of the pro-immigrant groups, making them less influential while creating a conflict within the centre-left political coalition. This became particularly evident when one considers that criticism was expressed by intellectuals such as Balbo and Manconi, who had previously founded the first anti-racist groups in Italy. By being criticised for their unconditional will to open the doors to all immigrants, non-political actors lost legitimacy and therefore influence on the process of decision making in the years that followed, as their position was discarded for being unachievable or simply unrealistic.[33]

The aims of the Martelli law were the following: the regularisation of illegal immigrants through a new sanatoria; the refusal to consider the country of origin as a criterion to grant a visa; the need for equal treatment and access to housing, jobs, health care and education for the immigrants; stronger support for the professional development of immigrants willing to work in the industrial sector; the approval of new guidelines for the census of foreigners and migrant communities within the country; the creation of a national monitoring centre for immigration (osservatorio sull'immigrazione), as at the time Italy only had an monitoring centre on emigration (osservatorio sull'emigrazione). The proposal, supported by the PCI (Italian Communist Party) and Verdi (Green Party), seemed to many quite unbalanced insofar as it responded only to the requests of the immigrants and the associations behind them (Melotti, 2004). The unconditional solidarity underlying Martelli's approach was not only justified by the general will of the Left to integrate immigrants and by the anti-racist stance mentioned above, but it also resulted from a comparison with other European countries such as France, seen as the epicentre of the new immigration. Looking at France led to an underestimation of the phenomenon by a considerably large part of the political world, not only on the Left but also by important representatives of the Christian democracy, such as the then Minister of Labour Carlo Donat-Cattin, who supported Martelli and actually demanded the opening of Italian borders and the possibility for immigrants holding only tourist visas to work in the country (Zincone, 2006; Einaudi, 2007: 144).

The 1990s, however, were also the years in which a debate on security and growing concerns linked to law and order started to emerge. New political parties and in particular the Northern League were rising to power and becoming recognised at a national level. Albeit not primarily concerned with immigration, at least not to the extent it is today, Bossi's party was certainly not in favour of unregulated immigration. Other, more traditional parties were undertaking structural changes, which influenced their attitude towards immigration, as for instance in the case of the MSI (Movimento Sociale Italiano). In 1993 its leader, Gianfranco Fini, founded Alleanza Nazionale (AN). The party held a relatively flexible position on immigration but it also drew a clear distinction between legal and illegal immigrants. While Fini and a number of his fellow party representatives agreed on the need to guarantee basic human rights to the former, they adopted a much firmer line with the illegal immigrants who, as Fini said in his speech delivered in 1995 at Fiuggi Congress, should be expelled immediately (cited in Anon. 1995).

According to political commentators, in choosing to be garantista, which is to say to opt for granting civil liberties and rights to those who had entered the country with a regular visa, Fini was publicly trying to take a distance from the extreme position traditionally held by the MSI[34] and from the close relationship he had always had with neo-Fascist movements and leaders, so as to avoid being perceived as racist and losing the legitimisation and credibility so much needed by his newborn party (Einaudi, 2007). However, all the smaller parties of the extreme Right opposed the draft of the law presented by Martelli or tried to modify a substantial number of its articles. The amendments put forward by the MSI and the Lega Nord were generally considered racist and therefore rejected, while those suggested by the PRI (Partito Repubblicano Italiano) – in the first instance also hostile to the law – were implemented. In particular, the Republicans managed to add to the text the need for rational planning of the arrivals, whereas the original law was more generous in not setting quotas (Campani, 1993). Moreover, they insisted on the need for work permits and rejected the idea of allowing foreigners in possession of tourist visas to be employed.

After various negotiations, the law that was approved was quite different from the original proposal, especially as far as the rule of escorting the illegal migrants to the borders and back to their countries of origin[35] or expulsion was concerned. Despite the fact that the rules on expulsion were hard to implement and indeed immigrants were rarely sent back to their countries, a difficulty due to lack of resources and the impossibility to identify them, Martelli's position shifted during this process of negotiation to the extent that towards the end of the writing of the legislative text he openly invoked the help of the police force in order to deal with the new – allegedly 'unexpected' – migratory waves (Einaudi, 2007: 161).

Eventually, the law left unsatisfied all the actors that had tried to influence its formulation: it created internal conflict within the Left, with the more radical groups arguing that it was too restrictive, as it limited the number of residence permits (Pugliese, 2002) and entirely neglected the concept of integration (Einaudi, 2007). The opposition was also very critical of the law, particularly since the Northern League's suggestion of introducing the 'crime of illegal entry',[36] whereby a migrant who had entered the country with no visa could be sent to jail even if they had not committed a crime other than that of, indeed, arriving in Italy, was not taken on board. It would take the party almost two decades to turn such a measure into part of an official law, the so-called 'security package' (pacchetto sicurezza), passed in 2008.[37] Nonetheless, albeit contradictory and limited by internal divisions and by the external constraints of international agreements such as Schengen, which Italy joined in 1990, the Martelli law represents the first structured attempt to regulate immigration without considering migrants solely as workers.

Immediately after the law was approved, Italy faced the consequences of the Albanian crises, which manifested themselves in two unprecedented waves of arrivals in 1990 and 1991.[38] The inadequacy of Italian institutions to respond to a situation of 'emergency' led to the appointment of the first minister for immigration.[39] Socialist MP Margherita Boniver was nominated by the Andreotti government on 12 April 1991.

While many Albanians were sent back to their country and others were rejected when still in international waters, the arrival in Bari of the ship Vlora on 8 August 1991[40] was destined to feature in national and international newspapers and to remain an example of Italian xenophobia. The Vlora had transported 20,000 people, turning the image of the crowded boat into an icon of the 'invasion' of the country by foreigners. For the first time the nature of the phenomenon appeared in its dramatic reality. The common reaction was one of incredulity: the arrival of the Vlora can be considered the watershed that divides the era of solidarity from the era of fear. The images linked to this particular group of immigrants and the boats that transported them became iconic in the Northern League's representation of 'an unsustainable and threatening invasion' – a concern shared by most centre-right parties. That fact that this 'landing' was so unexpected – or so it was portrayed – contributed to shock public opinion, a feeling explained by Palomba and Righi (1992: 1) in their 'Quel giorno che gli Albanesi invasero l'Italia',[41] in which the expression 'that day' (quel giorno) conveys both the suddenness and the irreversibility of an unforeseen event. The arrival of the Vlora to the Italian coast became symbolic not only of mass arrival and the changing face of immigration but also of Italians' xenophobia, while the pictures of the immigrants left for days in Bari's Vittoria football stadium[42] were published by the main newspapers around the world.

In subsequent years, the number of arrivals dropped consistently, while Italy tried to negotiate an agreement with Albania, training its police force to patrol the coasts while building infrastructure in and around Tirana and sending aid to the local population. However, the so-called 'invasion syndrome' (sindrome da assedio) reinforced by the mass media and the political discourse of the Right, had already spread across the country and awakened until then disinterested public opinion (Macioti and Pugliese, 1993: 203; Einaudi, 2007: 181).

After the political turmoil of 1992 and the disappearance of the traditional parties, the Ministry of Immigration was closed. Several proposals for new measures were put forward, although many of them were never passed. These proposals mainly focused on fighting racism, as in the case of Mancini's law[43] 205 of 1993, which aimed at fighting crimes linked to racial, ethnic and religious hatred, establishing that 'whoever spreads views based on racial superiority or ethnic hatred or encourages other persons to do so'[44] could be sentenced to up to three years in custody, a period that could be increased to four years for anyone who 'incites to commit or commits himself acts of violence for racial, ethnic, national and religious reasons'.[45] It also forbade the creation of groups or organisations that have among their aims incitement to racial discrimination or violence, punishable with disciplinary actions that range from the exclusion from electoral competition to up to six years in jail.[46] This law, albeit very much needed in the face of a growing number of racist attacks, shows how the focus of the debate was once again the racism of Italians, whereas immigration per se had not yet become relevant in the political rhetoric of that time.

The measure was bitterly opposed by the Northern League, which saw it as a limit to its members' freedom of expression and therefore fought to abolish it, achieving this goal in 2006. Many of the decrees formulated between 1991 and 1998 never became laws since the political instability of that time caused most governments to fall before the texts had been approved (Einaudi, 2007: 183). Berlusconi's government did not have enough time to approve a reform but it did express itself with regard to immigration with a draft proposal heavily influenced by AN. The proposal advocated giving more power to the police and introducing the crime of illegal entry as well as punishing illegal immigrants with several years in jail. The fact that associations and lobbies involved in the discussion managed once again to boycott the law should be interpreted as a lack of interest in the subject on the part of political parties, which tended not to hold a clear position on the matter, rather than a sign of strength on the part of these organisations. The Northern League itself did not get particularly involved in the discussion: not only was immigration not its primary interest until the late 1990s, but it was also still trying to gain national visibility and legitimacy. Berlusconi expressed a negative opinion on the idea of punishing the immigrants for illegal permanence in the country, since at that time it was a shared opinion that somebody should be sent to jail only if they had committed a crime or represented a danger for society (ibid.: 185–201).

In 1995, the approach to immigration adopted by the technocratic government led by Lamberto Dini was aimed instead at giving irregular immigrants a legal status, so as to reduce the number of undocumented workers and break the link with the black economy (Reyneri, 1999). The results of the amnesty included in the Martelli law were also the object of controversy: the limited number of illegal immigrants who had decided to come forward and be regularised was interpreted by some political actors – usually supporters of the measure – as a sign that there were not many illegal foreigners in the country, an interpretation that clearly neglected the fact that many could not afford the cost of social contributions needed to become official, while staying illegally employed was more convenient and often the only choice (Katrougalos and Lazaridis, 2003: 167–90). The fact that the necessary procedures for regularisation were not very clear (a constant factor in the Italian legislation on immigration) and that official information was not made easily accessible to applicants by the institutions in charge also contributed to this failure – a failure that, according to various commentators, resulted not only from the inability to discourage illegal entry into the country, but also from the lack of attention paid to promoting integration (Zincone, 2006).

From 1995 the political debate on immigration became more and more heated. The two coalitions were not homogeneous in their responses: on the Right, while the position of the Northern League started to become clear and exacerbate the debate with provocative statements and claims, Berlusconi was far less supportive of punitive policies. At the same time the Left was also internally divided between the most radical pro-immigrant interventionists (Radicals and the PRC) and representatives of the DS (Democratici di Sinistra), whose leader, Massimo D'Alema, seemed more worried about the threat posed by immigrants to the workers living in the metropolitan cities, who, in his view, were more exposed to security issues and therefore more in need of protection. Citizens' fears featured on the front pages of newspapers and magazines, which, in turn, arguably contributed to consolidate and increase the same fears with a series of recurrent references to crimes committed by immigrants (Colombo, 1997).

4 The Turco-Napolitano law: a humanitarian and solidarist perspective

After winning the 1996 elections Prodi and his government seemed to be oriented towards the introduction of an encompassing and more articulated legislation that would replace the previous partial laws. This will to revise the legislation came from an acknowledged need for a law that would not simply solve problems in times of emergency – the situation was at this point portrayed as one of constant emergency – but would also reflect the fact that the arrivals were not going to diminish in the foreseeable future. Moreover, a modification of the previous laws was seen as necessary in order to reassure other EU countries, such as France and Germany, that Italy would meet the Schengen criteria for border control (to be achieved by 1997) and would not become an open gate to Europe (Zincone, 2006: 352–53; Einaudi, 2007). With this in mind Minister of Social Solidarity Livia Turco and Minister of the Interior Giorgio Napolitano were called to formulate a new proposal, which became law in 1998.[47]

In presenting the proposal for public discussion, Turco insisted on three aspects: the need for a strict planning of the incoming flows of immigrants; the will to introduce new measures against organised crime linked to the smuggling of people across the borders; and the importance of citizenship and integration policies for the immigrants (Einaudi, 2007: 211; Zincone, 2006). During the preparatory phase of the new law, it became clear that the approach to the reform adopted by Turco and Napolitano was deeply different from that of their predecessors. The various steps of the negotiations followed a bottom-up style, based on a constant dialogue with the advocacy coalition: unions, religious associations, scout groups, feminist groups, evangelical representatives, political opponents and magistrates of the juvenile court. The clear will to start a 'negotiation' (concertazione) led to an awakening of the interlocutors and a reconfirmation of the central role that, as much as it had happened in the past, interest groups, organisation and charities could play again, after years of silence and weak participation on their part. These were not necessarily only Catholic associations, even though Turco was traditionally close to the Catholic world, but were also interfaith associations or groups linked to political parties such as ARCI (Associazione Ricreativa e Culturale Italiana), formerly a recreational association of the PCI. Academics, civil servants and observers were also directly asked to contribute to the discussion, bringing their specific expertise into the debate (Zincone, 2006: 353; Einaudi, 2007: 213). The same propensity towards policy learning was also confirmed by the attempt to compare the Italian situation with that of other countries – and particularly those which had opted for multiculturalism – in order to incorporate 'good practice' into social activities and legislative proposals.

However, this inclination towards an open dialogue during the preparation of the first draft of the law declined as it approached the stage of the final debate: once the Bill was made non-amendable and it was sent to be examined by technical committees, the role of the advocacy coalition proved to manage only to have a weak and indirect influence on the final text (Zincone, 2006: 354).

Looking closer at the content of the reform, the first innovation introduced was the compulsory annual entry flow planning as well as the possibility of establishing quotas of arrivals from countries that had signed bilateral agreements with Italy. Moreover, in order to fight the illegal employment of migrants, the law made available a new type of work visa for those who did not have a work contract but intended to enter the country and find a job once there. Foreigners were given 12 months to find a job: if they were still unemployed at the end of that period, they had to leave Italy. The Turco-Napolitano law also introduced the permesso di lavoro stagionale, a temporary visa for those employed in seasonal jobs, which could be extended to a maximum of nine months. The incentive to leave the country when the visa expired consisted in the possibility for those who left to re-enter legally a second time. Moreover, immigrants with a permanent job could apply for a two-year visa, which could be extended for two more years and then, after five years of residence, could become a 'residence card' (carta di soggiorno) – a residence permit with no expiry date which granted holders further rights than those guaranteed by a simple permesso di soggiorno (Einaudi, 2007: 216; Melotti, 2004).

In this way Italy was for the first time acknowledging the difference between temporary and permanent immigrants, already recognised in many other European countries. Following the 'humanitarian and solidaristic approach' to the issue, the law also introduced a 'social protection' permit for victims who collaborated with the authorities to fight prostitution and human trafficking (Zincone, 2006: 357). To defeat human trafficking, the measure established that those caught exploiting illegal immigrants would serve up to 15 years in jail. As for the most restrictive parts of the reform, the rejection of migrants at the borders, repatriation and the prohibition to re-enter the country for the following five years became an important part of the strategy to defeat illegal entry/residence: repatriation could also be imposed on those who had committed a crime and had to serve a certain period of time in prison or those who did not have valid identification. However, children under 16, pregnant women, permit holders and relatives of Italian citizens could not be expelled (Einaudi, 2007: 217).

Another new measure, bitterly criticised by the advocacy coalition, was the creation of the so-called CTP (Centri di permanenza temporanea, or centres for temporary detention), where illegal immigrants could be kept for 20 days (extensible to 30), the time supposedly needed to identify them and to obtain the authorisation from their countries of origin to receive them back. The committee in charge of writing the law, and particularly Livia Turco, never managed to reform the citizenship system as they were planning to do, since this would have necessarily entailed a change in the Constitution, which could only be modified by passing a separate specific measure. In 1999, Livia Turco and Minister of the Interior Rosa Russo Jervolino presented a proposal for such a law, with the aim of allowing migrants to apply for Italian citizenship after five years of residence in the country as well as giving immigrants' children who were born in Italy the same rights by the time they enrolled in primary school, as long as one of the parents was Italian or both of them had lived in Italy for five years (Zuccolini, 1999). Not only was this reform not approved then, but the issue of citizenship is still at the centre of a cross-party (polemical) debate today and the children of immigrants need to wait until they turn 18 to apply for citizenship – a process characterised as a series of bureaucratic steps[48] and which does not automatically grant them the status.[49] On that occasion, the most bitter criticism of the proposal to grant migrants citizenship and the right to vote came from Alleanza Nazionale's leader, Gianfranco Fini, who instead supported Forza Italia (FI) in its suggestion to make it easier for foreign citizens of Italian origin to acquire an Italian passport and vote in political elections.[50] Interestingly, Fini's position radically changed within a year, as we shall see.

Despite the fact that the Turco-Napolitano law was generally defined by members of the opposition (including representatives of AN and FI) as reasonable, well structured and coherent, it had to face the enraged criticism of the Northern League, which, having consolidated its electoral support at a national level, started turning its attention towards immigration, raising its voice in the public debate and very often embracing controversial and 'politically incorrect' stances. The Turco-Napolitano proposal, however, encountered various criticisms also within the Left, with the PRC and the Greens closer to the advocacy coalition in demanding more rights for immigrants, such as making expulsion illegal even for those immigrants who had committed a crime.

5 The years of transition: from a solidarist to an identitarian approach

The 1990s represent a transitional phase in the national debate on immigration, leading to profound changes in public opinion on the subject and marked by a new role played by the mass media in echoing the concerns of the political system as well as presenting the numbers of arrivals as constantly growing, an attitude also resulting, on the one side, from supposedly 'traumatic events' such as the Albanian crisis in 1997[51] and, on the other side, from the increase in episodes of intolerance. It is indeed at this point that the Lega starts formulating the anti-immigration rhetoric analysed in the previous chapter, although in this escalating intolerance it is still relatively isolated and criticised by its allies, and even perceived as racist by almost the entire Popolo delle Libertà (Zincone, 2006; Melotti, 2004; Balbo and Manconi, 2004). However, it did not take much longer before the League's position prevailed and became the trademark of an increasingly common (electoral) strategy on the part of a more united Right, responsible for pushing the debate to a new level of intolerance (Guolo, 2003). Statements such those of Borghezio and Maroni on the need to use plastic bullets against immigrants or to send them back to their countries on military planes to avoid the risk of them raping the hostesses marked the beginning of a new era of provocation and controversy (Stella, 1996).

The rhetoric of the Northern League was broadly examined in the previous chapter. What matters here is to try to explain what determined this shift from an inefficient response to immigration, which was nonetheless 'solidaristic' in its intentions, to a dramatically more exclusionary attitude towards the newly arrived. The spreading of institutional and social xenophobia since the mid-1990s invested not only Italy but Southern European countries in general (Daly and Barot, 1999). This growing hostility can be attributed to a number of factors. First of all, the concern of citizens living in poor suburban areas where immigration tended to concentrate at the beginning and where the competition for access to social services, such as council housing, was higher (Zinn, 1996). Moreover, the failure of the reforms mentioned above in achieving their goal of integration/regularisation and, more than anything else, the inability to address the issue of illegal employment in the black economy, had contributed to consolidating the links between immigration and criminality in the public understanding of the phenomenon (Colombo, 1997; Bonifazi, 1992).

The mechanism described in the previous chapter according to which the perception of a threat and its recognition and legitimisation on the part of the political system contribute to turn such feeling of endangerment into something 'real' sheds some light on the process of increasing suspicion on the part of Italians towards the foreign presence. Moreover, while the Right exploited the situation (and reinforced public anxiety) for electoral purposes, that part of the Left interested in discussing the possibility of a multicultural society focused exclusively on denouncing the racist attitudes of Italians, therefore blaming the latter for the intolerant turn taken by the debate. Intellectuals were part of this mechanism, since, as Melotti (2004: 162) recalls, influential opinion makers such as journalists Gad Lerner, Giorgio Bocca and many others never engaged with the need for structural reforms or more in general with the issue of immigration but rather blamed an 'abstract racism' as the only evil. It could be said that such an attitude in identifying the problem only in the citizens' innate racism probably favoured the emerging populist parties, which took this supposed intolerance on board and transformed it into a legitimate shared feeling on the basis of which citizens could (and indeed were encouraged to) reassert their own national and cultural identity (Campani, 1993: 507–35).

These populist political actors, neither adequately contrasted by other parties nor yet criticised or identified as dangerous by intellectuals and opinion makers, successfully managed to establish a link between national belonging and immigration and started to exploit such relation for electoral purposes, arguing for the need to defend a threatened national and Catholic identity and to fight against immigration. While the 'war between the poor' was escalating, the government seemed to neglect both the claims of Italian citizens demanding security and preferential access to resources and the rights of the migrants (Campani, 1993: 3).

The political discourse of these parties and their criticism of the Martelli and the Turco-Napolitano laws contributed to strengthening the idea that 'too much had been done for the immigrants' (Campani, 1993: 507–35). The influence of this rhetoric, and the salience acquired by the issue of immigration through constant exposition in the press[52] can be better understood in light of the studies on the effect of political elites on public opinion, according to which the attitude of party leaders and representatives are determinant in shaping public reaction, as it is freed from the stigma of being labelled 'intolerant' or 'unacceptable' (McLaren, 2001: 81–108).

After the turmoil of Tangentopoli and the contradictory responses to sudden emergencies linked to mass inward migration, Italians' traditionally weak sense of national identity (Putnam, 1993) found in this populist rhetoric a means to legitimise identification of an in-group and an out-group. Identifying the 'other' became synonymous with marginalisation (of the immigrants) (Dal Lago, 2004). The increasingly contradictory shifts in the position of high representatives of the Church, coupled with the Northern League's attempt to exploit the Church hierarchy's more controversial stances with the aim of finding a common ground with it on the defence of Catholicism as the traditional religion and the trademark of Italianness, contributed to legitimising the political action of Bossi's party, at least indirectly (Melotti, 2004). The social and political attitude of intolerance towards immigrants, widespread by the late 1990s, represents the pre-condition for a new season of exclusionary responses to foreigners, marked by the latest two measures on immigration: the above-mentioned Bossi-Fini law and the 'security package'.

6 Moving towards the Bossi-Fini law: the identitarian-legalitarian turn

In December 1998, the event that seemed to signal the legalistic identitarian turn in the Right's position on immigration was the collection, organised by the League with the support of the Movimento Sociale Italiano and Forza Nuova,[53] of 700,000 signatures of citizens demanding a referendum to abrogate the Turco-Napolitano law. For the first time the proposal for a new law came from common citizens and appeared to respond to shared needs and concerns as well as to be detached from that elitarian attitude that had characterised the previous debates on the theme. This does not necessarily mean that political parties were not the main agent behind this social mobilisation.

Despite the recurrent demonstrations and the mobilisation of a considerable number of citizens, the initiative was dismissed by the Constitutional Court in February 2000 as it contravened the conditions of the Schengen agreement (Einaudi, 2007: 294). Both AN and FI, concerned about the fact that the League was at that point the only party, apart from the neo-Fascist ones, responding to the growing fears of the citizens, decided not to let it benefit from this strategy and started themselves moving towards similar positions, even before they formed a coalition and while the Left was still in power (Zincone, 2006: 369).[54]

In March 1998, Fini, presenting his position as motivated by the fear that 'citizens would seek private justice' and as aimed at preventing racist episodes from taking place, put forward a proposal for a new law on immigration, also authored by MP Landi di Chiavenna and backed by MPs Maurizio Gasparri and Ignazio La Russa among others.[55] Officially presented as a reaction to the League's xenophobic position, the proposal was based on a distinction between legal and illegal immigration and it aimed to fight the latter without being hostile to the former. However, the proposal did share Bossi's suggestion of introducing the crime of illegal entry as well as that of collecting the immigrants' fingerprints. Furthermore, it backed Bossi's idea of assigning specific quotas of immigrants to single regions in order to avoid a concentration of people of the same ethnicity and/or religion in single areas, since such concentration could facilitate the creation of criminal organisations, whereas it was necessary to allow the local job market to receive these new workers and integrate them.[56] This proposal, opposed by coalition allies such as the CCD (the centrist party Centro Cristiano Democratico) representatives Marco Follini and Pierferdinando Casini, was never approved. However, this move contributed to pushing the League closer to Forza Italia. At the beginning of 2000, Bossi reached an agreement with his newfound ally Berlusconi based on a two-point programme: implementation of 'devolution' and stricter control of immigration.

Following the collection of 50,000 signatures, another law based on citizens' initiative (legge di iniziativa popolare), clearly informed by a combination of functionalist and identitarian approaches, was presented in 2000. On the one hand, functionalism is to be intended as an approach that 'aims to make entry and residence permits for immigrants dependent on the economic financial and demographic needs of the host country and consequently seeks to regulate immigration flows on the basis of present and future demand for labour', preventing immigrants from 'becoming a social security burden'. On the other hand, the identitarian perspective as already mentioned, gives priority to immigrants who are closer to the citizens of the receiving country in ethnic, cultural and religious terms (Zincone 2006: 351–52).

As Einaudi (2007: 296) put it, 'The law was aimed at contrasting immigration of any type'.[57] The introductory statements of the text, formulated by representatives of the Northern League, were a direct attack on the Left and its presumed intention to use the usual false buonismo in order to gain electoral support from the immigrants, an argument since then regularly put forward by the party in order to 'prove' the supposed hypocrisy of its political opponents. The measure's programmatic declaration referred to the need to contrast the 'Jacobin' model of society of the time with a 'Christian' one, which is to say with a model that would take into account not only the impact of globalisation but also the history and tradition of the country. What is striking here is the fact that such a goal reproduced the same rhetoric and the same language used by the Catholic Church and was characterised by the recurrent use of the terms Catholic and Italian as synonymous. The League had been clearly looking at the Church as an important ally, and an authoritative one both for its being trusted by Italians and for its use of a consolidated rhetoric aimed at claiming a fundamental role in shaping Italian national identity. The Lega only had to strengthen the links between such identity and the 'risks' of immigration.

On a more practical level, the Bossi-Fini law aimed to replace the 'logic of amnesties' with a strategy of 'prevention', the latter consisting in the systematic rejection of the new immigrants as well as in the denial for those who had been already expelled ever to re-enter the country. A logic based on a 'zero-tolerance' approach was presented by the League as the only adequate response to the phenomenon. The key requisite for immigration had to be necessarily linked to holding a work contract and proving to be paying taxes. The unavoidable tie between work and a visa was confirmed by the fact that in order to enter Italy legally, immigrants had to have a valid work contract already stipulated before leaving the country of origin, and could no longer reach the destination first and then be allowed a short period of time to find employment.

In this sense, the Bossi-Fini law recalls the first decrees on immigration analysed above and therefore is not as 'revolutionary' as sometimes described. What changed was the rhetoric, as the focus was on the immigrants' threat to national identity, whereas previously it was on the job market and the protection of Italian workers. Looking at the other norms made operational with this law, the first important change consisted in the fact that more power was allocated to the regions, whose mayors had to organise into a 'confederation' in order to establish different quotas, to be calculated according to the needs of the local economy and the direct requests of factories in each council. Moreover, illegal entry or permanence in the country would become a penal crime to be punished with immediate expulsion, whereby the immigrant was to be accompanied to the border by the police. This most extreme article of the law was never approved, mainly because of the opposition of centre parties CCD (Centro Cristiano Democratico) and CDU (Cristiani Democratici Uniti)[58] and that of Catholic associations such as Caritas, which appealed to Catholic MPs sitting on the benches of Forza Italia as well as to international organisations such as Amnesty International.

The main outcome of the measure was the introduction of a new residence permit, once again strictly linked to a work contract, only renewable for the same period, in this way turning the 'residence permit' into a private contract between employer and employee. The rule of verifying whether a particular job could be done by an Italian before employing an immigrant was reintroduced. At the same time, following a proposal by Minister Mirco Tremaglia,[59] citizens of Italian origin[60] were given priority, with the introduction of a protected special quota of permits reserved for them. Despite the fact that European guidelines had fixed at five years the maximum period of time regular immigrants had to wait before applying for the carta di soggiorno, in the first draft of the law it was raised to eight years, reduced to six in the final version. Notwithstanding the will to restrict immigration and prevent new arrivals, the measure had to include a new amnesty to mitigate the opposition of the industrialists lobbying with the Left and Catholic institutions.

Finally, the definitive bill established that the fingerprints of those applying for a visa (or renewing it) had to be collected and that illegal immigrants could be kept in the CTPs (now renamed CIE, Centri di identificazione ed espulsione – Centres for identification and expulsion) for up to 60 days (previously 20, extensible to 30). If the identification of the immigrant was not completed within 60 days, the individual was given five days to leave Italy: if the illegal migrant did not leave the country and if they re-entered the country within 12 years from the expulsion, they risked being punished with up to four years in prison.[61] The measure was finally approved on 11 July 2002.[62] Once again, the official law was somewhat far from the original draft, although this time the need to find a compromise was not due to the intervention of the advocacy coalition, excluded from the negotiations, but mainly linked to the action of the Constitutional Court, which rejected a number of norms contradicting international agreements or not complying with international law and violating human rights. As for internal criticism, while Alleanza Nazionale and the Lega Nord formed a fairly united front, Forza Italia, and particularly its leader as well as its Catholic representatives, tended to keep a low profile and to distance themselves from the more intolerant statements and in general from the aggressive political discourse of its allies (Zincone, 2006: 363; Anon. 2002a, 2002c).

The Bossi-Fini law has often been described as an empty box, given its inability to mark a real break with the previous legislation, which it actually reconfirmed. At the same time it was defended by scholars such as Melotti (2004), who claimed not to understand the strong criticism and charges of intolerance on the part of intellectuals such as Cavazzani (2002), De Giorgi (2002) and Dal Lago (2004). What Melotti was neglecting in considering the outcomes of the law is the fact that these cannot be measured merely in terms of articles passed and rejected, and that the balance between confirming the previous measures and breaking away from them needs to be judged also on the basis of the political discourse underlying the discussion of the law. Other scholars[63] seem to agree with Turco's definition of the Bossi-Fini law as 'a political manifesto, aimed mainly at sustaining an anti-immigrant rhetoric which, as Bossi often claims, can be summarised in the motto: "few immigrants, only to work, exclusively for the strictly necessary time, after which they should go home"'[64] (Turco, 2002, cited in Einaudi, 2007: 321). Nonetheless, this manifesto, 'which had a purely demagogic propaganda purpose and no operational capacity' (Zincone, 2006: 364) clearly contributed to turn immigration into a political issue of central importance in the electoral discourse of the Right and only to a certain extent of the Left. Indeed, the latter was forced to adapt and somehow to follow a similar path when reacting to crimes committed by immigrants in areas where it was in power, in order to avoid criticism from the public and to emerge as equally able to deal with citizens' concerns.[65]

Despite the antagonistic rhetoric informing the political discourse of the centre-right and, increasingly, the centre-left, a comparison between the laws passed by the two coalitions reveals that the final drafts of the bills passed are not dramatically different. According to scholars such as Colombo and Sciortino (2004), and Zincone and Di Gregorio (2002), there is a clear continuity between the immigration policies of the two governments, despite their radically different ideological positions, and despite a discrepancy in the decision-making style of the two reforms, with the centre-left bargaining between government and opposition and the centre-right acting unilaterally. I would argue that, in this sense, the Bossi-Fini law goes back to a position that, when considered on its practical goals rather than in terms of the language used, is fairly similar to the first law on the labour market passed in 1963, which for the first time linked entry into the country to a job contract.

This is not the only paradox: a high level of contradiction can be found within each coalition, in the discrepancy between the rhetoric and the actual legislation. On the one hand, albeit supporting a multicultural approach based on the immigrants' right to maintain their cultural identity and to access resources, the Left did not take concrete steps to integrate migrants or just left implementation of the measures to be carried out at a local level, depending on the amount of resources, the involvement of different associations and the councils' own initiatives. On the other hand, the Right's public discourse tended to stigmatise immigrants, while at the same time periodically regularising many of them in response to economic needs, particularly in those areas of the North where the League was the first party. In the case of the Left, the apparent discrepancy is due to the fact that at times of 'emergency' or when citizens express their fears, it has to respond by adopting more severe measures. When the Right turned immigration into a propaganda tool, the Left could only ignore the voters' requests at the risk of alienating them, therefore it had to compete with the Right on similar ground. Finally, some of the reasons for the inefficiency of the legislation are related to the difficulties in its implementation, its internal contradictions (for instance the blocking of new entries versus recurrent amnesties), the need to meet the expectations of the electorate and the seemingly growing demand for 'security'.

7 The 'security package'

Measures such as the Bossi-Fini law established fertile ground for more restrictive laws, by raising the bar of what is acceptable and what is not in dealing with immigration through an aggressive and occasionally violent rhetoric constantly reiterated through the years. The so-called 'security package' represents a dramatic turn in the state's reaction to immigration, which interrupted that process of continuity described above. Passed in 2008, it is referred to as a 'package' as it includes several measures: a law by decree (decreto legge), three legislative decrees (decreti legislativi), a draft law and a decree of the Council of Ministers. The different measures will now be analysed separately to explain more in depth the matters they deal with, and an analysis of the 'package' as a whole will follow in order to make sense of the changes introduced, the reactions in the public debate and in civil society, and finally their consequences.

A law by decree is a temporary law that has the immediate force of law once it is published in the official bulletin (*Gazzetta Ufficiale della Repubblica Italiana*) and which needs to be converted into law by Parliament within 60 days of its adoption (Merlino, 2009: 7). The law decree no. 92[66] 'concerning urgent measures to deal with public security' focuses, as implied in its title, on the formulation of ad hoc measures to be immediately implemented and aimed at guaranteeing the stability of the social order. It establishes that non-EU citizens have to be expelled and EU citizens 'removed' from the Italian territory if they are sentenced to more than two years in prison. Until 2008, according to article 235 of the Italian penal code, only non-EU citizens could be expelled and only when sentenced to more than ten years' imprisonment. Moreover, being an illegal immigrant became an 'aggravating circumstance' to be added to those already listed in article 61 of the penal code, which means that 'an individual who has been convicted for having committed a crime and whose administrative status of stay in the country is irregular will now face jail sentences that are a third longer than those applicable to Italians' (Merlino, 2009: 8). The measure also included a deterrent for landlords: those who let properties to irregular immigrants can spend from six months to four years in prison and have their property confiscated. The money coming from the sale of the confiscated properties is destined to prevent and counter offences linked to illegal immigration.

A particularly important change was introduced for what concerns local administrations: with the security package Italian mayors can adopt special measures for urgent security reasons, which means they finally have that discretionary power the League had fought long and hard for them to obtain, as emerged from the articles on the topic published in *La Padania*, analysed in the previous chapter. Finally, article 7 establishes that in circumstances of emergency, when citizens' security is believed to be at risk, the army can be employed in areas that need to be kept under control. This particular measure, resulting from an agreement between the Ministry of the Interior and the Ministry of Defence, can be authorised for a maximum period of six months during which the highest number of soldiers used at any point cannot exceed 3,000 units. The government planned to use 1,000 soldiers to monitor the CIEs, and to concentrate the others in metropolitan areas, particularly Milan, Rome and Naples, as well as in other provinces, according to the requests of the local prefects (Merlino, 2009: 9; Naletto, 2009).

The three legislative decrees,[67] formulated between 2007 and 2008, deal with matters related to family reunification, EU citizens' residence and asylum seekers. They establish respectively that: family reunion is allowed in case of wives, minors and disabled parents, although a DNA test can be required and this has to be paid for by the immigrant; EU citizens intending to stay in the country for more than three months need to prove they have an adequate income to support themselves and their families as well as to register with the concerned authorities within 10 days of the end of the three months, while the state has the right to deny entry for reasons linked to public security. Finally, the last decree introduces limits in the asylum seekers' right of free movement and establishes that those who enter or stay irregularly can be kept in the CIEs for up to 180 days.

The draft law on public security[68] is strictly connected to the decree law No. 92: it establishes that the acquisition of citizenship by marriage, previously obtainable in six months, can only be requested after two years of marriage. However, its main aim is to make illegal entry into the country a crime. This particular measure, which had been suggested by the League and AN at regular intervals for almost two decades but never passed, becomes official with this draft law, punishing 'illegal immigration' with a prison sentence from six months to two years. The immigrant caught in a situation of illegality faces a short trial and immediate arrest. In order to make illegality more difficult to sustain and force irregular immigrants to leave, the measure also establishes that agencies which deal with remittances need to request and photocopy the residence permits of those sending money back to their countries. The owners of money transfer agencies are not the only ones requested to denounce illegal immigrants: doctors and school teachers are also among the civil servants from whom the government expects collaboration. While the security package was still being discussed, many commentators looked at the idea of considering the status of illegal immigrant as a crime per se just as another provocative boutade on the part of the Right (Ludovico, 2007; Cottone, 2008). Both the idea of applying sanctions to illegal immigration and that of demanding citizens to report on individual cases, represent 'an open violation of the constitutional principle of equality of all before the law', as well as a clear contravention of the international agreements on basic human rights (Naletto, 2009: 2).

The final and equally controversial measure introduced with the security package was included in the decree signed by the Council of Ministers at a meeting in Bari in May 2008,[69] when a 'state of emergency' was declared in relation to the presence of nomadic communities in the regions of Latium, Lombardy and Campania. In case of states of emergency, defined by law 225/92 (article 5) as 'natural calamities, catastrophes, or other events that according to their intensity and reach need to be faced by extraordinary powers and means', the Council of Ministers is allowed to put forward ad hoc by-laws (ordinanze) to deal with the situation. The powers given in these circumstances to the Council of Ministers can be delegated to local 'commissioners'.

In 2008, such powers were transferred to the prefects, who became responsible for monitoring the camps, identifying and registering the individuals living in each settlement, mobilising the police against those illegal immigrants who therefore had to be expelled, evicting those not legally entitled to live there and 'fostering integration', which usually means dealing with the fears and protests of local residents. To carry on these duties and implement the changes, the prefects had at their disposal selected units of the military force (Merlino, 2009: 13; Naletto, 2009: 2). Moreover, unarmed citizens registered in specific associations can be used by mayors and prefects to patrol the streets and inform the police of security threats they encounter in supposedly socially degraded areas. The so-called 'ronde',[70] the patrols regulated by this measure, already existed and were carried out spontaneously by citizens organised in neighbourhood associations before the by-law was passed.[71] As Naletto recalls, many members of the ronde groups are also members of Right-wing organisations or individuals 'involved in acts of apology of Fascism', such as Gaetano Salva, leader of the patrols, prosecuted for racist propaganda and arrested in 2005 (Naletto, 2009: 2).

The first reactions to the measures contained in the security package began to arrive while the laws where still under Parliamentary scrutiny. Unlike the responses to the previous legislation on immigration, these reactions were not only immediate but also transversal to the political spectrum while the debate was animated by different sectors of civil society as well as representatives of foreign countries, particularly those whose citizens were targeted in the laws, such as Romania. Within the centre-right coalition, while the Northern League claimed the paternity of the security package, Alleanza Nazionale's leader, Fini, was the first to criticise bitterly some specific articles included in the draft version of the laws and particularly those on the so-called presidispia,[72] which established the need on the part of teachers and doctors to denounce illegal immigrants they encountered during their working activities. In a letter sent to Minister of the Interior Maroni, Fini expressed concern over the unconstitutionality of a measure which would inevitably lead to an open violation of migrants' human rights as defined by the EU:

> The measure, indeed, linking the access to public services to the exhibition of a valid residence permit to our administrative offices, prevents foreigners who do not hold such permits from benefiting from said services. At an operational level this results in a contradiction with other norms. Just to provide an example: a foreign minor[73] would not be allowed to enrol for schooling[74] whereas the right of education is granted, regardless of the person's status as a migrant, in the same way as it is granted to Italian citizens.[75]

Fini's intervention in the matter was welcomed and praised by representatives of the opposition such as the Partito Democratico (PD) MP Giuseppe Fioroni and Italia dei Valori (IdV) MP Vittorio Borghese, according to whom the measures would have the paradoxical effect of promoting integration by seg-regating foreigners (Anon. 2009a).[76] Centre-left parties, particularly the PD and its leader Dario Franceschini, attributed the responsibility for the law entirely to the Northern League, accused of blackmailing the government by guarantee-ing its loyalty to the majority coalition only when given full powers to pursue its federalist project and to introduce 'zero-tolerance' policies on immigration.

However, Berlusconi himself often remarked upon the fact that this was 'a law aimed at granting citizens unconcern, a law that I strongly desired'.[77] Equally satisfied by the approval of the draft were representatives of the AN such as Maurizio Gasparri who, taking a distance from Party Secretary Fini, supported Minister of the Interior Roberto Maroni and fellow Northern League politicians in their claim that the law was not racist, while defining the measure as 'a law for all Italians'[78] (Anon. 2009a). In responding to the accusation of bringing back Fascist racial laws, the Minister of the Interior issued an official statement, in which he argued that the security package did not forbid mixed marriages or the acquisition of legal status for those who entered the country legally. Such a statement was also a reaction to a petition against the law promoted by a group of Italian intellectuals, including Andrea Camilleri, Moni Ovadia, Dario Fo, Dacia Maraini and Antonio Tabucchi, launched in the pages of *MicroMega* magazine (Anon. 2009a, 2009e).

An immediate reaction from civil society came from the national associa-tions of doctors and teachers, particularly those represented by the CGIL union,[79] which took a clear stance against the supposed duty to denounce illegal immigrants. The main reasons for their protest were summarised in the slogans used for demonstration outside Montecitorio on 29 April 2009: '1 right to security for everybody; 2 no to the draft law on security; 3 no to citizens' patrols; 4 no to racism; 5 right to grant and to be granted access to health care for doctors and immigrants respectively.'[80]

According to the CGIL's manifesto, the draft law on security represented an intolerable restriction of human rights and was characterised by a great degree of racial discrimination and abuse, with the even more unacceptable strategy of recruiting different members of society, such as teachers, doctors, employers, and even landlords and common citizens, with the aim of turning them into informants and therefore pushing them towards the racial oppres-sion of the migrants. The manifesto also included reference to the fact that while the draft law was being discussed in Parliament, episodes of racism and violence were happening increasingly frequently and were attributed partly to an irresponsible press which incited citizens to commit such violent acts.[81] Similar charges of unconstitutionality and racism came from international organisations such as Amnesty International and Médecins Sans Frontières, as well as from the EU. Several representatives of the latter argued that the new 'package' and particularly its approach towards 'the Roma and Sinti emergency' would inevitably have led to the social stigmatisation of foreign citizens and was likely to determine an increase in violence and racism towards them.[82]

As Naletto (2009: 2) explains, 'the choice to intervene in the legal condition of foreigners only through safety laws and measures sends an important symbolic message: that so-called "insecurity" is due to the presence of foreigners, who, as they were born in another country, are inclined to criminality by nature'. Such measures are rooted in the rhetoric, consolidated by reiteration and years of anti-immigrant campaigns on the part of the League, shared by mainstream parties of the Right and not systematically opposed by antagonist political opponents. If the normalisation of exclusionary discourses contributes to reinforcing the idea that such laws are much needed by Italian citizens, these restrictive measures are in turn perceived as the official legitimation of citizens' fear.

As mentioned above, a certain degree of concern related to the security package started to emerge in those foreign countries whose citizens were targeted by the new laws, and particularly in Romania. The reaction of the then Prime Minister Calin Popescu Tariceanu arrived when the law was still under Parliamentary scrutiny: while confirming his will to cooperate with Italian authorities to reduce crime and monitor the movement of Romanian citizens, Tariceanu remarked upon the need to prevent and fight a spreading xenophobic attitude towards an entire population that was being discriminated against despite its contributing to the development of the Italian economy and society (Anon. 2008a).

Regarding the reaction to the law on the part of the Catholic Church, it has to be said that, despite a few ambiguous interventions of individual representatives on issues related to identity and (Muslim) immigration, most of the Catholic world proved critical of the pacchetto sicurezza since its first formulation.[83] The secretary for the Pastorale per i Migranti, Archbishop Agostino Marchetto, for instance, intervened to remark upon the need to avoid conflict with the newly arrived and to respect human rights. He openly criticised specific articles of the law (such as denying illegal immigrants education and health care), while praising others, such as expulsion, if used only as the 'extrema ratio'. The archbishop strongly remarked that opposing the aspect of the law that openly violated migrants' rights was his duty as a Catholic.[84] Several more cardinals intervened to criticise the law, often taking a clearer stance, as in the case of Archbishop of Milan Dionigi Tettamanzi who, in 2009, during the G8 in L'Aquila, reminded world leaders attending mass in Milan Cathedral that 'the rights of the weaker members of society are not weak rights'.[85] Tettamanzi (2008) also argued that this tends to be forgotten by those who exploit immigrants for personal and economic interest. This statement, in which the Lega was never mentioned, triggered a series of reactions on the part of leghisti, such as MP Calderoli, according to whom Tettamanzi and his supporters had to be considered as members of the opposition parties (and therefore 'communists').[86]

As support for Tettamanzi started to grow and more Catholic representatives, such as the archbishops of Lombardy and Sicily, openly declared their perplexities on the measure, the voices of those who had been relatively supportive of the new law tended to fade. This was also true of national newspapers and magazines of Catholic orientation, such as, for instance, *Avvenire*. Having defined the security package as 'a norm that should neither be praised nor blamed'[87] on 3 July 2009, journalist Pietro Chinellato rectified his statement the following day by writing that it was important not to neglect the signals of a 'xenophobic drift' (deriva xenofoba), and that 'security is a priority which cannot be given up, but that cannot be achieved to the detriment of an welcoming attitude'[88] (Carnevali and Gigante, 2009).

Leaving aside a more detailed analysis of the Church's reaction to the new measure, what is interesting to note is that once again the Church did not hold a uniform position on the matter but rather reproduced the same internal division previously shown in Chapter 2, with only the exception of several bishops who in these circumstances put forward their personal view in support of immigrants. The Vatican, however, limited its official intervention to taking a distance from those among its representatives who were critical of the new law.

The internal division within the Catholic hierarchy, confirmed on this occasion, has been interpreted by some commentators as a new challenge faced by the Church today. On the contrary, the Waldensian Church seemed to reach a unitary front in launching a campaign in protest against the security package. Such a campaign also involved a call for a national day of fasting to express solidarity with immigrants, defined as the victims of the law. The initiative was supported by several representative of centre-left parties, such as Paolo Ferrero (Partito della Rifondazione Comunista, or PRC), Emma Bonino (Partito Radicale, or PR), and Sonia Alfano (Italia dei Valori, or IdV) (Naso, 2009). Once again the Left jumped on the protest put forward by other public actors, proving not to have the capacity to organise itself as a united front and not to emerge as the main antagonist of the Lega.

Finally, a last reaction came from the CSM (Consiglio Superiore della Magistratura, the High Council of the Judiciary), which judged the law to be inefficient and actually counterproductive as it would obstruct judicial activity as well as violate the Constitution (Anon. 2009c). Several jurists noticed how the new law was also destined to have more practical consequences, such as that of a worsening of the situation of already overcrowded Italian prisons, with more people going to jail and being kept there for a longer time. According to them, given the impossibility of putting into practice some key measures such as the expulsion of illegal immigrants, the security package rather represented more than anything else a manifesto (norma-manifesto) inadequate to work as a deterrent. The law's repressive rhetoric, according to which jailing illegal immigrants solves the problem of criminality, becomes therefore an 'extra-juridical means employed within a global defensive strategy'.[89] Furthermore, it denies immigrants their basic human rights and particularly personal freedom: 'the right that has been historically most defended in the constitutions of all times is in this way suspended for long periods of time, following the provisions of an administrative authority (the police commissioner)'[90] (Viganò, 2008: 820).

The first general datum that emerges from the analysis of this new package of measures is the fact that it represents a clear moment of rupture with the previous legislation. After years of bills that in their final draft were not dramatically different from one another, where the most radical views on the most adequate response to a growing number of arrivals were blunted by the several modifications and amendments necessary for their approval, the latest measure exposed openly the paradoxical position of the Northern League. Its strategy was indeed aimed at reconciling an increasingly exclusionary attitude towards the newly arrived with the growing demand for more immigrants coming from the industrial areas of the North, where its anti-immigrant rhetoric contributed to secure it electoral consensus.

This paradox underlying the distance between the party's rhetoric and action can be explained and understood in light of Cento Bull's definition of the League's political action as 'simulative politics'.[91] Such a contradiction emerges when considering the centrality of identity politics in the party's ideology, typical of parties that focus on pre-material and non-economic issues (Bets, 1993). Starting from the premise that identity and interests are not necessarily antithetical and that in fact they can be 'mutually reinforcing', the scholar claims that the success of right-wing parties like the Northern League can be ascribed to 'their ability to reconcile apparently irreconcilable phenomena of both a material and pre-material nature' (Cento Bull, 2009: 3). The Northern League, indeed, aims to respond to the economic aspirations of strong global competitors while dealing with their fears and anxieties regarding the impact of globalisation. In this sense, simulation has to be intended as 'the use of symbols, signs and images which do not represent or refer to anything that is authentic, but which themselves produce or perform reality, and present themselves as evidence for this authenticity' (Blühdorn, 2007: 267).

According to Cento Bull, Bossi's party can be best understood within a framework of simulation, given the fact that competitive industrial areas can also be exposed to a widespread sense of anxiety and distress (Cento Bull, 2009: 5). 'In this context […] the Lega has developed a politics that "simulates" being able to reconcile irreconcilable material and cultural trends, for instance, by treating immigration as a "temporary" phenomenon', or providing 'a vision of a return to an idealized communitarian society which is both crime-free and (almost) immigrant-free' (Cento Bull, 2009: 143).

8 Conclusions

The analysis conducted to this point shows that the Italian legislation on immigration for decades reflected the same lack of consistency and long-term strategy that has characterised the cultural and political debate on the issue. The main trait of the laws passed until the early 1990s is their attempt to solve a series of unforeseen crises while regulating the internal job market following a protectionist approach. Until 1990, there is no reference to any of the models put forward by other European countries to deal with the phenomenon. References to multiculturalism as a fallacious model will appear a decade later and will become typical of the rhetoric of right-wing parties. Turco and Napolitano were the first politicians to look at multiculturalism as a point of reference that could be applied to the Italian situation as well, even though the implementation of policies inspired by this model did not go beyond an informal stage. Until the late 1990s, the approval of new measures was not accompanied by a general discussion on the most adequate means to foster integration, an attitude which helps to explain the sudden concern that invested the political world and civil society when immigration manifested itself at an unprecedented scale in terms of waves of arrivals and clashes with the local population. Even when, at the turn of the new century, immigration became a hot topic in political discourse and the two coalitions turned it into a decisive element in electoral campaigns characterised by heated polemic, the individual laws passed were all similar in their final drafts, showing mainly a degree of continuity.

The fact that, despite the deeply antagonistic views expressed by the different parties on the subject, these laws were overall homogeneous in what they established as well as in their consequences, can be explained by looking at a number of factors. First of all, the position of the Left shifted from a general will to welcome immigrants to an attitude much closer to that of the Right, with whom it chose to compete in reassuring the citizens, who seemingly demanded greater security. This change was triggered not only by the requests of public opinion but also by specific episodes of violence, when the Left reacted to the anger on the part of Italian citizens by closing various campi nomadi and threatening the mass expulsion of all illegal immigrants. The second reason why the laws passed until 2008 were similar in many respects is due to the tensions that emerged during the process of negotiation and Parliamentary scrutiny, when the more radical changes suggested by both extremes of the political spectrum were rejected by the Constitutional Court or simply balanced each other out. Moreover, international and EU organisations contributed to minimising or erasing the most controversial aspects of the laws.

By the end of the 1990s, immigration had become an important tool to gain electoral support and in this sense it started to represent the ground on which political parties would compete, sometimes almost blackmailing their allies, as in the case of the conditions posed by the Northern League to Forza Italia in order to remain part of the coalition. The language used by the different political actors shows some similarities: from the word 'sanatoria' – sanare means to heal – which implies an interpretation of immigration as an illness or a plague, to the term extracomunitario and its inward-looking perspective focused on the inside, the community. The main difference in the terminology used to formulate the laws until 2008 can be seen in the transformation of the centres of temporary stay into centres for identification and expulsion, where clearly the focus shifted from the fact that immigrants would only be temporarily deprived of their freedom, to the idea that expulsion was the only expectation they could have after identification.

As stated earlier, the Bossi-Fini law can be considered the last measure in this cycle, as it almost matched the law passed in 1963, which made entry dependent on the possession of a valid work contract. It can be said that the 1963 measure was even stricter, since it established that before employing a foreigner, an employer had to verify that no Italians were available for that job. However, it is also the case that the Bossi-Fini law began a new season of political discourse openly aimed at discouraging immigration and linking it to all the challenges Italy was facing, from pollution to crime and to economic decline. In this sense what had changed was the narrative behind the two laws, whereby the former still showed a certain degree of solidarity with the immigrants as persons, whereas the latter interpreted their presence exclusively within the framework of a victim-aggressor dynamic.

The 2008 law represents a clear turn and a clear departure from two decades of measures that, albeit lacking a long-term strategy, were the result of constant negotiation. The security package put the definitive word on a trend that had already started to outline an exclusionary attitude towards immigrants. With the introduction of the 'crime of illegal entry', they clearly become homines sacri, invisible in the public arena and exploited as scapegoats, the target of popular anger as well as the reassuring 'other', fundamental to place any blame outside the community.

The influence of the Northern League in this turn is self-evident. It can be said that until 2008 Italy did not seem to follow any coherent model in reacting to immigration, as the various measures were rather temporary responses to a series of critical periods of 'emergency'. Therefore the last hypothesis listed in the introduction to this chapter has to be considered true until the passing of the security package. After that there is a clear model emerging: the same permanent exclusion put forward by the League coincides with the strategy adopted by the state – a state in which the party represents the strongest voice among those debating immigration. The acquisition of such a prominent role within the public discussion on identity and otherness was to a certain extent facilitated by both the Left and the Church.

The former, indeed, despite its traditional welcoming attitude towards the newly arrived, lacked the strategic vision necessary to make a more inclusive discourse emerge and ended up competing with the League on the same ground: that of security.

The influence of the Church is much more difficult to assess: on the one hand, it cannot be said that it contributed to the affirmation of an exclusionary model of state and citizenship, as, on the contrary, often its representatives' voices were the only ones raised to compete against and condemn the Lega's arguments. On the other hand, its rhetoric, based on victimhood, and its call to protect a threatened Italian Catholic identity had definitely inspired and legitimised the discourse of the Northern League, which borrowed it and made it its own.

Notes

1 On pre-World War II migration to Italy, see Colombo and Sciortino, 2004b.
2 On the role of Catholic agencies and parishes in the recruitment process, see: Andall, 2000; Scrinzi, 2008.
3 On the link between the welfare system and migrants employed in the domestic sector, see also Sciortino, 2004.
4 The expression means literally 'those who look after'.
5 In the first trimester of 2014 the unemployment rate for the South was 21.7 per cent, while it was 13.9 per cent at national level and a higher 46 per cent for younger generations (age range 15–24) (data source: Istat, 2014).
6 See: Gavosto *et al.* 1999; Venturini, 1999; Reyneri, 2004.
7 Ministero del Lavoro e della Sicurezza Sociale.
8 Ministero dell'Interno.
9 Memorandum Ministeriale, 4 Dicembre 1963/4, in *Gazzetta Ufficiale della Repubblica Italiana*, No. 260, 4 Ottobre 1963.
10 Ufficio provinciale del lavoro.
11 Legge 30 Luglio 2002/189, 'Modifica alla normativa in materia di immigrazione e di asilo', in *Gazzeta ufficiale della Repubblica Italiana*, No. 199, 26 Agosto 2002.
12 Such expulsions were as frequent as to reach an average of 50 a week in 1972 (Einaudi, 2007: 102).
13 Disegno di legge 25 Luglio 1998/286, 'Testo unico delle disposizioni concernenti la disciplina dell'immigrazione e norme sulla condizione dello straniero emanate con decreto legislativo', in *Gazzetta Ufficiale della Repubblica Italiana*, No. 191, 18 Agosto 1998.
14 The blocking of entrance was a consequence of the economic crisis Italy was facing at the time, after a period of relative growth. Such a measure, which in Northern European countries had already started being put forward in the 1970s, resulted in an increasingly high number of immigrants entering the country illegally and applying for a visa through amnesty, which was granted on an average rate of one every four years (Einaudi, 2010).
15 Comitato interministeriale per l'emigrazione.
16 Legge 30 Dicembre 1986/943, 'Norme in materia di collocamento e di trattamento dei lavoratori extracomunitari e contro le immigrazioni clandestine', in *Gazzetta ufficiale della Repubblica Italiana*, No. 8, 12 Gennaio 1987.
17 'L'Italia non ha alcuna intenzione di diventare un paese di immigrazione. In quest'ottica e non essendo in grado di sopportare i costi economici e sociali che comporta nel lungo periodo l'accoglimento di un numero elevato di lavoratori stranieri, l'Italia non intende basare il proprio sviluppo economico sull'importazione di manodopera straniera' (Oscar Luigi Scalfaro, cited in Einaudi, 2007: 119).
18 'L'Italia ha una tradizione umanitaria degna della sua civiltà: porte spalancate a chi viene da noi per cercare libertà e fuggire a persecuzioni o a costretta clandestinità, e uguale comprensione per chi, malgrado queste stagioni povere di lavoro e di attività, viene per lavorare onestamente e inserirsi in una realtà sociale che ritiene valida. Porte spalancate anche per aiutare e potenziare il flusso turistico da ogni parte del mondo, fonte di attività, di lavoro e di ricchezza e mezzo non ultimo di reciproca conoscenza [...] Queste porte spalancate, dolorosamente trovano un limite, un setaccio per impedire abusi e pericoli' (Oscar Luigi Scalfaro, 'Premessa alla circolare del Ministero dell'Interno n.559/443/225388/2/4/6 del 19.8.85', p.1, cited in Bonini, 1987: 81; also cited in Dei, 2002: 16; Einaudi, 2007: 119).
19 On the ILO agreements, see: Bohning, 1991; Oelz, 2014; Anderson and Rogaly, 2005.
20 On the provisions of the ILO Conventions on the human rights of unauthorised migrant workers, see Lyon, 2006.

21 'Ogni membro per il quale la convenzione sia in vigore s'impegna a formulare ed attuare una politica nazionale diretta a promuovere e garantire, con metodi adatti alle circostanze ed agli usi nazionali, la parità di opportunità e di trattamento in materia di occupazione e di professione, di sicurezza sociale, di diritti sindacali e culturali, nonché di libertà individuali e collettive per le persone che, in quanto lavoratori migranti o familiari degli stessi, si trovino legalmente sul suo territorio' (ILO Convention No. 143, 4 June 1975, article 10).

22 '[U]na persona che emigra o è emigrata da un paese all'altro, in vista di occupazione altrimenti che in proprio conto: esso ammette qualsiasi persona ammessa regolarmente in qualità di lavoratore migrante' (Article 11).

23 Such interpretation of migrants as the international proletariat has previously been applied to Italians who left their countries in the many diasporas that marked Italian history. See Gabaccia, 1997.

24 'Nessuno è straniero nel mio Paese.'

25 'Nessuno è straniero nella Chiesa.'

26 See Shotwell, 1934.

27 'Diritto di mantenere la propria identità culturale.'

28 La legge era [...] basata su una concezione semplicistica del mercato del lavoro degli immigrati ma anche su meccanismi troppo complessi. Ignorava il lavoro autonomo e ambulante, come pure la richiesta si assumere con richieste nominative individui conosciuti personalmente e non con numeri e facce pescate a caso. Si scontrava anche con il grande problema, che né la legge 943/1986 né alcuna delle leggi successive riuscirono a risolvere: quello del ruolo determinante dell'economia sommersa nel fornire occupazione agli stranieri senza fornire le basi legali per ottenere il permesso di soggiorno' (Einaudi, 2007: 130).

29 Such a data set was recently questioned and problematised by Colombo and Sciortino (2004b), who explain how the rising numbers are also due to the fact that the Ministry of the Interior based the calculation on the number of visas issued each year, without taking out of the total number the expired visas that had not been renewed. The result of such a method was that there was no record of migrants leaving Italy.

30 While the 1990s are generally considered by scholars as revolutionary, such a mainstream interpretation has however been questioned by a number of studies which illustrate that phase of Italian history as one of continuity. On the issue, see Bull and Rhodes, 1997.

31 Legge 28 Febbraio 1990/39, 'Conversione in legge, con modificazioni, del decreto legge 30 Dicembre 1989 n. 416, recante norme urgenti in materia di asilo politico, di ingresso e soggiorno dei cittadini extracomunitari e di regolarizzazione di cittadini extracomunitari ed apolidi già presenti nel territorio dello Stato. Disposizioni in materia di asilo', in *Gazzetta Ufficiale della Repubblica Italiana*, No. 49, 28 Febbraio 1990.

32 Scarici, 2011.

33 Even though marginal, the idea that an 'open borders' policy could be of benefit for both the immigrants and Italian economic and cultural development is still suggested today. See Manconi and Brinis, 2013.

34 Anon. 1995.

35 'Misura di "accompagnamento alla frontiera".'

36 'Reato di immigrazione clandestina.'

37 Legge 24 Luglio 2008/125, 'Conversione in legge, con modificazioni, del decreto-legge 23 Maggio 2008/92', in *Gazzetta Ufficiale della Repubblica Italiana*, No. 173 del 25 Luglio 2008.

38 On the different migratory waves from Albany to Italy, see: Bonifazi and Sabatini, 2003; King and Mai, 2002. On the shift in the public perception of Albanian immigrants in Italy, see Zinn, 1996.

39 Margherita Boniver has been the only minister of immigration in Italy. However, Monti's government elected a minister for international cooperation and integration, Andrea Riccardi, who was in office from 16 November 2011 to 28 April 2013; in 2013 a new minister for integration, Cecile Kyenge, was elected under Bersani's government. Kyenge held the position from 28 April 2013 to 22 February 2014. At time of writing, Italy did not have a minister for integration.

40 Pini, 2011; Coppola and Ulivi, 2012. The story of the arrival of the Vlora in Italy is narrated in the film, *La nave dolce* (2012), directed by Daniele Vicari. See Vicari, 2012.

41 That day Albanians invaded Italy.

42 Quaranta, 2011.

43 Decreto legge 26 Aprile 1993/122 'Misure urgenti in materia di discriminazione razziale, etnica e religiosa', in *Gazzetta Ufficiale dela Repubblica Italiana*, No. 97, 27 aprile 1993, later converted into law, 25 Giugno 1993/205.

44 '[C]hi diffonde in qualsiasi modo idee fondate sulla superiorità o sull'odio razziale o etnico, ovvero incita a commettere o commette atti di discriminazione per motivi razziali, etnici, nazionali o religiosi' (Article 1, para. 1a).

45 '[I]n qualsiasi modo incita a commettere o commette violenza o atti di provocazione alla violenza per motivi razziali, etnici, nazionali o religiosi'. (Article 1, para. 1b).

46 Article 1, para. 2d.

47 Legge 6 Marzo 1998/40 'Disciplina dell'immigrazione e norme sulla condizione dello straniero', in *Gazzetta Ufficiale della Repubblica Italiana*, No. 59 del 12 Marzo 1998, later included in the Decreto legislativo, 25 Luglio 1998/286, 'Testo unico delle disposizioni concernenti la disciplina dell'immigrazione e norme sulla condizione dello straniero emanate con decreto legislativo', in *Gazzetta Ufficiale della Repubblica Italiana*, No. 191, 18 Agosto 1998.

48 As, for instance, the need to apply for citizenship during the period of time between the 18th and the 19th birthdays, or the need to prove residence in Italy, with no interruption, from birth to the moment of submitting the application.

49 The acquisition of Italian citizenship for children of immigrants regularly residing in Italy for at least five years is regulated by law, 5 February 1992, No. 91 'Nuove norme sulla cittadinanza', in *Gazzetta Ufficiale della Repubblica Italiana*, No. 38, 15 Febbraio 1992.

50 The measures regulating the right of Italians living abroad to vote in Italian general elections are law 17 Gennaio 2000/1, 'Modifica all'art. 48 della Costituzione concernente l'istituzione della circoscrizione Estero per l'esercizio del diritto di voto dei cittadini italiani residenti all'estero', in *Gazzetta Ufficiale della Repubblica Italiana* (Serie generale), No. 15, 20 Gennaio 2000; and law 27 Dicembre 2001/459 'Norme per l'esercizio del diritto di voto dei cittadini italiani residenti all'estero', in *Gazzetta Ufficiale della Repubblica Italiana*, No. 4, 5 Gennaio 2002. On the issue, see Tintori, 2009.

51 On the role of Italy in the solution of the Albanian crisis of 1997, see De Guttry and Pagani, 1999.

52 Academic studies have proven that visibility and prominence in the media of a specific issue can heavily influence the public agenda (Karapin, 2002). The fact that higher saliency leads the electorate to consider immigration issues as 'important to deal with' (Boomgaarden and Vliegenthart, 2007: 407) is particularly interesting as in Italy the media report on immigration, anti-immigration policies and neo-populist movements more than elsewhere in Europe. Schudson (2002) argues that rather than being just means useful to amplify politicians' voices and claims, the media should therefore be considered proper political actors/institutions capable of shaping public opinion.

53 Forza Nuova is an extreme right-wing party founded by Roberto Fiore and Massimo Morsello in 1997.

54 The competition aimed at 'appropriating' the issue of the relation between immigration and security in order to emerge as its 'rightful owner' in front of public opinion can be explained according to the influence of niche parties on mainstream parties, as illustrated in Chapter 5.

55 Disegno di legge 25 Luglio 1998/286, 'Testo unico delle disposizioni concernenti la disciplina dell'immigrazione e norme sulla condizione dello straniero emanate con decreto legislativo', in *Gazzetta Ufficiale della Repubblica Italiana*, No. 191, 18 Agosto 1998.

56 '[I]n quanto ciò può facilmente comportare l'insorgenza e la recrudescenza di consorterie, bande o cupole del crimine [...] così da assecondare la ricettività locale del mercato del lavoro, ove essa esiste, a tutto favore del processo di integrazione' (Landi di Chiavenna, cited in Einaudi, 2007: 295).

57 'La legge era tesa a contrastare l'immigrazione in tutte le sue forme.'

58 In 2002 the two parties merged together with the DE (Democrazia Europea) to form the UDC, Unione Democratici Cristiani e dei Democratici di Centro.

59 Tremaglia was then the minister of Italians abroad. The fact that Italy had at that time a Ministry of Emigration and a Ministry for Italians Abroad but no Ministry of Immigration is illustrative of the fact that Italy was still perceived as a sending country, rather than a receiving one.

60 These citizens of Italian origin living abroad sent an open letter to Tremaglia, demanding that Berlusconi's government 'reunite the Italian nation', which is to say give them the right to obtain an Italian passport automatically. See: penali_perpetrati. html; Anon. 'Lettera aperta e denuncia pubblica di reati penali perpetrati', www. ainei.org/052_Lettera_Aperta_e_denuncia_PUBBLICA_di_reati_Penali_perpetrati (accessed 14 June 2014).

61 Articles 12g and 13a, 13b.

62 Legge 30 Luglio 2002/189, 'Modifica alla normativa in materia di immigrazione e di asilo', in *Gazzeta ufficiale della Repubblica Italiana*, No. 199, 26 Agosto 2002.

63 As, for instance: Zincone, 2006; Einaudi, 2007.

64 '[U]n manifesto politico, soprattutto voluto per sostenere una retorica contro gli immigrati, che il ministro Bossi è solito sintetizzare nell'espressione: "immigrati pochi, solo per lavoro, solo per il tempo strettamente necessario e poi ritornino a casa".'

65 The obvious example of such a reaction is once again the Reggiani killing, mentioned in Chapter 3. On that occasion, Mayor Veltroni opted for a zero-tolerance policy, turning security into the priority of his coalition (Anon. 2007b; Battistelli and Lucianetti, 2010).

66 Decreto Legislativo 23 Maggio 2008/92 recante misure urgenti in materia di sicurezza pubblica, in *Gazzetta Ufficiale della Repubblica Italiana* (Serie generale), No. 122, 26 Maggio 2008.

67 Decreto legislativo 6 Febbraio 2007/30, 'Attuazione della direttiva 2004/38/CE relativa al diritto dei cittadini dell'Unione e dei loro familiari di circolare e di soggiornare liberamente nel territorio degli Stati membri', in *Gazzetta Ufficiale della Repubblica Italiana*, No.72, 27 Marzo 2007; Decreto legislativo 28 Gennaio 2008/25, 'Attuazione della direttiva 2005/85/CE recante norme minime per le procedure applicate negli Stati membri ai fini del riconoscimento e della revoca dello *status* di rifugiato', in *Gazzetta Ufficiale della Repubblica Italiana*, No. 40, 16 Febbraio 2008; Decreto Legislativo 23 Maggio 2008/92 recante misure urgenti in materia di sicurezza pubblica, in *Gazzetta Ufficiale della Repubblica Italiana* (Serie generale), No. 122, 26 Maggio 2008.

68 Disegno di legge 3 Giugno 2008, Atto Senato n. 733, XVI legislatura, 'Disposizioni in materia di sicurezza pubblica'.

69 Legge 24 Luglio 2008/125, 'Conversione in legge, con modificazioni, del decreto-legge 23 Maggio 2008/92', in *Gazzetta Ufficiale della Repubblica Italiana*, No. 173 del 25 Luglio 2008.

70 Anon. 2009d.

71 They had to a certain extent already been made operative in the Northern regions and provinces where the Lega was more popular.

72 From the words 'presidio' (garrison) and 'spia' (informer). The expression refers to schools and hospitals which, according to the security package, were to be turned into strongholds where the illegal immigrants could be recognised by teachers and doctors, who according to the law had to signal their presence to the authorities so that migrants could be identified and expelled.

73 Minore: a young person who is not yet of legal voting age.

74 Education in Italy is compulsory from the age of six to the age of 15 (Article 1 of the Circolare Ministeriale 30/12/2010, n. 101).

75 'La disposizione, infatti, subordinando la fruizione di pubblici servizi alla presentazione di documenti inerenti al soggiorno presso gli uffici della nostra amministrazione, impedisce che di questi servizi possano godere gli stranieri privi dei predetti documenti. Ciò fa sorgere, soprattutto a livello applicativo, un problema di compatibilità con altre norme. Un solo esempio delle conseguenza che ne deriverebbero: ai minori stranieri verrebbe negata l'iscrizione alla scuola d'obbligo ed il conseguente diritto all'istruzione che è attualmente tutelato, indipendentemente dalla regolarità della posizione in ordine al loro soggiorno, nelle forme e nei modi previsti per i cittadini italiani' (Fini, quoted in Anon. 2009a).

76 '[I]l nostro modo di integrare i bambini e gli studenti sarebbe quello di farli passare dal carcere' (Anon., 2009a).

77 'Una legge fatta per la serenità dei cittadini, da me fortemente voluta' (Anon. 2009a).

78 '[U]na legge per gli Italiani.'

79 Confederazione Generale Italiana del Lavoro.

80 1 Diritto alla sicurezza per tutti; 2 No al ddl sicurezza; 3 No alle ronde; 4 No al razzismo; 5 Libertà di cura per i medici e gli immigrati' (CGIL, 2009).

81 'Tutto l'impianto del ddl sicurezza [...] configura una restrizione intollerabile dei diritti umani e delle persone con un segno di forte discriminazione e vessazione razziale, in più cercando di arruolare, in questa guerra agli immigrati, intere categorie sociali (medici, infermieri, insegnanti, operatori pubblici, affittuari, datori di lavoro e comuni cittadini) spingendoli alla delazione e all'accanimento discriminatorio e razzista. Mentre il Parlamento discute di questi provvedimenti il clima e gli episodi di razzismo e di violenza si moltiplicano nel paese con un atteggiamento gravissimo e irresponsabile di certa stampa che istiga alla violenza razzista' (CGIL, 2009).

82 Hammarberg, 2009.

83 See Galeazzi, 2009.

84 Marchetto's statement has been perceived as a reply to the words of Father Federico Lombardi, head of Vatican press relations, who had taken distance from any member of the Church who had criticised the law (Anon. 'Pacchetto sicurezza e immigrazione: il silenzio del Vaticano, l'accusa dei vescovi', *Adista*, No. 79 (2009) www.adistaonline.it/?op=articolo&id=45758 (accessed 10 April 2014)).

85 'I diritti dei deboli non sono diritti deboli.'

86 Donaddio, 2009.

87 'Una legge senza infamia e senza lode.'

88 '[L]a sicurezza "è esigenza imprescindibile"; "non si afferma a scapito dell'accoglienza".'

89 'Strumento extrapenale, nel quadro di una strategia globale di tutela.'

90 'Il diritto storicamente più tutelato dalle Costituzioni di ogni epoca [...] viene così azzerato per periodi tutt'altro che brevi, sulla base del provvedimento di un'autorità amministrativa (il questore).'

91 The expressions 'symbolic politics' or 'simulative politics' (Blühdorn, 2007; Cento Bull, 2009) indicate a situation in which there exists a distance between party rhetoric and political action due to the strategy of the party to concentrate on issues that reflect the interests and anxieties of public opinion.

5 Recent debates on identity and otherness

Everything needs to change, so that everything stays the same?

1 Introduction

> Leave Italy now that you are still in time […] Italy is a country that should be destroyed: a beautiful and useless place, destined to die.[1]

The advice given by the professor to his student Nicola, in Marco Tullio Giordana's film *La meglio gioventù*,[2] a collective portrait of 40 years of Italian history through the life a family living in Rome, is representative of a widespread attitude amongst Italians who consider the nation as rolling down the inclined axis of decline. Such a pessimistic view, which often finds confirmation in intellectuals and opinion makers' analysis of the situation, is generally attributed to a number of factors: from the stagnating economy to the level of unemployment, from citizens' distrust of institutions and political elites to the anxieties linked to globalisation, to the ambiguous relationship with the EU. When labelling the nation as constantly 'at risk' or on the verge of a breakdown, a common attitude on the part of historians, economists and political observers is that of considering Italy as a special case, different from all its European counterparts. However, Europe in general has been going through a long series of institutional, financial, cultural and, in a certain sense, religious crises: increasingly often globalisation is perceived, rather than an opportunity, as a threat determining the beginning of a new era of egoism and retreat of contemporary democracies, which have witnessed in recent years the emergence throughout their territory of extreme right-wing parties 'fighting' for the protection of traditional values, parties which are progressively becoming relevant at national and international levels, as the vote in the 2014 European elections showed.

Italy, which is often referred to by Italian academics and public opinion as 'the sick man of Europe', represents no exception to this trend: despite the fact that recent surveys[3] show to what extent the country has moved forward in the last century in terms of education, lifestyle, health and welfare system, means of transport and green policies, to mention but a few, the forefront of the debate is still occupied by the unresolved and much discussed obstacles to the construction of a shared national identity, a difficulty to which new events seem to have added, as we shall see.

In reflecting on the present and future of the nation a century and half after its creation, scholars seem to have been following two paths of analysis: the first focuses on relatively recent events, such as the years of terrorism and the stragismo,[4] the two decades of Berlusconi's central role in Italian politics, the emerging of populist protest parties and movements and the consequent (supposed) death of representative democracy;[5] the second strand of investigation retraces the origins of the weak sense of national belonging by looking backwards to the events which have unquestionably contributed to the crystallisation of the idea that Italianness has always been weak and problematic. Among such turning points in the history of the nation, a prominent role is occupied by factors already mentioned in the previous chapters, from the end of the First Republic to the divided memory on Fascism and the Resistance, to the military inadequacy of the Italian army in World War I to a still contested process of Unification.

This analysis of the debate on national belonging, on the diverse, stratified, overlapping or conflicting definitions of Italianness, defined against an idea of 'otherness' incarnated by foreigners, was aimed at outlining a picture of how the phenomenon of immigration has or has not brought about a reflection on the meaning of Italian national identity, and how these traditional, original or antagonistic feelings of belonging have influenced the models of citizenship and integration put forward by the state, with a particular focus on public discourse and political rhetoric and their power to 'shape reality'. What emerged is an identity in a certain sense trapped in an outdated polarisation that absorbs the whole debate on what Italianità means, or ought to mean, today. The previous chapters accounted for the intellectuals' history-based, ideologically oriented and mostly Manichean interpretations as well as on the original and instrumental views on the matter put forward by the Northern League, passing through the more ambiguous and articulated discourse of the Church.

One of the aims of this book was to argue that the fixed framework applied to the issue of national identity described in the first chapter does not take into account the fact that the heated debates on Fascism and the Resistance, which beyond question have been pivotal in the definition of the national character, have contributed to preventing the public discourse from considering other recent 'challenges', which make necessary rethinking Italianness according to more inclusive criteria reflecting the changes occurring within a society today deeply different and less homogeneous and static from an ethno-cultural point of view. At the same time, the investigation conducted to this point was directed at problematising the position of the Church, generally perceived as one of complete and unconditional openness towards the newly arrived, exposing its much more nuanced, complex and certainly not univocal stance. Finally, the part on the League's discourse intended to unveil an exclusionary attitude, the consequences of which we are still witnessing and have often been underestimated in the past, as for instance the impact of its rhetoric on policy making.

This final chapter, while bringing together the different lines of investigation followed and their intersections, will deal with a number of events which, in the past three years, have brought back to the centre stage of public debate the two cardinal issues discussed: immigration and Italianità. These include the celebrations for the 150th anniversary of Unification, the resignation of Pope Benedict XVI and the ascent to the papal throne of Cardinal Jorge Mario Bergoglio, the scandals within the Northern League which marked the end of Bossi's era, the abrogation of the crime of illegal entry, and the reactions to the creation of the Ministry of Identity and Integration as well as the polemics against Minister Cecile Kyenge.

The analysis of these factors, while confirming or partially modifying the conclusions reached, leaves many questions open rather than saying the definitive word on the direction Italy is going to take vis-à-vis its model of citizenship and the future of national identity. If it is probably too early to draw conclusions, for instance, on the role of Pope Francis on issues such as interreligious dialogue or the hypothetical changes in the Catholic world's attitude towards immigrants and above all Muslim immigrants, in other cases, such as that of the Northern League, the consequences of the normalisation of the new nationalistic rhetoric are already clear enough to allow the description of a predictable future path. This last section will venture into the intricate realm of the mutual influence the different actors have on each other and which, on various recent occasions, has manifested itself more clearly than in the past, while briefly accounting for the absence in the debate of political actors such as Berlusconi's Forza Italia, Grillo's M5S (Movimento cinque stelle, or Five Star Movement) and the Left.

2 Branding or belonging? The 150th anniversary of Unification

'A Neapolitan from the ancient Kingdom and a Piedmontise from the sub-alpine Kingdom became Italian, not by rejecting their previous belonging but elevating and resolving it in that new belonging'.[6] It is with these words that Benedetto Croce described the Italian national identity emerging after Unification (1861–70), an identity that was more inclusive than previous regional and municipal affiliations. Looking back at the creation of the nation-state and its first difficulties in constructing a feeling of shared belonging, the philosopher and historian argued that at that point an even broader shared identity as Europeans was required. This, he claimed, could not be of any danger to national identity as it was not challenging but rather reinforcing it, since 'nations are not natural entities, but rather states of consciousness and historical constructions'.[7] Croce's optimistic view on the future on Italianness and its ability to enclose non-conflicting affiliations and loyalty at municipal, regional, national and European levels could not take into account, for it was expressed between the two world wars, the mark that World War II would leave on Italians and their sense of inadequacy, nor could the philosopher foresee that for a long time the interpretative keys of the 'new' form of belonging would be represented by the 'internal division', the divided memory rooted in the events revolving around the war. After at least three decades during which the dominant framework in the academic discussion on national identity had been that of the dichotomy between 'civil war' and 'struggle for freedom', the occasion to question this controversial identity once again and to frame it within more contemporary parameters was presented with the 150th anniversary of Unification (1861–2011) on 17 March 2011.

As early as in 2008, in preparation for the event, national newspapers and journals launched a series of opinion polls aimed at outlining a picture of how Italians interpreted national belonging and at measuring the levels of 'patriotism' within Italian civil society. According to one of these surveys,[8] when asked what national unity was, 52 per cent of respondents said 'a fundamental value' and 22 per cent 'an historical fact which could also change'. When solicited on whether patriotism as a value still existed, 75 per cent of interviewees answered positively, while, according to those interviewed, the feeling of national belonging was rooted in the Constitution (37 per cent), the language (25 per cent), the idea of the homeland (24 per cent), and the Catholic Church (14 per cent). Among the positive traits typical of Italianness, the respondents identified hospitality (11 per cent) and solidarity (8 per cent). When asked about what divides Italians, 50 per cent answered 'political parties'. Regarding the negative aspects of Italianness, only 4 per cent mentioned racism, whereas the majority (50 per cent) saw the low level of 'civic responsibility', 'indifference' (menefreghismo, 22 per cent) and individualism (11 per cent) as the main issues.

Despite the fact that patriotism was still acknowledged as an important value and that national unity was described in positive terms, Italians seemed also aware of the challenges that national identity had had to face during the last 150 years. The main issues were identified in a persistent divided memory on the Resistance, in globalisation and in the emergence of federalist and separatist ideas put forward by the Northern League. The disillusionment towards the political class and the anxieties linked to the economy, however, did not prevent a relevant number of the interviewees from declaring themselves 'proud of being Italian', even though such pride was hardly ever rooted in political or social aspects of life in Italy, and rather based on factors such as the artistic and cultural heritage, food, the natural beauty of the territory and the weather.[9]

As the anniversary of the birth of the new nation approached, official celebrations, exhibitions, lectures, talks in schools across the country were announced by government and opposition. A new round of opinion polls began, aimed once again at measuring the public perception of the 'homeland' while testing Italian knowledge of historical events and their expectations for the future. The fact that one of the recurrent questions concerned the possibility of reversing the process of unification or finding alternative solutions for a hypothetical non-unitary Italy already says something about the climate of uncertainty that preceded the anniversary.

Indeed, while the state representatives were busy channelling all the attention and efforts into the setting of an unprecedented marketing operation to foster participation in the various initiatives promoted, ranging from exhibitions to concerts, from public film screenings to the commercialisation of gadgets with the tricolore,[10] which had undergone an extraordinary (re)branding process, a number of journalists, historians and opinion makers intervened in the debate expressing their perplexities on the meaning of the anniversary and the cohesion of the nation. Such low expectations on the adhesion to the various appointments to mark the celebrations and the uneasiness of dealing with an anniversary that many found problematic, was reinforced by the fact that part of the political world, and particularly the representatives of the Northern League, had openly declared their intention not to take part in the events, bitterly criticising the celebrations when not directly taking the chance to speak against the nation and its 'fake unification'.[11] Distance from the celebration was also taken by the president of Bolzano province, Luis Durnwalder, who, despite the letter addressed to him by President of the Republic Giorgio Napolitano, declared that the German-speaking minority of his province had nothing to celebrate since its passage from Austria to Italy was decided (in 1919) without ever consulting the citizens.[12]

Far more conciliatory was the attitude of the Church, as proven by the letter written by Pope Benedict XVI to President Napolitano,[13] in which the pontiff retraced the history of the relationship between the Italian state and the Vatican. Ratzinger did not omit the difficult phases such relationship went through and rather focused on the importance of the Lateran Pacts and the Concordat of 1984 to reconcile the institutions of the Italian nation and those of the Vatican State – but not civil society, where citizenship and faith had never been contrasting values – while remarking upon the contribution given by the Church, the Vatican and individual Catholics to the history of the country. If the Pope did not miss the chance of reminding his readers that Italian identity finds in Catholicism its shared character and its unity – a sameness of values and belief that made Italy a nation before Unification and contributed to the overcoming of foreign domination – the letter was written in an appeasing style to the extent that Ratzinger argued that the view according to which Catholics were against Unification was far from true.[14]

Historians and intellectuals reflecting on the previous anniversaries of Unification seem to be of a different opinion and argue that all the important celebrations of Unification were marked by the protest or the absence of part of Italian society and by polemical stances of different political actors. The comparison made by Gentile between the 150th anniversary and the 100th and 50th celebrations (in 1961 and in 1911, respectively), shows how 'there has never been a united and unique Italy in the celebrations of the birth of the nation state, but rather three distinct Italies, different and even antithetical'.[15] The 50th anniversary was celebrated by the secular and liberal monarchy but harshly contested by Catholics, republicans, socialists and many others, without any of these groups ever suggesting that the process could be reversed and Italy brought back to being a 'geographical expression'. In 1961, the DC, whose representatives held the highest positions within the state, with the support of the Vatican, officiated the celebrations, which marked 'the symbiosis between state, nation and Italianness', with the opposition of most of the other political actors, from the communists to the neo-Fascists, but again none of them wished for the dismissal of the unitary state. Gentile dates back to this period the creation – through internal migration, television and mass consumption – of an identity which, albeit collective, was nonetheless detached from the state and indifferent to it, while it was more oriented to satisfy individuals' personal interests. According to the historian, the dissociation of Italianness from the state experienced a drastic acceleration in the following 50 years to the extent that, as mentioned above, the opportunity and the possibility of celebrating at all were questioned. The degeneration and the corruption of the state, coupled with citizens' growing disinterest in the nation, account for the surprised reactions of opinion makers when the celebrations did take place. Gentile concludes by stating that the link between Italianità and the nation is not unquestionable, today even more so than in the past, and therefore Italy could go either way, towards a revitalisation of such a link or towards the end of the nation (which does not mean the end of Italianità, which existed already centuries before Unification as a cultural common identity).

Gentile is certainly not alone in putting forward a seemingly pessimistic view of the future of the nation as other scholars' investigations into the state of the nation and Italianness reach similar conclusions.[16] Looking at the results of the various surveys mentioned above, Italian citizens, despite their disillusionment and their widespread individualism, appear to be slightly less pessimistic. Starting from the fact that in 2011 most of the interviewees answered correctly the questions related to the year of Unification (74 per cent) and the date of the celebrations (77 per cent), the most important datum is that 90 per cent of the respondents believed that 17 March was an important date to celebrate,[17] while the percentage of enthusiasts dropped slightly when they were queried about the future and in particular on whether they believed that Italy would still be a united nation in 50 years' time: 68 per cent answered positively. While just 66 per cent thought Rome to be the city that most represents Italy, the vast majority (90 per cent) recognised characters of the past such as Giuseppe Garibaldi, Giuseppe Verdi, Dante and Michelangelo as representative of Italy.[18]

However, Italians' worries about the future do emerge in other opinion polls whereby the idea that Italy is still today a partially divided country is shared by 67.5 per cent of the participants, a fragmented nation that will never be a unitary state (14.9 per cent), whereas only a minority (9.4 per cent) believe Italy to be a united country, and a dissident 2.1 per cent argue that it would have been better if it had never been unified.[19] This more unenthusiastic perception of the future is seemingly related to a negative view of political parties,[20] which have lost credibility throughout Europe, including in those countries, such as Germany, that have suffered less in the economic crisis. This was illustrated by a survey conducted by *The Guardian* in Spain, Poland, France, Germany and Britain in the same year, and which shows that just 6 per cent of the citizens interviewed trust their governments while only 9 per cent believed politicians to be 'honest'.

An important datum that emerges in the only Italian survey which took into account the opinion of immigrants residing in the country, and which was not commissioned by a newspaper or an Italian institution but was launched on the Internet,[21] is that 80 per cent of respondents stated that celebrating the anniversary was important and 78 per cent answered affirmatively the question 'will you celebrate?' The results seem to be confirmed by immigrants' participation in a number of events planned for 17 March and organised by the different foreign communities throughout Italian cities. Many of the observations left in the 'comment section' of the website interpret the celebrations as a means for and a sign of integration, while those who did not plan to celebrate still felt like 'strangers' or remarked on the fact that Italians themselves were divided on the issue of the anniversary.[22] However, before drawing any conclusion on the level of integration of immigrants and their inclusion in the public life of the nation, it should be added that in a previous survey on the same website the most popular answers of the 10,128 people responding to the question, 'Which word do you think is most representative of Italy?' were 'residence permit' (3,486), 'racism' (2,909), 'beautiful' (983), 'clandestine' (803) and 'anger' (381).

Once the celebrations, which – due to exemplary organisation and the reiteration of the idea that commemorating the homeland was a way of legitimising Italian institutions and re-launching Italianness – proved a success in terms of participation, were over and the cameras switched off, what was left? What was the impact of the festive frenzy after March 2011? The occasion of the anniversary was marked by the publication of a considerable number of volumes authored by historians, political scientists, representatives of government and public institutions. This vast literary production, catalogued and visible on the website of the Minister of the Interior can be roughly grouped into three categories: the (mainly academic) books which focused on specific protagonists of the process of Unification; the reflections of prominent representatives of the nation such as the presidents of the Republic; and volumes focusing on more original, sometimes provocative, contemporary interpretations of the idea of national identity.

The publications of the first type, albeit more important in terms of quantity and popularity as they were often advertised on institutional websites and presented at public meetings and seminars in the months preceding the celebrations, are less relevant in this context. These, indeed, focused almost entirely on the classical themes related to the construction of the Italian nation, sometimes insisting on the historical factors that prevented the feeling of belonging from becoming a common and unquestionable value and occasionally just resulting in rhetorical hagiographic accounts of the political and personal lives of the 'fathers of the homeland'. The books written by representatives of the highest institutions such as former President Carlo Azeglio Ciampi and President Giorgio Napolitano are characterised by their common attempt to reflect on past events and the exploitation of history for political purposes, while connecting the crucial moments of the process of nation building to the issues linked to national identity in contemporary Italy. Both Ciampi's and Napolitano's thoughts on the meaning of Italianness and on the past and future of the nation are aimed at sending out a message of hope addressed in particular to the younger generations, encouraging them to rediscover the value of patriotism through knowledge of national history, a story which needs to be told without omitting the difficult moments and the conflicts that the new nation went through. Both authors argue that the anniversary should be taken as an occasion to remind Italians that the word 'patria' can still be pronounced with pride and to dismantle the stereotypes resulting from a distorted use of history, such as labelling Unification as a conquest of the South on the part of Piedmont and the North in general. Despite the difference in tone – more bitter that of Ciampi, saddened by the recurrent attacks to the institutions and more enthusiastic that of Napolitano, convinced that the celebrations for the anniversary had shown a great awakening of a unitary and national conscience – both journeys through the history of the nation are aimed at showing the road ahead, a path to be walked without falling into the trap of nationalistic nostalgia or following the pursuit of material advantages to which is sacrificed the unity of the nation,[23] and certainly not reiterating that attitude and the discourses based on victimhood founded on past injustices and presented by many as the typical trait of the Italian character.[24]

The concept of victimhood surfaced recurrently in the debates on contemporary Italy and the future of the nation, often in relation to the supposed attitude of Italians to 'feel sorry for themselves' (piangersi addosso).[25] In his *La repubblica del dolore*, De Luna (2011) identifies in the institutionalisation of the status of victim the main distortion of Italian national identity. The scholar begins by stating that collective memory is a pact through which nations make choices on what to forget and what to retain of the events of the past; the weaker a state is, the more it will need to construct emotionally moving memories, privileging the subjective point of view of the victims of historical and political events and processes rather than the facts themselves, with the result that history becomes a weapon to be used against political opponents. In arguing this, De Luna is referring to the supposed link between the decline of a state and the institution on the part of different Italian governments of days of remembrance for an increasing number of groups labelled as victims, from those who lost their lives in the Holocaust, to those killed by the Mafia, to the victims of terrorist attacks. As a consequence, he argues, the shared memory of Italians seems to be rooted almost exclusively in their suffering or, even better, in the mediatisation and popularisation of the claims of diverse groups representing victims, which contend with each other over the sympathy of public opinion in the TV show arena, and according to a logic that responds to a typically commercial demand/supply mechanism. De Luna takes the phenomenon as a clear sign of marketing erosion of the public sphere whereby the criteria of belonging to the nation are negotiated. This view is highly problematic, not least because it assumes the existence of antagonistic groups exhibiting solidarity as a political strategy to pursue private interests in the public space, with the consequence that in order to restore the primacy of 'true history' and prove the instrumental nature of such strategy, the scholar goes as far as to group this memory centred on the role of the victim together with the political strategy of the Northern League, whose rhetoric of victimhood serves the end of acquiring relevance and legitimation while securing compensation for the supposed injustice or discrimination experienced.

3 The resurrection of the Northern League and the mainstreaming of fear

While the comparison with the Lega's rhetoric seems out of place and controversial in the context of the analysis of Italians' unity resulting from the shared memory of traumatic events, the fact that Bossi's party turned the politics of victimhood into a means of retaliation is undeniable, as Chapter 3 showed. The spreading of a selfish national priority founded on prima noi ('Italians first') has been normalised through reiteration and this is certainly the main effect that the League's discourse has produced in Italian society, together with the idea that freedom of expression should prevail over political correctness and that today Italians are denied the right to protect their identity and fight against the threats to which such identity is exposed. In continuity with the analysis of the latest updates in the debate on Italianness on the part of intellectuals it is opportune at this point to ask the same question about the Lega: What is left? What is the heritage of a party for which many have recently predicted the death? Has the leghista parable really been completed?

The Italian political world has recently been the epicentre of several earthquakes, which have brought about significant changes in the past two years, from the seemingly unstoppable rise of Beppe Grillo's M5S to Berlusconi's troubles with the judiciary, his expulsion from Parliament in November 2013,[26] and the re-founding of a new Forza Italia, marked by the defection of Angelino Alfano, who became the leader of the 'moderate' fringe converged in the Nuovo Centrodestra. Many observers, busy trying to make sense of these new 'revolutions', allowed the League to drift out of public attention, and the difficulties experienced by his leader, Bossi, were interpreted by political scientists and opinion makers as the final word of a concluded chapter in Italian political history.[27] It has to be said that in 2012 the Lega dominated the front pages of national newspapers, which reported in detail on the scandals[28] investing Bossi's family and his closest fellow party representatives, but the headlines all pointed in the direction of a terminal decline for the Padanian saga. Despite his first attempts to remain party leader, Bossi, following charges of corruption, lost consensus and was forced to resign,[29] while Roberto Maroni – the moderate face of the League, who believed that the party had always been ruled by passion and instinct (pancia) but needed to start being guided by reason[30] (pensare con la testa) – became party secretary.[31]

The transitional phase of the 'Maroni era' can be seen as one of institutionalisation and responsibility, an attitude aiming to reinforce the legitimation of the party and pull it out of the storm,[32] while reassuring coalition partner Berlusconi of the reliability of his allies. This period was characterised by a lowering of tone and the disappearance from the Lega's public discourse of the theme of immigration, which did not resurface even with the approaching 2013 general election.

Such silence, which extended to the other parties and their electoral campaigns, as it clearly emerges from the analysis of party manifestos and electoral programmes, seems even more paradoxical in the light of two facts: the first is that in 2008 immigration had been the most exploited issue in terms of political propaganda, also used by Berlusconi who had previously held a low profile and delegated the Lega to do the 'dirty work'; the second fact is that immigration had never been so present and discussed in the national media, which confirms that the choice to ignore the issue was not due to a sudden irrelevance of the theme. The manifestos of the two main coalitions of centre-right and centre-left only devoted a few lines each to the issue, the former incorporating (in the paragraph devoted to security) a single sentence on the intention to approve bilateral agreements with the sending countries to facilitate repatriation, and the latter putting forward a vague intention of formulating a proposal to extend citizenship to second generations, while grouping immigrants together with other 'minorities' such as gays and women. The Northern League presented its own separate manifesto which was, however, identical to that of Forza Italia, and therefore equally laconic for concerns on immigration.[33] Even the departure of a growing number of immigrants since 2008, following the economic crisis and the resulting drop in job opportunities, does not explain the choice of not tackling immigration directly, particularly because the rhetoric of the 'invasion' had not been dismissed. On the contrary, the paradox results from the fact that issues related to immigration and particularly to the arrival in Lampedusa of hundreds of refugees and asylum seekers and to the polemics arising from their conditions of detention in the Sicilian CIE, featured daily in national newspapers.[34]

One of the possible explanations for the general disinterest in the subject during the last general election could be the economic slump that Italy, as most Southern European countries, was experiencing (and continued to experience at the time of writing) and the increasingly pressing tax burden, which, together with the growing anti-party sentiment on the part of public opinion, tested and proven by the surveys mentioned above, forced political actors to provide concrete answers to more practical issues, as demanded by citizens. The electoral debates were, indeed, almost entirely centred on fiscal issues, the negotiations on the national public debt with the EU, the re-launching of the Italian economy and the revitalisation of the job market.

In the specific case of the Northern League, the choice of complying with the political strategy of Forza Italia can also be understood as the price to be paid for Berlusconi's support for Maroni's candidature as governor of the region of Lombardy.[35] Berlusconi's tone during the election campaign was for the first time apologetic and surprisingly unassuming,[36] as he, too, probably felt the need to reassure public opinion on the governability of the country and the efficiency of a party which promised to lead Italy out of the crisis, not to mention the need to reassure citizens on the stability of his own leadership. In this sense, if in 2008 Forza Italia seemed to have appropriated the language of the League, at least on immigration, in 2013 it repositioned itself on a more traditional mainstream line. It should also be added that the Lega kept employing its anti-immigrant, pro-traditional identity rhetoric in the electoral campaigns conducted at regional level, where it proved successful.

At the end of February a new left-wing coalition had won the elections, Maroni had become governor of Lombardy[37] and a new phase of transition opened for the Northern League with the election of a new party secretary, the two front runners being Flavio Tosi, already the Northern League's secretary for the region of Veneto and mayor of Verona, and Matteo Salvini, MEP and party vice-secretary for the region of Lombardy, and both well known for their strenuous opposition to immigration and for their verbal aggressiveness. If Maroni tried to present the respectable face of his party, with the election of Salvini as party secretary on 7 December the League seems to have gone back to Bossi's golden days of controversial statements and violent tones, a new turn that also heavily affects the rhetoric on immigration.[38] Just to provide an example, Salvini commented on the 'disinfestation' of immigrants at the Lampedusa CIE with these words: 'in the end the true victims are not those who get disinfected in Lampedusa: the real victims are the citizens of Lampedusa and Bergamo, who will get mugged by those who have been disinfected.'[39] In line with the rhetoric that presents Italians as the victims, threatened by immigrants and discriminated against by the state, Salvini also distinguished himself in the ferocious criticism directed at the creation of a new minister of identity and integration, and at the minister herself, Cecile Kyenge, targeting her for her Congolese origins which, supposedly, automatically made her an enemy of Italians.[40]

Since the beginning of her time in office, the minister, elected within the centre-left coalition, had been the League's number one enemy: a violent denigratory campaign was launched on Facebook and in the pages of *La Padania*. Kyenge was accused of plotting against the state, of being willing to allow polygamy in Italy and introduce *ius soli* to grant citizenship to all foreigners born in Italy; she was compared to an orangutan, threatened and had bananas thrown at her; various political representatives (from Forza Italia as well) who jumped on the bandwagon of racism called for 'somebody to come and rape her' or 'kill her please'; supporters of the Northern League were incited to show up at her meetings and insult her and *La Padania* started publishing the diary of her public appearances on a daily basis, to facilitate the objective of delegitimising her and bringing about her abolition from the ministry.[41]

The identitarian rhetoric, which presents the natives as victims, was adopted by mainstream parties too and certainly by Berlusconi, who began to talk about the need to 'fight cultural relativism' and protect 'our identity, our history' and 'the Christian roots of Europe'.[42] Whether the rise to power of Grillo's party, characterised by aggressive language and a polemical stance, played a role in the more institutionalised parties' decision once again to raise the tone of the debate is difficult to assess. Its electoral success in the 2013 elections certainly hit hard the established political equilibrium and probably determined the reinvigoration of the protest and rupture elements in the discourse of other parties. With the results of the 2014 European elections, whereby the Lega achieved an unexpected (after the low performance in the 2013 general elections) 6.16 per cent,[43] political observers, including those who had thought it dead a few months earlier, started to acknowledge that, in fact, it was still in good health[44] and, due to its reinforced alliance with Le Pen's Front National, back to the forefront of national and European politics.

I would argue that, regardless of the party links with the European radical Right, regardless of Salvini's effect on the revitalisation of the anti-immigration stance, regardless of the results of the last European elections, the party was not finished for another reason: namely, the fact that its violent exclusionary rhetoric rooted in the 'us versus them' dichotomy has produced a profound and long-lasting change in both the spreading of intolerant attitudes and their perception on the part of political actors and public opinion as legitimate, being justified by a situation of emergence that puts at risk the nation and its citizens. Such a 'normalisation' of belief, tone and content would once have been labelled without hesitation as extreme and controversial, typical of niche parties, but this 'mainstreaming of fear' was made possible by a number of factors and can be explained according to the mechanisms that regulate the relationship between 'niche'[45] and 'mainstream' parties. Indeed, far from being exclusively linked to the circumstances (for instance, economics) in which they operate, these parties' success depends on their own strategies (Kitschelt, 1997) but even more on the way in which other more established parties react to their claims, which is to say on the mainstream parties' own political (and electoral) tactics (Wagner, 2011).

According to the literature, established parties can compete with niche parties by putting forward thee different kinds of strategy: dismissive, accommodative and adversarial. In the first case the mainstream parties do not consider the issue worthy of attention and therefore ignore it, while in the second case, they recognise the importance of the issue and, by adopting a position similar to that of the niche party, try to delegitimise the party while presenting themselves as 'the rightful owner of that issue'. In the third case, by adopting an adversarial strategy, the mainstream party acknowledges the relevance of the issue and emphasises it but from a point of view that stands in direct opposition to that of its competitor. By influencing mainstream competitors, a niche party can significantly change the political debate even if it remains electorally small. Hence 'strategies directed against short-term threats [...] may have a lasting impact' (Meguid, 2005). Wagner (2011: 5) describes parties' status, their being mainstream or niche, as dynamic, which is to say that a niche party can become mainstream (and vice versa), for instance, through participation in government, a situation that would force it to deal with a broader number of issues not originally included in its political interests, such as economic matters. Finally, Wagner (2011) explains that the shift from niche to mainstream can also be motivated by the party's need to achieve a stronger consensus, for instance after an electoral defeat.

In the case of the Northern League, it can be said that the reaction of the most proximal mainstream party, Forza Italia, was an accommodative one, whereby Berlusconi's party, recognising the appeal of the Lega's arguments on certain key issues, tried to compete by means of issue appropriation, which is to say by adopting similar positions on the issue while at the same time presenting itself as more capable of dealing with it. By competing on the same ground, Forza Italia has also contributed to giving the issue of immigration more salience while legitimising the Lega's claims.

Contrarily, the Left has chosen an adversarial strategy, thereby acknowledging the importance of the issue but dealing with it in a directly opposing way. The fact that the Left was not particularly coherent in its strategy and occasionally, following the pressure of public opinion, adopted an accommodative strategy contributed to weaken its own position, with the result that it appeared less 'efficient' in dealing with certain issues such as, for instance, problems of law and order related to immigration. This was the case in the change in strategy after the Reggiani killing of 2007, when the Left was forced to reassure citizens on the security front, thereby sacrificing its previous position to the appeasement of a concerned part of the public.

Meguid argues that a dismissive and an accommodative strategy will each weaken the niche party, while an adversarial strategy will strengthen its standing. However, the case of the Lega proves that this is not always the case,[46] while clearly participation in government did contribute to turn claims and stances that would once have been considered extreme into legitimate, 'normal', mainstream claims. The institutionalisation and the mainstreaming of fear is to be understood within this process.

4 And yet it moves: Pope Francis and the accidental abolition of the crime of illegal entry

The views on national identity and immigration that emerge from the analysis of recent discussions seem to confirm the bleak picture of an Italianness which on the one hand is trapped in a pessimistic interpretation anchored to an outdated polarisation between antagonistic ideological interpretations of the history of the country, and on the other hand is constructed through a generally tolerated exclusionary rhetoric rooted in an irreconcilable resentment insiders feel towards outsiders, against whom their own identity is constantly redefined. The divided memory, the sense of inadequacy, the anxiety linked to a state of economic and cultural uncertainty, the battle against a threatening otherness, all contribute to the construction (or demolition) of an immobile nation that lives in the past and fears for the future – a disillusioned nation in constant retreat while the meaning of Italianness shrinks and is reduced to a fragile bone. While Italy seems to be missing every chance to revitalise itself through contamination or through the enlargement of possible forms of belonging, the models of citizenship put forward by the actors interacting in the public arena appear to converge. Amid the distinctions that need to be made between the different rationales behind each of them and the instrumental employment of the discourses for which this book has accounted, what matters here are the consequences of such convergence.

Is there any hope then? Can we see on the horizon any sign contradicting the idea that the only answer to the changes within a society that has apparently exhausted its vitality and its capacity to adapt is closure and diffidence? Two new facts seem to contradict the rather pessimistic view put forward until this point: the first is the role of Pope Francis in the spread of a more inclusive discourse and in the promotion of inter-religious dialogue; the second is the abolition in April 2014 of the crime of illegal entry, following a proposal put forward by a number of M5S MPs.[47]

When in February 2013 Pope Benedict XVI announced his resignation to the Cardinals gathered at the consistory for the canonisation of Otranto's martyrs, the first reaction was one of shock. Rumours about such an eventuality had already circulated, following an interview Ratzinger had given to Peter Seewald in 2010,[48] but such an idea had always been denied by the Vatican. The announcement, given in Latin to a somewhat confused audience, was received with incredulity by the media and a public unaware that the right of a Pope to retire to private life is ratified by Canon Law. There are five historical precedents of successors of Peter who ceased to be Pope while still living: the first was Ponziano, who was exiled to the isle of Tavolara, in Sardinia, in 235; the more famous Celestine V, cited by Dante in the *Divine Comedy*, who abdicated in 1294; while we need to go back to 1415 to find the most recent pontiff, Gregory XII, to resign.

The silence of the thousands of people gathered in Saint Peter's Square when the new Pope appeared on the balcony and that of many observers commenting live on the conclave says a lot about the fact that Bergoglio's election was completely unexpected, while the cardinals who participated in the voting recalled afterwards that the name of the Argentine cardinal emerged as an increasingly likely choice even at the second scrutiny. The experts in Vatican affairs who intervened on various TV shows that evening devoted most of their talking to the profiles and chances of a restricted number of possible 'papabili',[49] as for instance Cardinal Angelo Scola, perceived as the strongest candidate and, according also to the international press, nearly four times more likely to be selected Pope than the next highest-ranked favourite,[50] an expectation triggered by the fact that Italy has more cardinal electors.[51] While the result of the conclave exposed two internal currents within the Roman curia that, by means of (large) simplification, can be labelled traditional and progressive, respectively, the ascension to the papal throne of Jorge Mario Bergoglio was presented by national and international media as a 'revolution' – a sign of profound change within a Church weakened by the scandals linked to sexual abuse and the IOR (the Vatican bank).

Leaving aside the criticism directed at Bergoglio, which will be briefly addressed later on, what is relevant in this context is the fact that, despite being closer to his predecessor than many realise, Bergoglio's election did represent a moment of rupture, at least for what concerns his style in communicating with his audience. From his first words ('brothers and sisters ... good evening'), interspersed with extended periods of silence, the new Pope sent out a message of informality, simplicity and normality, a message reinforced by concrete actions, such as taking the bus with the cardinals after the election, or going back to the hostel where he stayed during the conclave and paying the bill, or calling the newsagent where he used to buy newspapers in Argentina to tell him not to save any more for him. What is particularly relevant in this context is the fact that such an original style seems also to inform the interventions Pope Francis made on a variety of issues related to immigration, religious diversity and, more generally, the welcoming attitude promoted by the social doctrine of the Catholic Church. As the pontiff himself recalled after his election, the choice of his name, a homage to Saint Francis of Assisi, was meant to symbolise the two pillars of his mission: building peace and caring for the poor. Since then, Bergoglio has given course to this mission on several occasions, all of which have attracted some degree of criticism, from the washing of the feet of men and – a first for a Pope – women during the Maundy Thursday rite to his visit to Lampedusa, from the message to Muslims for the end of Ramadan to the intervention in support of the Roma and Sinti of Italy, which are all worth brief analysis.

The fact that the visit to Lampedusa on 8 July 2014 was the pontiff's first official visit to Italy made the event even more significant, as it implied that the Pope considered the immigration 'emergence' of those days a priority. The national newspapers reporting on the event remarked on the 'spontaneous gestures' of a Pope who, staring at the sea, interrupted the reading of the official discourse for the celebration of the 50th anniversary of the encyclical *Pacem in terris* to cry out loudly: 'Shame! This is a shame!' Breaking protocol, the Pope then shook hands with a group of migrants, exhorting the public to pray for them and for those who had died while, during the celebration of mass, he criticised the 'globalisation of indifference' and addressed Muslim immigrants using an expression typical of the dialect of Lampedusa and reassured them that the Church supports them in their search for a more dignified life for themselves and their families.[52]

What is interesting in this first speech concerning the Church's solidarity towards the immigrants, including those of Muslim faith, is the fact that the pontiff in referring to the spreading indifference of Italians towards the tragedies of the migrants chose to use the word 'globalisation', which as has been argued elsewhere in this book, recalls a number of concerns related to the economy and to diversity in religious, cultural and ethnic terms. In this sense, the idea of exploiting an expression commonly associated with fear or anyway perceived as carrying a negative connotation and associating it with the issue of indifference towards the newly arrived seems particularly apt as the 'no more globalisation' message is a message with which public opinion is familiar: the Pope is just adding indifference to the negative products of globalisation. The reference to this specific idea of globalisation is probably a coincidence rather than the actuation of a thought-through plan; nonetheless, this is the case for most slogans that later become powerful symbols of well-articulated stances. Moreover, whether intentional or not, this slogan works on the same level as the Lega's anti-globalisation slogans and once it was picked up by all the main newspapers and repeated in talk shows and quoted in experts' interviews, it became an interesting means to exploit the popularity of anti-globalisation sentiment, just orienting it in a different direction and counterbalancing an exclusionary discourse from within the same framework.

The opening towards Muslim citizens on the part of Bergoglio was confirmed on a number of occasions after the visit to Lampedusa, through highly symbolic gestures as well as through public speeches. An event that generated great surprise and great criticism took place in March 2013, when the Pope during the rite of Maundy Thursday, washed the feet of a number of disabled men and women. The event attracted strong criticism on the part of the most conservative/traditionalist fringe of the Catholic hierarchy and the most conservative part of civil society, as well as from a number of observers, who remarked on the fact that the rite implies the washing of the feet of selected men (never women), which is to say of men chosen for their rectitude. Clearly, if the presence of women was perceived as inopportune and as a sign of rupture with tradition, the main discontent of those in disagreement with the gesture was related to the presence of a Muslim woman amongst those chosen and their fear that the Pope's washing and kissing of her feet would be perceived as a sign of subordination to her religion, not to mention the fact that the ceremony had taken place in a youth detention centre, the Don Gnocchi, in Rome, rather than in a church.[53]

Among the many other circumstances in which Bergoglio divided public opinion by showing the will to dialogue with the Muslim community we should include his message for the end of Ramadan. Benedict XVI had already done the same, sending his wishes for the beginning of Ramadan, and therefore Bergoglio's message was not perceived as dangerous or out of place in itself. What raised concern, more than the content of the message, was the difference in the communicative style adopted. Pope Ratzinger addressed Muslims in September 2006 just after the polemic raised by his Regensburg lecture, which, as mentioned, triggered heated reactions around the globe, and in this sense can be perceived as a late attempt to mend a seemingly compromised relationship between the Vatican and the Muslim countries just before his (much-contested) visit to Turkey. In his message Benedict XVI reiterated the idea that the Church looks at individuals of Muslim faith with respect while addressing, immediately afterwards, the issue of terrorism and the idea that Muslims are the first victims of such violence and exhorting the public to pray to God to give Muslim religious and political leaders of the world faith and strength. Despite the fact that the main issue with the Regensburg lecture consisted in the use by the Pope of a quotation that points to the implicit violence of Islam, the pontiff chose to go back to such a controversial interpretation of Islam that devoted Muslims had contested the first time around.[54]

Bergoglio's message, in continuity with the spirit of the Second Vatican Council and with the declaration *Nostra Aetate*, remarked upon the importance of inter-religious dialogue intended as a moment of mutual enrichment. The new element in this message was represented by the fact that the respect the Pope referred to was directed at the religion, Islam, and not only at its followers, even though the Pope did specify that this respect did not imply a recognition of the validity of Islam's principles. However, if the part on Muslims in the *Nostra Aetate* has to be considered an 'accidental document within the document', as it was written with the intention of including only a dialogue with the Jewish communities, and if since then every message inciting to the pursuit of such a dialogue has always insisted on the distinction between the respect for those of Muslim religion and the religion itself,[55] this time Francis made clear that the religion and the religious sites were to be respected as well. The fact that such a difference is not irrelevant is proven by the enthusiastic reaction of the Italian Muslim communities,[56] and the improvement in the Church's perception among Italian Muslims,[57] a process which already started within the first hours of Francis's pontificate.[58]

If Bergoglio attracted the sympathy of the Muslim world, he also raised concerns and has been harshly criticised. Among the most frequent charges coming from sectors of society and intellectuals who can, broadly speaking, been defined as close to the Right,[59] are those referring to the 'populism' of the new Pope, his strategy of addressing issues in a vague manner in order not to displease anybody and not to touch on the most controversial issues. Moreover, the idea of an unconditional opening to Islam spread by media interested in showing the element of discontinuity with his predecessor Ratzinger was also at the centre of recent polemic. With regard to the idea of dialogue with Islam which emerges in the *urbi et orbi* Christmas speech 'Evangelii gaudium', for instance, some Vatican experts noticed that in paragraphs 252 and 253, the Pope 'bravely' refers to those Christians in Muslim countries who have been denied the right to practise their religion. This part of the discourse was neglected by commentators and newspapers, or it was underestimated, as it proved alignment of Bergoglio's thought with that of Ratzinger, therefore dismantling the idea of a turn in the Church's position. Many observers pointed to the doctrinal and substantial correspondence[60] between the two pontiffs and remarked upon the 'courage' of Benedict XVI in denouncing the violence of Islam, while accusing Bergoglio of being more ambiguous and more interested in 'appearing', in becoming the centre of attention rather than a means for conveying the Church's message.

Apart from his view on Islam, the Pope was criticised for his rupture with the liturgical tradition[61] as well as for his opening to non-believers. If Ratzinger, the guardian of the doctrine, had considered Islam and secularism as a united front representing a challenge for the Church and a threat for Christian societies and their traditional identity, Bergoglio showed the will to engage in a religious dialogue.[62] He also included a series of categories previously left at the margins of the 'Christian family', such as the homosexuals and the divorced. To testify this will to reach the most diverse public the Pope did not hesitate to use a provocative and paradoxical language, as for instance when, during a mass, while addressing the need to open a dialogue with all kinds of interlocutors, he jokingly said: 'If ... an expedition of Martians arrives and some of them come to us ... and if one says: "Me. I want to be baptised!", what would happen?' and 'who are we to close the doors?', implying that nobody can be deliberately excluded by the Church.[63] Magister and other commentators have identified in Francis's most recurrent statement 'who am I to judge?' a clear sign of both his demagogic rhetoric and a dangerous relativism, strategically employed to put himself forward as the face of a renewed Church, despite the fact that doctrinally speaking he remains a Jesuit, which is to say an intransigent traditionalist.[64]

An occasion when the criticism towards Francis came directly from political representatives of the Right was offered by the Pope's meeting with the national directors of the Pastoral for Gypsies,[65] organised to discuss the condition of the Roma and Sinti residing in Rome. The pontiff argued that they live on the margins of society, suffer the highest rate of unemployment within the country, are denied basic civic rights and are looked upon with suspicion.[66] If the Roma and Sinti thanked Bergoglio for his solidarity – albeit asking him not to refer to them as 'gypsies' (zingari)[67] – the opinions Bergoglio expressed were perceived as unacceptable by members of the right-wing party Fratelli d'Italia and the Lega Nord, whose leader, Salvini, intervened to explain 'with respect' that if Roma and Sinti are perceived as 'thieves' there must be a reason. If the League's secretary in addressing the Pope left aside his usual aggressive tone, his statement on Twitter was commented upon by fellow Lega members, supporters and sympathisers who were much less diplomatic: their position can be summarised with their suggestion that the Vatican welcome into its territory as many 'gypsies' as the Pope liked, thus implying that the Pope can set the rules in his own state, but not in 'our homeland'.[68]

Bergoglio, however, was not the first Pope to meet the Roma and Sinti of Europe, as Paul VI and Benedict XVI had already done so, in 1965 and 2011, respectively, while John Paul II had met them several times during his papacy. The reason why such criticism from the League was not officially expressed in 2011 could be twofold: the first explanation might be the fact that in 2011 Maroni was party secretary and, as has been argued, he had an interest in keeping a low profile and promoting a 'more respectable' Lega. The second is the fact that what changed with Bergoglio was that, regardless of his theological perspective, the rhetoric, tone and symbolic gestures employed have all contributed to the perception of his discourse as 'revolutionary', or at least unconventionally progressive and inclusive, whereas the League had previously exploited Ratzinger's concern about the threats posed by Islam to Italian (Christian) identity.

The criticism experienced by the League proves once again that beyond the intentions of the actors who put their views forward, the rhetoric they employ does contribute to shaping reality as well as the perception of it. The fact that the Lega has understood the danger (for itself) of a Pope who talks about the 'globalisation of indifference', which is to say a Pope whose messages stand in opposition to its own and are equally familiar to/attractive for public opinion, emerges when one realises that Salvini replied to the Pope by talking of the risks of a 'globalisation of clandestinity'.

The rhetoric used by the Pope contributed to changing the debate on immigration and public perception of both the discussion and the phenomenon itself, even though according to Bergoglio's detractors, nothing changed. As argued elsewhere in this book, the importance of public discourse in shaping 'reality' is of central importance as it allows new 'meanings' to alter the mainstream discourse or vision of the world, which through a constant negotiation of the role of single signifiers renews itself and evolves. The Parliamentary approval of the abolition of the crime of illegal entry proves that a lack of public discourse on a certain issue, even when the situation is changing substantially, is sometimes less efficient than a reiterated discourse, at least in the public perception of such change.

The proposal to abrogate the crime of illegal entry was first put forward to the Parliamentary Committee on Justice in October 2013 by two Five Star Movement MPs, Maurizio Cioffi and Andrea Buccarella, despite not featuring in the party programme. Beppe Grillo and Gianroberto Casaleggio immediately took a distance from the proposal, writing on the party blog that the idea had never been discussed and had therefore to be considered a personal, unauthorised initiative by the two MPs, defined as two 'Drs Strangelove' out of control who needed to be stopped.

The two party leaders, while remarking on their disagreement both with the idea and the methods used to put it forward, also added that if the Movement had included in its manifesto such a proposal, it would have been dramatically penalised in electoral terms. They defined the amendment for the abolition of clandestinity as a clear invitation to African and Middle Eastern migrants to come to Italy at a time when the situation in Lampedusa was near collapse and one Italian in eight had not got enough money to eat regularly. Moreover, they argued that the crime of illegal entry had been introduced in other 'more civilised countries', such as France, Britain and the United States. A meeting between the Movement's members was then held without the participation of Grillo, whereby the base (party members), who had also collected 70,000 signatures to support their move, decided to go ahead, demanding a public online referendum on the issue. The voting process took place even though the supporters of the proposal lamented that members were not informed of the possibility to vote until the process had already started and that the window of time – seven hours – during which members could cast their vote coincided with the working day and therefore all those who had no access to the Internet were excluded from the decision.

The reaction of the other parties followed soon afterwards. Forza Italia[69] and Antonio Di Pietro's Italia dei Valori contested the proposal, although the most heated reaction came from the Northern League, whose members interrupted a regular sitting of the Upper Chamber of Parliament to protest and show a series of signs reading 'No to security, yes to clandestines', 'No to pensioners, yes to illegal immigrants', 'Clandestines back to their own countries'. The same MPs later occupied the office of Pietro Grasso, president of the Senate.

Solidarity with Cioffi and Buccarella's proposal came from Nichi Vendola's SEL (Sinistra Ecologia e Libertà) and the PD (Partito Democratico), whose leader, Matteo Renzi, declared himself in favour of the proposal since the Bossi-Fini law was a measure that exploited citizens' fear.[70] Nevertheless, Renzi also specified that being in favour of the abolition of the crime of illegal entry does not imply being in favour of unregulated immigration. The interventions of the Left were pretty much limited to these statements and in terms of visibility and impact were much less efficient than the protest of the Lega.

The first step for the abolition of the crime of illegal immigration was the approval of the proposal by the Senate[71] in October. Grillo commented on the decision with a post on his blog, in which he stated that 'after the amendment illegal immigrants are still illegal immigrants, but it will be easier to proceed with the expulsions'[72] – probably written to reassure the right-wing spectrum of the Five Star Movement's electorate. Six months later, on 1 April, the measure was approved by the Lower chamber and became law, with 332 votes in favour and 124 against: illegal entry went back to being an administrative rather than a criminal offence, at least the first time an immigrant enters Italy illegally, while repeat offences and refusal to comply with the expulsion still represent criminal offences punishable by detention.[73]

The discussion on the amendment is particularly interesting as it exposed the lack of awareness on the part of both media and public opinion of the norms that regulate immigration in Italy, as proven by the fact that most newspaper commentators, and even political actors, Renzi among them, when discussing the crime of illegal entry, kept referring to the need to change or to retain the Bossi-Fini law, despite the fact that the crime of illegal entry was not introduced with the 2002 measure, as at that time the proposal of the Northern League was rejected, but rather in 2009 with decree number 92 included in the 'security package' law, as explained in Chapter 4.[74]

In the end, if on the one hand the change to the security package can be seen as a concrete one, on the other hand the importance of such a change is diminished by two factors. The first is the fact that the crime of illegal entry is no longer a criminal offence only for migrants entering the country illegally for the first time and, in this sense, it has to be said that those who end up in jail for such a crime have never been numerous[75] for all sorts of reasons, from overcrowded prisons to the difficulty of identifying foreigners to the impossibility of making sure that once identified they do not escape before the sanction is inflicted.[76] The second factor that explains why the law does not represent a radical measure in terms of immigration policy is the fact that the proposal for the abrogation of the crime was not preceded or accompanied by any coherent discussion on the part of those supporting it, while the voices raised against it were loud and clear.

The suggestion for a change was rather considered by media and public opinion as a sudden about-turn or eradication of previous legislation (colpo di spugna), which, as already stated, did not in fact alter much. The fact that the process was perceived as triggered by two individual (new) politicians also ties in with the silence of the Left, not only on this occasion but from 2009 onwards, which is to say since the security package became law. The effect of the position of the Left can be explained within the processes that regulate the mainstream-niche parties' relations, previously mentioned. Once again, indeed, the Left remained silent, ignoring the issue and letting other (new) actors appropriate it. The fact that the M5S did not emerge as the 'rightful owner of the issue' is mainly due to the reaction of the party leader, which contributed to presenting the movement as fragmented (far more than was actually the case, as proven by the internal referendum), and therefore less efficient in setting the agenda. However, the Left appeared even less efficient, since it allowed both the M5S and the Lega to become the only actors influencing the debate on a theme that is supposed to be closer to its own interests and not even putting forward an antagonistic rhetoric, much less exploiting this occasion to delegitimise the security package and suggest more ideologically articulated reasons to justify the need for a change in state policies on immigration.

As a result, the most prominent (and legitimate) actor dealing with immigration is still a Northern League intentioned to fight for the reintroduction of the crime of illegal entry, as Salvini, galvanised by the consensus achieved by his party in the last European election, recently declared.[77] The lack of solid rhetoric in support of the idea that the status of migrants cannot be considered a crime contributes to the possibility that in the end the position of the League will prevail. The main issue with the abrogation of clandestinity therefore does not consist in the fact that it only refers to migrants arriving in

Italy for the first time, but in the fact that its symbolic value – never exploited by the Left – was completely overlooked with the result that the new measure had very little impact on public perceptions of immigration. Finally, the fact that the M5S managed to make this change in such a short time and without the employment of a powerful discourse exposed even more the lack of strategy and competency of the Left.

5 Conclusions

The analysis of recent debates on Italianness and immigration involving the public actors analysed in the previous chapters, intellectuals, and particularly historians, members of the Catholic hierarchy and representatives of political parties, seems to point to the conclusion that not much has changed in the last three years. Concerning the views put forward on the state of national identity, the reflections related to the 150th anniversary of Unification generally reproduced the previous debates, very much focused on the polarised and antagonistic views of the role played by historical factors, and above all the Resistance, in the construction of a belonging presented as weak and divided. Such a debate has not moved much further from the discussion that started in the late 1980s, and certainly immigration has not been included in the number of factors that could trigger a renegotiation of the idea of Italianità.

Amid the legitimacy of the idea that immigration does not matter, or more simply the lack of interest on the part of intellectuals in this issue, what is relevant in this contest is the effect that such silence has had in allowing other public actors to occupy the space left vacant in the debate. Among such actors the most influential is unquestionably the Northern League, which, for the reasons already mentioned elsewhere, is inclined to exploit the theme strategically in order to put at the forefront of political debate a set of claims and aims that, in the course of the last 20 years, have evolved noticeably.

The analysis on the League and the latest shifts within the party, particularly after the election of Salvini as party secretary, shows that immigration has become increasingly important in the party's rhetoric on Italianness. If the construction of an exclusionary and selective identity has been facilitated by a political conjuncture whereby the return to the days of aggressive statements and polemical *vis* proved fruitful in terms of electoral consensus, particularly after the rise to power of the Five Star Movement, the main change to be noticed is, in this case, what has been described as 'the normalisation' of anti-immigrant feelings within the country. The mainstreaming of fear, which found fertile ground in a society increasingly concerned with globalisation and with a seemingly imminent Islamisation of Italy, represents the main consequence of the Lega's appropriation of the debate, as its voice is by far the most heard in the public sphere. Therefore, if Italian intellectuals seem to be engaged in a debate that has not changed at all, the League has managed to radicalise its own discourse as well as that of other interlocutors, turning intolerance into something, indeed, 'normal'.

The last two cases taken into account, the rhetoric of Pope Francis and the lack of rhetoric that accompanied the abolition of the crime of illegal entry, represent two specular moments. On the one hand, despite the recurrent remarking on the part of observers on the continuity between Ratzinger and Bergoglio from a purely doctrinal point of view, the current pontiff has managed to inject a dose of optimism into the debate on immigration, showing the advantage of a welcoming attitude in the revitalisation of Italian society while reinforcing such rhetoric with concrete actions that, no matter how populist, have been efficient in triggering the sympathy of public opinion both for himself and for immigrants. Leaving aside the effect such a strategy could have on the actual integration of foreigners who see their difficulties publicly acknowledged, the message of the Pope seems at the moment the only authoritatively inclusive message in the Italian public arena.

By contrast, the abrogation of part of the security package, despite representing the only factual change in the state's attitude towards the newly arrived, took place in a vacuum facilitated by the silence of the Left and, therefore, had very little impact on the debate itself. It could be argued that, if anything, the passing of the new measure has allowed the Northern League to regain control of the debate and to reinvigorate its exclusionary idea of citizenship and Italianness.

Notes

1 'Lasci l'Italia finché è in tempo [...] L'Italia è un paese da distruggere: un posto bello e inutile, destinato a morire.'
2 *The best of Youth* (2003).
3 Survey 'Italia in cifre 2011', conducted by Istat for the anniversary of Unification.
4 The strategy of terror aimed at creating a climate of tension and destabilise the political and social order through violent actions, which in Italy reached its peak in the 1970s. On the subject, see: Barbagallo, 2001; Tullio, 1980; Antonello and O'Leary, 2009; Cento Bull, 2007.
5 Diamanti, 2014a.
6 'Un napoletano dell'antico regno o un piemontese del regno subalpino si fecero italiani non rinnegando l'esser loro anteriore ma innalzandolo e risolvendolo in quel nuovo essere' (Croce, 1993: 314).
7 '[L]e nazioni non sono dati naturali, ma stati di coscienza e formazioni storiche' (Croce, 1993: 15).
8 SWG survey for *Il Venerd; di Repubblica*, 1 March 2008.
9 This datum is also confirmed by the results of the Demos survey conducted in November 2009 for *La Repubblica*. According to this survey, Italians who are proud of their national identity also link such feeling to the 'glorious past' of the country.
10 The Italian flag.
11 Anon., 2011e.
12 Anon., 2010a, 2011d, 2011a.
13 *Messaggio di Benedetto XVI a S.E. l'Onorevole Giorgio Napolitano, Presidente della Repubblica Italiana, in occasione dei 150 anni dell'Unità Politica d'Italia*, March 2011. On the letter and its meaning see: Anon.,2011b, 2011c.
14 However, before the publication of the letter and within the debate on the anniversary of Unification, a new polemic was opened with the interventions of a

minority of Catholic historians and intellectuals who argued that in order to reach a real pacification with the Church, the Italian state should have apologised to the Vatican for a number of reasons related to the 'Roman question', from the expropriation of its territories to the selling (svendita) of the papal possessions. See Pellicciari, 2009.

15 '[N]on c'è stata un'unica e identica Italia a festeggiare il compleanno dello stato nazionale, ma tre Italie diverse, fra di loro persino antitetiche' (Gentile, 2012).

16 On the fact that the celebrations exposed once more the diffulties faced by Italians to come to terms with their history while showing that if in the past there has not been great enthusiasm for the anniversaries, the criticism towards the anniversary of 2011 has been much sharper than in 1911 and in 1961. See Romano *et al.* 2011.

17 According to other surveys the percentage is lower. In the one conducted by IPSO for *Corriere della Sera*, 81 per cent of Italians believe Unification is valuable and 79 per cent think it is right to celebrate it.

18 Data from IPR Marketing survey commissioned by *Il Sole 24 Ore* in 2011.

19 Eurispes survey, presented in Rome on 28 January 2011.

20 In the case of Italy, citizens declared themselves 'fed up' with the exasperating contrasts relating to Berlusconi, the Judiciary and the Northern League (Ipsos survey: 'Italiani stanchi delle contrapposizioni politiche', 26 March 2011).

21 More than 3,000 people answered the question on the website dedicated to foreigners in Italy, www.stranieriinitalia.it, in March 2011.

22 Even though there is no objective way of establishing how relevant this survey was in statistical terms, it is important to report on it as it represents one of the few occasions on which immigrants' opinions emerge, and can therefore be considered qualitatively interesting.

23 The reference to the secessionist claims of the Northern League is rather clear in the thought of both presidents.

24 As Romano *et al.* (2011) explain, such rhetoric of victimhood is not just peculiar of Italy but typical of all kinds of nationalism.

25 On the need to overcome the rhetoric of victimhood, see Cazzullo, 2011.

26 Anon. 2013i.

27 Damilano, 2013; see also Diamanti, 2013.

28 Such scandals include the illegal personal use of public money on the part of Bossi's entourage and family, and particularly his youngest son Renzo Bossi. For further details see: Serafini, 2012; Colonnello, 2012; Viviano, 2012.

29 Anon. 2012b.

30 Interview with Maroni, cited in Giudici, 2012.

31 Sala, 2012; Bacchiddu, 2012.

32 The fact that the scandals were related to corruption and private use of state money represented the worst possible blow for a party born with the aim of fighting the corruption of the Italian central state. The slogan 'Roma ladrona' (from the word ladro, which means thief) hit back when Bossi's detractors started referring to the party as 'Lega ladrona'.

33 Immigration did feature in the manifestos of parties positioned at the extreme Right (Casa Pound) and extreme Left (Rifondazione Comunista) of the political spectrum, which suggested stopping immigration tout court and opening the doors to all immigrants, respectively. These positions, both highly ideological, had very little impact on the electoral campaign.

34 The two main facts concerning Lampedusa reported by national newspapers were the shipwreck of October which caused the death of hundreds of migrants and the broadcast of the video on the inhuman proceedings used in the CIE during disinfestation of scabies, when migrants were forced to line up naked, facing a wall, and were sprayed with disinfectant. See: Galullo, 2013; Rubino, 2013; Tonacci and Viviano, 2013; Sciacca, 2013.

35 Anon. 2012c; Zulin, 2007.
36 'Non ricordo nella mia vita un momento più difficile di questo: la gente è davvero sfiduciata.' 'Ho già chiesto scusa agli italiani [...] Tuttavia i nostri anni di governo non sono passati invano.'
37 Anon. 2013b.
38 Anon. 2013j.
39 '[P]erchè i poverini non sono quelli di Lampedusa che vengono disinfettati: i poverini sono i cittadini di Lampedusa e di Bergamo che poi vengono derubati da chi viene disinfettato' (Anon. 2013k).
40 Anon. 2014b.
41 Anon. 2013f.
42 Popolo delle Libertà, *Carta dei valori*, 2013.
43 In 1994 it had achieved 6.65 per cent, in 1999 4.49 per cent, in 2004 4.96 per cent and in 2009 10.2 per cent.
44 See Diamanti, 2014b.
45 Niche parties are characterised by the fact that they focus on a limited number of (mainly uneconomical) ideological issues, which are usually ignored or under-discussed by other, more traditional parties and for this reason they can potentially gain consensus from across the political spectrum. The three main categories of niche parties, according to the literature, include green parties, radical right-wing parties and ethno-territorial parties (Meguid, 2005; Wagner, 2011).
46 Cento Bull and Garau, 2013.
47 Anon. 2014a.
48 Anon. 2013a.
49 Slang for 'cardinals more likely to be elected Pope'.
50 However, Bergoglio reportedly had already come second in the 2005 conclave which resulted in the election of Joseph Ratzinger, when he reportedly begged his fellow cardinals to stop voting for him. Albeit neglected by the media and observers, he cannot, therefore, be described as a 'rank outsider'.
51 Lyman, 2013.
52 Anon. 2013e.
53 Scalfari, 2013.
54 Accattoli, 2006.
55 Such a difference between Ratzinger and Bergoglio is not acknowledged by some Italian observers who, aiming to minimise the novelty in the latter's papacy, tend to perceive his action as coherent with that of his predecessor. See Burini, 2013.
56 See the answer from the UICOI (the Association of the Muslim Communities in Italy) to Pope Francis's message at the end of Ramadan.
57 Daconto, 2013.
58 Anon. 2013c.
59 Anon. 2013d; Rodari, 2013; Ingrao, 2013.
60 See Tornielli, 2013. On the differences between the two as presented in the media, see Grana, 2013. See also Sandro Magister's blog for *L'espresso/La Repubblica*, in particular 'La svolta di Francesco', published online (www.chiesa.espressonline.it) on 3 October 2013.
61 In particular, the Lefebvrians have accused Bergoglio of using a paradoxical and confusing rhetoric, and of being responsible for the death of many Christians killed in Muslim countries. They also expressed their disapproval at the continuity, evident in their view, between the spirit and guidelines of the *Nostra Aetate* and the Second Vatican Council, which they always rejected. See Speciale, 2013.
62 Marroni, 2013.
63 Anon. 2014g.
64 Magister, 2013b.

65 The meeting was organised within the activities of the Pastoral for Migrants in June 2014.
66 Anon. 2014h.
67 Giansoldati, 2014. As argued in Chapter 3, the labelling of all groups characterised by a nomadic lifestyle as 'zingari' is discriminatory itself, as it does not account for the differences in terms of nationality, country of origin, ethnic and religious background. However, the term is so commonly used in Italy that not only did the Pope use it, but also a number of national newspapers, reporting on the meeting and the speech, used the word in their titles. See, for instance, Anon., 2011f.
68 Paudice, 2014.
69 On 10 October Maurizio Gasparri (PDL) tweeted: 'Clandestinità: perfino Casaleggio blocca le follie 5 stelle. Correggere subito il tiro!'
70 Gallori and Nardinocchi, 2013.
71 Anon. 2013g, 2013h.
72 '[D]opo l'emendamento del M5S il clandestino rimane comunque clandestino, ma da oggi sarà più facile procedere con le espulsioni.'
73 Daconto, 2014; Anon. 2014c, 2014d; Greco, 2014.
74 See Sarzanini, 2013; Giustiniani, 2013.
75 The data on the website of the Ministry of the Interior are quite confusing as the total refers to people arrested for crimes related to illegal entry, and it is impossible to know how many immigrants were sentenced to prison for entering Italy illegally for the first time.
76 Moreover, from the moment of the definitive approval, the government had 180 days to enforce the law, which meant that even if the main reason behind the proposal was the dramatic situation in Lampedusa, nothing was going to change for at least another year.
77 Anon. 2014e, 2014f.

6 Conclusion

The previous chapters have provided a broad overview of contemporary debates on Italian national identity and immigration, considering the two strands of discussion separately as well as following their intersecting trajectories. The aim of this investigation was to assess what model of integration, if any, Italy is putting forward in reacting to the new challenges immigration poses to the definition of citizenship and shared or antagonistic interpretations of belonging. The choice of analysing the subject within the theoretical framework of discourse analysis, employed as an interpretative tool to examine the most significant events that marked the past 50 years of Italian political history, has contributed to bringing to light the key concepts around which the debates revolve as well as the interactions between the different political actors participating in the discussion, their political strategies, the internal tensions and disagreements within each group, the evolution of these different interpretations of citizenship and otherness, their influence one on another and, finally, their overall impact on state policy making. Thus, this book has accounted for the role played by intellectuals, historians, political observers, Catholic representatives and politicians in the ongoing reflections on the meaning of Italianness, while addressing the silence or marginality of other political actors, and particularly the Left, in the same debate.

The importance of looking at the core issues of identity and otherness through the lenses of discourse theory also resides in the opportunity offered by such a methodological approach to understand the mechanisms behind the creation, promotion and consolidation of each of the 'views of the world' examined, whose ideological orientation reveals itself precisely in their being presented as objective and unproblematic. Moreover, the centrality of articulation, which is to say conflict between different narratives put forward by political actors aiming to achieve, retain or gain power and visibility in the public sphere by imposing their own ideas of the world, proved fundamental in this investigation. Indeed, it fully exposed, on the one hand, the processes according to which meaning is created through politics and by politics and, on the other hand, how meaning is linked to performance or, in other words, how it takes shape through a routinely executed series of actions, whereby coherence and reiteration represent powerful instruments that political actors exploit in order to present themselves as the most efficient and competent 'issue owners'.

Furthermore, the application of discourse theory to the discussions on Italianness and immigration has allowed the close relationship between discourse and legislation and their mutual influence to become manifest, showing not only how the legislative text is informed by the rhetoric accompanying its formulation but also as the law provides an authoritative source of legitimation for said rhetoric, conferring on it a quasi-normative status. Finally, the interpretation of meaning as constantly evolving has also been a pillar of this investigation, as such dynamic connotation contributes to explain how new meanings are relational, negotiated through competition between antagonist views, and how the fact that a definitive agreement cannot be achieved is not necessarily a negative aspect, as we shall see.

After restating the rationale behind the methodological choices that informed this book, it is now worth asking what, on a more practical level, the results are of the investigation conducted, what questions it answered and what new interrogatives it left open.

The contributions of Italian intellectuals to a discussion on national identity, which slowly started developing in the early 1990s after decades of silence during which any public reflection on Italianness would have been perceived as a sign of a nationalist disposition inherited from Fascism, are characterised by the centrality of historical factors accounting for the weakness of Italians' collective sense of belonging. The ideologically oriented dichotomy between the interpretations of the Resistance as, on the one hand, the founding myth of the Republic and, on the other hand, as a civil war ultimately won by foreigners, represents beyond any doubt the core of the debate. The voice of the so-called revisionist historians and their negative judgement of events in the immediate aftermath of World War II is by far the most influential within the public sphere. The focus of the narrative put forward by these intellectuals resides in the inadequacy of Italian citizens, army and institutions rooted in the historical events of the time, which resulted in the weakening of the sense of belonging and, ultimately, in the so-called 'death of the homeland'.

The reason behind this strong involvement of those who, generalising, can be defined Right-leaning historians in the questioning of the 'real' meaning of the Resistance is seemingly motivated by the rejection on their part of what they perceive to be the 'history written by the winners', whereby the expression refers to the dominant (until the mid-1970s) 'communist' interpretation of the Resistance as a guerra di liberazione, a struggle for freedom. The idea, put forward by this group of historians, according to which the divided and problematic Italian identity has reached today an unprecedented degree of weakness, to a certain extent seems to be supported by Italians' self-perception, as it emerged in the surveys carried out in 2011 before and during the celebrations of the 150th anniversary of Unification.

Even though Italian citizens acknowledge the many issues that contributed to the weakening of such collective identity, and among them most interviewees identify the clash in the irreconcilable interpretations of the Resistance, I would argue that such a perception was indeed facilitated by the narrative employed by intellectuals and the reiteration on their part and in the national media of such view. The interesting datum in this debate is that the historians involved tend to limit their reflections to remarking on how the concepts of 'patria', 'nationalism' and 'Italianness' have in time become a sort of collective tabù, while at the same time they seem unable to move forward in the debate, which in a certain sense has been stagnating around the same recriminations for decades.

It could be argued that recently the debate on Fascism and the Resistance has become a mere political strategy borrowed by political parties in order to attract consensus. The language used by political representatives to delegitimise their opponents, particularly during electoral campaigns, is indicative of this strategy, as the epithets 'fascist' and 'communist' are still used to indicate in derogatory terms and with one symbolic word the whole set of stereotyped values and faults attributed to two separate universes. This is the case despite the fact that such contrasting narratives are nowadays completely inadequate to provide a reliable map of Italian politics, in a progressive de-ideologised world where substantial differences between the Right and the Left emerge only moving towards the extremes of the political spectrum, in Italy as well. Such a perspective, which acquires authoritativeness through reiteration, can contribute to explain the tendency to adopt an inward-looking approach in the assessment of the nodal challenges posed to Italianness, while accounting for the lack of interest on the part of intellectuals in seemingly external factors, among them immigration – but also European integration, corruption, secularism, just to provide a few examples – in the redefinition of the meaning of national belonging. The impact of such a trend will be assessed in due course in relation to the role of other actors who engaged in the same debates.

If Italian intellectuals only appear to take part in the debate on national identity, while they show little interest in the relation between immigration and Italianness, the ecclesial documents and the interventions of many representatives of the Catholic hierarchy taken into account suggest that the Church has played a pivotal role both in the two separate debates as well as in connecting them one to another. The Church has proven a high degree of awareness of the fact that the migratory waves of the 1950s were not to be considered a temporary phenomenon, although the Catholic discourse on migration, until well after the Second Vatican Council, seems primarily concerned with the conditions of life of Catholics living abroad and with the role that 'foreign parishes' have in providing them with spiritual assistance and pastoral care. The Church's discourse on migration to Italy reflects the same delays as the Italian political world, as for instance until the late 1990s the idea of migration was still limited to the internal movement of Italians migrating from the South to the North of the country and Southerners represented the foreign component of an increasingly multicultural society, an interpretation quite similar to that of the Northern League and, more in general, of the majority of political parties.

The most interesting datum in the Church's narrative on immigration consists in the shift, illustrated by the two case studies of Ratzinger's and Biffi's documents, from a unconditional love for the newly arrived to the more careful doctrinal specifications and internal guidelines put forward to deal with immigrants of Muslim faith. The criterion for integration emerging from these documents points in the direction of conversion to Catholicism as the only real means for immigrants to free themselves from the status of 'strangers'. The process behind this mechanism of inclusion has its roots in the Catholic twofold recurrent discourse, which on the one hand claims for the Church a fundamental role in the definition of Italian identity, presenting all Italians as Catholics, while on the other hand grouping together secularism and Islam as 'challenges' threatening such traditional collective identity and its shared values.

While actively fighting all kinds of discrimination and racism, the Church seems to suggest a model of citizenship based on a social ladder of different categories of immigrants to be included, which has at its top Catholics, followed by non-Catholic Christians and, going down the ladder, Jews and, finally, Muslims, relegated to the lower level of what appears to be a hierarchically structured society. Such a model of citizenship, whereby national identity and religious belonging conflate and coincide works according to a mechanism which this book has referred to as 'selective solidarity'. The principle of selective solidarity is based on a theoretical premise – the principle of Truth and the superiority of Catholicism on other faiths, based on fundamental mistakes when not on superstition or violence – as well as on an utilitarian criterion, which is that of privileging immigrants who are easier to assimilate. The results of both strategies point in the same direction: granting priority to Catholic immigrants.

The original aspect of the Church's discourse is neither that of granting recognition to (potential) Catholics (which is coherent with its mission), nor that of linking Catholicism with Italianness (which to a certain extent is understandable for all sorts of historical reasons), but rather that of making the boundaries of citizenship overlap and coincide with those of Catholicism, leaving difference outside – a difference that, the Church is clear in this sense, needs to be respected, engaged in a dialogue, perceived as potentially possible to include (convert) but that, until this process of 'enlightenment' is completed, is still 'external'.

The analysis of the role of the Church in the debates under scrutiny provides a clear example of the importance of rhetoric in shaping public perception, often beyond the intentions of those who employ such rhetoric. As previously mentioned, the Church does not represent a united form, as dissent has emerged across time and from individual representatives, to the point that such internal division has been perceived by observers as a further sign of the Church's decline manifesting itself at the centre of its empire, Rome. However, these dissenting voices, even when authoritative, have not prevented – and could not do so by any means – other political actors from appropriating and exploiting for political purposes certain views put forward by the Catholic hierarchy, just turning them into far more controversial stances. The influence, reinforced by the media, of a discourse expressed by representatives of the most trusted institution in Italy in legitimising more exclusionary claims is self-evident. Among the most exploited traits of the Catholic narrative are the recurrent references to an identity threatened by alternative 'lifestyles' (namely religious relativism and Islam), the idea that Catholics are victims to whom the right of freedom of speech is denied (and therefore in need of protection from the state), the critique of political correctness as a sign of false tolerance and the idea that the state should establish utilitarian criteria to decide which categories of immigrants can be integrated.

The importance of rhetoric is also proven by the fact that despite what has been assessed by experts as a high degree of continuity in doctrinal terms between the last three Pontiffs, John Paul II, Benedict XVI and Francis, the different rhetoric employed by each of them together with a series of symbolic gestures performed by some and not by others has greatly influenced the perception of both their personas and their attitudes towards immigrants, while also marking a clear distance between their ideas of solidarity.

However, the Church's influence on the state policies on immigration seems to go in the opposite direction, as most of the adverse reactions to the stricter laws on immigration, such as the Bossi-Fini law and the security package, came from the Catholic world and represented the most critical voices within that debate, far more incisive than those expressed by the Left, which very often limited intervention to remarking upon the criticism expressed by others. Such apparent incongruence between the Church's position on national identity and otherness and its interventions on the legislative measures passed in the last decade by the Right, can be explained with the idea, already expressed in previous chapters, that criticism towards the law and support for immigrants has generally been inversely proportional to the role occupied in the Catholic hierarchy.

This study has indeed shown that, with the few exceptions already mentioned, the most prominent representatives of the Church are also the most involved in politics (and in recent times have been moving closer to the Right), whereas doubts about the texts of the last two measures on immigration were expressed by Catholic associations and priests more exposed to direct contact with the migrants, with those exceptions already mentioned elsewhere. This explanation can be considered valid until the ascent of Jorge Mario Bergoglio to the papal throne in 2013. Whether the 'revolution' brought about by Pope Francis is going to hold its ground or fade is impossible to assess at this stage, but it can be said that the new Pope certainly represents the main sign of a trend of inversion within the Church since 2000.

The party that more than any other has exploited the most controversial arguments put forward by Catholic representatives and particularly those mentioned above and which has emerged as the most influential actor involved in the debates on identity and otherness is beyond doubt the Northern

League. The nationalism put forward by the party represents a clear example of a 'performative way of doing politics', an 'inauthentic posture' aimed at achieving recognition, legitimation and, ultimately, electoral consensus. The Lega has managed to become the most recognised 'issue owner' when it comes to Italianità and immigration, an achievement facilitated by a Left whose contradictions and internal division have prevented it from appearing equally 'efficient' and coherent in approaching the issue of immigration. While the Left has never suggested a link between a shared feeling of belonging and the presence of foreigners, the Northern League has turned such a link into a political means of negotiation with other political parties as well as an ideal Trojan Horse to achieve more articulated objectives, from federalism to the delegitimation of political competitors to public perception of the party as closer to common citizens' anxieties and more active in dealing with them. The League has built its success through the 'manufacturing of reality', via a self-feeding system whereby immigrants are turned into aggressors and Italians into victims. Its political action has proven, once again, the centrality of rhetoric and its impact on state policy making.

The previous chapter has already described the continuity between the first law on immigration of 1963 and the 2002 Bossi-Fini law for what concerns the actual rules established by the two measures as well as their incommensurably different rhetoric (the latter being much more aggressive and exclusionary, directly influenced by the Northern League), and how the employment of such rhetoric has prepared the ground for policies that are much stricter vis-à-vis migrants' rights. Furthermore, the party's harsh discourse on immigration has never prevented the Lega from being the primary supporter of the regular amnesties that allowed more immigrants to be employed in Italy, mainly, but not exclusively, in the domestic sector.

While this double strategy has been framed within the interpretation of 'simulative politics', which to a certain degree is once again a sign of that 'inauthentic nationalism' previously mentioned, the most long-lasting effect of the League's political action has been that of mainstreaming fear. The party has indeed been successful in injecting fear into public opinion, forcing other more established parties of the Right, but occasionally the Left as well, to adopt a similar approach towards immigration. There are two main consequences of this process: the first is the fact that the front of anti-immigration parties within the Italian (and European) political scenario has sensibly extended. The second is that not only has the League legitimised intolerant attitudes and an openly discriminatory discourse justifying the right of Italians to react to the 'assault' on the part of Islam, but it has also constantly raised the bar of what it is acceptable to say in the name of a freedom of speech for which Italians have to fight.

The model of citizenship put forward by the League has been defined as a model of an 'institutionalised state of exception', where the immigrants represent the living sign of the boundaries of Italian identity. This model, in which the outsider has to change to become Italian, to whom no conversion to

Catholicism can grant a place in society and where they are destined to live on the margins, coincides with the model of citizenship put forward by the state with the security package.

It is, therefore, possible to conclude that if until 2009 the fourth hypothesis suggested in the Introduction, that Italy was not following any specific model but was rather reacting to 'emergencies' with ad hoc measures aimed at protecting the national economy and dealing with a temporary phenomenon, had to be considered correct, since the security package Italy seems to have taken the path of a systematic exclusion of immigrants, following the model suggested by the Northern League. This model has been supported by a narrative perceived by public opinion as 'coherent' and convincing, which has granted the discourse of the Lega a degree of solidity that has left it almost unquestioned even when the party's electoral destiny was perceived as one of decline. I would argue that even the recent abolition of the crime of illegal entry has not changed the situation. As already mentioned, the lack of 'discourses' accompanying the law on the part of the political actors putting the proposal forward or supporting it – namely the Five Star Movement and the Democratic Party – has made the change far less significant than it could have been and has actually exposed how little the abrogation of the offence from the penal code has meant. On the contrary, it has worked as an occasion for the Northern League to add new fuel to an almost exhausted debate, providing party leader Salvini and his fellow leghisti with a new battle to fight, which makes the chance of the reato di clandestinità being reintroduced in the near future quite high.

In this generally gloomy scenario there seem to be two reasons to think that the formulation of a more inclusive idea of shared belonging is still possible. The first, as already mentioned, is the role of Pope Bergoglio whose rhetoric, no matter how populist or instrumental it has been judged, emerged as the only charismatic and authoritative pro-immigrant voice in the public debate. The second source of hope for migrants, and arguably for Italians, comes from migrants themselves, their organisations, the initiatives they promote and the claims they put forward to demand the right to participate in Italian public life as well as from those Italian citizens who rejected the imposition on the part of the state of denouncing illegal immigrants, condemning them to be sent to jail or back to the countries they had fled. Moreover, one should reflect on the fact that even if political actors do not seem ready to recognise multiculturalism *de jure*, they could not prevent Italy from becoming a multiethnic country, albeit so *de facto*.

Establishing the direction Italy is going to take vis-à-vis the issue of citizenship in coming years is not easy to assess. I would suggest that moving on from ideological and outdated understandings of the nodal points in the construction (or demolition) of Italian identity and looking at those events with the distance one should apply to the study of history would allow new interpretations of Italianità to emerge. Moreover, rebalancing the conception of national identity in favour of second-generation immigrants born in Italy (with a long-due reform of citizenship) rather than mending the necessarily weak ties with third- and fourth-generation Italians abroad could be another way to foster a process of revitalisation of an identity which has in time been essentialised into fixed schemes.

Finally, interpreting the weakness of Italianness as a sign of malleability and strength, as has been done by a number of mainly international observers, and considering such weakness as a starting point for a necessary renewal of national belonging in a more inclusive sense could be a first step towards a society that would more closely reflect its internal – already existing – dynamism.

Bibliography

Books and articles

Accattoli, L., 'Il Papa saluta la fine del Ramadan: "Serenità e pace ai musulmani"', *Corriere della Sera*, 23 October 2006.

Acerbi, A., *La Chiesa e l'Italia. Per una storia dei loro rapporti negli ultimi due secoli* (2003) Milan: Vita e Pensiero.

Agamben, G., *Homo Sacer: Sovereign Power and Bare Life* (1998) Stanford, CA: Stanford University Press.

Agnew, J., 'The Rhetoric of Regionalism: The Northern League in Italian Politics', *Transactions of the Institute of British Geographers*, Vol. 20, No. 2 (1995): 156–72.

Albertazzi, D., '"Back to our Roots" or Self-confessed Manipulation? The Use of the Past in the Lega Nord Positioning of Padania', *National Identities*, Vol. 8, No. 1 (2006): 21–39.

——'Addressing "the People": A Comparative Study of the Lega Nord's and Lega dei Ticinesi's Political Rhetoric and Styles of Propaganda', *Modern Italy*, Vol. 12, No. 3 (2007): 327–47.

Alessandri, A., 'Difendiamo la nostra terra dal furto della nostra identità', *La Padania*, 6 October 2007.

Allam, M., 'Troppa libertà: in Olanda integrazione fallita', *Corriere della Sera*, 19 December 2004.

——'Mussulmani in Italia, identità e integrazione', *Corriere della Sera*, 28 April 2005.

——'L'Islam in Italia? Tutto bene. Un DVD (idilliaco) per le scuole', *Corriere della Sera*, 20 November 2006a.

——'Una scuola. Due stati', *Corriere della Sera*, 1 September 2006b.

Allum, P., 'From Two into One. The Faces of the Italian Christian Democratic Party', *Party Politics*, Vol. 3, No. 1 (1997): 23–52.

Alvaro, C., *L'Italia rinunzia?* (1986 [1944]) Palermo: Sellerio.

Andall, J., *Gender, Migration and Domestic Service* (2000) London: Ashgate.

——'La vittoria della Lega: immigrazione e cittadinanza in Veneto', in G. Baldini and A. Cento Bull (eds), *Politica in Italia* (2009) Bologna: Il Mulino, pp. 261–80.

Anderson, B. and Rogaly, B., *Future of Labour Law* (2005) Cambridge: Cambridge University Press.

Andini, 'Caso immigrazione. Il Cardinale Biffi ha tolto la sordina', *Avvenire*, 1 October 2000.

Anon. 'Fini: "La nostra svolta non è finita"', *Corriere della Sera*, 26 January 1995.

——'Biffi: immigrazione, prima i cattolici', *La Padania*, 14 September 2000a.

——'Non è xenofobo. Salvaguarda la razza cattolica. Il sostegno del Vaticano al Cardinal Biffi', *Avvenire*, 23 September 2000b.

——'Al bivio il dialogo con gli Altri', *La Stampa*, 2 October 2000c.

——'Il parroco ribelle denuncia il Cardinal Biffi', *La Stampa*, 2 October 2000d.

——'Don Vitaliano denuncia il Cardinale Biffi', La *Repubblica*, 2 October 2000e.

——'Prodi replica a Biffi. La libertà di credo non si tocca', *Corriere della Sera*, 2 October 2000f.

——'Libertà religiosa in Europa', *La Repubblica*, 2 October 2000g.

——'Dominus Iesus, Verità senza arroganza', *Avvenire*, 4 October 2000h.

——'Legge Bossi-Fini: carta schiavista', *La Repubblica*, 6 May 2002a.

——'Moschea, ricorso della Lega', *Corriere della Sera*, 30 June 2002b.

——'La Caritas attacca la legge Bossi-Fini sugli immigrati', *La Repubblica*, 7 November 2002c.

——'Chiusa scuola musulmana, scoppia la polemica', *Il Tempo*, 9 September 2005a.

——'Sul concordato la discussione è chiusa', *Corriere della Sera*, 16 November 2005b.

——'Aperta tra le polemiche la nuova scuola araba di Milano', *La Repubblica*, 9 October 2006.

——'Tor di Quinto: donna aggredita e violentata', *Corriere Romano*, 31 October 2007a.

——'Sicurezza, Veltroni contro la Romania. Per le espulsioni varato decreto legge', *La Repubblica*, 31 October 2007b.

——'Giovanna Reggiani è morta', *Corriere della Sera*, 1 November 2007c.

——'Sicurezza, l'avvertimento di Bucarest, "Non consentiremo misure xenofobe"', *Corriere della Sera*, 12 May 2008a.

——'Omicidio Reggiani, condannato Mailat, al giovane rumeno 29 anni di carcere', *La Repubblica*, 29 October 2008b.

——'All'esame la norma sui presidi-spia. Fini scrive a Maroni: "è negativa"', *Corriere della Sera*, 4 May 2009a.

——'Milano, la proposta della Lega. "Carrozze metro solo per milanesi"', *La Repubblica*, 7 May 2009b.

——'Il CSM sul pacchetto sicurezza. "Paralizzerà gli uffici giudiziari"', *La Repubblica*, 10 June 2009c.

——'Il pacchetto sicurezza diventa legge. Sì alle ronde, la clandestinità è reato', *La Repubblica*, 2 July 2009d.

——'Oltre 35 mila firme contro il ddl sicurezza', *MicroMega*, 2 July 2009e.

——'Immigrati: scontro Vaticano–Lega. Il Ministro Calderoli ci offende', *La Repubblica*, 25 August 2009f.

——'Unità d'Italia, la sparata di Calderoni: celebrazioni inutili. Scoppia la polemica', *Il Messaggero*, 3 May 2010a.

——'Che cosa significa essere italiani? Dibattito sull'identità nazionale', *Il Giornale*, 28 May 2010b.

——'Unità d'Italia, scontro aperto tra Napoletano e Durnwalder', *Corriere della Sera*, 11 February 2011a.

——'Papa: "Cattolici decivisi nella costruzione dell'identità italiana"', *Il Giornale*, 16 March 2011b.

——'Messaggio del Papa a Napolitano. "Fondamentale il contributo cattolico"', *La Repubblica*, 16 March 2011c.

——'150 anni Unità d'Italia, Borghezio: "Inno sfigatello. Facciamo come in Belgio"', *Il fatto quotidiano*, 17 March 2011d.

——'Unità d'Italia, festa e polemiche. La Lega boicotta la celebrazione', *La Stampa*, 17 March 2011e.

——'Il Papa riceve zingari e Rom. "Mai più vessazioni e disprezzo"', *La Repubblica*, 11 June 2011f.

——'Papa Francesco, più dialogo con l'Islam, costruiamo ponti', *Il Messaggero*, 22 March 2012a.

——'"Dimissioni irrevocabili": Umberto Bossi non è più il segretario della Lega Nord', *Il Fatto Quotidiano*, 5 April 2012b.

——'Berlusconi alla Lega: "Accordo globale o niente Lombardia"', *Corriere della Sera*, 30 December 2012c.

——'Interviste, libri e "profezie": già da mesi voci di dimissioni', *La Repubblica*, 11 February 2013a.

——'Lombardia a Maroni: "Missione compiuta"', *Corriere della Sera*, 26 February 2013b.

——'L'Islam sorride a Papa Francesco', *Panorama*, 15 March 2013c.

——'La prime critiche dei siti conservatori agli strappi liturgici', *Corriere della Sera*, 2 April 2013d.

——'Papa Francesco a Lampedusa: 'No a globalizzazione dell'indifferenza"', *Corriere della Sera*, 8 July 2013e.

——'Cento giorni di insulti alla Kyenge', *L'Espresso*, 19 August 2013f.

——'Il reato di clandestinità è abolito. Passa in Senato proposta M5s', *La Repubblica*, 9 October 2013g.

——'Via il reato di immigrazione clandestina. Il Senato approva l'emendamento del M5s', *Corriere della Sera*, 9 October 2013h.

——'Berlusconi decaduto, si del Senato. FI: è un colpo di Stato. Il Pd: "Ora la legge è uguale per tutti"', *Il Messaggero*, 27 November 2013i.

——'Gay, immigrati, Roma (ladrona): con Salvini torna la Lega che ce l'ha duro', *Libero*, 21 December 2013j.

——'Salvini show a Chiuduno: Immigrati disinfettati? Poi vengono da noi a rubare', *Corriere della Sera/Bergamo*, 21 December 2013k.

——'Grillo, gli iscritti del M5S dicono no al reato di immigrazione clandestina', *Corriere della Sera*, 13 January 2014a.

——'Caso Kyenge, Salvini: il ministro lavora contro gli italiani', *La Repubblica*, 16 January 2014b.

——'Immigrazione, abolito il reato di clandestinità', *Libero*, 2 April 2014c.

——'Stop al reato di clandestinità. Via libera della Camera', *L'Unità*, 2 April 2014d.

——'Raccolta di firme: "introdurre il reato di clandestinità"', *La Repubblica*, 7 April 2014e.

——'Salvini: firme per reintroduzione reato immigrazione clandestina', *Il Fatto Quotidiano*, 11 April 2014f.

——'Papa Francesco: "Sacramenti anche ai marziani. Chi siamo noi per chiudere le porte?"', *La Repubblica*, 12 May 2014g.

——'Papa: contro Rom ostilità e disprezzo, istituzioni si impegnino per garantire diritti', *La Repubblica*, 5 June 2014h.

Antonello, P. and O'Leary, A. (eds) *Imagining Terrorism: The Rhetoric and Representation of Political Violence in Italy (1969–2009)* (2009) Oxford: Legenda.

Anzaldùa, G., *Borderlands/La Frontera* (1999) San Francisco, CA: Aunt Lute Books.

Astorri, R., 'Stato e Chiesa in Italia: dalla revisione concordataria alla Seconda Repubblica', *Quaderni di diritto e politica ecclesiastica*, No. 1 (2004).

Bacchiddu, P., 'Acclamazione per Maroni, lacrime per Bossi, ecco la nuova Lega Nord', *Panorama*, 2 July 2012.

Balbo, L. and Manconi, L., *I razzismi possibili* (1990) Milan: Feltrinelli.

——*Razzismi. Un vocabolario* (1993) Milan: Feltrinelli.

——*I razzismi reali* (2004) Milan: Fabietti.

Baldi, F., 'Cota: "La nuova legge è una vittoria culturale"', *La Padania*, 7 May 2009.

Balibar, E., *We, the People of Europe? Reflections on Transnational Citizenship* (2004) Princeton, NJ: Princeton University Press.

Banti, A.M., *La nazione del Risorgimento. Parentela santità e onore alle origini dell'Italia unita* (2000) Turin: Einaudi.

Banti, A.M. and Ginsgborg, P. (eds), 'Per una nuova storia del Risorgimento', in *Storia d'Italia, Annali, 22, Il Risorgimento* (2007) Turin: Einaudi.

Banton, M., *International Action Against Racial Discrimination* (1996) Oxford: Oxford University Press.

Barbagallo, F., 'Il doppio Stato, il doppio terrorismo, il caso Moro', *Studi Storici*, Vol. 42, No. 1 (2001): 127–38.

Barnes, P., *Building Societies: The Myth of Mutuality* (1984) London: Pluto.

Barry, B., *Culture and Equity: An Egalitarian Critique of Multiculturalism* (1999) Cambridge: Polity Press.

Bassi, P., 'Manifestare per difendere la nostra identità', *La Padania*, 12 May 2007a.

——'Rifugiati, fatto fuori un altro pezzo di Bossi-Fini', *La Padania*, 28 July 2007b.

——'Reagire subito o saremo colonizzati', *La Padania*, 11 April 2007c.

——'Non hanno voluto evitare l'emergenza Rumeni', *La Padania*, 1 May 2007d.

——'Il Rom della strage è già fuori', *La Padania*, 6 October 2007e.

Battaglia, F.M. and di Paolo, P., *Scusi, lei si sente italiano?* (2010) Rome and Bari: Laterza.

Battaglia, M., 'Il popolo di Radiopop: con la Lega abbiamo eclissato l'Arcobaleno', *Panorama*, 17 April 2008.

Becker, G., 'A Theory of Competition Among Pressure Groups for Political Influence', *Quarterly Journal of Economics*, Vol. 48 (1983): 371–99.

Bell, D., *Communitarianism and its Critics* (1993) Oxford: Oxford University Press.

Bellah, R., Madsen, R., Sullivan, W., Swidler, A. and Tipton, S., *Habits of the Heart: Individualism and Commitment in American Life* (1985) Berkeley and Los Angeles: University of California Press.

Belluati, M, Grossi, G. and Viglongo, E., *Mass-media e società multietnica* (1995) Milan: Anabasi.

Bencivenga, E., *Oltre la tolleranza: per una proposta politica esigente* (1992) Milan: Feltrinelli.

Benda, J. (ed.) *The Betrayal of the Intellectuals*, trans. Richard Aldington (1980) London: Norton.

Bentham, J., *Principles of Morals and Legislation* (1781), in J.H. Burns and H.L.A. Hart (eds), *An Introduction to the Principles of Morals and Legislation* (1996) Oxford: Clarendon Press.

Berger, P.L., *Resurgent Religion and World Politics* (1999) Grand Rapids, MI: The Ethics and Public Policy Center and Wm. B. Eerdmans Publishing Co.

Berry, J.M., *The Interest Group Society* (1997) New York: Longman.

Bets, H.G., 'The New Politics of Resentment: Radical Right-Wing Populist Parties in Western Europe', *Comparative Politics*, Vol. 25 (1993): 413–27.

Betts, G.G., *The Twilight of Britain: Cultural Nationalism, Multiculturalism and the Politics of Toleration* (2002) New Brunswick, NJ: Transaction Publishers.

Biffi, G., *Nota Pastorale 'La città di San Petronio nel terzo millennio'* (2000) Bologna: EDB.

Biggeri, L., 'L'immigrazione straniera in Italia e il ruolo della statistica', in *La presenza straniera in Italia: l'accertamento e l'analisi*, Rome: Atti del Convegno Istat, 15–16 Dicembre 2005.

Billings, D.B., 'Religion as Opposition: A Gramscian Analysis', *The American Journal of Sociology*, Vol. 96, No. 1 (July 1990): 1–31.

Biorcio, R., *La Padania promessa* (1997) Milano: Il Saggiatore.

——'The Lega Nord and the Italian Media System', in G. Mazzoleni, J. Stewart and B. Horsfield (eds), *The Media and Neo-populism: A Contemporary Comparative Analysis* (2003) Westport, CT: Greenwood Publishing Group, pp. 71–95.

——'Democrazia e populismo nella seconda Repubblica', in M. Maraffi (ed.) *Gli italiani e la politica* (2007) Bologna: Il Mulino, pp. 187–207.

Blanchard, P., Bancel, N. and Lamaire, S. (eds) *La fracture coloniale. Le société française au prisme de l'héritage colonial* (2005) Paris: La Découverte.

Blühdorn, I., 'Sustaining the Unsustainable: Symbolic Politics and the Politics of Simulation', *Enviromental Politics*, Vol. 16, No. 2 (2007): 251–75.

Bobbio, N., *Eguaglianza e libertà* (1995) Turin: Einudi.

——'Bobbio risponde a De Felice. Storia: scorretto assimilarla alle scienze fisiche, i fatti non bastano. Per comprendere bisogna scegliere', *La Stampa*, 23 March 1996.

Bobbio, N., De Felice, R. and Rusconi, G.E., *Italiani: amici, nemici* (1996) Roma: Donzelli.

Bocca, G., *La disunità d'Italia* (1990) Milan: Garzanti.

——*Italiani strana gente* (1998) Milan: Mondadori.

Bodei, R., *Il noi diviso* (1998) Turin: Einaudi.

Bohning, R., 'The ILO and the New UN Conventions on Migrant Workers: The Past and Future', *International Migration Review*, Vol. 25, No. 4 (1991): 698–709.

Boiocchi, S., 'Picchiato e in galera chi manifesta contro il terrorismo', *La Padania*, 12 September 2007.

Bolgiani, I. (ed.) *La Chiesa cattolica in Italia. Normativa pattizia* (2009) Milan: Giuffrè.

Bollati, G., *L'italiano. Il carattere nazionale come storia e come invenzione* (1983) Turin: Einaudi.

Bonifazi, C., 'Italian Attitudes and Opinions Towards Foreign Migrants and Migration Policies', *Studi Emigrazione*, Vol. 30 (1992): 21–41.

Bonifazi, C. and Sabatini, D., 'Albanian Migration to Italy: What Official Data and Survey Results can Reveal', *Journal of Ethnic and Migration Studies*, Vol. 2, No. 6 (2003): 967–95.

Bonini, D., 'Politica immigratoria e bisogni sociali dell'immigrato. Una prima riflessione', in N. Sergi (ed.) *L'immigrazione straniera in Italia* (1987) Rome: Edizioni lavoro.

Bonnett, A., *Anti-racism* (2000) London: Routledge.

Boomgaarden, H.G. and Vliegenthart, R., 'Explaining the Rise of Anti-immigrant Parties: The Role of News Media Content', *Electoral Studies*, Vol. 26, No. 2 (2007): 404–17.

Borooah, K.V. and Mangan, J., 'Multiculturalism versus Assimilation: Attitudes Towards Immigrants in Western Countries', *International Journal of Economic Science and Applied Research*, Vol. 2, No. 2 (2009): 35–50.

Bossi, U., *Il mio progetto* (1996) Milano: Sperling & Kupfer.

——'La Lega mantiene le promesse. Federalismo e stop ai clandestini', *La Padania*, 7 June 2009.

Bossi, U. and Vimercati, D., *La rivoluzione. La Lega: storie e idee* (1993) Milan: Sperling & Kupfer.

Boswell, J., *Community and the Economy: The Theory of Public Co-operation* (1994) London: Routledge.

Bottoni, G., *Fine della cristianità? Il cristianesimo tra religione civile e testimonianza evangelica* (2000) Bologna: Il Mulino.

Bozzo, B., 'Noi e l'Islam', *La Padania*, 6 September 2000.

Breuilly, J., *Nationalism and the State* (1992) Cambridge, MA: Harvard University Press.

Brubaker, R., *Citizenship and Nationhood in France and Germany* (1992) Cambridge, MA: Harvard University Press.

Brzozowski, S., *A Legend of Modern Poland* (1910) Lwòw: Wydanie Drugie.

Bull, M. and Rhodes, M., 'Between Crisis and Transition: Italian Politics in the 1990s', *West European Politics*, Vol. 20, No. 1 (1997): 1–13.

Burini, M., 'Da Assisi ad Allah, passando per Ratisbona. Il nuovo Pontefice e l'Islam', *Il Foglio*, 2 April 2013.

Cachafeiro, M., *Ethnicity and Nationalism in Italian Politics* (2002) Aldershot: Ashgate.

Caciagli, M., 'La destinée de la subculture rouge dans le Centre Nord de l'Italie', *Politix*, No. 30 (1995): 45–60.

——'Quante Italie? Persistenza e trasformazione delle culture politiche subnazionali', *Polis*, Vol. 3 (1988): 429–57.

Calhoun, C., *Critical Social Theory* (1995) Oxford: Blackwell.

Campani, G., 'Immigration and Racism in Southern Europe: The Italian Case', *Ethnic and Racial Studies*, Vol. 16, No. 3 (1993): 507–35.

Canovan, M., *Populism* (1981) New York: Harcourt Brace Jovanovich.

Cappadocia, E., 'The Christian Democratic Party in Italian Politics', *International Journal*, Vol. 16, No. 4 (1961): 383–98.

Carcano, F., 'Chiudiamo le porte di casa nostra a chi arriva dai Paesi Mussulmani', *La Padania*, 19 September 2006.

——'Calderoli: "Lega in piazza contro l'immigrazione"', *La Padania*, 1 May 2007.

Caritas-Migrantes, *Immigrazione Dossier Statistico* (2000) Rome: Nuova Anterem.

——*Immigrazione Dossier Statistico* (2008) Rome: Idos.

——*Immigrazione Dossier Statistico* (2010) Rome: Idos.

Carnevali, E. and Gigante, V., 'Mistero Boffo, ovvero l'ombra di Ruini', *MicroMega*, 5 February 2009.

Cartocci, R., *Fra Lega e chiesa. L'Italia in cerca di integrazione* (1994) Bologna: Il Mulino.

Cavazzani, A., 'Oltre la cittadinanza: nuovi spazi di esistenza politica dei migranti', intervento al convegno 'Potere politico e globalizzazione', Università della Calabria, Rende, 26–27 September 2002.

Cazzullo, A., *L'Italia s'è ridesta* (2011) Milan: Mondadori.

Ceccarini, L., 'The Church in Oppositon. Conflict, Lobbying and Catholic Voters in Italy', in J. Haynes (ed.) *Religion and Politics in Europe, the Middle East and North Africa. Challenges to Citizenship, Secularisation and Democracy* (2009) London: Routledge.

Cento Bull, A., 'Regionalism in Italy', in P. Wagstaff (ed.) *Regionalism in the European Union* (1999) Exeter: Intellect Books.

——*Social Identities and Political Cultures in Italy* (2000) Oxford: Berghahn.

——*Italian Neofascism: The Strategy of Tension and the Politics of Nonreconciliation* (2007) Oxford: Berghahn Books.

——'Lega Nord: A Case of Simulative Politics?', *South European Society and Politics*, Vol. 14, No. 2 (2009): 129–46.

Cento Bull, A. and Garau, E., 'The Lega Nord: From Niche to Mainstream and Back to Niche?', paper presented at the conference 'Mainstreaming the Extreme Right', held at the University of Bath, 21 November 2013.

Cento Bull, A. and Gilbert, M., *The Lega Nord and the Northern Question in Italian Politics* (2001) London: Palgrave.

Chabod, F., *L'idea di nazione* (1961) Bari: Laterza.

Chirico, J., 'Humanity, Globalisation, and Worldwide Religious Resurgence: A Theoretical Explanation', *Sociology of Religion*, Vol. 46, No. 3 (1985): 219–42.

Ciampi, C.A., *Non è il paese che sognavo. Taccuino laico per 150 anni dell'Unità d'Italia* (2010) Milan: Il Saggiatore.

Ciarlo, P., 'Federalismo amministrativo e Regioni speciali', *Quaderni costituzionali*, Vol. 1 (2000): 129–30.

Cigler, A.J. and Loomis, B.A., *Interest Group Politics* (2011) Washington, DC: CQ Press.

Clark, M., *Modern Italy. 1871 to the Present* (2008, third edition) Harlow: Pearson Education Ltd.

Cochran, C.E., 'Introduction', in T.G. Jelen and M.C. Segers (eds) *A Wall of Separation? Debating the Public Role of Religion* (1998) Lanham, MD: Rowman and Littlefield, ix–xix.

Colombo, A., 'Hope and Despair: Deviant Immigrants in Italy', *Journal of Modern Italian Studies*, Vol. 2, No. 2 (1997): 1–20.

Colombo, A. and Sciortino, G., *Gli immigrati in Italia* (2004a) Bologna: Il Mulino.

——'Italian Immigration: The Origins, Nature and Evolution of Italy's Migratory System', *Journal of Modern Italian Studies*, Vol. 9, No. 1 (2004b): 49–70.

Colonnello, P., 'Scandalo Lega, si dimette Belsito. I fondi usati per la famiglia Bossi. Maroni: "Ora pulizia"', *La Stampa*, 3 April 2012.

Conklin, A., *A Mission to Civilize: The Republican Idea of Empire in France and West Africa, 1895–1930* (1997) Stanford, CA: Stanford University Press.

Conover, P.J., *Group Identification and Group Sympathy: Their Political Implications* (1986) Midwest Political Science Association Annual Meeting.

Cook, E., 'Measuring Feminist Consciousness', *Women and Politics*, Vol. 9 (1989): 71–88.

Coppa, F.J., 'Giolitti and the Gentiloni Pact between Myth and Reality', *The Catholic Historical Review*, Vol. 53, No. 2 (1967): 217–28.

Coppola, A. and Ulivi, S., 'Quel maxi sbarco e le storie dei migranti. La Vlora ventuno anni dopo', *Corriere della Sera*, 31 October 2012.

Corecco, E., 'La presenza dei migranti nella Chiesa particolare: segno dell'immanenza reciproca tra Chiesa universale e particolare', in *Orizzonti pastorali oggi* (1987) Padua: Editrice Emp.

CO.RE.IS, Comunicato Stampa, 'Ratzinger, Biffi e i Musulmani. Si salvi chi può!', 2000.

Cota, R., 'Nuove BR e Jihad, bomba sulla nostra testa', *La Padania*, 2 August 2007.

——'Siamo più padroni a casa nostra e più artefici del nostro destino', *La Padania*, 25 March 2009.

Cotta, M., 'Elite Unification and Democratic Consolidation in Italy: A Historical Overview', in J. Higley and R. Gunther (eds) *Elites and Democratic Consolidation in Latin America and Southern Europe* (1992) Cambridge: Cambridge University Press.

Cottone, N., 'Il reato di immigrazione clandestina entra nel pacchetto sicurezza', *Il Sole 24 Ore*, 21 May 2008.

Croce, B., *Storia d'Europa nel secolo decimonono* (1993 [1932]) Milan: Adelphi.

Daconto, C., 'Papa Francesco sei il nostro idolo', *Panorama*, 8 July 2013.

——'L'immigrazione clandestina non è più reato. E ora?', *Panorama*, 3 April 2014.

Dal Lago, A., *Non-persone. L'esclusione dei migranti in una società globale* (2004) Milan: Feltrinelli.

Dalla Torre, G., *La città sul monte. Contributo ad una teoria canonistica sulle relazioni fra Chiesa e Comunità politica* (1996) Rome: An Veritas Editrice.

——'Aspetti di giustizia vaticana', *Stato, Chiese e pluralismo confessionale*, No. 18 (2013).

Daly, F. and Barot, R., 'Economic Migration and Social Exclusion: The Case of Tunisians in Italy in the 1980s and 1990s', in F. Anthias and G. Lazaridis (eds), *Into the Margins – Migration Exclusion in Southern Europe* (1999) London: Ashgate, 35–54.

Damilano, M., 'Buone notizie: la Lega è morta', *L'Espresso*, 3 June 2013.

Davie, G., 'Global Civil Religion: A European Perspective', *Sociology of Religion*, Vol. 62, No. 4 (2011): 455–73.

Davies, L., 'Pope Francis Calls for Better Links between Islam and Christianity', *The Guardian*, 22 March 2013.

Davis, D., *Religious Liberty in Northern Europe in the Twenty-first Century* (2000) Waco, TX: Baylor University.

Debray, R., *Teachers, Writers, Celebrities: The Intellectuals of Modern France* (1981) London: Verso.

De Felice, *Il Rosso e il nero* (1995) Milan: Baldini & Castoldi.

——'Il sogno di una storia normale. Il biografo di Mussolini risponde a Bobbio', *La Stampa*, 19 March 1996.

De Franciscis, M.E., *Italy and the Vatican: The 1984 Concordat between Church and State* (1989) New York: Peter Lang.

De Giorgi, A., 'Guerra imperiale e controllo metropolitano: note sulla condizione dei migranti dopo l'11 settembre', intervento al convegno 'Potere politico e globalizzazione', Università della Calabria, Rende, 26–27 September 2002.

De Guttry, A. and Pagani, F. (eds), *La crisi albanese del 1977. L'Azione dell'Italia e delle organizzazioni internazionali* (1999) Milan and Rome: Franco Angeli.

Del Pero, M., *L'alleato scomodo: gli USA e la DC negli anni del centrismo (1948–1955)* (2011) Rome: Carocci.

De Luna, G., *Figli di un benessere minore. La Lega 1979–1993* (1994) Florence: La Nuova Italia.

——*La Repubblica del dolore. Le memorie di un Italia divisa* (2011) Milan: Feltrinelli.

De Paolis, V., *Chiesa e migrazioni* (2005) Rome: Urbaniana University Press.

Desideri, C. and Santantonio, V., 'Building a Third Level in Europe: Prospects and Difficulties in Italy', *Regional and Federal Studies*, Vol. 6, No. 2 (1996): 96–116.

Destro, A., 'A New Era and New Themes in Italian Politics: The Case of Padania', *Journal of Modern Italian Studies*, Vol. 2, No. 3 (1997): 358–77.

De Winter, L. and Tursan, H., *Regionalist Parties in Western Europe* (1998) London: Routledge.

Diamanti, I., *La Lega. Geografia, storia e sociologia di un nuovo soggetto politico* (1993) Rome: Donzelli.

——*Il male del Nord. Lega, localismo, secessione* (1996) Rome: Donzelli.

——'Allarme senza solide basi. La Lega e la Chiesa anti-Islam', *Il Sole 24 Ore*, 5 November 2000.

——*Mappe dell'Italia politica. Bianco, rosso, verde, azzurro e … tricolore* (2009) Bologna: Il Mulino.

——'Cosa significa essere italiani?', *Limes*, 27 January 2010.

——*Un salto nel voto. Ritratto politico dell'Italia di oggi* (2013) Rome, Bari: Laterza.

——*Democrazia Ibrida* (2014a) Rome and Bari: Laterza.

——'La Lega partito nazionale alla conquista del Sud', *La Repubblica*, 2 June 2014b.

Diani, M., 'Linking Mobilisation Frames and Political Opportunities in Italy', *American Sociological Review*, Vol. 61, No. 6 (1996): 1053–69.

Donaddio, M., 'La Lega attacca Tettamanzi. Il Cardinale: "Sono tranquillo"', *Il Sole 24 Ore*, 7 December 2009.

Donovan, M., 'The Italian State: No Longer Catholic, No Longer Christian', *West European Politics*, Vol. 26, No. 1 (2003): 95–116.

Durand, J.D., *Storia della Democrazia cristiana in Europa: dalla rivoluzione francese al postcomunismo* (2002) Milan: Guerini e Associati.

——(ed.), *Christian Democrat Internationalism: Its Action in Europe and Worldwide from Post-World War 2 Until 1990s: vol. 1, The Origins, vol. 2, The Development (1945–1979): The Role of Parties, Movements, People* (2013) Brussels: Peter Lang.

Einaudi, L., *Le politiche dell'immigrazione in Italia dall'Unità a oggi* (2007) Bari: SEDIT.

——'Le politiche dell'immigrazione in Italia dall'Unità a oggi', in *Treccani Storia* (2010) Rome: Treccani.

Eldersveld, S., *Political Parties: A Behavioural Analysis* (1964) Chicago, IL: Rand McNally.

Entzinger, H. and Biexeveld, R., 'Benchmarking in Immigrant Integration', report for the European Commission (2003).

Fallaci, O., 'La rabbia e l'orgoglio', *Corriere della Sera*, 29 July 2001a.

——*La rabbia e l'orgoglio* (2001b) Milan: Rizzoli.

Fassin, E., 'Aveugles à la race ou au racisme? Une approche strategique', in D. Fassin and E. Fassin (eds), *De la question sociale 'a la question raciale?* (2006) Paris: La Decouverte.

Favell, A., *Philosophies of Integration: Immigration and the Idea of Citizenship in France and Britain* (1998) London: Palgrave.

Fernando, M.L., 'Exceptional Citizens: Secular Muslim Women and the Politics of Difference in France', *Social Anthropology*, Vol. 17, No. 4 (2009): 379–92.

Ferrari, G., 'Popolazione in crescita? Troppi stranieri', *La Padania*, 6 June 2007.

Ferrari, S., 'The Secularity of the State and the Shaping of Muslim Representative Organizations in Western Europe', in J. Cesari and S. McLoughlin (eds), *European Muslims and the Secular State* (2006) Aldershot: Ashgate.

Ferrera, M., 'The Southern Model of Welfare in Social Europe', *Journal of European Social Policy*, Vol., No. 1 (1996): 17–35.

Fogarty, M.P. and Dame, N. (eds) *Christian Democracy in Western Europe, 1820–1953* (1957) Paris: University of Notre Dame Press.

Formigoni, G., *La democrazia cristiana e l'alleanza occidentale (1943–1953)* (1996) Bologna: Il Mulino.

Forno, F., 'Protest in Italy During the 1990s', paper presented at the workshop 'New Social Movements and Protest in Southern Europe', University of Edinburgh, 28 March–2 April 2003.

Fortier, A.M., 'Queer Diasporas', in D. Richardson and S. Seidman (eds), *Handbook of Lesbian and Gay Studies* (2000) London: Sage.

Foucault, M., *Power/Knowledge: Selected Interviews and Other Writings 1972–1977* (1981) Hemel Hempstead: Harvester Press.

Francis, J.G., 'The Evolving Regulatory Structure of European Church-State Relationships', *Journal of Church and State*, Vol. 34, No. 4 (1992): 775–804.

Franzina, E., 'Inni e canzoni', in M. Isnenghi, *I luoghi della memoria. Simboli e miti dell'Italia unita* (1996) Rome and Bari: Laterza.

Fulton, J., 'Religion and Politics in Gramsci. An Introduction', *Sociology of Religion*, Vol. 48, No. 3 (1987): 197–216.

Furedi, F., *Where have all the Intellectuals Gone?* (2004) London: Continuum.

Furlong, P., 'Political Catholicism and the Strange Death of the Christian Democrats', in S. Gundle and S. Parker (eds) *The New Italian Republic. From the Fall of the Berlin Wall to Berlusconi* (1996) London: Routledge, pp. 59–71.

Gabaccia, D., 'Diaspora or International Proletariat? Italian Lobor, Labor Migration, and the Making of Multiethnic States, 1815–1939', *Diaspora: A Journal of Transnational Studies*, Vol. 6, No. 1 (1997): 61–84.

——*Italy's Many Diasporas* (2000) London: UCL Press.

Galeazzi, G., 'Strali vaticani sulla Lega', *La Stampa*, 25 August 2009.

Galeazzi, M., *Togliatti e Tito: tra identità nazionale e internazionalismo* (2005) Rome: Carocci.

Galeotti, A.E., *La tolleranza. Una proposta pluralista* (1994) Naples: Liguori Editore.

Galli della Loggia, E., *La morte della patria* (1996) Rome and Bari: Laterza.

——*L'identità italiana* (1998) Bologna: Il Mulino.

Gallizzi, G, 'Mafia cinese, il nostro futuro è a rischio', *La Padania*, 26 April 2007.

Gallori, P. and Nardinocchi, C., '70.000 firme per abolire la Bossi-Fini. Si da Renzi e dal sindaco di Lampedusa', *La Repubblica*, 10 October 2013.

Galullo, R., 'Lampedusa, la più grande tragedia del mare: centinaia di morti', *Il Sole 24 Ore*, 3 October 2013.

Garavaglia, M., 'Sveglia Padani, tocca a noi', *La Padania*, 4 November 2007.

Garibaldi, I., 'Classi temporanee biennali per gli allievi stranieri', *La Padania*, 6 June 2007a.

——'Decreto sicurezza. Vivono i Talebani di Rifondazione', *La Padania*, 28 November 2007b.

——'Tragiche emarginazioni frutto di un'accoglienza demagogica', *La Padania*, 20 November 2007c.

Gavosto, A., Venturini, A. and Villosio, C., 'Do Immigrants Compete with Natives?', *Labour*, Vol. 13, No. 3 (1999): 603–21.

Gazzotti, G., 'Leggi più severe contro le centrali del terrore', *La Padania*, 14 September 2007.

Gellner, E. *Nations and Nationalism* (1983) Ithaca, NY: Cornell University Press.

Gentile, E., *Il mito dello stato nuovo dall'antigiolittismo al fascismo* (1982) Rome and Bari: Laterza.

——*Le religioni della politica. Fra democrazie e totalitarismi* (2001) Rome and Bari: Laterza.

——*Italiani senza padre. Intervista sul Risorgimento* (2003a) Rome and Bari: Laterza.

——*Renzo De Felice. Lo storico e il personaggio* (2003b) Rome and Bari: Laterza.

——*Le religioni della politica: fra democrazie e totalitarismi* (2007) Rome and Bari: Laterza.

——'Unità d'Italia, un domani a rischio', *Corriere della Sera*, 10 April 2012.

Giannini, G. *La Folla* (2002 [1945]) Catanzaro: Rubbettino Editore.

Giansoldati, F., 'Papa: "troppo disprezzo per gli zingari". I Rom polemizzano: "Non usi quel termine"', *Il Mattino*, 6 June 2014.

Gibelli, A., 'La UE dei nostri figli: turchi, cinesi e arabi', *La Padania*, 25 April 2007a.

——'Questo laicismo che ci mortifica', *La Padania*, 10 May 2007b.

——'Dove sono finiti i doveri degli ospiti?', *La Padania*, 17 May 2007c.

——'La Lega in piazza per salvare i Cristiani', *La Padania*, 7 July 2007d.

——'Moschee: bomba a orologeria', *La Padania*, 22 July 2007e.

——'Questo Governo punta a minimizzarela gravità della situazione', *La Padania*, 25 July 2007f.

——'Più campi nomadi, più danni al Paese', *La Padania*, 31 July 2007g.

——'Il Rom della strage è già fuori', *La Padania*, 6 October 2007h.

Gilroy, P., *Against Race: Imagining Political Culture beyond the Color Line* (2000) Cambridge, MA: Harvard University Press.

Giovagnoli, A., *Il partito italiano: la Democrazia cristiana dal 1942 al 1994* (1996) Rome and Bari: Laterza.

Girardin, S., 'Il Carroccio torna a chiedere la moratoria sulle moschee', *La Padania*, 20 January 2009.

Giudici, C., *Padania perduta. Che ne sarà della Lega dopo Bossi?* (2012) Venice: Marsilio.

Giustiniani, C., 'Immigrazione, non basta cambiare la Bossi-Fini', *L'Espresso*, 9 October 2013.

Goffman, E., *Relazioni in pubblico* (1981) Milan: Bompiani.

Goldberg, D.T., *Racist Culture. Philosophy and the Politics of Meaning* (1993) Malden, MA: Blackwell.

Golini, A. and Bonifazi, C., 'Demographic Trends and International Migration', in *The Future of Migration* (1987) Paris: Organisation for Economic Co-operation and Development.

Gordon, M.M., *Assimilation in American Life: The Role of Race, Religion and National Origins* (1964) Oxford: Oxford University Press.

Gouldner, A.W., *The Future of Intellectuals and the Rise of the New Class* (1979) New York: Seabury Press.

Gramsci, A., *Selections from the Prison Notebooks*, ed. and trans. Q. Hoare and G. Nowell Smith (1971) New York: International Publishers, pp. 312–13.

——*Quaderni dal carcere* (1948–51), ed. V. Gerratana (1975) Turin: Einaudi.

Grana, F.A., 'Papa Francesco e Ratzinger, la distanza tra il "parroco del mondo" e il professore', *Il Fatto Quotidiano*, 23 March 2013.

Greco, A.M., 'Via il reato di clandestinità: Lega pronta al referendum', *Il Giornale*, 3 April 2014.

Greenberg, A., 'The Church and the Revitalization of Politics and Community', *Political Science Quarterly*, Vol. 115, No. 3 (2000): 377–94.

Grimoldi, P., 'Schierare la marina per fermare gli sbarchi', *La Padania*, 27 July 2007.

Gualtieri, R., *L'Italia dal 1943 al 1992* (2006) Rome: Carocci.

Guolo, R., *Xenofobi e xenofili. Gli italiani e l'Islam* (2003) Rome and Bari: Laterza.

——'Chi brandisce la croce', *La Repubblica*, 6 January 2004.

Gurin, P., 'Women's Gender Consciousness', *Public Opinion Quarterly*, Vol. 49, No. 2 (1985): 143–63.

Habermas, J., *The Structural Transformation of the Public Sphere: An Inquiry into a Category of Bourgeois Society* (1989a) Cambridge, MA: The MIT Press.

——*Critical Theory and Society: A Reader* (1989b) New York: Routledge, pp. 136–42.

Haddad, Y. and Balz, M.J., 'The October Riots in France: A Failed Immigration Policy or The Empire Strikes Back?', *International Migration*, Vol. 44, No. 2 (2006): 24–32.

Hague, E., Giordano, B. and Sebesta, E.H., 'Witness, Multiculturalism and National-ist Appropriation if Celtic Culture: The Case of the League of the South and the Lega Nord', *Cultural Geographies*, Vol. 12, No. 2 (2005): 151–73.

Hammond, P., Shibley, M.A. and Solow, P.M., 'Religion and Family Values in Pre-sidential Voting', *Sociology of Religion*, No. 55 (1994): 277–90.

Hanley, D. (ed.), *Christian Democracy in Europe: A Comparative Perspective* (1994) London: Pinter.

——(ed.) *Christian Democracy in Europe* (1996) London: Continuum.

Hayes, B., 'The Impact of Religious Identification on Political Attitudes: An Interna-tional Comparison', *Sociology of Religion*, No. 56 (1995): 457–74.

Heidegger, M., *Being and Time* (1972 [1927]) New York: Harper and Row.

Hobbes, T., *Leviathan* (2009 [1651]) New York: Cosimo.

Hollifield, J.F., *Immigrants, Markets and States* (1992) Cambridge, MA: Harvard University Press.

Horniziel, L.M., *La condizione degli immigrati stranieri in Italia. Rapporto del Ministero del Lavoro dell'Istituto per gli Studi sui Servizi Sociali* (1990) Milan: Franco Angeli.

Hornsby-Smith, M., 'The Catholic Church and Social Policy in Europe', in *Welfare and Culture in Europe: Towards a New Paradigm in Social Policy* (1999) London: Jessica Kingsley Publishers, pp. 172–289.

Howarth, D. and Stavrakakis, Y., 'Introducing Discourse Theory and Political Analy-sis', in D. Howarth, A.J. Norval and Y. Stavrakakis (eds) *Discourse Theory and Political Analysis: Identities, Hegemony and Social Change* (2000) Manchester: Manchester University Press, pp. 1–23.

Hunter, J.D., *Culture Wars: The Struggle to Define America* (1991) New York: Basic Books.

Huysseune, M., 'A Eurosceptic Vision in a Europhile Country: The Case of the Lega Nord', *Modern Italy*, Vol. 15, No. 1 (2010): 63–75.

Iacopini, R. and Bianchi, S., *La Lega ce l'ha crudo. Il linguaggio del Carroccio nei suoi slogan, comizi e manifesti* (1994) Milan: Mursia.

Iezzi, I., 'L'Emilia riscopre la sua identità', *La Padania*, 2 February 2007a.

——'Sul litorale è allarme, basta con il buonismo', *La Padania*, 31 July 2007b.

——'Si scrive libertà religiosa, si legge islamizzazione', *La Padania*, 27 July 2007c.

——'Ce li hanno portati in casa', *La Padania*, 5 March 2009.

Impagliazzo, M. (ed.), *La nazione cattolica: Chiesa e società in Italia dal 1958 a oggi* (2004) Milan: Guerini e Associati.

Indini, A., 'Alessandri: "L'Islam non ci ha mai dimostrato di essere moderato', *La Padania*, 24 July 2007a.

——'Sicurezza. Comuni boicottati dalle leggi buoniste di Prodi', *La Padania*, 24 July 2007b.

Ingrao, I., 'Se Papa Francesco ricuce con l'Islam', *Panorama*, 16 April 2013.

Jacoby, R., *The Last Intellectuals: American Culture in the Age of Academe* (1987) Durham, NC: Duke University Press.

Jelen, T.G. and Chandler, M.A., 'Patterns of Religious Socialisation: Communalism, Associationalism and the Politics of Lifestyle', *Review of Religious Research*, Vol. 38, No. 2 (1996): 142–58.

Jelen, T.G. and Segers, M. (eds), *A Wall of Separation? Debating the Public Role of Religion* (1998) Cambridge: Cambridge Univesity Press.

Jelen, T.G. and Wilcox, C., *Religion and Politics in Comparative Perspective: The One, The Few and the Many* (2002) Cambridge: Cambridge University Press.

Jennings, J. and Kemp-Welch, T. (eds) *Intellectuals in Politics: From the Dreyfus Affair to Salman Rushdie* (1997) London: Routledge.

John Paul II, 'Messaggio per la Giornata Mondiale del Migrante e del Rifugiato', *Notiziario della Conferenza Episcopale Italiana*, 30 November 2004: 251–53.

Kalyvas, S.N., *The Rise of Christian Democracy in Europe* (1996) Ithaca, NY: Cornell University Press.

——'From Pulpit to Party. Party Formation and the Christian Democratic Phenomenon', *Comparative Politics*, Vol. 30, No. 3 (1998): 293–312.

Karapin, Roger, 'Far-Right Parties and the Construction of Immigration Issues in Germany', in M. Schain, A. Zolberg and P. Hossay (eds) *Shadows over Europe: The Development and Impact of the Extreme Right in Western Europe* (2002) New York: Palgrave Macmillan.

Katrougalos, G. and Lazaridis, G., *Southern Europe Welfare States: Problems, Challenges and Prospects* (2003) London: Palgrave.

Keating, M. and Wilson, A., 'Federalism and Decentralisation in Italy', paper presented at the 2010 PSA conference, Edinburgh.

Kellstedt, L.A., Green, J.C., Guth, J.L. and Smidt, C.E., 'The Rapture of Politics: The Christian Right as the United States Approaches the Year 2000', *Sociology of Religion*, Vol. 55, No. 3 (1994): 307–26.

Kertzer, D., *Comrades and Christians. Religion and Political Struggle in Communist Italy* (1980) Cambridge: Press Syndicate of the University of Cambridge.

King, M.L., *Why We Can't Wait* (2000) New York: Signet Classic.

King, R., 'Tackling Immigration into Italy: Ten Years of the *Immigrazione Dossier Statistico*', *Journal of Ethnic and Migration Studies*, Vol. 28, No. 1 (2002): 173–80.

King, R. and Mai, N., 'Of Myths and Mirrors: Interpretations of Albanian Migration to Italy', *Studi Emigrazione*, Vol. 39, No. 145 (2002): 161–200.

Kitschelt, H.A.J., with McGann, A.J., *The Radical Right-Wing in Western Europe: A Comparative Analysis* (1997) Ann Arbor: University of Michigan Press.

Klein, E., *Gender Politics* (1984) Cambridge, MA: Harvard University Press.

Kollman, K., *Outside Lobbying: Public Opinion and Interest Groups Strategies* (1998) Princeton, NJ: Princeton University Press.

Krase, J., 'Italian American Space', in M.J. Bona and A.J. Temburri (eds), *Through the Looking Glass: Italian and Italian/American Images in the Media* (1996) New York: American Italian Historical Association, pp. 241–65.

Kymlicka, W., *Multicultural Citizenship* (1995) Oxford: Oxford University Press.

Laclau, E. and Mouffe, C., *Hegemony and Socialist Strategy. Towards a Radical Democratic Politics* (1985) London: Verso.

Lanaro, S., *L'Italia nuova. Identità e sviluppo (1961–1988)* (1988) Turin: Einaudi.

Lanzillo, M., *Tolleranza* (2001) Bologna: Il Mulino.

La Porta, R., Lopes de-Silener, F., Shleifer, A. and Vishny, R.W., 'Trust in Large Organizations', *American Economic Review*, Vol. 87, No. 2 (1997): 333–38.

Lawson, K., *Political Parties and Linkage: A Comparative Perspective* (1980) New Haven, CT: Yale University Press.

Lazaridis, G. and Katrougalos, G., *Southern European Welfare States: Problems, Challenges and Prospects* (2003) Basingstoke: Palgrave/Macmillan.

Leege, D.C. and Kellstedt, L.A. (eds) *Rediscovering the Religious Factor in American Politics* (1993) New York: M.E. Sharpe.

Leopardi, G., *Discorso sopra lo stato presente dei costumi degli italiani* (1991 [1824]) Milan: Feltrinelli.

Lerner, G., 'S.O.S razzismo. Stranieri d'Italia', *L'Espresso*, 3 September 1989: 6–11.

Levitt, P., '"You Know, Abraham was Really the First Immigrant": Religion and Transnational Migration', *International Migration Research*, Vol. 37, No. 3 (2003): 847–73.

Lewis, R., *Anti-racism: A Mania Exposed* (1988) London: Quartet.

Lingua, G., 'Religioni e sfera pubblica contemporanea. Alcune questioni preliminari', in G. Lingua (ed.) *Religioni e ragione pubblica. Percorsi nella società post-secolare* (2010) Pisa: Edizioni ETS.

Locke, J., *Two Treatises on Government* (1988 [1689]) Cambridge: Cambridge University Press.

Ludovico, M., 'Ecco il pacchetto sicurezza del Governo', *Il Sole 24 Ore*, 10 October 2007.

Lyman, E.J., 'Italians Miffed Papacy didn't Return to Homeland', *USA Today*, 16 March 2013.

Lyon, B., 'New International Human Rights Standards on Unauthorized Immigrant Workers Rights: Seizing an Opportunity to Pull Governments out of the Shadows', Villanova University School of Law, School of Law Working Papers Series, 2006, Paper 45.

Maccanti, E., 'Impronte digitali per gli immigrati', *La Padania*, 29 July 2007.

Macioti, M.A. and Pugliese, E., *Gli immigrati in Italia* (1993) Rome and Bari: Laterza.

Magatti, M., *Tra disordine e scisma, le basi sociali per la protesta del Nord* (1998) Turin: Bollati Boringhieri.

Magister, S. 'La Chiesa italiana esporta il suo modello in Spagna', *L'Espresso online*, 23 February 2007.

Magni, R., 'Gli immigrati e il lavoro in Italia', *La XXI Regione, gli stranieri in Italia*, No. 9 (1995): 13–15.

Manconi, L. and Brinis, V., *Accogliamoli tutti. Una ragionevole proposta per salvare l'Italia, gli italiani e gli immigrati* (2013) Milan: Il Saggiatore.

Mannheim, K., 'The Sociology of the Intellectual', *Theory, Culture and Society*, Vol. 10 (1993): 69–80.

Maraini, D., 'Ma il dolore non ha una bandiera', *Corriere sella Sera*, 5 October 2001.

Margiotta Broglio, F. (ed.) *Relazioni tra Stato e Chiesa: lineamenti storici e sistematici* (1991) Bologna: Il Mulino.

——*Italia e Santa Sede: dalla grande guerra alla conciliazione: aspetti politici e giuridici* (1996) Rome and Bari: Laterza.

Mariani, G., 'Dal '98 la CO.PA.M aiuta i Paesi più poveri a casa loro', *La Padania*, 20 August 2006.

Marks, G. and Wilson, C.J., 'The Past in the Present: A Cleavage Theory of Party Response to European Integration', *British Journal of Political Science*, Vol. 30, No. 03 (2000): 433–59.

Maroni, R., Gibelli, A. and Bricolo, F., 'Rapporti con i soli Paesi islamici che non perseguitano i cristiani', *La Padania*, 14 June 2007.

Marroni, C., 'Papa Francesco: dialogo con l'Islam e con chi non crede', *Il Sole 24 Ore*, 23 March 2013.

McDonnell, D., 'A Weekend in Padania: Regionalist Populism and the Lega Nord', *Politics*, Vol. 26, No. 2 (2006): 126–32.

McLaren, L.M., 'Immigration and the New Politics of Inclusion and Exclusion in the European Union: The Effects of Elites and the EU on Individual-level Opinions Regarding European Immigrants', *European Journal of Political Research*, Vol. 39 (2001): 81–108.

Meguid, B., 'Competition Between Unequals: The Role of Mainstream Party Strategy in Niche Party Success', *American Political Science Review*, Vol. 99, No. 3 (August 2005): 347–59.

Meletti, J., 'Immigrazone, dai cattolici plausi e silenzi', *La Repubblica*, 3 October 2000.

Meli, M.T., 'Boselli: D'Alema sbaglia. Sul concordato vado avanti', *Corriere della Sera*, 7 November 2005.

Melotti, U., *L'immigrazione: una sfida per l'Europa* (1992) Milan: Edizioni Associate.

——*Migrazioni, nazionalità, cittadinanza. Sui pregiudizi e sul razzismo* (1996) Rome: Il Mondo 3.

——*Migrazioni internazionali. Globalizzazione e culture politiche* (2004) Milan: Mondadori.

Melucci, A., 'Movimenti sociali negli anni 80: alla ricerca di un oggetto perduto?', *Stato e Mercato*, No. 14 (1985).

Melucci, A. and Diani, M., *Nazioni senza stato. I movimenti etnico-nazionali in Occidente* (1992) Milan: Feltrinelli.

Merlino, M., 'The Italian (In)Security Package. Security vs. Rule of Law and Fundamental Rights in the EU', *Liberty and Security* research paper No. 14 (2009).

Messina, P., *Regolazione politica dello sviluppo locale. Veneto ed Emilia Romagna a confronto* (2001) Turin: Utet.

Miles, R. and Brown, M., *Racism* (2003) London: Routledge.

Miller, A., Gurin, P. and Gurin, G., 'Stratum Identification and Consciousness', *Social Psychology Quarterly*, Vol. 43, No. 1 (1980): 30–47.

——'Group Consciousmess and Political Participation', *American Journal of Political Science*, Vol. 25 (1981): 494–511.

Mirabile, T., 'Chiudere subito le moschee che fomentano odio', *La Padania*, 12 April 2007a.

——'Cittadinanza agli immigrati: un trucco della sinistra', *La Padania*, 25 July 2007b.

——'Le leggi del governo incoraggiano le stragi di clandestini', *La Padania*, 19 June 2007c.

Moia, L., *Federalisti di Dio? Incontri e scontri tra Lega e Chiesa* (1997) Milan: Ancora.

Moioli, V., *Il tarlo delle Leghe* (1991) Brescia: ComEdit 2000.

Moller Okin, S., *Justice, Gender and the Family* (1989) New York: Basic Books.

Montanari, A., 'Lega ultimo baluardo contro l'invasione', *La Padania*, 29 July 2007a.

——'La legge sulla libertà religiosa islamizzerà il Paese', *La Padania*, 24 July 2007b.

——'Castelli: "Sinistra razzista e colpevole"', *La Padania*, 3 November 2007c.

Montefiore, A., 'The Political Responsibility of Intellectuals', in I. Maclean (ed.), *The Political Responsibility of Intellectuals* (1990) Cambridge: Cambridge University Press, pp. 201–28.

Mughini, L., *Non passa lo straniero. L'Italia, gli italiani e l'immigrazione* (2002) Venice: La Meridiana.

Musaragno, R., *Studenti esteri in Italia (1960–2000). Un itinerario d' impegno per la testimonianza missionaria* (2001) Rome: Ucsei.

Mussa, G. (ed.), *Padania, identità e società multirazziali* (1998) Ed. Enti Padani Locali Federali.

Napolitano, G., *Una e indivisibile. Riflessioni sui 150 anni della nostra Italia* (2011) Milan: Rizzoli.

Nelsen, B.F., Guth, J.L. and Fraser, C.R., 'Does Religion Matter? Christianity and Public Support for the European Union', *European Union Politcs*, Vol. 2, No. 2 (2001): 191–217.

Nevola, G., *Altre Italie: identità nazionale e regioni a statuto speciale* (2003) Rome: Carocci.

Norris, P. and Inglehart, R., *Sacred and Secular. Religion and Politics Worldwide* (2004) New York: Cambridge University Press.

Oelz, M., 'The Ilo's Domestic Workers Convention and Recommendation: A Window of Opportunity for Social Justice', *International Labour Review*, Vol. 153, No. 1 (2014): 143–72.

Olivetti, M., *Nuovi statuti e forma di governo delle Regioni* (2002) Bologna: Il Mulino.

Oneto, G., *L'invenzione della Padania* (1997) Ceresola: Foedus Editore.

——'Cinque mosse contro i nuovi sbarchi', *La Padania*, 29 September 2004.

Pace, E., *L'Unità dei cattolici in Italia* (1995) Milan: Guerini e Associati.

Paci, M., 'Il sistema italiano di welfare tra tradizione clientela e prospettiva di riforma', in U. Ascoli (ed.) *Welfare State all'italiana* (1987) Rome and Bari: Laterza, pp. 297–326.

Pagani, I., 'Riflessioni in margine al Convegno sui 50 anni di Trieste Italiana. Senato della Repubblica, 19 Ottobre 2004', *Storia del mondo*, No. 30 (25 October 2004).

Paganini, G. and Tortarolo, E., *Pluralismo e religione civile: una prospettiva storica e filosofica* (2004) Milan: Mondadori.

Palomba, R. and Righi, A., 'Quel giorno che gli Albanesi invasero l'Italia. Gli atteggiamenti dell'opinione pubblica e della stampa italiana sulla questione delle migrazioni dall'Albania' (1992) working paper Ipr-Cnr.

Pandini, M., 'Per bloccare le moschee Calderoli arruola i suini', *La Padania*, 12 September 2007.

Panebianco, A., 'Representation without Taxation: l'idea di cittadinanza in Italia', *Il Mulino*, Vol. 1 (January–February 1991): 54–60.

——*Le relazioni internazionali* (1992) Milan: Jaka Book.

——'Patti pericolosi', *Corriere della Sera*, 5 August 2005.

Pansa, G., *Carte false* (1986) Milan: Rizzoli.

Parisi, A. and Pasquino, G. (eds), *Continuità e mutamento elettorale in Italia. Le elezioni del 20 Giugno 1976 e il sistema politico italiano* (1977) Bologna: Il Mulino.

Parrenas, R.S., *Servants of Globalisaton: Women, Migration and Domestic Work* (2001) Stanford, CA: Stanford University Press.

Patriarca, S., 'Italian Neopatriotism: Debating National Identity in the 1990s', *Modern Italy*, Vol. 6, No. 1 (2001): 21–34.

Paudice, C., 'Matteo Salvini vs. Papa Francesco sui Rom: "Sui bus di Roma dicono 'occhio al portafogli'? Chissà perché." La Rete: "Se li prenda il Vaticano"', *Huffington Post Italia*, 6 June 2014.

Pavone, C., *Una guerra civile. Saggio storico sulla moralità della Resistenza* (1991) Turin: Bollati Boringhieri.

Pellicciari, A., 'Scuse al Vaticano per l'Unità d'Italia', *Libero*, 12 September 2009.

Pini, V., 'Vent'anni fa lo sbarco dei 27.000. Il primo grande esodo dall'Albania', *La Repubblica*, 6 March 2011.

Piretti, M.S., 'La strategia politica di Gentiloni e il fallimento dell'intransigentismo cattolico', *Ricerche di Storia Politica*, Vol. IX (1995): 5–40.

Pivato, S., *La storia leggera. L'uso pubblico della storia nella canzone italiana* (2002) Bologna: Il Mulino.

Pivetti, I., 'I cattolici vanno alla Lega', *Autonomia Lombarda*, 5 March 1992.

Pizzorno, A., 'Introduzione allo studio della partecipazione politica', *Quaderni di sociologia*, Vol. 9 (1966): 273–77.

Poli, G., 'Fondazione federalista al via per salvare una cultura che muore', *La Padania*, 30 May 2007.

Polledri, M. and Maraventano, A., 'Il Carroccio: Lampedusa è stanca di pagare per mantenere i clandestini all'interno del Ctp', *La Padania*, 21 August 2007.

Polli, G., 'Borghezio: aiutiamo le nostre genti a riappropriarsi della loro identità', *La Padania*, 1 June 2007a.

——'Censire le moschee? Meglio tardi che mai', *La Padania*, 15 May 2007b.

——'Fondamentale tutelare le nostre radici', *La Padania*, 22 May 2009.

Pugliese, E., *L'Italia tra migrazioni internazionali e migrazioni interne* (2002) Bologna: Il Mulino.

Putnam, R. *Making Democracy Work: Civic Traditions in Modern Italy* (1993) Princeton, NJ: Princeton University Press.

Putnam, R.D., Leonardi, R., Nanetti, R.Y. and Pavoncello, F., 'Explaining Institutional Success: The Case of Italian Regional Government', *The American Political Science Review*, Vol. 77, No. 1 (1983): 55–74.

Putnam, R.D., Leonardi, R. and Nanetti, R.Y., *Making Democracy Work: Civic Traditions in Modern Italy* (1993) Princeton, NJ: Princeton University Press.

Quaranta, L., 'E 20.000 disperati finirono prigionieri. Lo sbarco della Vlora venti anni fa', *Corriere del mezzogiorno*, 5 August 2011.

Rawls, J., *A Theory of Justice* (1971) Cambridge, MA: Harvard University Press.

Renan, E., 'What is a Nation?', in H. Bhabha (ed.) *Nation and Narration* (1990) London: Routledge, pp. 8–22.

Rex, J. and Singh, G., 'Multiculturalism and Political Integration in Modern Nation States', *International Journal of Multicultural Societies*, Vol. 5, No. 1 (2003): 3–19.

Reyneri, A., 'The Mass Legalisation of Migrants in Italy: Permanent or Temporary Emergence from the Underground Economy?', in M. Baldwin *et al.* (eds), *Immigrants and the Informal Economy in Southern Europe* (1999) London: Frank Cass, pp. 83–104.

Reyneri, E., 'Immigrants in a Segmented and Often Undeclared Labour Market', *Journal of Modern Italian Studies*, Vol. 9, No. 1 (2004): 71–93.

Robbers, G., *Church Autonomy* (2001) Frankfurt: Lang.

Rodari, P., 'Basta con samba e gay, l'anatema dei tradizionalisti contro le svolte di Francesco', *La repubblica*, 6 August 2013.

Romanelli, R., *Storia dello Stato italiano dell'unità a oggi* (1995) Rome: Donzelli.

Romano, S., *Memorie di un conservatore* (2005) Milan: TEA.

Romano, S., Lazar, M. and Canonica, M., *L'Italia disunita* (2011) Milan: Longanesi.

Roselli, G., 'Se torniamo al governo via i romeni', *La Padania*, 4 November 2007.

Roux, C., 'Italy's Path to Federalism. Origins and Paradoxes', *Journal of Modern Italian Studies*, Vol. 13, No. 3 (2008): 325–39.

Rubino, M., 'Lampedusa, strage di migranti. Barcone a picco, centinaia di morti', *La Repubblica*, 3 October 2013.

Rusconi, G.E., 'Se l'identità italiana non è più motivo di solidarismo', *Il Mulino*, Vol. 1 (1991).

——*Se cessiamo di essere una nazione* (1993) Bologna: Il Mulino.

——*Possiamo fare a meno di una religione civile?* (1999) Rome and Bari: Laterza.

Sahlins, P., *Boundaries: The Making of France and Spain in the Pyrenees* (1989) Los Angeles: University of California Press.

Sahliyeh, E., 'Religious Resurgence and Political Modernization', in E. Sahliyeh (ed.) *Religious Resurgence and Politics in the Contemporary World* (1990) New York: State University of New York Press.

Said, E., *Representation of the Intellectuals* (1994) New York: Pantheon Books.

Sala, R., 'Lega, è il giorno di Maroni segretario', *La Repubblica*, 11 July 2012.

Sandel, M., *Liberalism and the Limits of Justice* (1982) Cambridge: Cambridge University Press.

Sartori, G., 'Ma quanto è laico Eminenza!', *L'Espresso*, 28 September 2000a.

——*Pluralismo, multiculturalismo e estranei. Saggio sulla società multietnica* (2000b) Milan: Mondadori.

——'Uditi i critici ha ragione Oriana', *Corriere della Sera*, 15 October 2001.

Sarzanini, F., 'Cambiare la Bossi-Fini, la prudenza di Alfano', *Corriere della Sera*, 7 October 2013.

Satta, S., *De Profundis* (2003 [1945]) Nuoro: Ilisso.

Scalfari, E., 'Il Papa lava i piedi a giovani detenuti: anche due ragazze, una è musulmana', *La Repubblica*, 7 August 2013.

Scarici, E., 'Villa Literno, la visita del neo-ministro sulla tomba del martire Jerry Masslo', *Corriere del Mezzogiorno*, 24 November 2011.

Schain, M.A., *The Politics of Immigration in France, Britain and the United States: A Comparative Study* (2008) New York: Palgrave Macmillan.

Schiavone, A., *Italiani senza Italia* (1998) Turin: Einaudi.

Schlesinger, P. and Foret, F., 'Political Roof and Sacred Canopy?', *European Journal of Social Theory*, Vol. 9, No. 1 (2006): 59–81.

Schmidtke, O., 'The Northern League: Changing Friends and Foes, and its Political Opportunity Structure', in D. Cesarani and M. Fulbrook (eds), *The New Italian Republic. From the Fall of the Berlin Wall to Berlusconi* (1996) London: Routledge, pp. 179–208.

Schnapper, D., *La communautè des citoyens* (1994) Paris: Gallimard.

Schudson, M., 'The News Media as Political Institutions', *Annual Review of Political Science*, Vol. 5, No. 1 (2002): 249–69.

Sciacca, A., 'Lampedusa: in fila, nudi e al freddo. La disinfezione shock dei migranti', *Corriere della Sera*, 18 December 2013.

Sciortino, G., 'Le politiche di controllo in Italia', in I. Fondazione Cariplo (a cura di) *Terzo rapporto sulle migrazioni* (1998) Milan: Franco Angeli, pp. 71–84.

——*L'ambizione della frontiera. Le Politiche di controllo migratorio in Europa* (2000) Milan: Franco Angeli.

——'Immigration in a Mediterranean Welfare State: The Italian Experience in Comparative Perspective', *Journal of Comparative Policy Analysis: Research and Practice*, Vol. 6, No. 2 (2004): 111–29.

Scoppola, P., 'Una incerta cittadinanza italiana', *Il Mulino*, Vol. 1 (1991).

——*25 Aprile. Liberazione* (1995) Turin: Einaudi.

Scrinzi, F., 'Migration and the Restructuring of the Welfare System in Italy: Change and Continuity in the Domestic Sector', in H. Luts (ed.), *Migration and Domestic Work. A European Perspective on a Global Theme* (2008) Ashgate: Aldershot.

Seidler, J., 'Contested Accommodation: The Catholic Church as a Special Case of Social Change', *Social Forces*, Vol. 64, No. 4 (1986): 847–74.

Serafini, M., 'Intercettazioni, assegni, documenti: l'inchiesta che ha travolto il Senatùr', *Corriere della Sera*, 5 April 2012.

Shotwell, James Thomson (ed.), *The Origins of the International Labor Organization: Documents*, Vol. 2 (1934) New York: Columbia University Press.

Shupe, A., 'The Stubborn Persistence of Religion in the Global Arena', in E. Sahliyeh (ed.) *Religious Resurgence and Politics in the Contemporary World* (1990) Albany, NY: State of New York University Press.

Silverstein, P., *Algeria in France* (2004) Bloomington: Indiana University Press.

Singh, G., 'Multiculturalism in Contemporary Britain: Reflections on the Leicester Model', *International Journal of Multicultural Societies*, Vol. 5, No. 1 (2003): 40–54.

Sivini, G., 'Socialisti e cattolici dalla società allo stato', in G. Sivini (ed.), *Sociologia dei partiti politici* (1971) Bologna: Il Mulino, pp. 21–105.

Speciale, A., 'Lefebvriani contro il Papa che dialoga con l'Isalm', *La Stampa*, 23 August 2013.

Spectorowski, A., 'Ethnoregionalism: The Intellectual New Right and the *Lega Nord*', *Global Review of Ethnopolitics*, Vol. 2, No. 3 (2003).

Spotts, F. and Wieser, T., *Italy. A Difficult Democracy* (1986) Cambridge: Cambridge University Press.

Stella, G.A., *Dio Po. Gli uomini che fecero la Padania* (1996) Milan: Baldini e Castoldi.

Stucchi, G., 'Rivolta a Chinatown. Esplode la banlieue milanese', *La Padania*, 13 April 2007.

Taggart, P.A., *Populism*, Vol. 3 (2000) Buckingham: Open University Press.

Taguieff, P.A., *Les Fins de l'antiracisme* (1995) Paris: Michalon.

Tajfel, H., *Human Groups and Social Categories: Studies in Social Psychology* (1981) Cambridge: Cambridge University Press.

Tambini, D., *Nationalism in Italian Politics: The Stories of the Northern League* (2001) London: Routledge.

Tarchi, M., *L'Italia populista: dal qualunquismo ai girotondi* (2003) Bologna: Il Mulino.

Taylor, C., *Sources of the Self: The Making of the Modern Identity* (1989) Cambridge, MA: Harvard University Press.

——*A Secular Age* (2007) Cambridge, MA: Harvard University Press.

Thomas, C. (ed.) *First World Interest Groups: A Comparative Perspective* (1993) Westport, CT: Greenwood Press.

Thomas, W.I., *The Child in America* (1928) New York: Knopf.

Tintori, G., *Fardelli d'Italia? Conseguenze nazionali e transnazionali delle politiche di cittadinanza italiane* (2009) Rome: Carocci.

Tonacci, F. and Viviano, F., 'CIE Lampedusa, gli immigrati del video shock: "Urlavano di spogliarci e ci deridevano"', *La Repubblica*, 18 December 2013.

Tornielli, A., 'Benedetto XVI e "la stessa linea teologica" di Francesco', *La Stampa*, 17 December 2013.

Traniello, F., 'Religione e nazione', in *La costruzione dello Stato-nazione in Italia* (2012) Rome: Viella.

Triandafyllidou, A. and Gropas, R., *European Immigration. A Sourcebook* (2007) Padstow: T.J. International.

Trigilia, C., *Le subculture politiche territoriali* (1981) Milan: Fondazione Feltrinelli.

Tullio, B., *Il terrorismo in Italia negli anni '70* (1980) Milan: Bibliografica.

Turco, L., 'Immigrati. La faccia feroce del governo', *L'Unità*, 19 February 2002.

Turner, J.H., Singleton, R. and Musick, D., *Oppression: A Socio-history of Black-White Relations in America* (1984) Chicago, IL: Nelson Hall.

Udina, M. (ed.), *Gli accordi di Osimo: lineamenti introduttivi testi annotati* (1979) Trieste: Edizioni LINT.

Vallier, I., *The Roman Catholic Church: A Transnational Actor* (1971) Madison: University of Wisconsin Press.

Valsecchi, F., *Alle radici di una protesta* (1997) Genoa: Marietti.

Van Hecke, S. and Gerard, E. (eds), *Christian Democratic Parties in Europe since the End of the Cold War* (2004) Leuven: Leuven University Press.

Veneziani, M. *et al.*, *Socialismo e nazione* (1983) Frosinone: Ciarrapico.

Venturini, A., 'Do Immigrants Working Illegally Reduce the Natives' Legal Employment? Evidence from Italy', *Journal of Population Economics*, Vol. 12 (1999): 135–54.

Vernizzi, P., 'Appello dei musulmani moderati: "Chiudete la scuola islamica"', *Il Giornale*, 5 September 2011.

Veronesi, A., 'No al voto agli immigrati. Ragioni economiche, sociali e sanitarie', *La Settimana di Saronno*, 9 June 2004.

Vertone, S., *La cultura degli italiani* (1994) Bologna: Il Mulino.

Vicari, D., 'I giorni della nave Vlora e il ritorno di una storia rimossa', *La Repubblica*, 5 November 2012.

Viganò, F., 'Pacchetto sicurezza ed espulsione: intenti legislativi e vincoli europei', *Diritto penale e procedurale*, No. 7 (2008): 813 ss.

Vincent, G., *Religions et transformations de l'Europe* (1993) Strasbourg: Presses Universitaires de Strasbourg.

Viviano, F., 'I pm: a Lugano la cassaforte di Belsito. "Sui conti di Aurora i milioni della Lega"', *La Repubblica*, 30 April 2012.

Voye, L., 'Secularization in a Context of Advanced Modernity', *Sociology of Religion*, Vol. 60, No. 3 (1999): 275–88.

Wagner, M., 'Defining and Measuring Niche Parties', *Party Politics* (2011) online.

Walicki, A., *Stanislaw Brzozowski and the Polish Beginnings of 'Western Marxisms'* (1989) Oxford: Clarendon Press.

Warner, C.M., *Confessions of an Interest Group: The Catholic Church and Political Parties in Europe* (2000) Princeton, NJ: Princeton University Press.

Warnink, H., *Legal Position of Churches and Church Autonomy* (2001) Leuven: Peeters.

Weil, P. and Crowley, J. 'Integration in Theory and Practice: A Comparison of France and Britain', *West European Politics*, Vol. 17, No. 2 (1994): 110–26.

Wertman, D.A., 'The Catholic Church and Italian Politics: The Impact of Secularisation', *West European Politics*, Vol. 5, No. 2 (1982).

Wetherell, M. and Potter, J., *Mapping the Language of Racism: Discourse and the Legitimation of Explotaition* (1992) New York: Harvester Wheatsheaf.

Westerlund, D., *Questioning the Secular State. The Worldwide Resurgence of Religion in Politics* (1996) London: C. Hurst & Co.

Wilcox, C., Jelen, T.G. and Leege, D., 'Religious Group Identifications: Toward a Cognitive Theory of Religious Mobilization', in D. Leege and L. Kellstedt (eds) *Rediscovering the Religious Factor in American Politics* (1993) Armonk, NY: M.E. Sharpe, 72–99.

Willaime, J.P., *Sociologie des Religions* (1995) Paris: Presses Universitaires de France.

Williams, R., *Keywords* (1988) London: Fontana.

Wood, D., 'Pockets of Resistance to Globalisation: The Case of the Lega Nord', *Patterns of Prejudice*, Vol. 43, No. 2 (2009): 161–77.

Young, I.M., *Justice and the Politics of Difference* (1990) Princeton, NJ: Princeton University Press.

Zaslove, A., 'Closing the Door? The Ideology and Impact of the Radical Right Populism on Immigration Policy in Austria and Italy', *Journal of Political Ideologies*, Vol. 9, No. 1 (2004): 104.

Zega, 'L'inferno sono gli altri. La Chiesa e gli immigrati', *La Stampa*, 2 October 2000.

Zeigler, H., *Political Parties in Industrial Democracies: Imagining the Masses* (1985) Mason, OH: Thomson Learning.

Zincone, Giovanna, 'The Making of Policies: Immigration and Immigrants in Italy', *Journal of Ethnic and Migration Studies*, Vol. 32, No. 3 (2006): 347–75.

Zincone, Giovanna and Di Gregorio, L., 'Il processo delle politiche di immigrazione in Italia: uno schema interpretative integrato', *Stato e Mercato*, No. 3 (2002): 433–66.

Zincone, Giuliano, 'I coltivatori di dubbi e la spada di Oriana', *Corriere della Sera*, 17 October 2001.

Zinn, D., 'Adriatic Brethren or Black Sheep? Migration in Italy and the Albanian Crisis', *European Urban and Social Studies*, Vol. 3, No. 30 (1996): 241–49.

Zuccolini, L., 'Jervolino: ora la doppia cittadinanza', *Corriere della Sera*, 11 February 1999.

Zulin, G., 'Lombardia, Maroni trionfa ma ora ha un problema: restare segretario per non perdere la Lega', *Libero*, 27 February 2007.

Conciliar documents

Acta et documenta, Series II, Vol. II, Part III: 729–31.

Acta synodalia, Vol. II, III.

Declaration *Nostra Aetate*, 28 October 1965.

Decreto *Christus Dominus*, 28 October 1965, N. 18.

Ecclesial documents

CEI, *Nota Pastorale* 'Stranieri dal terzo mondo. I nuovi poveri tra noi e il nostro impegno' (1982) Bologna: EDB.

——'Dichiarazione sull'accordo di revisione del Concordato lateranense', 18 febbraio 1984, in Enchiridion della Conferenza Episcopale Italiana, 3 (1980–85), Bologna: EDB, 1989: 931.

——*Nota Pastorale* 'La Chiesa di fronte al razzismo. Per una società più fraterna' (1989) Bologna: EDB.

——*Nota Pastorale* 'Uomini di culture diverse; dal conflitto alla solidarietà' (1990) Bologna: EDB.

——*Nota Pastorale* 'Ero forestiero e mi avete ospitato' (1993) Bologna: EDB.

——*Nota Pastorale* 'Nella Chiesa nessuno è straniero' (2000) Bologna: EDB.

——*Catechismo della Chiesa Cattolica* (ed.) (2003) Milan: Edizioni Piemme.

Commissione episcopale per le migrazioni e il turismo, 'Ero forestiero e mi avete ospitato', 4 October 1993.

——'Il mondo come una casa: dalla diffidenza all'accoglienza', 21 November 2004.

Commissione teologica internazionale, 'Fede e inculturazione', 8 October 1988.

——'Il Cristianesimo e le religioni', 30 September 1996.

Francis, Apostolic exhortation *Evangelii Gaudium*, 24 November 2013.

John XXIII, encyclical *Pacem in Terris*, 11 April 1963.

John Paul II, speech for the World Congress on Migration, 'Migrazioni: l'impegno della Chiesa', 15 March 1979.

——encyclical *Laborem exarcens*, 14 September 1981.

——Speech for the World Day of the Pastoral for Migrants, 'La Chiesa testimone e promotrice dell'integrazione dei migranti', 17 October 1985.

——Speech for the World Day of Migrants, 'Gravi, dolorose e complesse le condizioni le condizioni delle famiglie coinvolte nella dura situazione dell'emigrante', 15 August 1986.

——'Operatori di pace nel pensiero e nell'azione, con la mente e col cuore, rivolti all'unità dell'intera famiglia umana', 27 October 1986.

——encyclical *Redemptoris mission*, 7 December 1990.

——Opening speech for the IV General Episcopal Conference of Latin-American Bishops, 'Nuova evangelizzazione, promozione umana, cultura cristiana: Gesù Cristo ieri, oggi e domani', 12 October1992.

——Message for the Day of the Migrant and the Reugee, 'Nella Chiesa nessuno è straniero', 25 July 1995.

——Post-Synodal Apostolic Exhortation *Ecclesia in Africa*, 14 September 1995.

——'Lo spirito di Dio e "i semi di verità" presenti nelle religioni non cristiane', 9 September 1998.

——encyclicals *Fides et ratio*, 14 September 1998.

——'Fede, speranza e carità nella prospettiva del dialogo religioso', 29 November 2000.

——Message for World Peace Day, 'Dialogo tra le culture per una civiltà dell'amore e della pace', 1 January 2001.

——Messaggio per la 90 giornata mondiale del migrante e del rifugiato, 'Migrazioni in visione di pace', 21 November 2004.

Paul VI, encyclical *Ecclesiam suam*, 6 August 1964.

——Apostolic exhortations *Evangelii Nuntiandi*, 8 December 1975.

Pius XII, Constituzione *Exul Familia*, 1 August 1952.

Pontificio Consiglio della Cultura, 'Per una pastorale della cultura', 23 May 1999.

Pontificio Consiglio per la giustizia e per la pace, 'La Chiesa di fronte al razzismo', 3 November 1988.

Pontificio Consiglio per la Pastorale dei Migranti e degli Itineranti, 'Chiesa e mobilità umana', 26 May 1978.

Pontrificio Concilio per il dialogo religioso, 'Dialogo e annuncio', 19 May 1991.

Ratzinger, J., 'Dichiarazione *Dominu Iesus* circa l'unicità e l'universalità salvifica di Gesù Cristo e della Chiesa', 6 August 2000b.

Legal documents (listed in chronological order)

Costituzione della Repubblica Italiana, in *Gazzetta Ufficiale della Repubblica Italiana*, 27 Dicembre 1947.

Memorandum Ministeriale 4 Dicembre 1963/4, in *Gazzetta Ufficiale della Repubblica Italiana*, No. 260, 4 Ottobre 1963.

ILO *Convention on Migrant Workers* (Supplementary Provisions) No.143 (1975).

Legge 25 Marzo 1985/121, 'Modificazioni al Concordato lateranense dell'11 Febbraio 1929 tra la Repubblica Italiana e la Santa Sede', in *Gazzetta Ufficiale della Repubblica Italiana*, No. 85, 10 Aprile 1985.

Legge 30 Dicembre 1986/943, 'Norme in materia di collocamento e di trattamento dei lavoratori extracomunitari e contro le immigrazioni clandestine', in *Gazzetta ufficiale della Repubblica italiana*, No. 8, 12 Gennaio 1987.

Legge 28 Febbraio 1990/39, 'Conversione in legge, con modificazioni, del decreto legge 30 Dicembre 1989 n. 416, recante norme urgenti in materia di asilo politico, di ingresso e soggiorno dei cittadini extracomunitari e di regolarizzazione di cittadini extracomunitari ed apolidi già presenti nel territorio dello Stato. Disposizioni in materia di asilo', in *Gazzetta Ufficiale della Repubblica Italiana*, No. 49, 28 Febbraio 1990.

Legge 5 February 1992, No. 91, 'Nuove norme sulla cittadinanza', in *Gazzetta Ufficiale della Repubblica Italiana*, No. 38, 15 Febbraio 1992.

Legge 24 Febbraio 1992/225, 'Istituzione del servizio nazionale della protezione civile', in *Gazzetta Ufficiale della Repubblica Italiana*, No. 64, 17 Marzo 1992.

Decreto legge 26 Aprile 1993/122, 'Misure urgenti in materia di discriminazione razziale, etnica e religiosa', in *Gazzetta Ufficiale della Repubblica Italiana*, No. 97, 27 Aprile 1993.

Legge 6 Marzo 1998/40, 'Disciplina dell'immigrazione e norme sulla condizione dello straniero', in *Gazzetta Ufficiale della Repubblica Italiana*, No. 59 del 12 Marzo 1998.

Disegno di legge 25 Luglio 1998/286, 'Testo unico delle disposizioni concernenti la disciplina dell'immigrazione e norme sulla condizione dello straniero emanate con decreto legislativo', in *Gazzetta Ufficiale della Repubblica Italiana*, No. 191, 18 Agosto 1998.

Legge Costituzionale 17 Gennaio 2000/1, 'Modifica all'art. 48 della Costituzione concernente l'istituzione della circoscrizione Estero per l'esercizio del diritto di voto dei cittadini italiani residenti all'estero', in *Gazzetta Ufficiale della Repubblica Italiana* (Serie generale), No. 15, 20 Gennaio 2000.

Legge 27 Dicembre 2001/459, 'Norme per l'esercizio del diritto di voto dei cittadini italiani residenti all'estero', in *Gazzetta Ufficiale della Repubblica Italiana*, No. 4, 5 Gennaio 2002.

Legge 30 Luglio 2002/189, 'Modifica alla normativa in materia di immigrazione e di asilo', in *Gazzeta ufficiale della Repubblica Italiana*, No. 199, 26 Agosto 2002.

Decreto legislativo 8 Gennaio 2007/5, 'Attuazione della direttiva 2003/86/CE relativa al diritto di ricongiungimento familiare', in *Gazzetta Ufficiale della Repubblica Italiana*, No.25, 31 Gennaio 2007.

Decreto legislativo 6 Febbraio 2007/30, 'Attuazione della direttiva 2004/38/CE relativa al diritto dei cittadini dell'Unione e dei loro familiari di circolare e di soggiornare liberamente nel territorio degli Stati membri', in *Gazzetta Ufficiale della Repubblica Italiana*, No.72, 27 Marzo 2007.

Decreto legislativo 28 Gennaio 2008/25, 'Attuazione della direttiva 2005/85/CE recante norme minime per le procedure applicate negli Stati membri ai fini del riconoscimento e della revoca dello *status* di rifugiato', in *Gazzetta Ufficiale della Repubblica Italiana*, No. 40, 16 Febbraio 2008.

Decreto Legislativo 23 Maggio 2008/92 recante misure urgenti in materia di sicurezza pubblica, in *Gazzetta Ufficiale della Repubblica Italiana* (Serie generale), No. 122, 26 Maggio 2008.

Disegno di legge 3 Giugno 2008, Atto Senato n. 733, XVI legislatura, 'Disposizioni in materia di sicurezza pubblica'.

Legge 24 Luglio 2008/125, 'Conversione in legge, con modificazioni, del decreto-legge 23 Maggio 2008/92', in *Gazzetta Ufficiale della Repubblica Italiana*, No. 173 del 25 Luglio 2008.

Online resources

Anon., 'Lettera aperta e denuncia pubblica di reati penali perpetrati', n.d., www.ainei. org/052_Lettera_Aperta_e_denuncia_PUBBLICA_di_reati_Penali_perpetrati (accessed 14 June 2014).

——'Islam in Italia. Libertà religiosa, diritti e doveri', n.d., www.radioradicale.it (accessed 8 April 2009).

——'Pacchetto sicurezza e immigrazione: il silenzio del Vaticano, l'accusa dei vescovi', *Adista*, No. 79 (2009) www.adistaonline.it/?op=articolo&id=45758 (accessed 10 April 2014).

Battistelli, F. and Lucianetti, L.F., 'La sicurezza urbana tra politics and policy' (2010) www.astrid-online.it/rassegna/Rassegna-28/02-09-2009/5_BATTISTELLI_Sicurezza-urbana_23_07_09.pdf (accessed August 2014).

Bossi, U., 'Superare lo stato centralizzato' (1983) www.leganordromagna.org/lega-nord/programma-lega-nord.php (accessed 12 January 2009).

——Discorso di Cà San Marco: 'Fino alla nostra libertà' (2006) www.giovanipadani.leganord.org/articoli.asp?ID=5822 (accessed 14 April 2008).

CGIL, 'Presidio 29 Aprile contro il pacchetto sicurezza' (n.d.) www.CGIL.it (accessed 30 September 2009).

Dei, A., 'La politica dell'immigrazione in Italia attraverso le sanatorie' (2002) www.liberimigranti.it/download/AnnaDei.doc (accessed 20 February 2014).

De Magistris (2005) www.blogautore.espresso.repubblica.it (accessed 20 April 2014).

Hammarberg, T., *Report by Thomas Hammarberg, Commissioner for Human Rights of the Council of Europe, following his visit to Italy on 13–15 January 2009* (n.d.) wcd.coe.int/ViewDoc.jsp?id=1428427&Site=CommDH&BackColorInternet=FEC65B&BackColorIntranet=FEC65B&BackColorLogged=FFC679 (accessed 23 April 2010).

Lega Nord, 'Rispettate le nostre leggi o tornatevene al vostro paese', Comunicato Stampa Giovani Padani, 30 October 2004, www.giovanipadani.leganord.org/articoli.asp?ID=2475 (accessed 9 January 2009).

——'Grazie alla Lega finalmente non ci saranno solo Muhammed nelle graduatorie per le case popolari', 3 February 2005, www.giovanipadani.leganord.org/articoli.asp?ID=2475 (accessed 9 Janaury 2009).

Lautsi and Others vs. Italy (Application no. 30814/06), European Court of Human Rights, Grand Chamber, 18 March 2011, www.uniroma2.it/didattica/Ecclesiastico/deposito/Esempi_di_pronunzie.pdf (accessed 7 April 2014).

Magister, S., 'La svolta di Francesco', 3 October 2013a, www.chiesa.espressonline.it (accessed 15 March 2014).

——'I nodi del pastore Bergoglio', 29 October 2013b, www.chiesa.espressonline.it (accessed 15 March 2014).

Matarazzo, R., 'L'Italia e l'immigrazione. Tra fobie e integrazione' (2009) www.affarinternazionali.it (accessed 23 March 2010).

Naletto, G., 'The Institutionalisation of Racism and Xenophobia in Italy', in European Social Watch Report, *Migrants in Europe as Developed Actors. Between Hope and Vulnerability* (2009) www.socialwatch.eu/wcm/ … /European_Social_Watch_Report_2009.pdf (accessed 7 March 2010).

Naso, P., 'La forza di una minoranza' (2009) www.chiesavaldese.org/page/sinodo/sinodo2009/sinodo2009.php (accessed 7 April 2009).

Pedersen, O.K., 'Discourse Analysis', Working paper No. 65 (2009) openarchive.cbs.dk/bitstream/handle/ … /WP%20CBP%202009-65.pdf (accessed 11 May 2010).

Provenza, M., 'Chiesa, stato e politica: un rapporto complesso', Ateneonline (2003) www.ateneonline-aol.it/030117promAP.html (accessed 18 June 2008).

Ratzinger, J., *Nota sull'espressione 'Chiese sorelle'* (2000a) www.facoltateologica.it/Semeraro.pdf (accessed 18 June 2008).

——*Presentazione 'Dominus Jesus'* (2000c) www.vatican.edu/roman_curia/congregations/cfaith/documents/rc_con_cfaith_doc_20000905_dominus-iesus-ratzinger_it.html (accessed 15 June 2009).

Ricca, P., *Official Note from the Press Office of the Italian Waldesian Church*, 6 September 2000, www.google.it/search?hl=it&rlz=1R2ADBF_it&q=nota+ufficiale+chiesa+valdese&meta=&aq=f&aqi=&aql=&oq=&gsrfai= (accessed 7 May 2008).

Tettamanzi, D., (2008) www.vita.it/news/view/93674 (accessed 16 September 2008).

Index

Alfano (Angelino): 172; 189.
AN: 154; 156; 160; 162; 165; 169.
Andreotti (Giulio): 149; 155.
assimilation: 13–16; 70–71; 91.

Berlusconi (Silvio): 25; Ch I note 6, p.47; 68; Ch III note 6, p.140; 156–57; 163; 170; 182–83; 189–93; Ch V note 20, p.204.
Boniver (Margherita): 155; Ch IV note 39, p.178.
Borghezio (Mario): 111–12; 123; 128; Ch III note 16, p.141; 161.
Bossi (Umberto): 25; 83–84; 108; 112; 116–17; 119–20; 126; 128; 140; Ch III note 37; 141; Ch III note 61; 143; 154; 162–66; 189; 190; Ch V note 28, p.204.

Calderoli (Roberto): 125; 171.
Casini (Pierferdinando): 163.
Catholicism: 42; 55; 60–63; 66; 70; 72–74; 77; 80–83; 86; 88–89; Ch II note 30, p. 96–97; 120; 129–31; 139; Ch III note 56, p.142; 162; 185.
CCD (Centro Cristiano Democratico): 163.
CDU (Cristiani Democratici Uniti): 164.
CEI: 53; 64; 66–70; 79; 82; 84–85; 90; Ch II note 30, p.96–97.
christian identity: 76–77; 129; Ch III note 39, p.142.
christianisation: 68; 72.
Ciampi (Carlo Azeglio) 1; 188.
civil religion: 37; 57–58; Ch II note 8, p.95.
colonialism: 72; Ch II note 81, p.99; 106; 112.

colonisation: 106; 116.
communities: (imagined) 35 (of place; of memory; of hope; psychological) 13.
Craxi (Bettino): Ch I note 8, p.48.
crime: 41; 43; 115; 118; 122–23; 127; 133; 137; Ch III note 81, p.144; 156–58; 166; 171; 173; 175; 194; 199–201; (of illegal entry) 130; 163–64.
criminality: Ch II note 38, p.97; 118–19; 122; 127; 133; 138; 161; 171–72.

D'Alema (Massimo): 157.
DC: 24; 28; 33; 37; Ch I note 9, p.48; Ch I notes 51 and 52, p.51; 66–67; Ch II note 13, p.95; Ch II note 31, p.97; 105; 107–9; 130–31; Ch III note 7, p. 140; 186.
dialogue: 42; (inter-religious) Ch I note 64, p. 52; 54; 59; 69–70; 72–76; 79; 85–86; 88–89; 91; Ch II notes 63; 72 and 74, p.99; 129; 131–32; 158; 194; 196–98.
Dini (lamberto): 154.
discrimination: 9; 35; 64; 71; 87; Ch II note 42, p.98; 110; 113; 119; 135; Ch III note 66, p. 143; 156; 170; 189.

emigration: 6; Ch I note 47, p.50; 90; Ch II note 40, p. 97–98; 147; 149; 152; 154; Ch IV note 59, p. 179.
ethnism: 106–7.
ethno-reglionalism: 109; 116; Ch V note 45, p. 205.
ethno-territorialism: 107.
EU: (citizenship) 25; 40–41; 56; 60 (integration) 25; 60; 117; 209.
extracomunitari: 111; 124; 137–38; Ch III notes 30 and 32, p. 141; 151; 174.

Fascism: 29–31; 33; 36; Ch I notes 19 and 25, p. 48–49; Ch I notes 52 and 61, p.51; 116; 134; 138; 169; 182; 208.

Federalism: 106; 131; Ch III note 28, p.141; 212; (federal state) 125 (federalist revolution) 117 (federalist culture) 121 (federal project) 170.

Fini (Gianfranco): 154; 160; 163; 169–70.

First Republic: 67; 105; Ch III note 7, p. 140; 182.

Follini (Marco): 163.

Forza Italia: 25; 68; 156–57; 160; 163; 183; 190–91; 193; 200.

Franceschini (Dario): 170.

freedom: (of conscience) 76 (cultural) 87 (of expression) 62; 83; 92; 128; 134 (of speech): 16; 75; 92; 103; 211–12 (of religion) 66; 88; 93.

Gasparri (Maurizio): 163; 170; Ch V note 69, p. 206.

globalisation: 15; 24–25; 35–36; 44; 54; 56–57; 60; 72; 81; 118; 120; 123; Ch III note 34, p.141; Ch III note 61, p.143; 164; 173; 181; 184; 196; (Globalisation of indifference) 195; (Globalisation of fear/clandestinity) 199.

Grillo (Beppe): 183; 189; 192; 199–200.

IDV (Italia dei Valori): 159; 172.

integration: 10; 14–16; 37; 42; 44; Ch I, note 47, p.50; 65; 71; 76; 80; 82; 86; 91; 103; 124; 138; Ch III note 38, p.141; 158; 161; 169–70; 174; Ch IV note 39, p. 178; 182–83; 187; 191; (European) 25; Ch I note 14, p.48; 60; 117; 146; 151–52; 157; 209–10 (models of) 6–8; 69; 132; (social) 39.

interest groups: 57; 60–61; Ch II note 12, p.95; 151; 158.

Islam: 42; 72; 79; 82–85; 93–94; Ch II note 62, p.99; Ch II note 89, p. 100; 122–24; 130; 132; 197–99; 210–12.

Islamisation: 43; 81; 119–20; 121; 123; 129; 202.

Kyenge (Cecile): Ch IV note 39, p.178; 183; 191.

La Russa (Ignazio): 163.

Lateran Pacts: 65–66; Ch II note 1, p.94; 185 (Concordat) 65–66; Ch II notes 27 and 28, p.96; Ch II note 30, p.96–97; 185.

law and order: 119; 122; 154; 193.

Mani Pulite: 26; Ch I note 49, p.50; p.131 (Tangentopoli) 67; 162.

Maroni (Roberto): 121; 130; 140; 161; 169–70; 190–91; 199; 201–2; 213.

Martelli (Claudio): 153–54; 155.

memory: 58; 81; 189; (collective) 188; (shared) 7; 30–32; 36; 38 (divided)182; 184; 194.

M5S (Movimento Cinque Stelle): 183; 189; 192; 194; 199; 201–2; Ch V note 72, p. 206; 213.

MSI (Movimento Sociale Italiano): 154; 162; 166.

multiculturalism: 2; 15–16; 39; 71; Ch II note 42, p. 98; 117–18; 158; 174.

Napolitano (Giorgio): 158; 174; 185; 188; Ch V note 13, p.203.

nationalism: 24–26; 33; 35; Ch I note 40, p. 50; Ch I note 51, p.51; 60; 106; 109; Ch V note 24, p.204; 209; 212.

nation-state: 1–2; 7; 16; 24–25; 33; 35; 40; 44; 57; 60; 62; 64; 108; 113; 183.

NCD (Nuovo centrodestra): 189.

neutrality: 7; 11–12; 44; 59; 63; 67; 93.

North-South divide: 18; 35; 102; 106.

Padania: 103; 111; 116–18; (Padanian identity) 120–21; 127; 129–31; 137–38; Ch III note 2, p. 140.

participation: 10–14; 22; 34; Ch I note 28, p.49; 56–57; 61; 89.

PCI: 24; 32–33; 37; Ch I note 39, p.50; Ch I notes 51 and 52, p.51.

PD (Partito democratico): Ch I note 8, p.48; 169–70; 200.

Pivetti (irene): 131.

Populism: 109; Ch III note 8, p.140; 161; 172; Ch IV note 52, p.178; 182; 197; 203; 213.

PRC (Partito della Rifondazione Comunista): 24; 157; 160; 172.

PRI (Partito Repubblicano Italiano): 48; 154–55; 186.

Prodi (Romano): Ch I note 8, p.48; 85; 88; 158.

PSI (Partito Socialista Italiano): Ch I note 9, p.48; Ch I note 49, p.50; Ch II note 23, p.96; 186.

racism: 15–16; 22; 39–41; 71; 111–15; 118; 126; 133–34; 152–53; 156; 161; 170; 184; 187; 191–92; 210.

regions: 103; 105–6; 108; 111; 117; Ch III note 5, p.140; (Regionalism): 25; 109;116; (Regional identity): 60; 107.

relativism: 16; 21; 55; 71–72; 74–76; 81–83; 120; 192; 198; 211.

Renzi (Matteo): 200.

Resistance: 18; 23–24; 27–33; 37; 45–46; Ch I note 36, p.50; 182; 184; 202; 208–9.

rethoric of victimhood: 55; 75–76; 92; 94; 106; 114; 116; 118; 127–28; 133–34; 138–39; 175; 188–89; 191–92; 197; Ch V notes 24 and 25, p. 204; 211; 212.

Roma and sinti: 90; 127; Ch III note 63, 143; 170; 195; 198–99.

Russo Jervolino (Rosa): 160.

Salvini (Matteo): 112; 140; 191–92; 198.

Scalfaro (Oscar Luigi): 149.

Second Vatican Council: 54; 69; 87; 93; Ch II note 62, p.99; Ch V note 61, p.205; 209.

secularisation: 14; 56; 67–69; Ch II notes 5 and 6, p.95; 106; 108; 118.

secularism: 56; 60; 84; 129; 198; 209–10.

security: 115–16; 118–19; 126; 145; 150–51; 154; 157; 162–63; 166–72; 174; Ch IV notes 54 and 65, p.179; 190; 193; 200.

self-determination: 106; 116–17; 119; 127; 131.

solidarity: 29; 32; 35; 38; 55; 62; 71; 78; 81; 91–93; 103–4; 112; 118; 125; 127–31; 139; 149; 153–55; 172; 175; 184; 189; 196; 198–200; 210–11.

stereotype: 9; 11; 115; 119; 127; 136; 188; 209.

subcultures: 36–39; Ch II note 5, p.95; 105; 107; 108–9; 150–51.

territory: 36; 38; 65; Ch II note 30, p.96–97; 106–7; 109; 115; 117–18; 120; 124–25; 127; 133–34; Ch V note 45, p.205.

terrorism: 119; 1214; 137; 182; 197.

tolerance: 13; 15–16; 44; Ch I note 72, p. 52; 75–76; 80–83; 90–92; 110–12; 115; 118–19; 126–27; 130; 134; 137; 148.

Tosi (Flavio): 191.

Turco (Livia): 85; 88; 158–60; 165; 174.

UDC (Unione Democratici Cristiani): Ch IV note 58, p.179.

Vatican: Ch I note 51, p.51; 62; 64–70; Ch II note 31, p.97; 185–86; 197–98; Ch V note 14, pp.203–4.

Veltroni (Valter): Ch III note 63, p.143; Ch IV note 65, p.179.

Verdi (Green party): 154; 160.